Accessing SAS® from Microsoft Office Applications

Course Notes

Accessing SAS® from Microsoft Office Applications Course Notes was developed by Johnny Johnson and Andy Ravenna. Additional contributions were made by Kathy Kiraly, Linda Mitterling, Warren Repole, Christine Riddiough, Eric Rossland, Stacey Syphus, Melinda Thielbar, and Cynthia Zender. Editing and production support was provided by the Curriculum Development and Support Department.

Accessing SAS® from Microsoft Office Applications Course Notes

Book code E70002, course code SBIAMO, prepared date 29Aug05.

Table of Contents

Course Description

This course provides an overview of the SAS Add-In for Microsoft Office and shows how it can be used to directly access SAS information from Microsoft Office applications. You learn how to run SAS Stored Processes and use SAS tasks for processing data directly from inside a Microsoft Excel or Microsoft Word document. In addition, you learn how to access and work with existing SAS data from Microsoft Excel.

To learn more…

SAS Education

A full curriculum of general and statistical instructor-based training is available at any of the Institute's training facilities. Institute instructors can also provide on-site training.

For information on other courses in the curriculum, contact the SAS Education Division at 1-919-531-7321, or send e-mail to training@sas.com. You can also find this information on the Web at support.sas.com/training/ as well as in the Training Course Catalog.

SAS Publishing

For a list of other SAS books that relate to the topics covered in this Course Notes, USA customers can contact our SAS Publishing Department at 1-800-727-3228 or send e-mail to sasbook@sas.com. Customers outside the USA, please contact your local SAS office.

Also, see the Publications Catalog on the Web at support.sas.com/pubs for a complete list of books and a convenient order form.

Prerequisites

There are no formal prerequisites for this course.

Chapter 1 SAS Business Intelligence and Course Introduction

1.1 SAS Business Intelligence Overview

What Is Business Intelligence?

Business intelligence uses knowledge management, data warehouse[ing], data mining and business analysis to identify, track and improve key processes and data, as well as identify and monitor trends in corporate, competitor and market performance. – BETTERMANAGEMENT.COM

SAS Business Intelligence includes

- a set of client applications
- SAS server processes
- a centralized metadata management facility.

The SAS®9 Intelligence Platform is enterprise software with components that exist on multiple machines throughout the organization.

3 ...

Multiple Tier Environment

The SAS Intelligence Platform consists of a multiple tier environment that is typically represented by the

- client tier
- middle tier
- server tier.

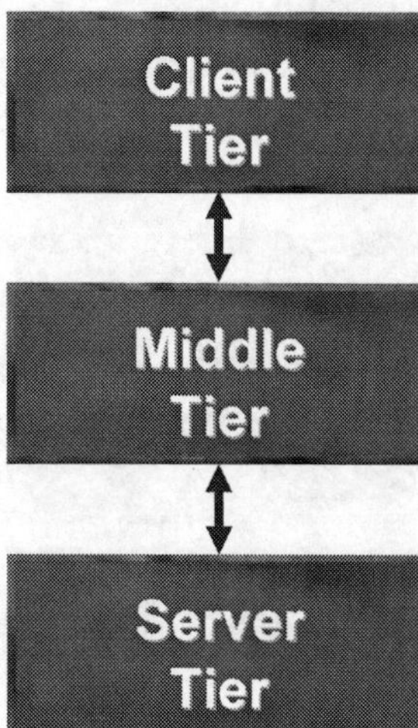

4

The SAS Add-In for Microsoft Office utilizes only the client and server tiers.

Client Tier

In the most basic terms, if an application is installed on the machine that the user is sitting at, that machine is the client tier.

The SAS Add-In for Microsoft Office is considered a ***Windows Client*** because it is

- run in the Microsoft Windows environment
- installed on the machine where it will be used.

5

The other two types of SAS client applications are Java Clients and Browser Clients.

The SAS Business Intelligence (BI) client tools cannot execute SAS code on their own. They have to request code submission and other services from a SAS server.

Server Tier

The server tier is where one or more SAS servers is installed and accessed by the BI tools.

The SAS Add-In for Microsoft Office uses the following types of SAS servers:

Metadata Server	enables centralized metadata delivery and management to SAS applications across the enterprise.
Workspace Server	executes SAS code on behalf of the client applications.
Stored Process Server	executes and delivers results from SAS Stored Processes.

Most interactions with SAS Servers are transparent to the add-in user.

6 ...

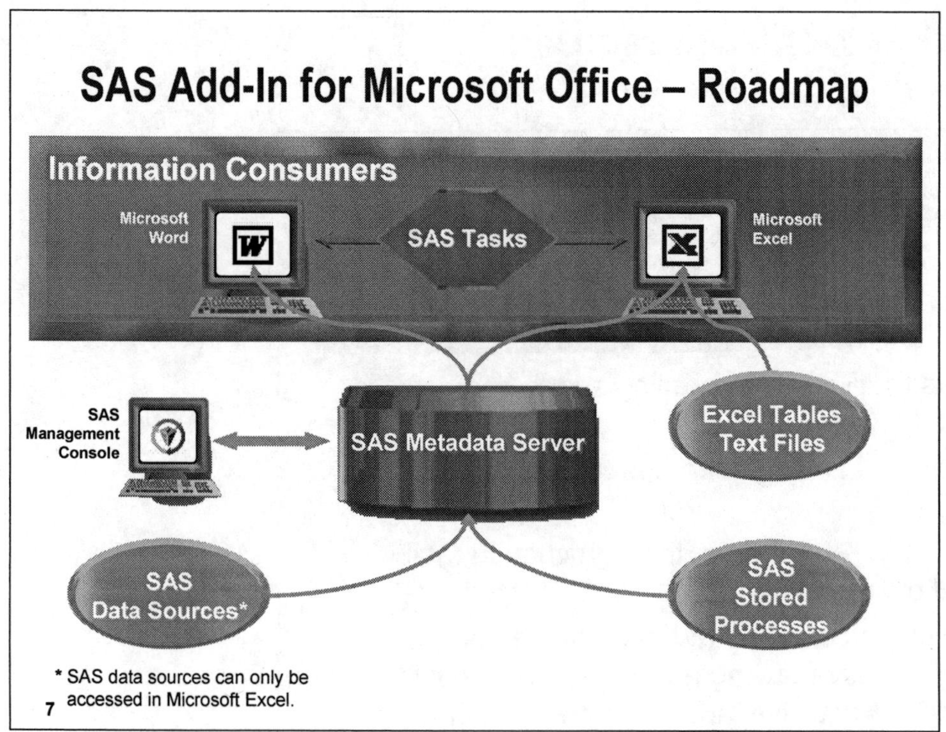
SAS Add-In for Microsoft Office – Roadmap
Information Consumers
Microsoft Word
SAS Tasks
Microsoft Excel
SAS Management Console
SAS Metadata Server
Excel Tables Text Files
SAS Data Sources*
SAS Stored Processes
* SAS data sources can only be accessed in Microsoft Excel.
7

1.2 Introduction to the Course Data

Course Data

The data used in this course is from *Orion Star Sports & Outdoors*, which

- is a fictitious retail company selling sports and outdoor products
- has retail stores in many countries throughout the world
- sells products in retail stores, through catalog mail orders, and over the Internet
- utilizes the Orion Star Club to track purchases, enabling analyses of buying patterns and providing a basis for CRM activities and targeted product offerings.

9

Orion Star Data – General

The data used in the course from the Orion Star organization consists of the following:

- data ranging from 1998 through 2002
- employee information for the employees located in many different countries as well as the United States headquarters
- approximately 5,500 different sports and outdoor products
- approximately 90,000 customers worldwide
- approximately 750,000 orders
- 64 suppliers.

10

Orion Star Data – General

There are many data tables and files that have the various information collected and used at Orion Star.

The tables used in this course include:

- **ORDERS**
- **ORDERFACT**
- **CUSTOMER_DIM**
- **PROFIT**.

The files used in this course include:

- **PRODUCT.XLS**.

11

Orion Star Data – ORDERS

The **ORDERS** table contains general information about each order across all order types.

Order ID	Order Type	Employee ID	Customer ID	Date Order was placed by Customer	Date Order was Delivered
1230000033	Internet Sale	99999999	8818	01JAN1998	07JAN1998
1230000204	Internet Sale	99999999	47793	01JAN1998	04JAN1998
1230000268	Internet Sale	99999999	71727	01JAN1998	03JAN1998
1230000487	Internet Sale	99999999	74503	01JAN1998	04JAN1998
1230000494	Internet Sale	99999999	8610	01JAN1998	07JAN1998
1230000689	Internet Sale	99999999	19278	01JAN1998	05JAN1998

12

Order ID	Order Type	Employee ID	Customer ID	Date Order was placed by Customer	Date Order was Delivered
1230000033	Internet Sale	99999999	8818	01JAN1998	07JAN1998
1230000204	Internet Sale	99999999	47793	01JAN1998	04JAN1998
1230000268	Internet Sale	99999999	71727	01JAN1998	03JAN1998
1230000487	Internet Sale	99999999	74503	01JAN1998	04JAN1998
1230000494	Internet Sale	99999999	8610	01JAN1998	07JAN1998
1230000689	Internet Sale	99999999	19278	01JAN1998	05JAN1998

Orion Star Data – ORDERS

The **ORDERS** table contains 6 columns, 747,953 rows, and uses the ORDER_TYPE user-defined format in addition to SAS date formats.

Alphabetic List of Variables and Attributes					
#	Variable	Type	Len	Format	Label
4	Customer_ID	Num	8	12.	Customer ID
6	Delivery_Date	Num	4	DATE9.	Date Order was Delivered
3	Employee_ID	Num	5	12.	Employee ID
5	Order_Date	Num	4	DATE9.	Date Order was placed by Customer
1	Order_ID	Num	8	12.	Order ID
2	Order_Type	Num	3	ORDER_TYPE.	Order Type

FORMAT NAME: ORDER_TYPE LENGTH: 13 MIN LENGTH: 1 MAX LENGTH: 40 DEFAULT LENGTH 13 FUZZ: STD		
START	END	LABEL (VER. 9.1 08AUG2003:10:05:32)
1	1	Retail Sale
2	2	Catalog Sale
3	3	Internet Sale

13

Alphabetic List of Variables and Attributes					
#	Variable	Type	Len	Format	Label
4	Customer_ID	Num	8	12.	Customer ID
6	Delivery_Date	Num	4	DATE9.	Date Order was Delivered
3	Employee_ID	Num	5	12.	Employee ID
5	Order_Date	Num	4	DATE9.	Date Order was placed by Customer
1	Order_ID	Num	8	12.	Order ID
2	Order_Type	Num	3	ORDER_TYPE.	Order Type

FORMAT NAME: ORDER_TYPE LENGTH: 13 MIN LENGTH: 1 MAX LENGTH: 40 DEFAULT LENGTH 13 FUZZ: STD		
START	END	LABEL (VER. 9.1 08AUG2003:10:05:32)
1	1	Retail Sale
2	2	Catalog Sale
3	3	Internet Sale

Orion Star Data – ORDERFACT

The **ORDERFACT** table contains detailed information about each item ordered.

Order ID	Product ID	Quantity Ordered	Total Retail Price for This Product	Cost Price Per Unit	Order Type	Date Order was placed by Customer	Date Order was Delivered	Year Order was Placed	Quarter Order was Placed
1230000033	220101400065	3	$28.50	$4.55	Internet Sale	01JAN1998	07JAN1998	1998	1
1230000204	220100100228	2	$113.40	$28.45	Internet Sale	01JAN1998	04JAN1998	1998	1
1230000204	220101100031	2	$41.00	$9.25	Internet Sale	01JAN1998	04JAN1998	1998	1
1230000268	240100200004	1	$35.20	$14.80	Internet Sale	01JAN1998	03JAN1998	1998	1
1230000487	240200100007	1	$24.70	$11.80	Internet Sale	01JAN1998	04JAN1998	1998	1
1230000494	240200100224	1	$136.10	$66.10	Internet Sale	01JAN1998	07JAN1998	1998	1
1230000689	230100100012	2	$358.60	$82.00	Internet Sale	01JAN1998	05JAN1998	1998	1

14

Order ID	Product ID	Quantity Ordered	Total Retail Price for This Product	Cost Price Per Unit	Order Type	Date Order was placed by Customer	Date Order was Delivered	Year Order was Placed	Quarter Order was Placed
1230000033	220101400065	3	$28.50	$4.55	Internet Sale	01JAN1998	07JAN1998	1998	1
1230000204	220100100228	2	$113.40	$28.45	Internet Sale	01JAN1998	04JAN1998	1998	1
1230000204	220101100031	2	$41.00	$9.25	Internet Sale	01JAN1998	04JAN1998	1998	1
1230000268	240100200004	1	$35.20	$14.80	Internet Sale	01JAN1998	03JAN1998	1998	1
1230000487	240200100007	1	$24.70	$11.80	Internet Sale	01JAN1998	04JAN1998	1998	1
1230000494	240200100224	1	$136.10	$66.10	Internet Sale	01JAN1998	07JAN1998	1998	1
1230000689	230100100012	2	$358.60	$82.00	Internet Sale	01JAN1998	05JAN1998	1998	1

Orion Star Data – ORDERFACT

The **ORDERFACT** table contains 12 columns, 951,669 rows, and uses the ORDER_TYPE user-defined format in addition to SAS date and dollar formats.

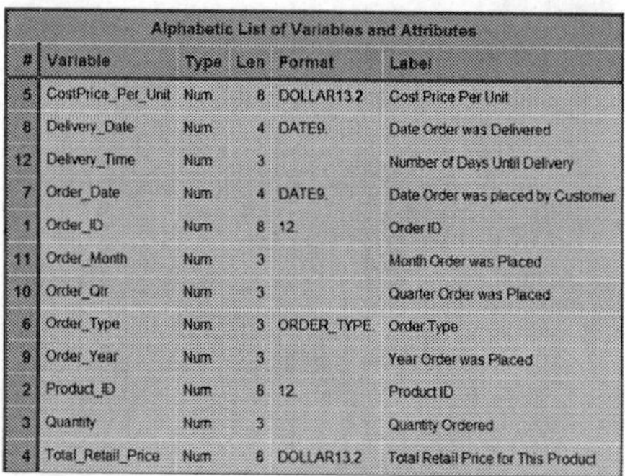

Alphabetic List of Variables and Attributes					
#	Variable	Type	Len	Format	Label
5	CostPrice_Per_Unit	Num	8	DOLLAR13.2	Cost Price Per Unit
8	Delivery_Date	Num	4	DATE9.	Date Order was Delivered
12	Delivery_Time	Num	3		Number of Days Until Delivery
7	Order_Date	Num	4	DATE9.	Date Order was placed by Customer
1	Order_ID	Num	8	12.	Order ID
11	Order_Month	Num	3		Month Order was Placed
10	Order_Qtr	Num	3		Quarter Order was Placed
6	Order_Type	Num	3	ORDER_TYPE.	Order Type
9	Order_Year	Num	3		Year Order was Placed
2	Product_ID	Num	8	12.	Product ID
3	Quantity	Num	3		Quantity Ordered
4	Total_Retail_Price	Num	8	DOLLAR13.2	Total Retail Price for This Product

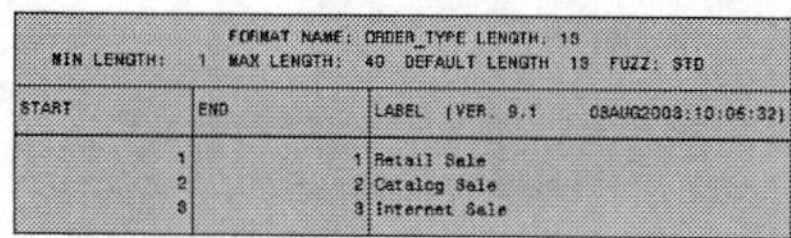

```
FORMAT NAME: ORDER_TYPE LENGTH: 13
MIN LENGTH:   1  MAX LENGTH:  40  DEFAULT LENGTH  13  FUZZ: STD
```

START	END	LABEL (VER. 9.1 08AUG2003:10:05:32)
1	1	Retail Sale
2	2	Catalog Sale
3	3	Internet Sale

15

Alphabetic List of Variables and Attributes					
#	Variable	Type	Len	Format	Label
5	CostPrice_Per_Unit	Num	8	DOLLAR13.2	Cost Price Per Unit
8	Delivery_Date	Num	4	DATE9.	Date Order was Delivered
12	Delivery_Time	Num	3		Number of Days Until Delivery
7	Order_Date	Num	4	DATE9.	Date Order was placed by Customer
1	Order_ID	Num	8	12.	Order ID
11	Order_Month	Num	3		Month Order was Placed
10	Order_Qtr	Num	3		Quarter Order was Placed
6	Order_Type	Num	3	ORDER_TYPE.	Order Type
9	Order_Year	Num	3		Year Order was Placed
2	Product_ID	Num	8	12.	Product ID
3	Quantity	Num	3		Quantity Ordered
4	Total_Retail_Price	Num	8	DOLLAR13.2	Total Retail Price for This Product

```
FORMAT NAME: ORDER_TYPE LENGTH: 13
MIN LENGTH:   1  MAX LENGTH:  40  DEFAULT LENGTH  13  FUZZ: STD
```

START	END	LABEL (VER. 9.1 08AUG2003:10:05:32)
1	1	Retail Sale
2	2	Catalog Sale
3	3	Internet Sale

Orion Star Data – CUSTOMER_DIM

The **CUSTOMER_DIM** table contains information about each customer.

Customer ID	Customer Country	Customer Gender	Customer Name	Customer First Name	Customer Last Name	Customer Birth Date	Customer Age Group	Customer Type Name	Customer Group Name	Customer Age
1	France	Male	Albert Collet	Albert	Collet	24NOV1940	61-75 years	Orion Club Gold members high activity	Orion Club Gold members	63
13	Germany	Male	Markus Sepke	Markus	Sepke	21JUL1984	15-30 years	Orion Club Gold members low activity	Orion Club Gold members	19
19	Germany	Male	Oliver S. Füßling	Oliver S.	Füßling	23FEB1960	31-45 years	Orion Club Gold members high activity	Orion Club Gold members	44

16

Customer ID	Customer Country	Customer Gender	Customer Name	Customer First Name	Customer Last Name	Customer Birth Date	Customer Age Group	Customer Type Name	Customer Group Name	Customer Age
1	France	Male	Albert Collet	Albert	Collet	24NOV1940	61-75 years	Orion Club Gold members high activity	Orion Club Gold members	63
13	Germany	Male	Markus Sepke	Markus	Sepke	21JUL1984	15-30 years	Orion Club Gold members low activity	Orion Club Gold members	19
19	Germany	Male	Oliver S. Füßling	Oliver S.	Füßling	23FEB1960	31-45 years	Orion Club Gold members high activity	Orion Club Gold members	44

Orion Star Data – CUSTOMER_DIM

The **CUSTOMER_DIM** table contains 11 columns, 17,157 rows, and uses the $GENDER and $COUNTRY user-defined formats in addition to a SAS date format.

Alphabetic List of Variables and Attributes					
#	Variable	Type	Len	Format	Label
11	Customer_Age	Num	3		Customer Age
8	Customer_Age_Group	Char	12		Customer Age Group
7	Customer_BirthDate	Num	4	DATE9.	Customer Birth Date
2	Customer_Country	Char	2	$COUNTRY.	Customer Country
5	Customer_FirstName	Char	20		Customer First Name
3	Customer_Gender	Char	1	$GENDER.	Customer Gender
10	Customer_Group	Char	40		Customer Group Name
1	Customer_ID	Num	8	12.	Customer ID
6	Customer_LastName	Char	30		Customer Last Name
4	Customer_Name	Char	40		Customer Name
9	Customer_Type	Char	40		Customer Type Name

FORMAT NAME: $GENDER LENGTH: 6 NUMBER OF VALUES: 2 MIN LENGTH: 1 MAX LENGTH: 40 DEFAULT LENGTH 6 FUZZ: 0		
START	END	LABEL (VER. V7|V8 08AUG2003:10:05:33)
F	F	Female
M	M	Male

FORMAT NAME: $COUNTRY LENGTH: 24 NUMBER OF VALUES: 238 MIN LENGTH: 1 MAX LENGTH: 40 DEFAULT LENGTH 24 FUZZ: 0		
START	END	LABEL (VER. V7|V8 08AUG2003:10:05:33)
AD	AD	Andorra
AE	AE	United Arab Emirates
AF	AF	Afghanistan
AG	AG	Antigua/Barbuda
AI	AI	Anguilla
AL	AL	Albania
⋮	⋮	⋮
YT	YT	Mayotte
YU	YU	Yugoslavia
ZA	ZA	South Africa
ZM	ZM	Zambia
ZW	ZW	Zimbabwe

17

Alphabetic List of Variables and Attributes					
#	Variable	Type	Len	Format	Label
11	Customer_Age	Num	3		Customer Age
8	Customer_Age_Group	Char	12		Customer Age Group
7	Customer_BirthDate	Num	4	DATE9.	Customer Birth Date
2	Customer_Country	Char	2	$COUNTRY.	Customer Country
5	Customer_FirstName	Char	20		Customer First Name
3	Customer_Gender	Char	1	$GENDER.	Customer Gender
10	Customer_Group	Char	40		Customer Group Name
1	Customer_ID	Num	8	12.	Customer ID
6	Customer_LastName	Char	30		Customer Last Name
4	Customer_Name	Char	40		Customer Name
9	Customer_Type	Char	40		Customer Type Name

FORMAT NAME: $GENDER LENGTH: 6 NUMBER OF VALUES: 2 MIN LENGTH: 1 MAX LENGTH: 40 DEFAULT LENGTH 6 FUZZ: 0		
START	END	LABEL (VER. V7|V8 08AUG2003:10:05:33)
F	F	Female
M	M	Male

FORMAT NAME: $COUNTRY LENGTH: 24 NUMBER OF VALUES: 238 MIN LENGTH: 1 MAX LENGTH: 40 DEFAULT LENGTH 24 FUZZ: 0		
START	END	LABEL (VER. V7|V8 08AUG2003:10:05:33)
AD	AD	Andorra
AE	AE	United Arab Emirates
AF	AF	Afghanistan
AG	AG	Antigua/Barbuda
AI	AI	Anguilla
AL	AL	Albania
YT	YT	Mayotte
YU	YU	Yugoslavia
ZA	ZA	South Africa
ZM	ZM	Zambia
ZW	ZW	Zimbabwe

Orion Star Data – PROFIT

The **PROFIT** table contains information about costs, sales, salaries, and profit for each company in Orion Star.

Obs	Company	YYMM	Sales	Cost	Salaries	profit
1	Board of Directors	98M01	.	.	$113,028	$-113,028
2	Board of Directors	98M02	.	.	$113,028	$-113,028
3	Board of Directors	98M03	.	.	$113,028	$-113,028
4	Board of Directors	98M04	.	.	$113,028	$-113,028
5	Board of Directors	98M05	.	.	$113,028	$-113,028
6	Board of Directors	98M06	.	.	$113,028	$-113,028

18

Obs	Company	YYMM	Sales	Cost	Salaries	profit
1	Board of Directors	98M01	.	.	$113,028	$-113,028
2	Board of Directors	98M02	.	.	$113,028	$-113,028
3	Board of Directors	98M03	.	.	$113,028	$-113,028
4	Board of Directors	98M04	.	.	$113,028	$-113,028
5	Board of Directors	98M05	.	.	$113,028	$-113,028
6	Board of Directors	98M06	.	.	$113,028	$-113,028

Orion Star Data – **PROFIT**

The **PROFIT** table contains 6 columns and 960 rows. It is sorted by YYMM.

Alphabetic List of Variables and Attributes					
#	Variable	Type	Len	Format	Label
1	Company	Char	30		Company
4	Cost	Num	8	DOLLAR13.	Cost
5	Salaries	Num	8	DOLLAR12.	
3	Sales	Num	8	DOLLAR13.	Sales
2	YYMM	Num	4	YYMM5.	Year-Month
6	profit	Num	8	DOLLAR12.	Profit

19

Alphabetic List of Variables and Attributes					
#	Variable	Type	Len	Format	Label
1	Company	Char	30		Company
4	Cost	Num	8	DOLLAR13.	Cost
5	Salaries	Num	8	DOLLAR12.	
3	Sales	Num	8	DOLLAR13.	Sales
2	YYMM	Num	4	YYMM5.	Year-Month
6	profit	Num	8	DOLLAR12.	Profit

Orion Star Data – `PRODUCT.XLS`

The **`PRODUCT.XLS`** workbook contains information about men's shoes in the Orion product line.

	A	B	C	D
1	Product_ID	Product_Name	Product_Ref_ID	Product_Group
2	220100400007	Big Guy Men's Cortez Nb-Street Shoes	220100400000	LSF
3	220100400014	Cross Nubuck Women's/Men's Street Shoes	220100400000	LSF
4	220100400018	Osprey Men's Street Cat Nubuck Street Shoes	220100400000	LSF
5	220100400019	Osprey Men's Streetcat Leather Street Shoes	220100400000	LSF
6	220100400020	Ultra M802 All Terrain Men's Shoes	220100400000	LSF
7	220100400021	Ultra M803 At Men's Street Shoes	220100400000	LSF
8	220100400022	Ultra M803 Ng Men's Street Shoes	220100400000	LSF
9	220100400026	Vector Low Men's Shoes	220100400000	LSF
10	220100700001	Classic Men's Leisure Shoes	220100700000	Orion
11	220100700010	Men's Running Shoes Burn	220100700000	Orion
12	220100700013	Rugged Men's Walking Shoes	220100700000	Orion
13	220100700023	Armadillo Road Dmx Men's Running Shoes	220100700000	Orion
14	220100700039	Power Men's Dmx Wide, Walking Shoes	220100700000	Orion
15	220100700044	Quickstyle Dmx Men's Running Shoes	220100700000	Orion
16	220100700046	Tcp 6 Men's Running Shoes	220100700000	Orion
17	220100700049	Trailblaze Dmx Lite Men's Running Shoes	220100700000	Orion
18	220100700052	Trooper Ii Dmx-2x Men's Walking Shoes	220100700000	Orion
19	220100700054	Trooper Lx Dmx-2x Men's Walking Shoes	220100700000	Orion
20	220200100005	4men Men's Air Golden Shoes	220200100000	Eclipse Shoes
21	220200100006	4men Men's Air Presto Shoes	220200100000	Eclipse Shoes
22	220200100007	Atmosphere Acma Men's Running Shoes	220200100000	Eclipse Shoes

20

	A	B	C	D
1	Product_ID	Product_Name	Product_Ref_ID	Product_Group
2	220100400007	Big Guy Men's Cortez Nb-Street Shoes	220100400000	LSF
3	220100400014	Cross Nubuck Women's/Men's Street Shoes	220100400000	LSF
4	220100400018	Osprey Men's Street Cat Nubuck Street Shoes	220100400000	LSF
5	220100400019	Osprey Men's Streetcat Leather Street Shoes	220100400000	LSF
6	220100400020	Ultra M802 All Terrain Men's Shoes	220100400000	LSF
7	220100400021	Ultra M803 At Men's Street Shoes	220100400000	LSF
8	220100400022	Ultra M803 Ng Men's Street Shoes	220100400000	LSF
9	220100400026	Vector Low Men's Shoes	220100400000	LSF
10	220100700001	Classic Men's Leisure Shoes	220100700000	Orion
11	220100700010	Men's Running Shoes Burn	220100700000	Orion
12	220100700013	Rugged Men's Walking Shoes	220100700000	Orion
13	220100700023	Armadillo Road Dmx Men's Running Shoes	220100700000	Orion
14	220100700039	Power Men's Dmx Wide, Walking Shoes	220100700000	Orion
15	220100700044	Quickstyle Dmx Men's Running Shoes	220100700000	Orion
16	220100700046	Tcp 6 Men's Running Shoes	220100700000	Orion
17	220100700049	Trailblaze Dmx Lite Men's Running Shoes	220100700000	Orion
18	220100700052	Trooper Ii Dmx-2x Men's Walking Shoes	220100700000	Orion
19	220100700054	Trooper Lx Dmx-2x Men's Walking Shoes	220100700000	Orion
20	220200100005	4men Men's Air Golden Shoes	220200100000	Eclipse Shoes
21	220200100006	4men Men's Air Presto Shoes	220200100000	Eclipse Shoes
22	220200100007	Atmosphere Acma Men's Running Shoes	220200100000	Eclipse Shoes

1.3 Introduction to the Course Scenarios

Orion Star Information Consumers

There are many people and groups at Orion Star who use SAS software, including

- information systems staff
- business analysts
- management and C-level executives (such as CEO, CFO).

22

The Information Systems Department has built a data warehouse by extracting data from Online Transactional Processing Systems (OLTP) and Enterprise Resource Planning (ERP) systems, as well as data from external sources.

The business users use the data warehouse

- to create data marts
- to perform advanced analyses
- for querying and reporting.

Management and C-level executives use the SAS Business Intelligence tools to access the information stored in the data warehouse.

Business Intelligence Personae

IT Support

IT Admin (Ahmed)
- User administration
- Reporting administration
- Software administration

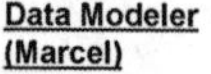

Data Modeler (Marcel)
- Business View manager
- Understands physical data model
- SQL programmer

Report Administrator (Robert)
- Report Builder
- Schedule reports
- Monitor queue

Power Users

Business Analyst (Jacques)
- No DBMS or programming
- Strong Excel
- Ad hoc queries
- OLAP
- Create reports
- Publish reports
- Custom reports
- Understands business metrics

Power User (Gloria)
- Some DBMS and programming
- Strong Excel
- Ad hoc queries
- Custom reports
- Modeling
- Analytics
- Detail data
- Understands business domain

Information Consumers

C-level Execs
- Annotation
- E-mail

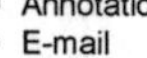

Middle Management (Henri)
- Drill down
- Manipulation
- Annotation

Operational Consumers
- Sales
- Marketing
- Customer Service
- Finance
- Tech Support

23

Business Intelligence Personae

For this course, we'll assume the identity of Jacques, a business analyst with strong Excel and reporting skills.

Business Analyst (Jacques)
- No DBMS or programming
- Strong Excel
- Ad hoc queries
- OLAP
- Create reports
- Publish reports
- Custom reports
- Understands business metrics

The tables were created by Marcel, the data modeler.

Data Modeler (Marcel)
- Business View manager
- Understands physical data model
- SQL programmer

24

Lecture Scenario

During the demonstrations, business problems will be addressed by

- filtering and summarizing one million orders
- performing a sales forecast
- creating charts of customer data.

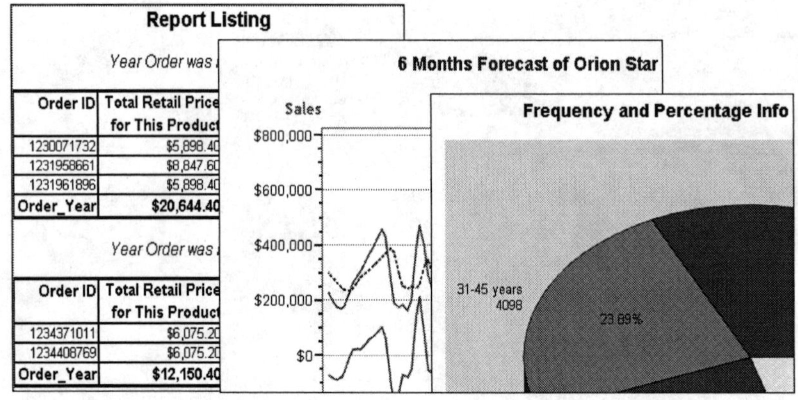

25

Exercise Scenario

During exercises, you will

- filter and sort customer data
- execute a stored process, send the results to Microsoft Word, and modify the output style
- analyze and graphically present retail sales data.

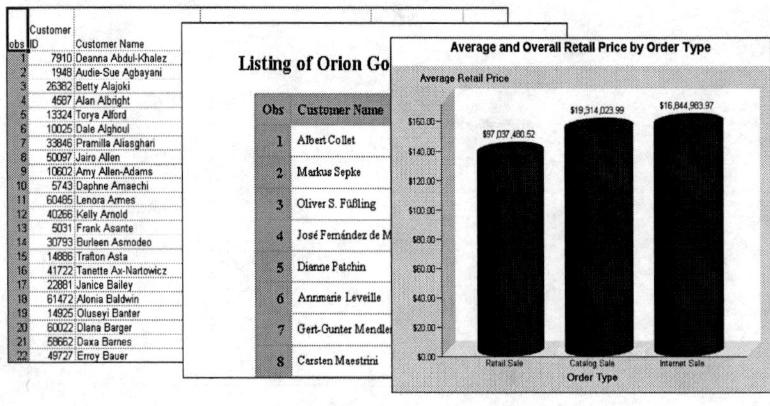

26

Chapter 2 Exploring the SAS Add-In for Microsoft Office

2.1 Overview of the SAS Add-In for Microsoft Office

The SAS Add-In for Microsoft Office

The SAS Add-In for Microsoft Office is a Component Object Model (COM) add-in that extends the functionality of Microsoft Office.

From *within* Microsoft Word and Microsoft Excel, users can harness the power of SAS analytics and access SAS data sources.

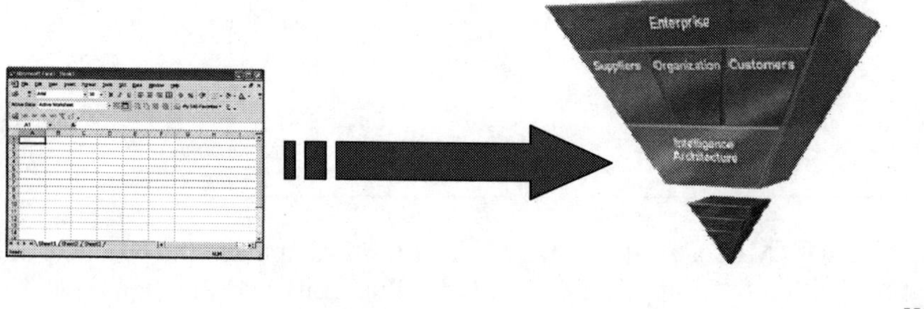

3

COM technology is a Microsoft standard that is used in many Microsoft Office products.

The SAS Add-In for Microsoft Office

You can use the add-in for ad hoc reporting or to execute stored processes dynamically and embed the results in your documents and spreadsheets.

In general, you can use the add-in to

- access and view SAS data sources
- access and view any other data source that is available from your SAS server
- analyze SAS or Excel data using analytic tasks.

4

Why Is the SAS Add-In for Microsoft Office Important?

Many business users can benefit from the power of SAS analytics without having to work in a traditional programming environment.

Users already familiar with Microsoft Word and Microsoft Excel are not required to learn a new application.

The add-in brings SAS analytics, data access, and SAS content to the Microsoft Office environment.

5

These business users are familiar with Microsoft Excel and Microsoft Word and use the products daily. The ability to run SAS programs within these applications provides flexibility and functionality.

Capabilities

With the SAS Add-In for Microsoft Office, you can

- embed SAS reports and analytics into Microsoft Office applications using stored processes
- access SAS data on one or more servers within Microsoft Excel
- manipulate results and distribute them with existing Microsoft Office functionality
- access and analyze more than 65,536 rows and 256 columns of data in Microsoft Excel.

6

Requirements

These are the system requirements for installing and using the SAS Add-In for Microsoft Office:

- Windows NT 4, Windows 2000, Windows XP
- Office 2000 or greater
- SAS Intelligence Platform
- the SAS Add-In for Microsoft Office.

7

The SAS Add-In for Microsoft Office must be installed on each client machine.

2.2 Using the SAS Add-In for Microsoft Office in Excel

The SAS Add-In for Microsoft Office

The SAS Add-In for Microsoft Office adds a

- SAS menu to the menu bar
- SAS Analysis Tools toolbar
- SAS Data Analysis toolbar (for Excel only).

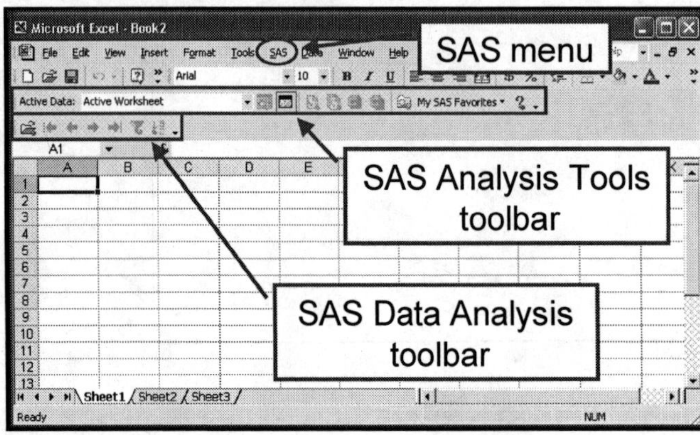

9 ...

SAS Menu for Microsoft Excel

The SAS menu in Microsoft Excel provides access to the following functionality:

- ability to run stored processes and SAS tasks
- tools to work with a SAS data source
- options for the add-in
- ability to specify the server
- the style manager to customize the appearance of results returned to Microsoft Excel.

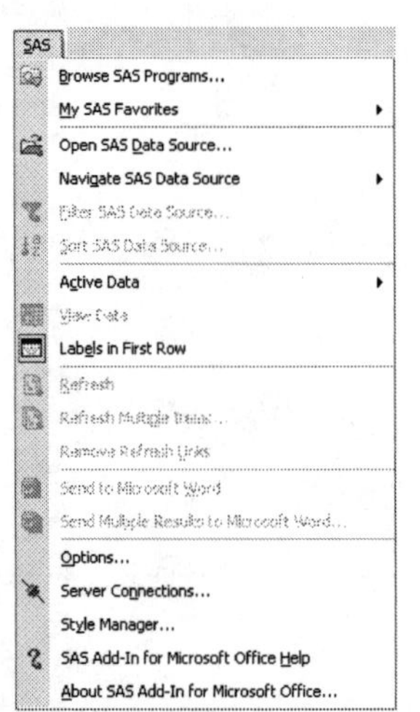

13

SAS Analysis Tools Toolbar for Excel

The SAS Analysis Tools toolbar provides access to some of the same options as the SAS menu.

Some of the tasks that can be performed include the following:

- changing the active data source
- showing labels in the first row
- refreshing the results
- viewing the data
- browsing SAS programs
- exporting results to Microsoft Word
- accessing your SAS Favorites.

14

SAS Data Analysis Toolbar for Excel

The SAS Data Analysis toolbar provides access to options for working with SAS data.

The tasks that can be performed include the following:

- opening a SAS data source
- navigating through the data
- using a filter
- sorting the data
- selecting columns.

The SAS Data Analysis toolbar is not available in Microsoft Word.

15

SAS Add-In Options for Excel

With the SAS Add-In for Microsoft Office options, you can

- modify the settings for handling SAS data
- specify the default formats for graphs and results
- choose settings for how SAS Tasks are surfaced
- modify settings for handling stored processes.

16

SAS Add-In Options for Excel

Access the options for the SAS Add-In for Microsoft Office for Excel by selecting **SAS** ⇨ **Options…**.

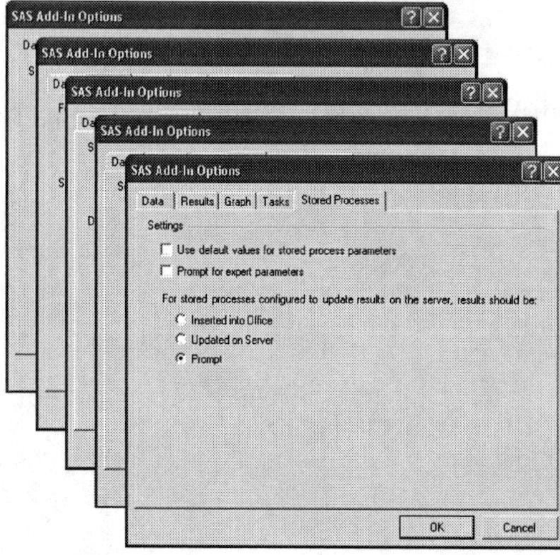

17

Connecting to the SAS Metadata Server

When you use the SAS Add-In for Microsoft Office for the first time in Excel, you will have to log in to the SAS Metadata Server.

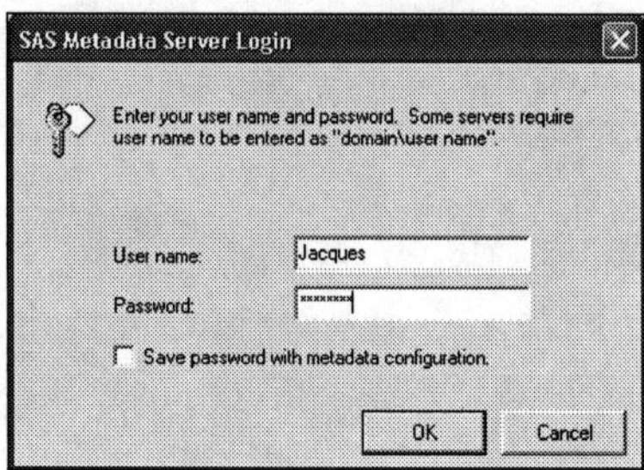

18

If the metadata server definition in your configuration does not contain a user name and password, you will be prompted to enter it. You can choose to save this password in your configuration so that you will not be prompted again.

You can modify your connection to the SAS Metadata Server by selecting Server Connections from the SAS menu.

In the SAS Intelligence Platform, security consists of both authentication and authorization. *Authentication* is the process of verifying the identity of a person or process within the guidelines of a specific security policy. *Authorization* is the process of determining which permissions the user has for which resources. Authentication is a prerequisite for authorization.

Using the SAS Add-In for Microsoft Office in Excel

In this demonstration you will use Microsoft Excel to explore some of the key features of the SAS Add-In for Microsoft Office. This demonstration will cover various features at a high level, which will then be covered in detail during the remaining chapters of the course.

For this demonstration, you will

- extract data from a SAS table that contains nearly one million records
- produce a yearly summary report of products that have a retail price greater than $5,000.

Output (partial listing):

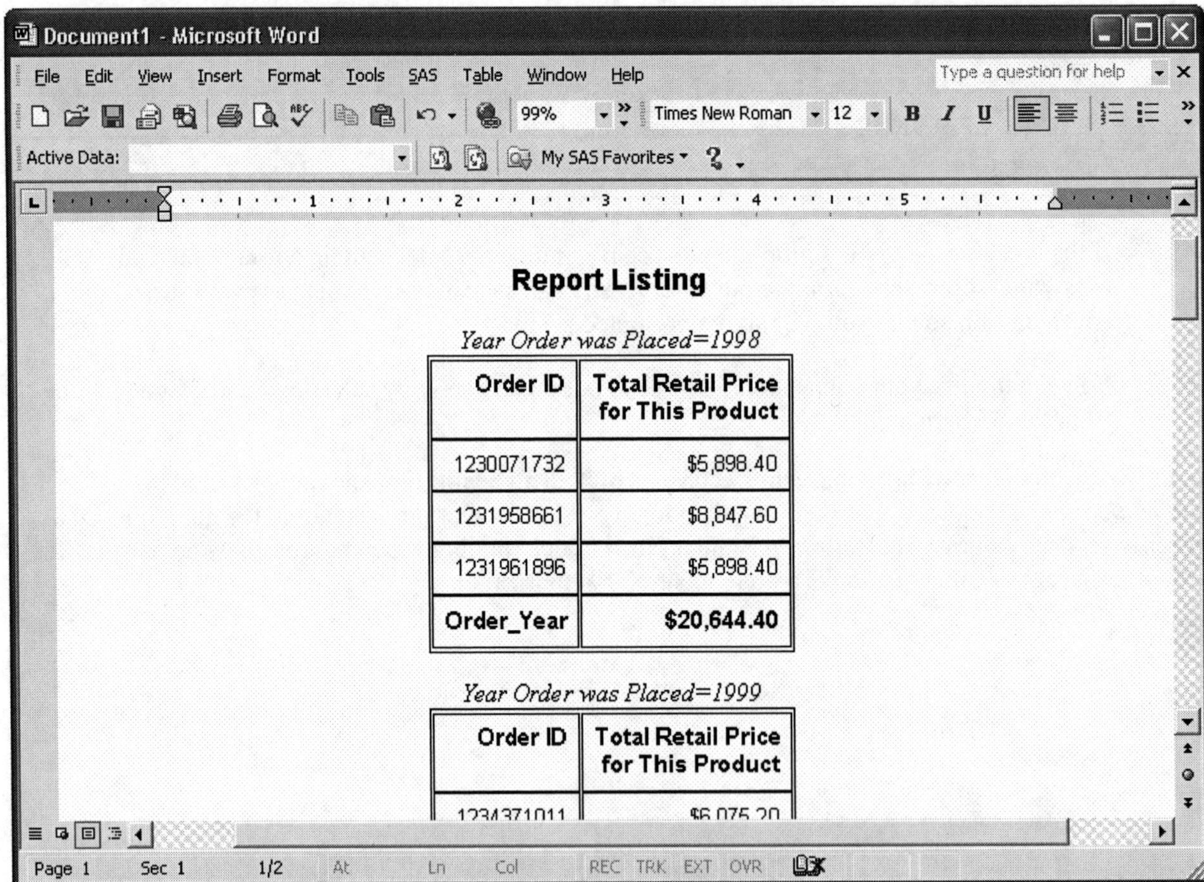

Use the SAS Menu for Microsoft Excel

The SAS Add-In for Microsoft Office enables you to customize how the tool integrates with both Microsoft Excel and Microsoft Word. These features are set using the SAS Add-In Options window. Use the SAS Menu for Microsoft Excel to set the default SAS server.

1. Invoke Microsoft Excel by selecting **Start** ⇨ **All Programs** ⇨ **Microsoft Office** ⇨ **Microsoft Excel**.

2. Select **SAS** ⇨ **Options** from the pull-down menu.

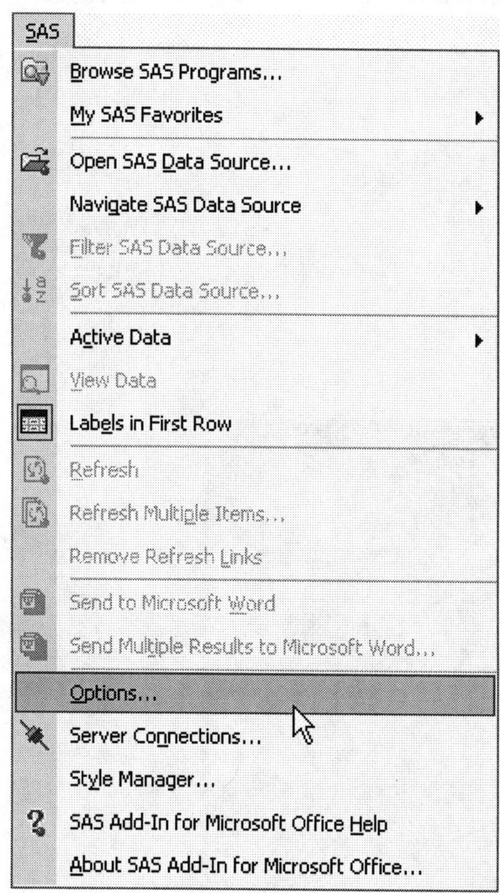

If prompted, enter the user name and password provided by the instructor.

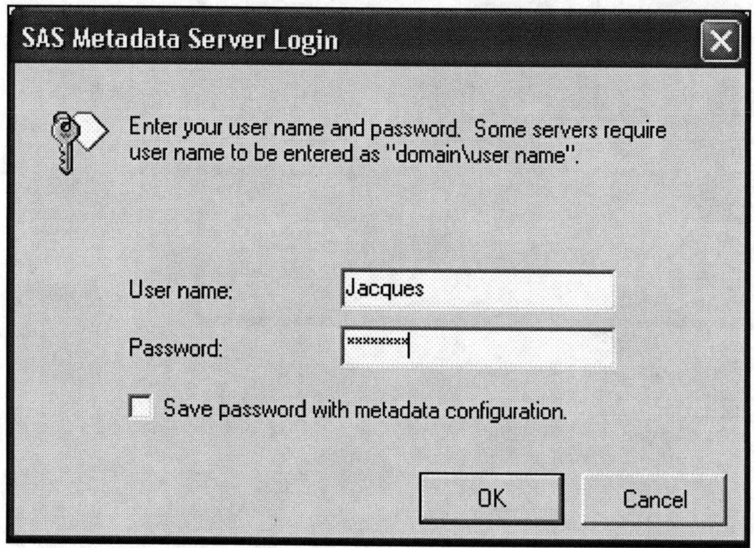

✎ The values shown above may be different from those used in class.

3. Select OK.

The add-in displays an information window while it connects to the SAS Metadata Server, and then the SAS Add-In Options window opens.

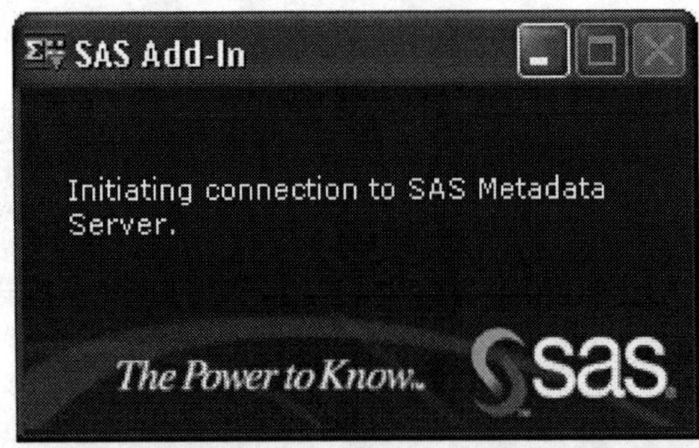

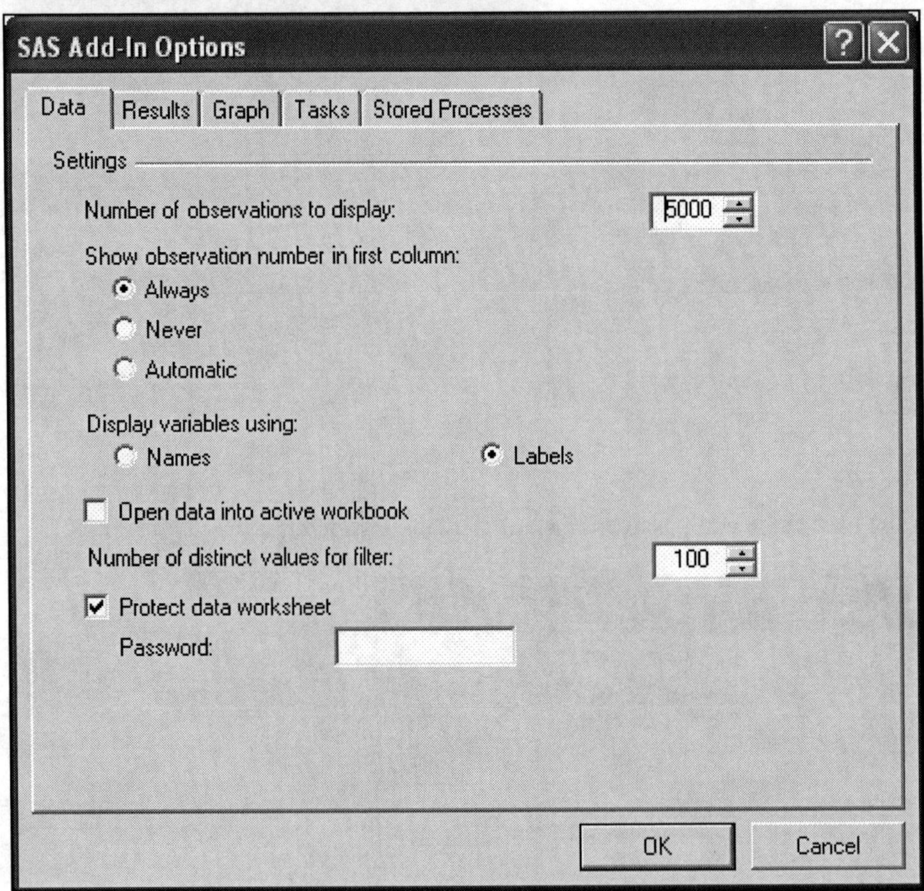

4. Use the SAS Add-In Options window to set the default server.

   a. Select the **Tasks** tab.

   b. Set **SASMain** as the Default SAS server.

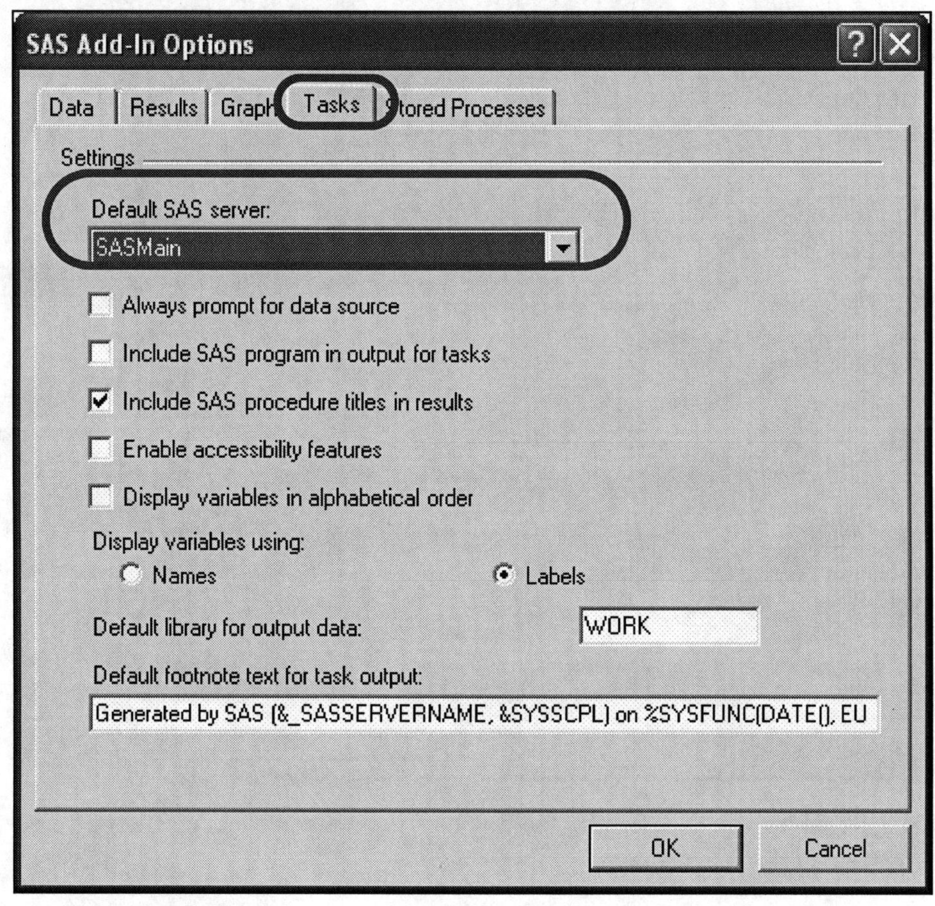

Select OK.

Other SAS Add-In Options windows:

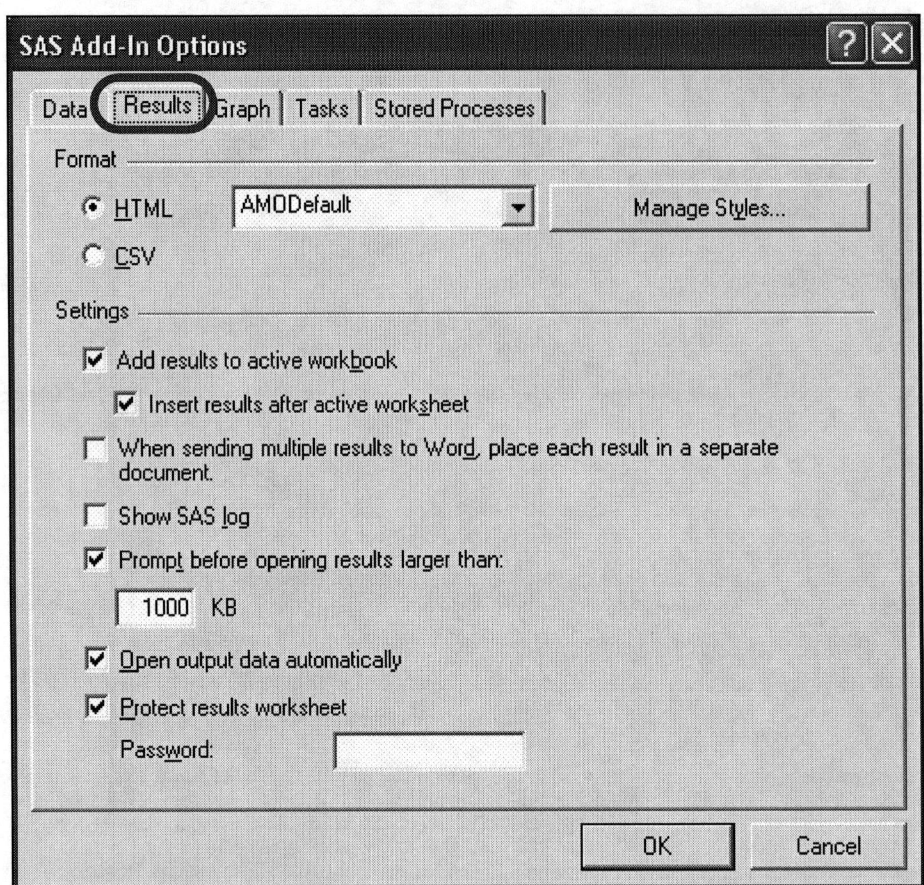

The Results tab enables you to customize the way data is streamed back to Microsoft Excel.

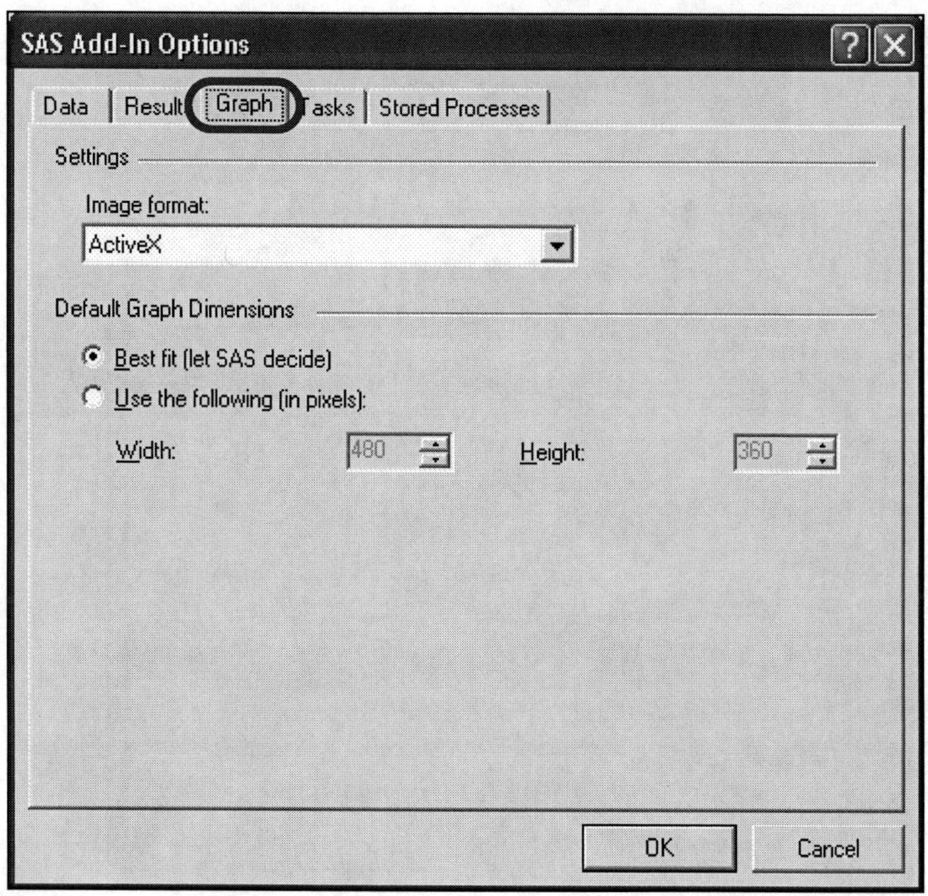

The Graph tab allows you to customize the image format and graph dimensions.

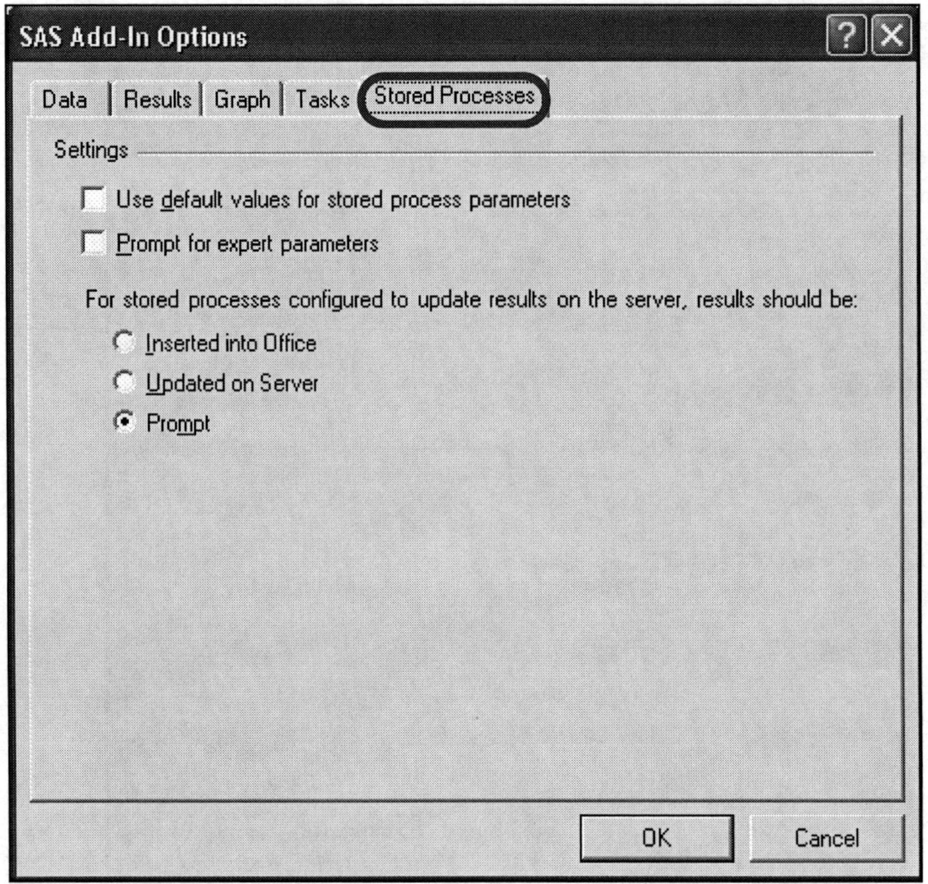

The Stored Process tab enables you to customize parameter usage and updates.

Use the SAS Data Analysis Toolbar for Excel

The SAS Add-In for Microsoft Office enables Excel to access SAS data on a server, which can then be added to a workbook. The SAS Data Analysis toolbar can be used to add data, navigate through the data, apply a filter, sort the data, and restrict which columns to display. Use the SAS Data Analysis toolbar to add a SAS table to Microsoft Excel and then apply a filter to the table.

1. Select the Open SAS Data Source button from the SAS Data Analysis toolbar (or **SAS** ⇨ **Open SAS Data Source...**).

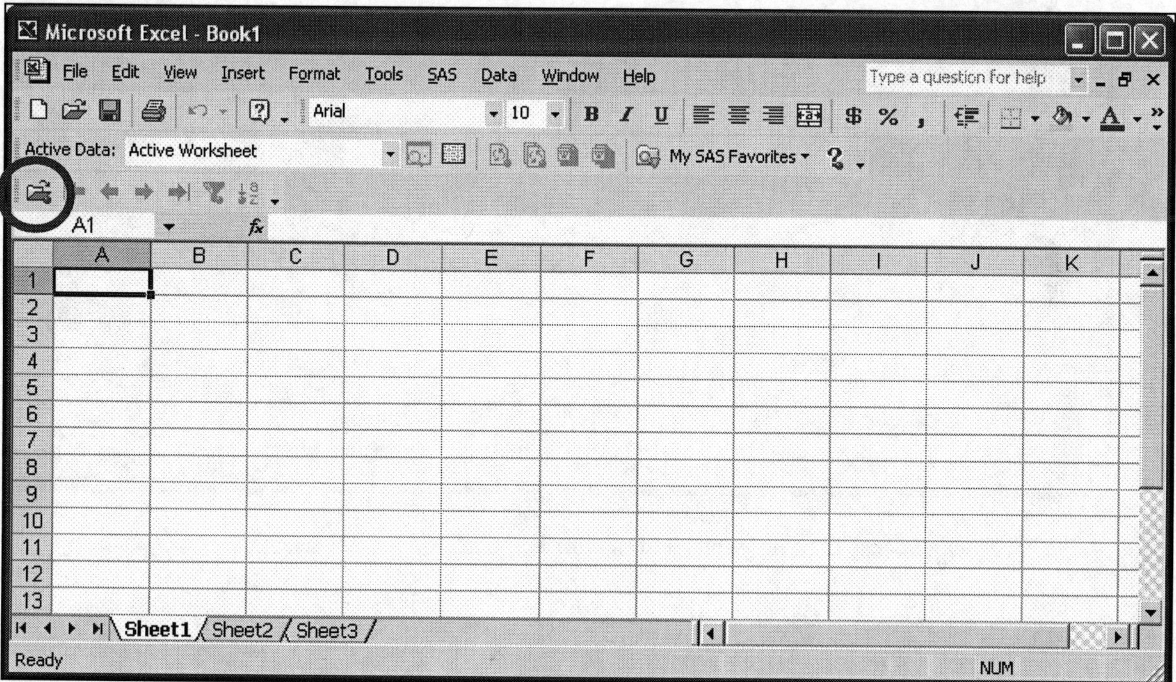

2. In the Open SAS Data Source window, select **Servers** from the shortcut bar. Then, choose **SASMain** and select Open.

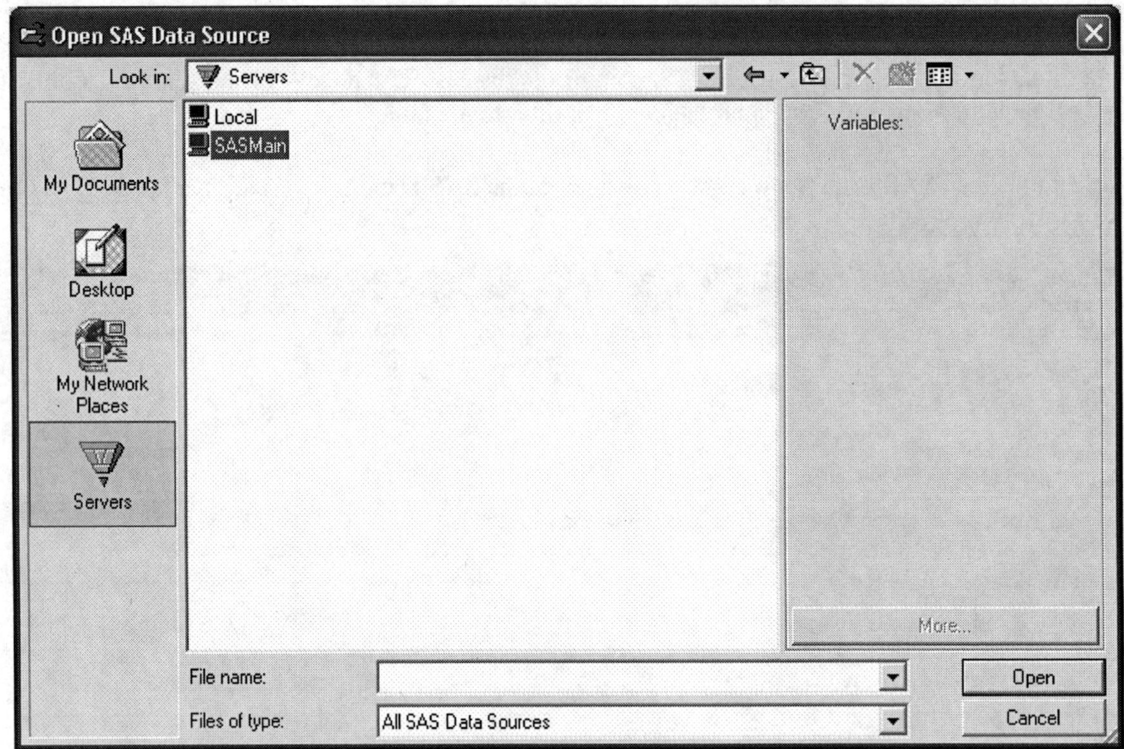

You can access data on your local machine or through a SAS server.

a. Choose **MDM Target Tables Library** and select Open.

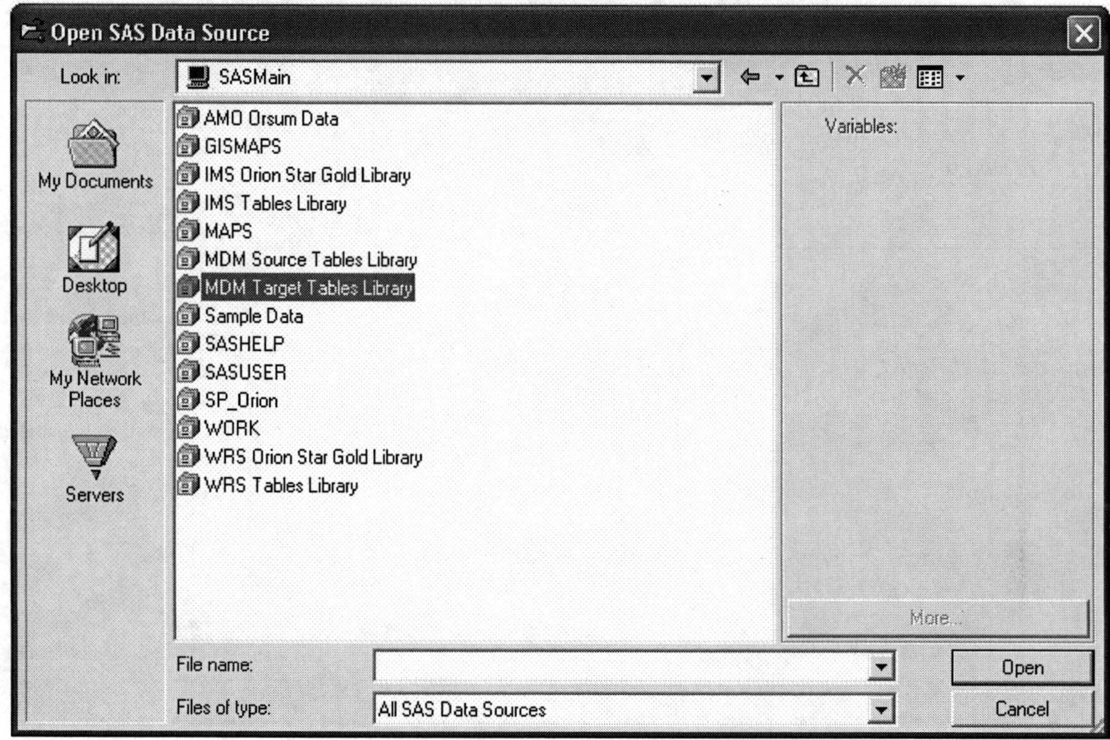

Libraries provide an organizational system for data sources on a specific server. A SAS data library is a collection of SAS files that are recognized as a unit by SAS.

b. Choose the **MDM_OrderFact** table, then select Open.

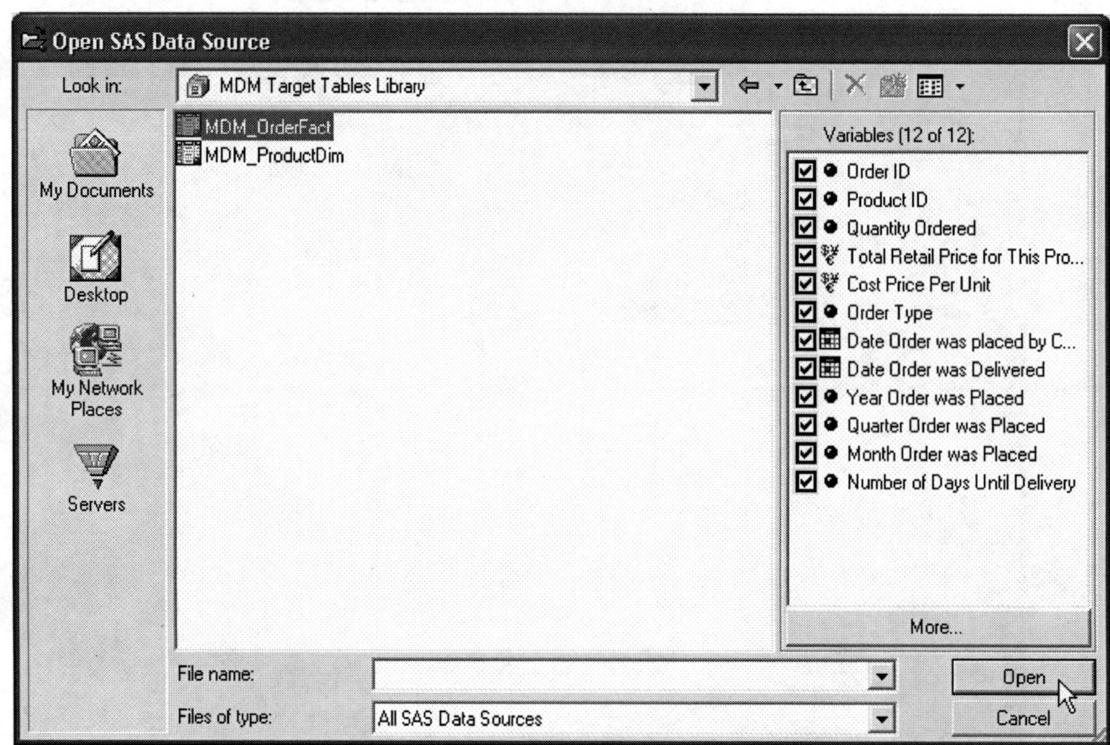

If you cannot read the entire name of a table, use the View Mode icon on the toolbar to change the view to Detail or List.

From the Variables pane, you can deselect any columns that you choose not to include from the data source.

By default, the first 5000 rows of data from the server are retrieved into the worksheet:

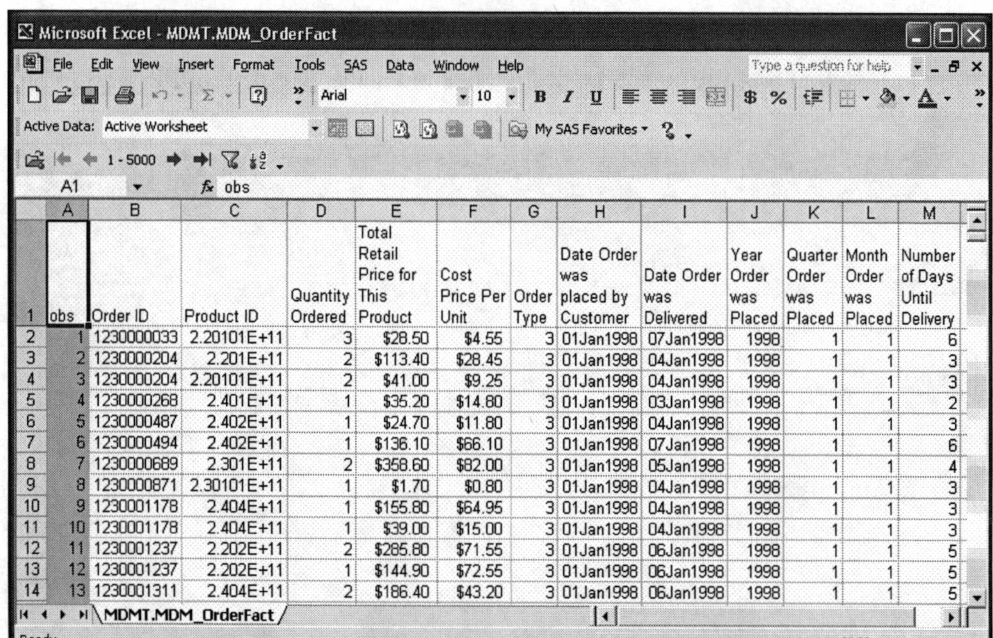

obs	Order ID	Product ID	Quantity Ordered	Total Retail Price for This Product	Cost Price Per Unit	Order Type	Date Order was placed by Customer	Date Order was Delivered	Year Order was Placed	Quarter Order was Placed	Month Order was Placed	Number of Days Until Delivery
1	1230000033	2.20101E+11	3	$28.50	$4.55	3	01Jan1998	07Jan1998	1998	1	1	6
2	1230000204	2.201E+11	2	$113.40	$28.45	3	01Jan1998	04Jan1998	1998	1	1	3
3	1230000204	2.20101E+11	2	$41.00	$9.25	3	01Jan1998	04Jan1998	1998	1	1	3
4	1230000268	2.401E+11	1	$35.20	$14.80	3	01Jan1998	03Jan1998	1998	1	1	2
5	1230000487	2.402E+11	1	$24.70	$11.80	3	01Jan1998	04Jan1998	1998	1	1	3
6	1230000494	2.402E+11	1	$136.10	$66.10	3	01Jan1998	07Jan1998	1998	1	1	6
7	1230000689	2.301E+11	2	$358.60	$82.00	3	01Jan1998	05Jan1998	1998	1	1	4
8	1230000871	2.30101E+11	1	$1.70	$0.80	3	01Jan1998	04Jan1998	1998	1	1	3
9	1230001178	2.404E+11	1	$155.80	$64.95	3	01Jan1998	04Jan1998	1998	1	1	3
10	1230001178	2.404E+11	1	$39.00	$15.00	3	01Jan1998	04Jan1998	1998	1	1	3
11	1230001237	2.202E+11	2	$285.80	$71.55	3	01Jan1998	06Jan1998	1998	1	1	5
12	1230001237	2.202E+11	1	$144.90	$72.55	3	01Jan1998	06Jan1998	1998	1	1	5
13	1230001311	2.404E+11	2	$186.40	$43.20	3	01Jan1998	06Jan1998	1998	1	1	5

Because **`Product ID`** is a numeric column, it is displayed with a default Excel format.

3. The arrow tools on the SAS Data Analysis toolbar enable scrolling through the data. The arrows with the bars next to them take you all the way to the beginning or end of the data.

   a. Select [➡|] on the SAS Data Analysis toolbar (or **SAS** ⇨ **Navigate SAS Data Source** ⇨ **Go to End**) to navigate to the last rows of the table.

   The last 5000 rows of data from the server are retrieved into the worksheet:

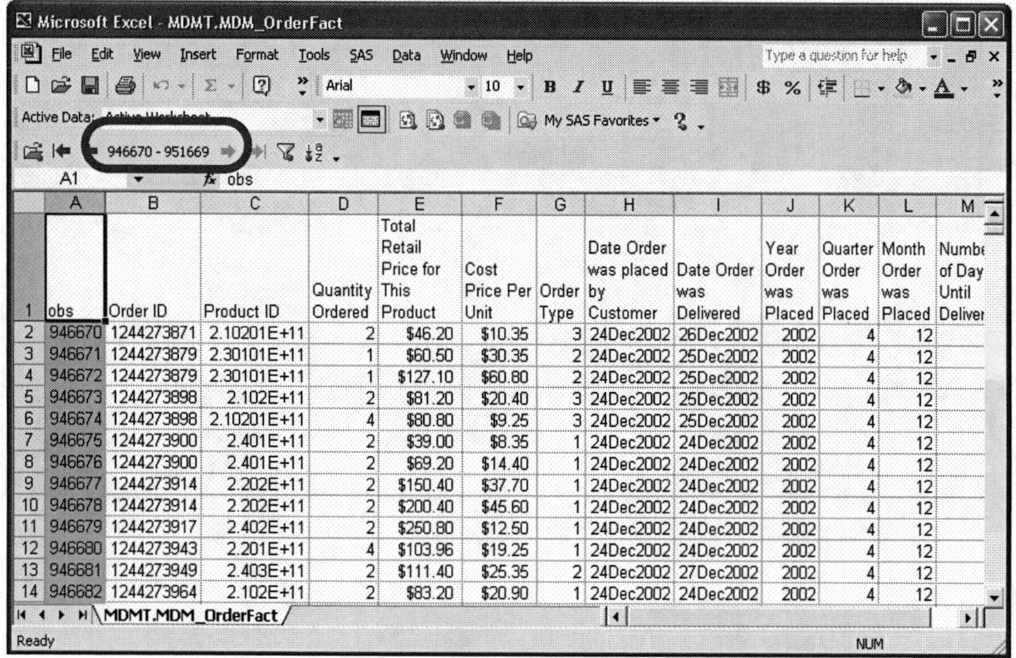

obs	Order ID	Product ID	Quantity Ordered	Total Retail Price for This Product	Cost Price Per Unit	Order Type	Date Order was placed by Customer	Date Order was Delivered	Year Order was Placed	Quarter Order was Placed	Month Order was Placed	Numbe of Day Until Delive
946670	1244273871	2.10201E+11	2	$46.20	$10.35	3	24Dec2002	26Dec2002	2002	4	12	
946671	1244273879	2.30101E+11	1	$60.50	$30.35	2	24Dec2002	25Dec2002	2002	4	12	
946672	1244273879	2.30101E+11	1	$127.10	$60.80	2	24Dec2002	25Dec2002	2002	4	12	
946673	1244273898	2.102E+11	2	$81.20	$20.40	3	24Dec2002	25Dec2002	2002	4	12	
946674	1244273898	2.10201E+11	4	$80.80	$9.25	3	24Dec2002	25Dec2002	2002	4	12	
946675	1244273900	2.401E+11	2	$39.00	$8.35	1	24Dec2002	24Dec2002	2002	4	12	
946676	1244273900	2.401E+11	2	$69.20	$14.40	1	24Dec2002	24Dec2002	2002	4	12	
946677	1244273914	2.202E+11	2	$150.40	$37.70	1	24Dec2002	24Dec2002	2002	4	12	
946678	1244273914	2.202E+11	2	$200.40	$45.60	1	24Dec2002	24Dec2002	2002	4	12	
946679	1244273917	2.402E+11	2	$250.80	$12.50	1	24Dec2002	24Dec2002	2002	4	12	
946680	1244273943	2.201E+11	4	$103.96	$19.25	1	24Dec2002	24Dec2002	2002	4	12	
946681	1244273949	2.403E+11	2	$111.40	$25.35	2	24Dec2002	27Dec2002	2002	4	12	
946682	1244273964	2.102E+11	2	$83.20	$20.90	1	24Dec2002	24Dec2002	2002	4	12	

4. Filter the data so that only products with a total retail price of $5000 or more are displayed.

   a. Select on the SAS Data Analysis toolbar (or select **SAS** ⇨ **Filter SAS Data Source**).

   b. Select in the first box and select the desired column name, **Total Retail Price for This Product**.

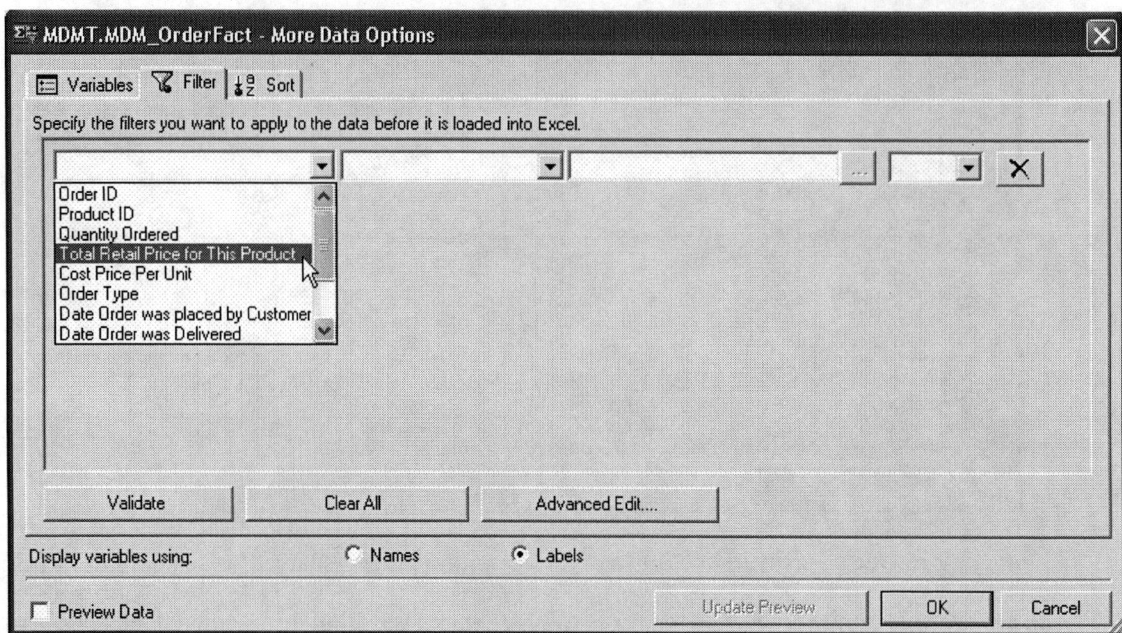

   c. Select in the second box and specify the filter criterion **Is greater or equal to**.

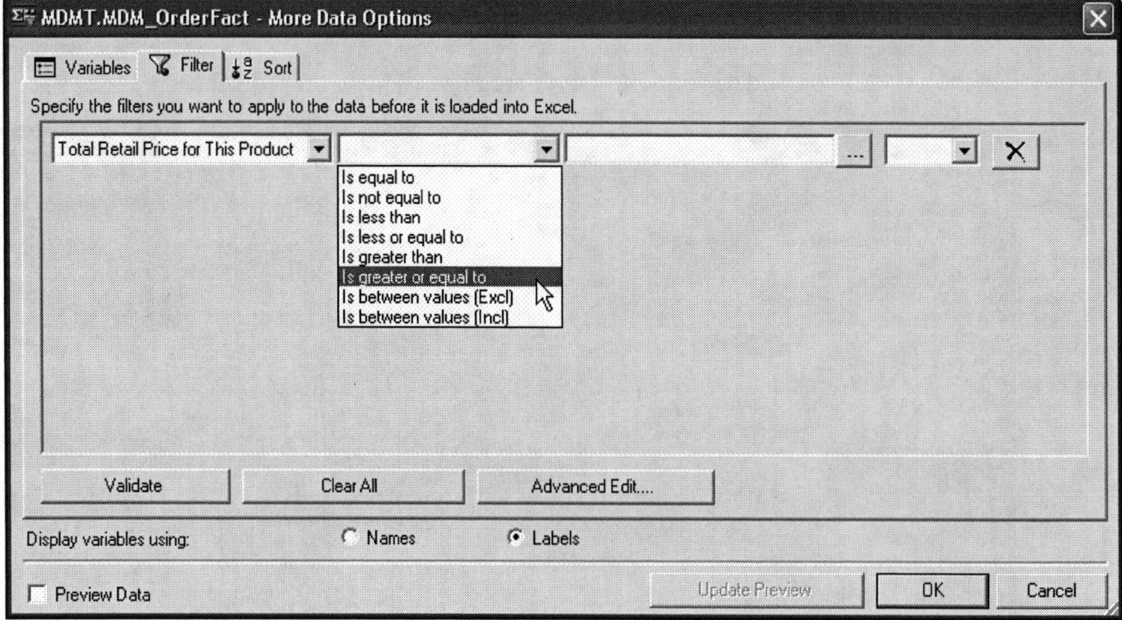

d. In the third box, type in the desired value **5000** and select OK.

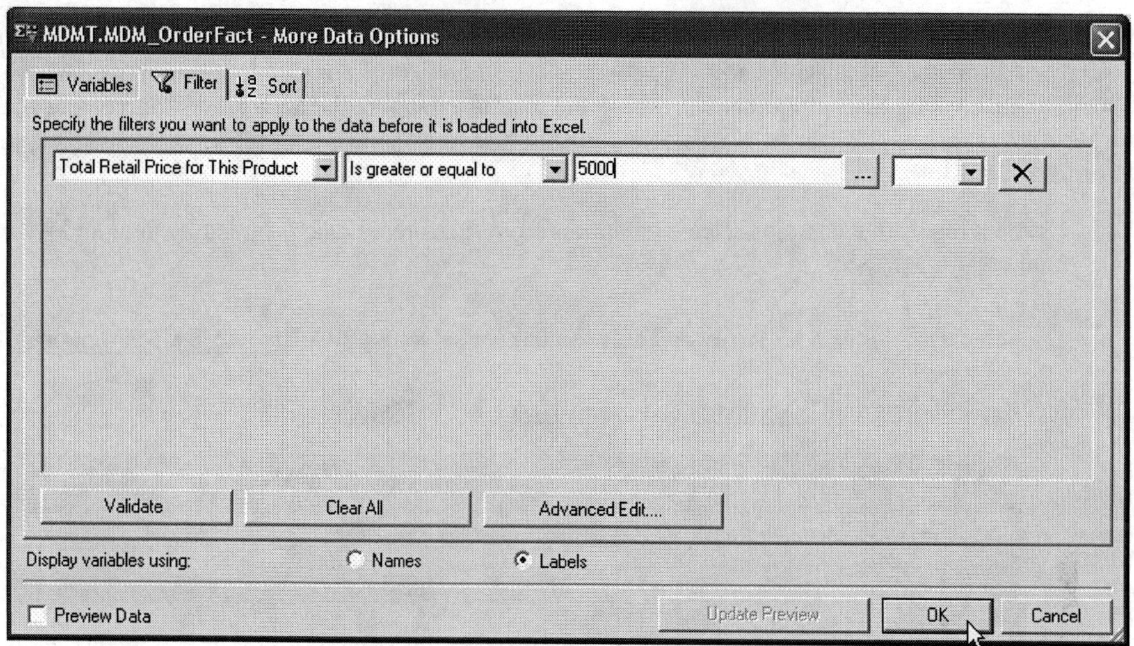

All rows of the data are filtered on the SAS Workspace Server; 14 rows are returned to Excel:

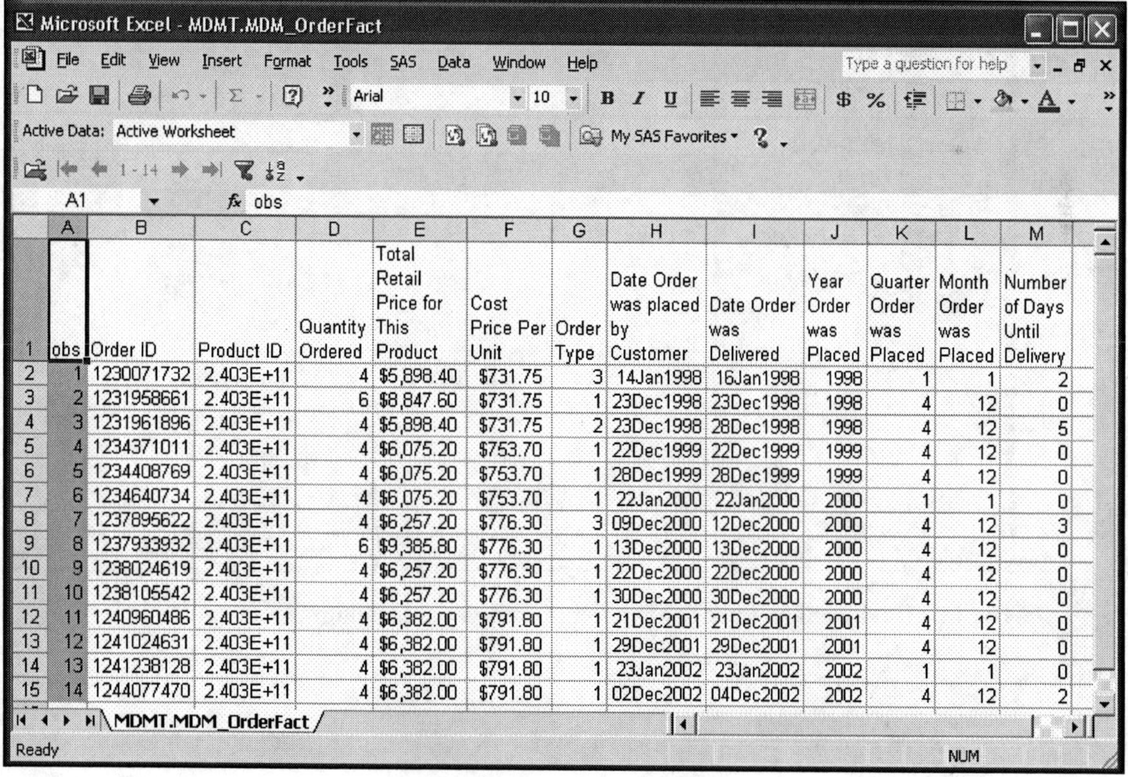

obs	Order ID	Product ID	Quantity Ordered	Total Retail Price for This Product	Cost Price Per Unit	Order Type	Date Order was placed by Customer	Date Order was Delivered	Year Order was Placed	Quarter Order was Placed	Month Order was Placed	Number of Days Until Delivery
1	1230071732	2.403E+11	4	$5,898.40	$731.75	3	14Jan1998	16Jan1998	1998	1	1	2
2	1231958661	2.403E+11	6	$8,847.60	$731.75	1	23Dec1998	23Dec1998	1998	4	12	0
3	1231961896	2.403E+11	4	$5,898.40	$731.75	2	23Dec1998	28Dec1998	1998	4	12	5
4	1234371011	2.403E+11	4	$6,075.20	$753.70	1	22Dec1999	22Dec1999	1999	4	12	0
5	1234408769	2.403E+11	4	$6,075.20	$753.70	1	28Dec1999	28Dec1999	1999	4	12	0
6	1234640734	2.403E+11	4	$6,075.20	$753.70	1	22Jan2000	22Jan2000	2000	1	1	0
7	1237895622	2.403E+11	4	$6,257.20	$776.30	3	09Dec2000	12Dec2000	2000	4	12	3
8	1237933932	2.403E+11	6	$9,385.80	$776.30	1	13Dec2000	13Dec2000	2000	4	12	0
9	1238024619	2.403E+11	4	$6,257.20	$776.30	1	22Dec2000	22Dec2000	2000	4	12	0
10	1238105542	2.403E+11	4	$6,257.20	$776.30	1	30Dec2000	30Dec2000	2000	4	12	0
11	1240960486	2.403E+11	4	$6,382.00	$791.80	1	21Dec2001	21Dec2001	2001	4	12	0
12	1241024631	2.403E+11	4	$6,382.00	$791.80	1	29Dec2001	29Dec2001	2001	4	12	0
13	1241238128	2.403E+11	4	$6,382.00	$791.80	1	23Jan2002	23Jan2002	2002	1	1	0
14	1244077470	2.403E+11	4	$6,382.00	$791.80	1	02Dec2002	04Dec2002	2002	4	12	2

The filter icon changes from [icon] to [icon] to indicate that a filter is applied.

Use the SAS Analysis Tools Toolbar for Excel

The SAS Add-In for Microsoft Office enables you to execute almost any type of SAS analysis. The SAS Analysis Tools toolbar provides access to some of the same features available through the SAS Menu, including browsing SAS programs, refreshing the results, changing the active data source, and accessing your SAS favorites. Use the SAS Analysis Tools toolbar to execute a SAS task in Excel and export the results to Word.

1. Create a report that contains selected columns from the filtered data grouped by year and with a grand total.

   a. Select [icon] on the SAS Analysis Tools toolbar (or select **SAS** ⇨ **Browse SAS Programs**).

   b. Expand the group **SAS Tasks** and select **Describe** ⇨ **List Data**. Then select [Run].

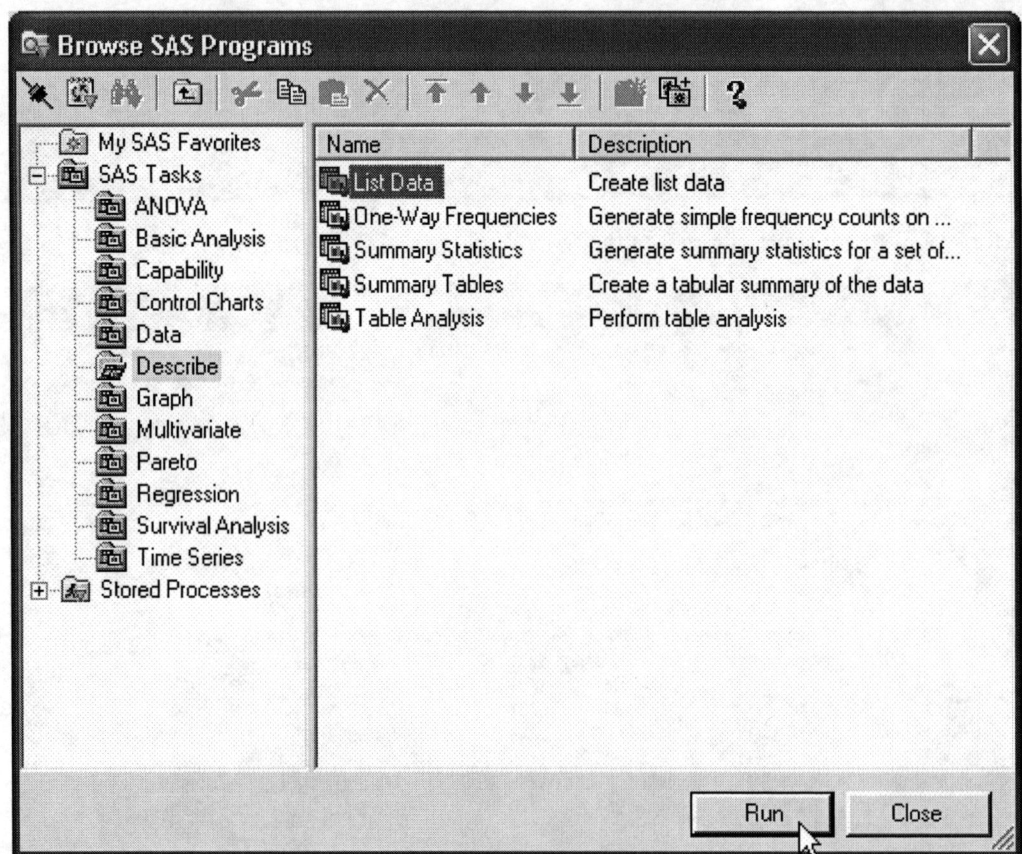

The List Data window opens with a list of the available columns.

c. Drag the **Order ID** and **Total Retail Price for This Product** columns from the Variables pane to the List Data Task Roles pane. Drop each column in the List Variables role. The columns placed in this role will be printed in the report in the order in which they are listed.

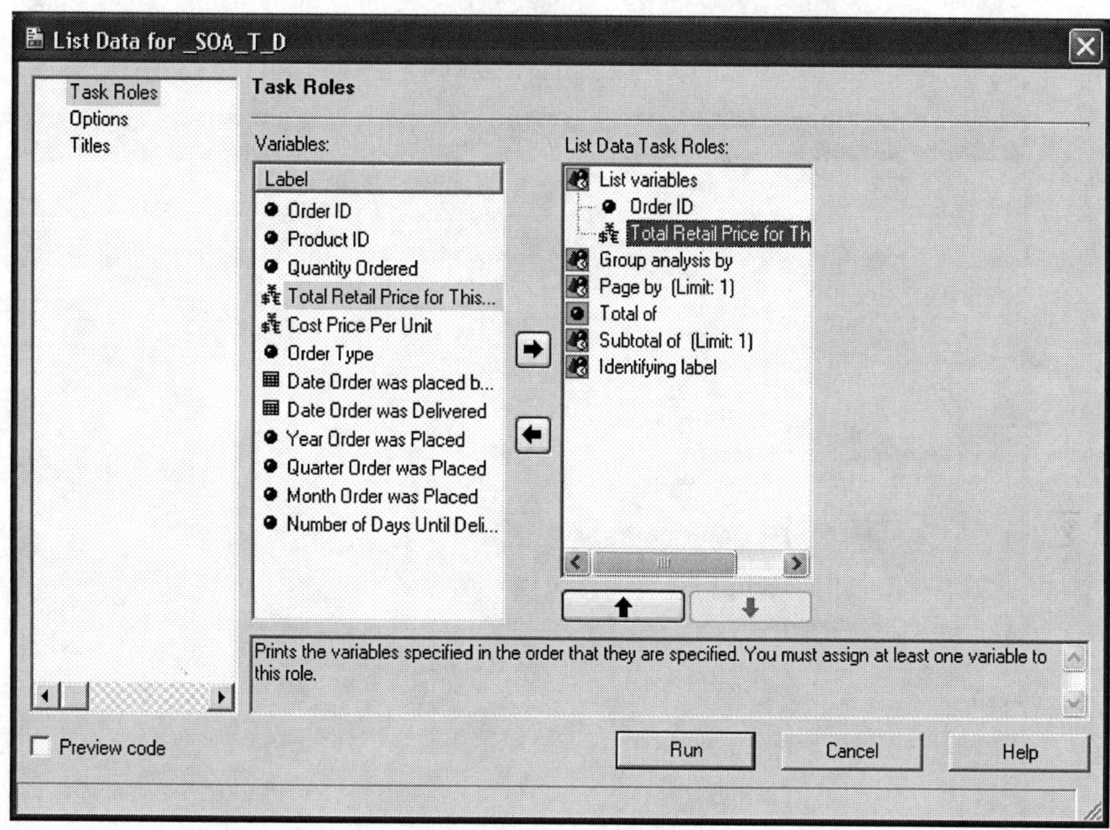

The ➡ button can also be used to assign variable(s) to roles.

d. Drag **Year Order was Placed** to the Group analysis by role. Assigning a column to this role causes the table to be sorted and grouped by the specified column.

To specify the sort order for a column in the Group analysis by role, select either **Ascending** or **Descending** from the sort order drop-down list. For this demonstration, retain the default value of ascending order for Year Order was Placed.

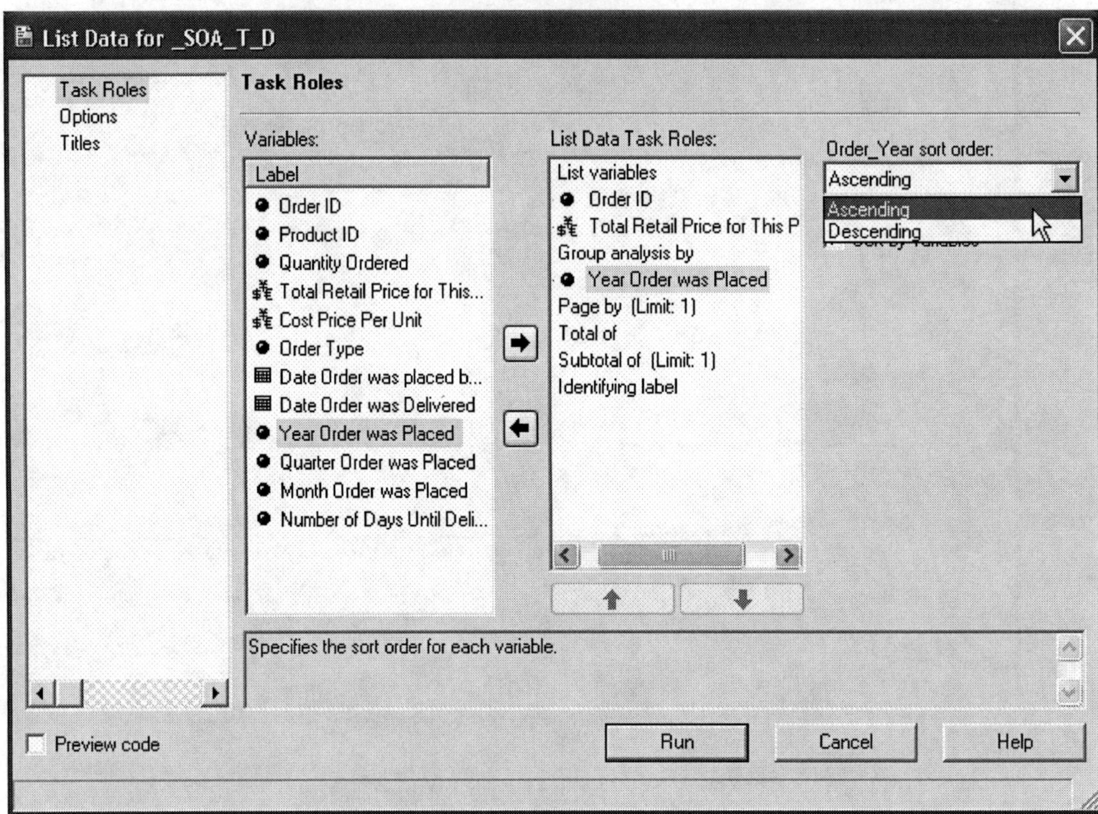

e. Drag the **Total Retail Price for This Product** column to the Total of role. The numerical columns placed in this role will display grand totals at the bottom of the listing report.

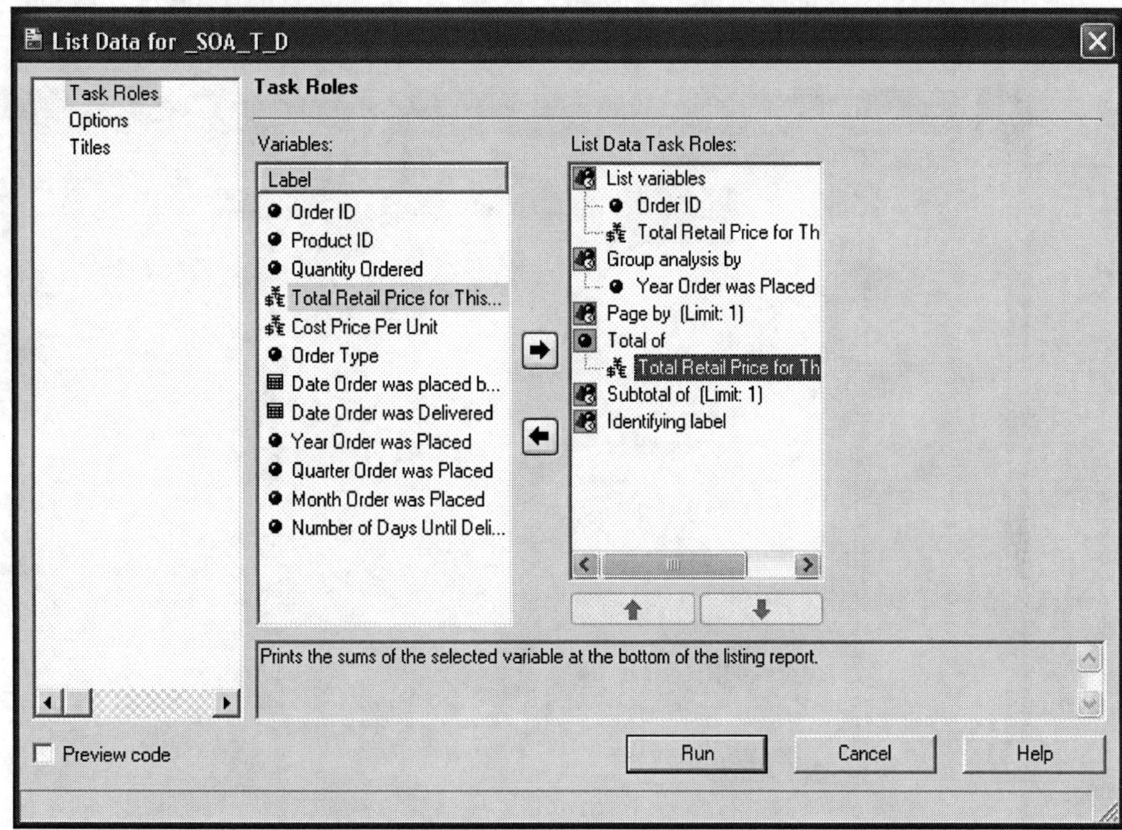

f. To specify additional report options, select **Options** in the Selection pane.

g. To suppress the printing of the row numbers in the report, deselect the **Print the row number** check box in the Options pane. Then select Run.

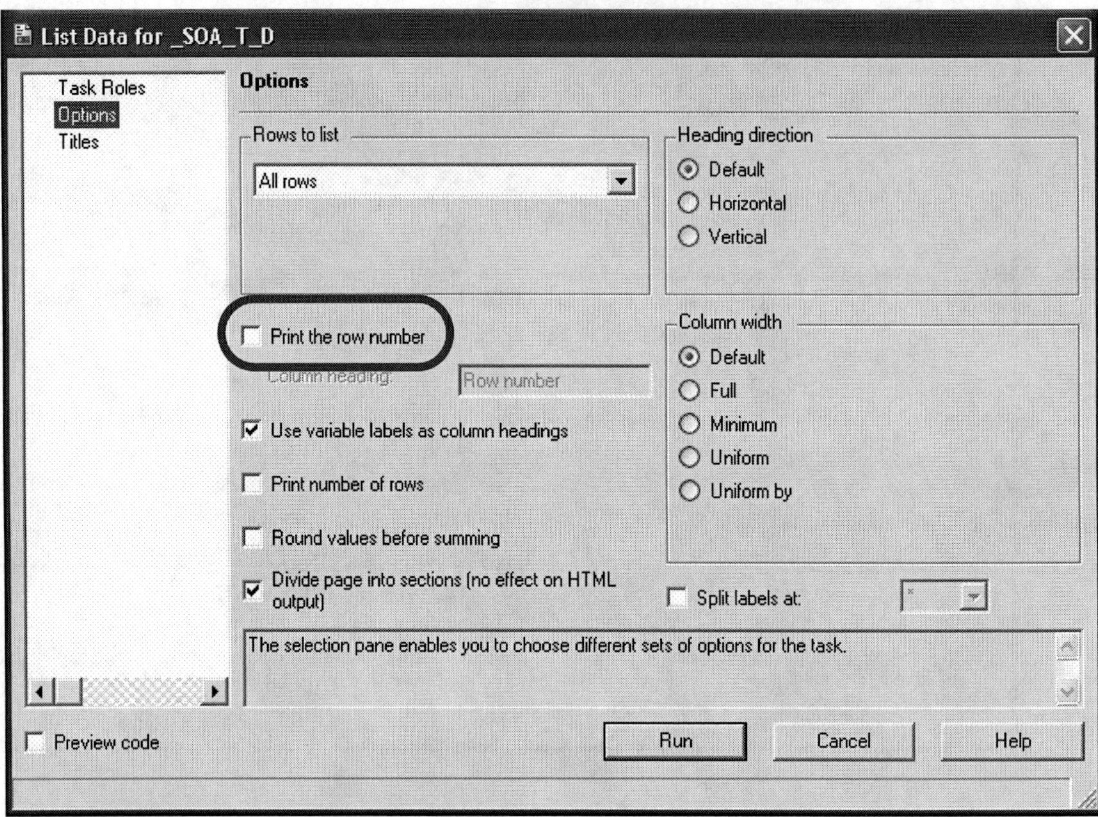

The List Data task runs and displays the report in the worksheet.

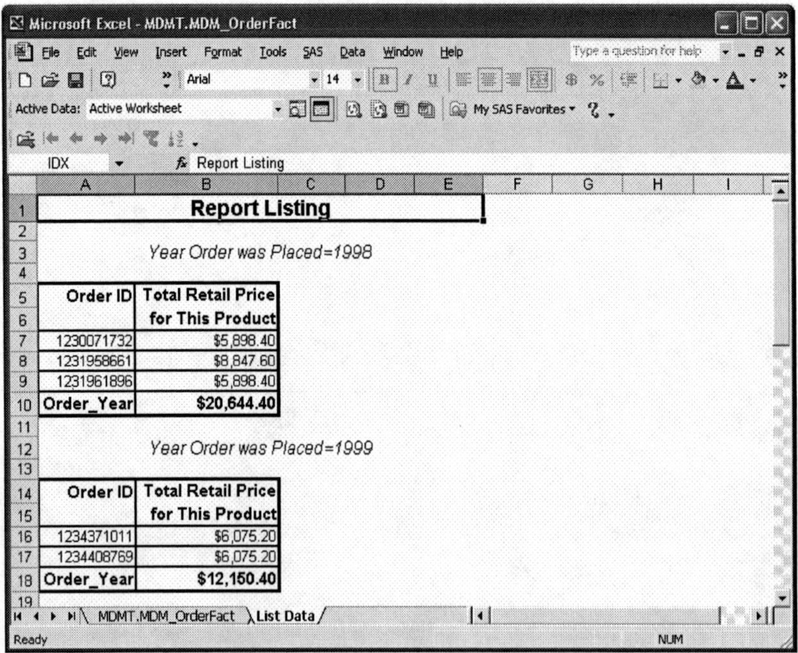

Send Results from Excel to Word

1. Send the results of the List Data task currently in Microsoft Excel directly into a new Microsoft Word document.

   a. Select on the SAS Analysis Tools toolbar (or select **SAS** ⇨ **Send to Microsoft Word**).

   When an analysis is selected to be sent to Word, the SAS task runs again to incorporate any changes that were made to the data source before the analysis is seen in Word.

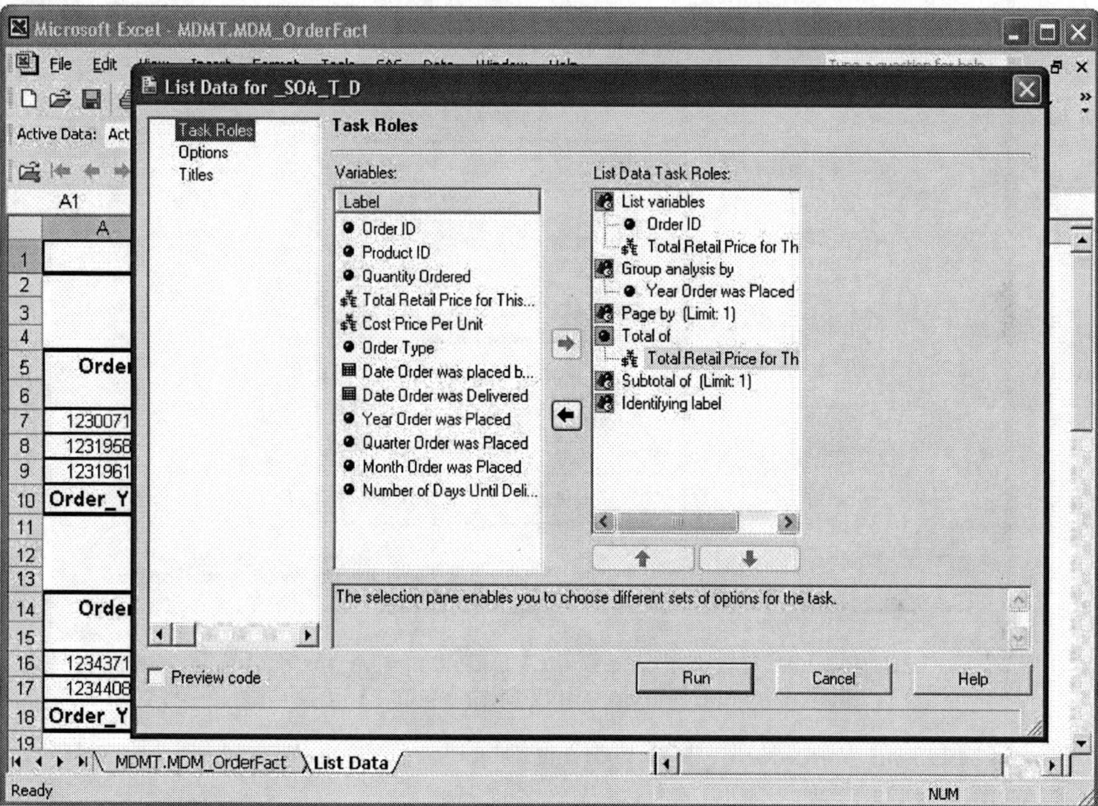

   b. Select Run.

The List Data task runs a second time and displays the report in Word.

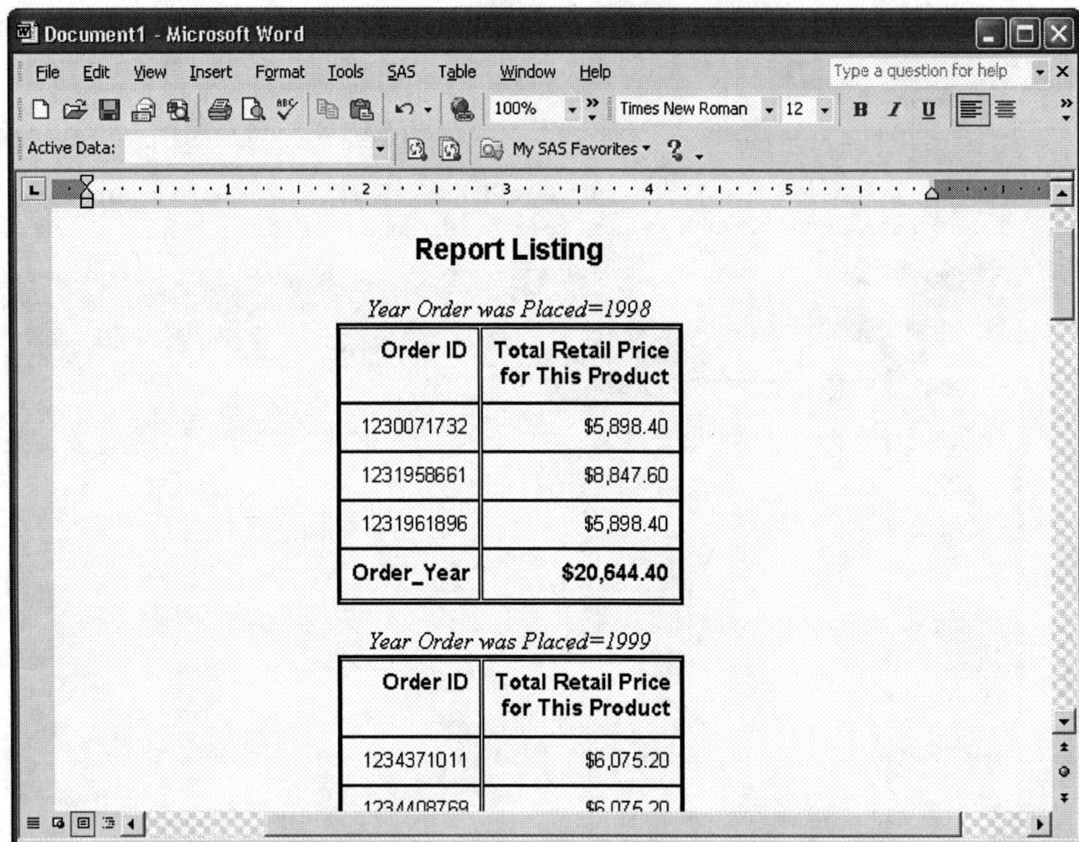

✎ After the output is available in the Word document, the document can be edited and new text added using the functionality of Microsoft Word.

c. In Microsoft Word, select **File** ⇨ **Exit** and do not save the changes.

2.3 Using the SAS Add-In for Microsoft Office in Word

The SAS Add-In for Microsoft Office

The SAS Add-In for Microsoft Office adds a

- SAS menu to the menu bar
- SAS Analysis Tools toolbar

to Microsoft Word.

SAS menu

SAS Analysis Tools toolbar

21

SAS Menu for Microsoft Word

The SAS menu in Microsoft Word provides access to the following functionality:

- ability to run stored processes and SAS tasks
- options for the add-in
- ability to specify the server
- style manager to customize the appearance of results returned to Microsoft Word.

22

SAS Analysis Tools Toolbar for Word

The SAS Analysis Tools toolbar provides access to some of the same options as the SAS menu.

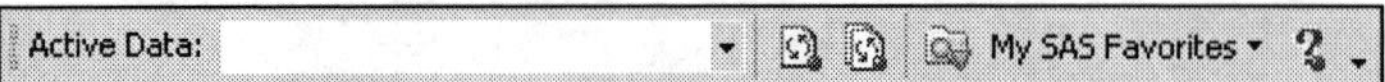

Some of the tasks that can be performed include

- changing the active data source
- refreshing the results
- browsing SAS programs
- accessing your SAS Favorites.

23

SAS Add-In Options for Word

With the SAS Add-In for Microsoft Office options, you can

- specify the default formats for graphs and results
- choose settings for how SAS tasks are surfaced
- modify the settings for handling stored processes.

24

SAS Add-In Options for Word

Access the options for the SAS Add-In for Microsoft Office for Word by selecting **SAS** ⇨ **Options...**.

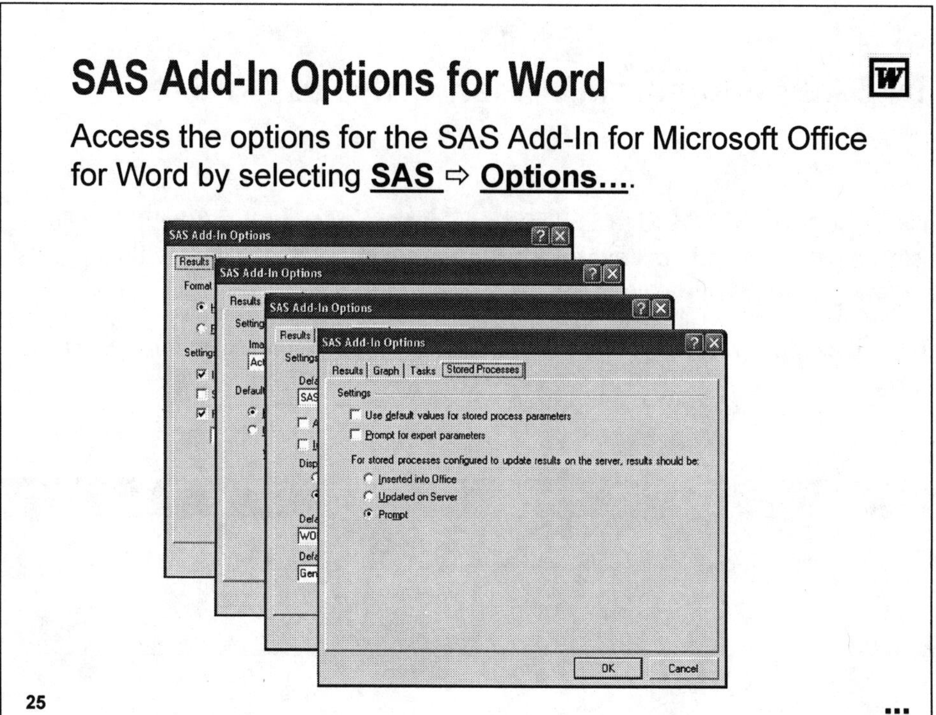

25

Connecting to the Metadata Server

When you use the SAS Add-In for Microsoft Office for the first time in Word, you will have to log in to the SAS Metadata Server.

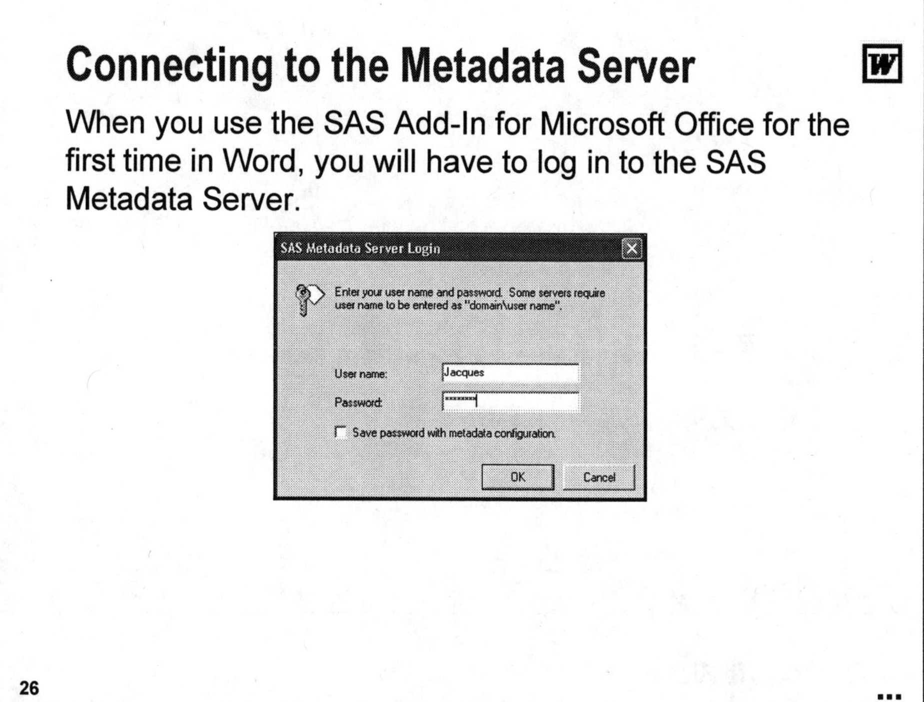

26

If the metadata server definition in your configuration does not contain a user name and password, you will be prompted to enter it. You can choose to save this password in your configuration so that you will not be prompted again.

Using the SAS Add-In for Microsoft Office in Word

In this demonstration you will use Microsoft Word to explore some of the key features of the SAS Add-In for Microsoft Office. This demonstration will cover various features at a high level, which will then be covered in detail in the remaining chapters of the course.

For this demonstration, you will execute a stored process that creates a six-month forecast for U.S. sales with 95% confidence bands.

Output:

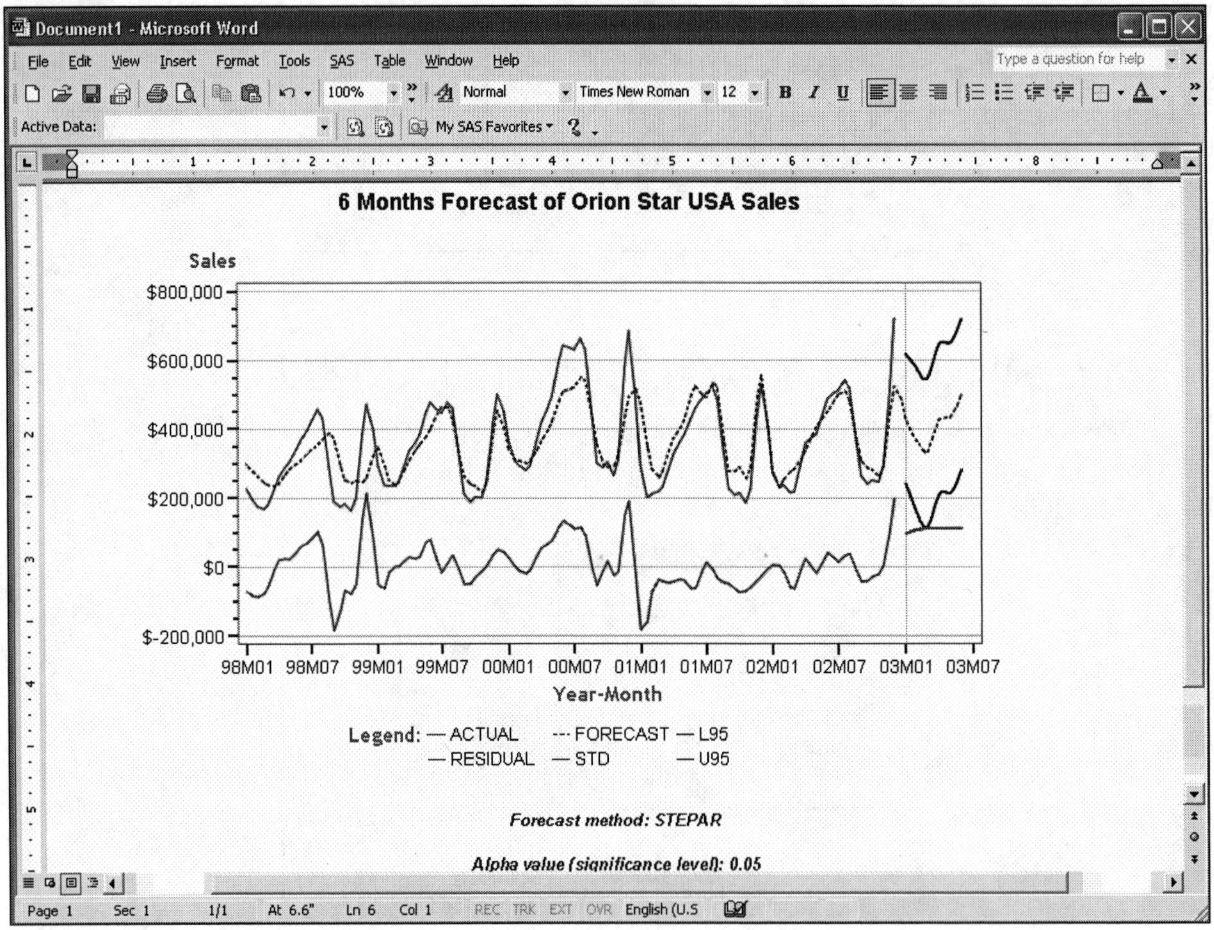

Document1 - Microsoft Word

6 Months Forecast of Orion Star USA Sales

Sales

$800,000
$600,000
$400,000
$200,000
$0
$-200,000

98M01 98M07 99M01 99M07 00M01 00M07 01M01 01M07 02M01 02M07 03M01 03M07

Year-Month

Legend: — ACTUAL --- FORECAST — L95
— RESIDUAL — STD — U95

Forecast method: STEPAR

Alpha value (significance level): 0.05

Use the SAS Menu for Microsoft Word

The SAS Add-In for Microsoft Office enables you to customize how the tool integrates with Microsoft Word. These features are set using the SAS Add-In Options window. Use the SAS Menu for Microsoft Word to accept default parameters for stored processes.

1. Invoke Microsoft Word by selecting **Start** ⇨ **All Programs** ⇨ **Microsoft Office** ⇨ **Microsoft Word**.

2. Select **SAS** ⇨ **Options** from the pull-down menu.

If prompted, enter the user name and password provided by the instructor.

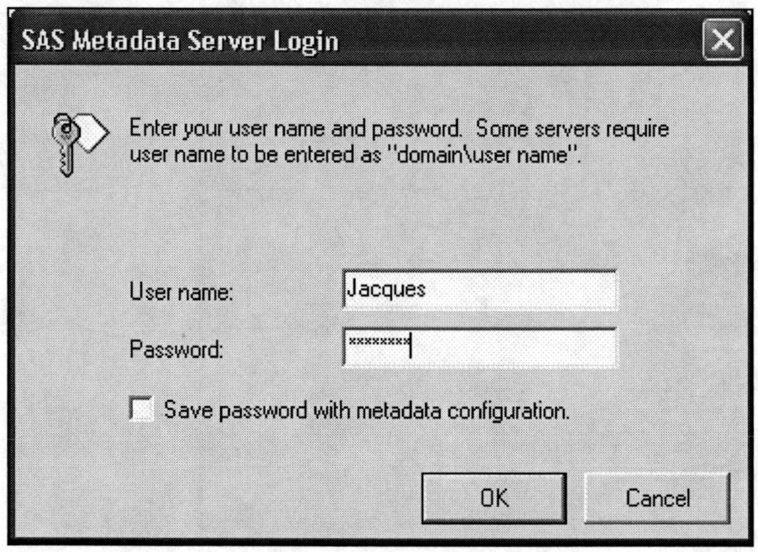

✎ The values shown above may be different than those used in class.

3. Select OK.

The add-in displays an information window while it connects to the SAS Metadata Server, and then the SAS Add-In Options window opens.

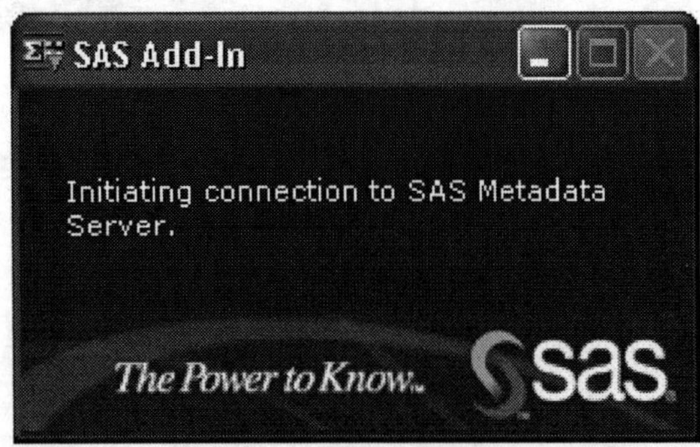

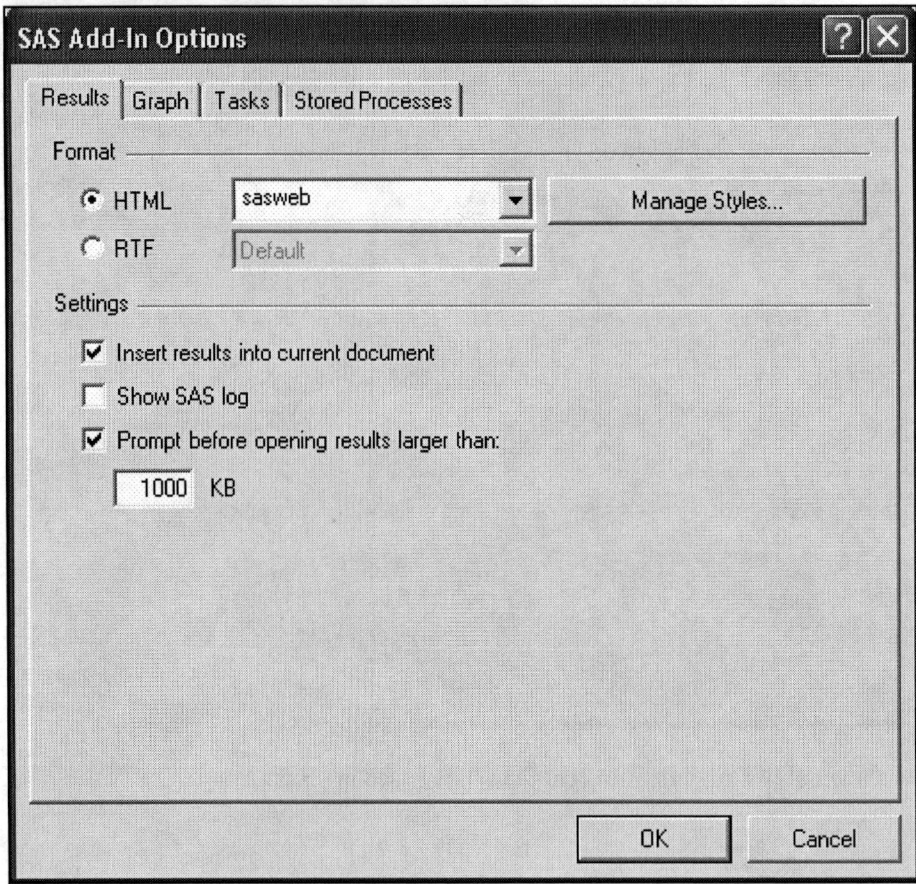

4. Use the SAS Add-In Options window to use default parameters for stored processes.

   a. Select the **Stored Processes** tab.

   b. Select **Use default values for stored process parameters**.

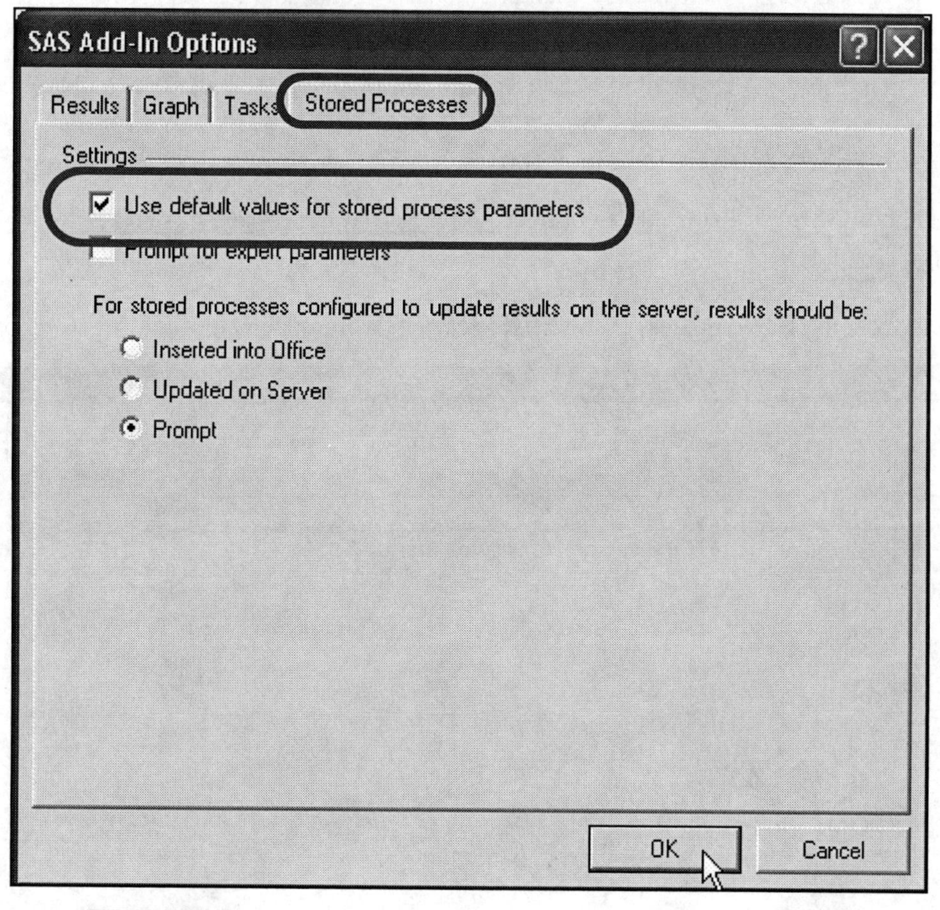

Select OK.

Use the SAS Analysis Tools Toolbar for Word

The SAS Add-In for Microsoft Office enables you to execute a SAS stored process. The SAS Analysis Tools toolbar provides access to some of the same features available through the SAS Menu, including browsing SAS programs, refreshing the results, changing the active data source, and accessing your SAS favorites. Use the SAS Analysis Tools toolbar to execute a stored process in Word.

1. Create a graph that displays a six-month forecast of U.S. sales with the default alpha level of 5%.

   a. Select [icon] on the SAS Analysis Tools toolbar (or select **SAS** ⇨ **Browse SAS Programs**).

   b. Expand the group **Stored Processes** and select **AMO Stored Processes** ⇨ **AMO Sales Forecast**. Then select [Run].

   The output from the stored process is streamed back to a Word document.

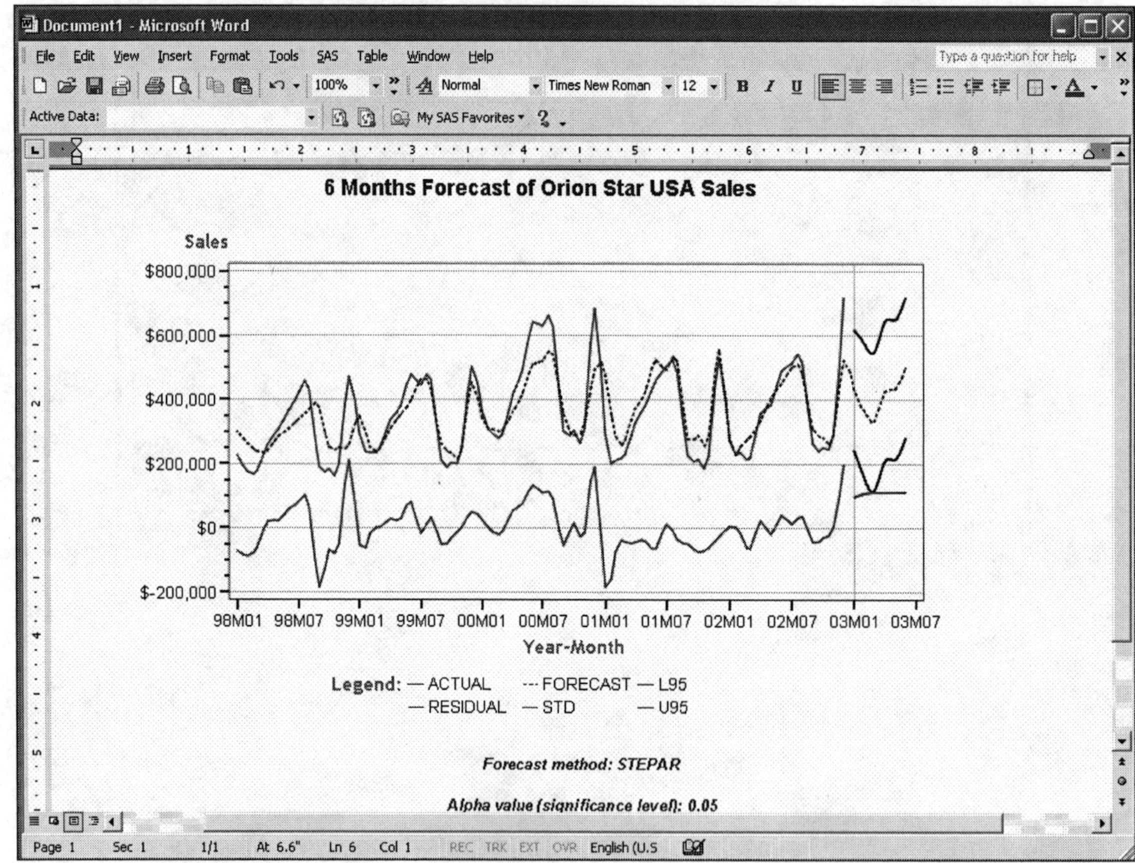

   After the output is available in the Word document, the document can be edited and new text added using the functionality of Microsoft Word.

   c. To set the parameters option back to the default, go to **SAS** ⇨ **Options** ⇨ **Stored Processes** and deselect **Use default values for stored process parameters**. Then select [OK].

   d. In Microsoft Word, select **File** ⇨ **Exit** and do not save the changes.

Chapter 3 Inserting SAS Data into Microsoft Excel

3.1 SAS Data Set Concepts and Terminology

Data Terminology

Traditionally, SAS has used alternative terminology to describe the structure of data. Similarly, other products, such as SQL, use their own unique method of referring to data and data structures.

Data Processing	SAS	SQL
file	data set	table
record	observation	row
field	variable	column

3

A **file** is a rectangular table of rows and columns of values that represent all of the data stored for a collection of entities that usually have something in common. An entity is anything that is of importance, and of interest, to an organization. Example entities include

- a person (such as a customer or employee)
- a product
- a purchase
- a policy
- an account.

A **record** is any one of the horizontal rows of a file that represents all of the data maintained for a single entity.

A **field** is any one of the vertical columns in a file. A field represents a single piece of information about all of the entities, such as name, address, or account number.

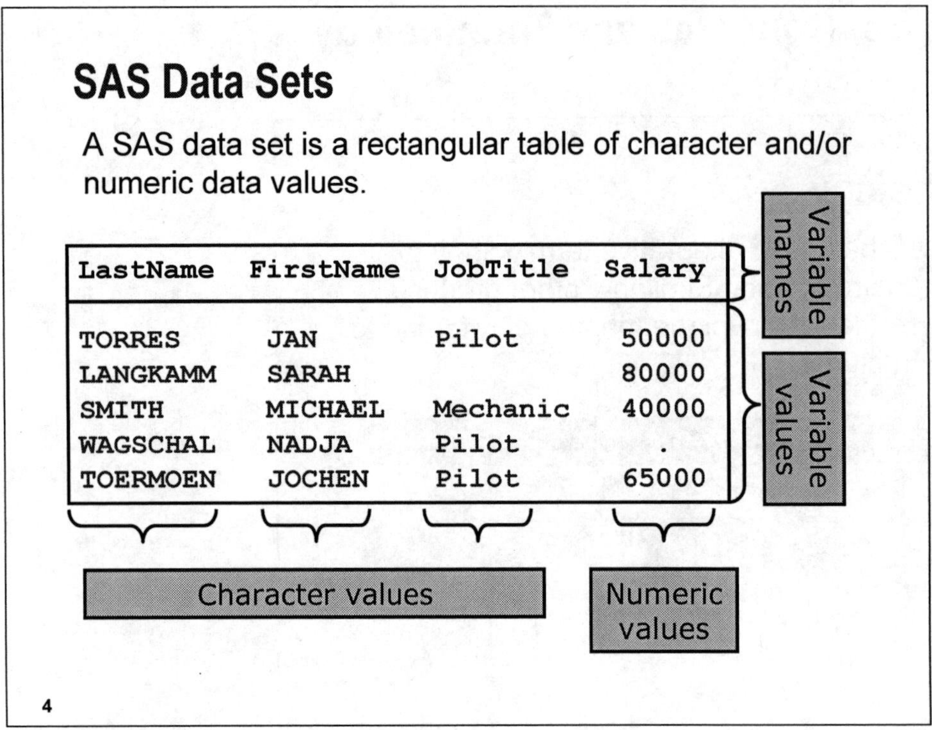

Missing character values are stored and displayed as a single blank space. Missing numeric values are stored and displayed as a period.

Data Types

Variables (columns) in a SAS data set can be one of the following:

- Character
- Numeric
- Date

A variable's type determines how it can be used. For example, you cannot compute an arithmetic average or standard deviation of the character variable **`FirstName`**.

5

Character data is stored in 1 to 32,767 bytes. Numeric data is stored in 8 bytes by default.

Data Types - Character

Character variables can contain

- letters (A – Z, a – z)
- numbers (0 – 9)
- special characters (~ ! @ # $ % ^ & * ? and so on).

6

Data Types - Numeric

Numeric variables can contain

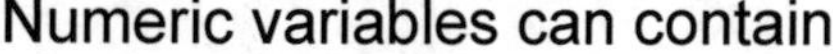

- digits (0 – 9)

and optionally

- one sign (+ or -)
- one decimal point (.)
- the letter 'E' to indicate the exponent for scientific notation.

Numeric values are stored **without** dollar signs or commas.

7

Data Types - Date

SAS dates

- are stored as numeric values
- represent the number of days between January 1, 1960, and a specific date
- are typically stored with a date format to display a calendar date.

8

Microsoft Excel uses January 1, 1900, as its start date. SAS dates that are stored as numbers without a date format could be misinterpreted in Excel.

SAS Formats

A SAS format is a writing instruction. It tells SAS how variable values are to appear in a report. A SAS format does **not** change the stored value.

SAS provides an extensive group of formats that are used with either numeric or character data. SAS also permits the creation of user-defined formats.

9

SAS Formats

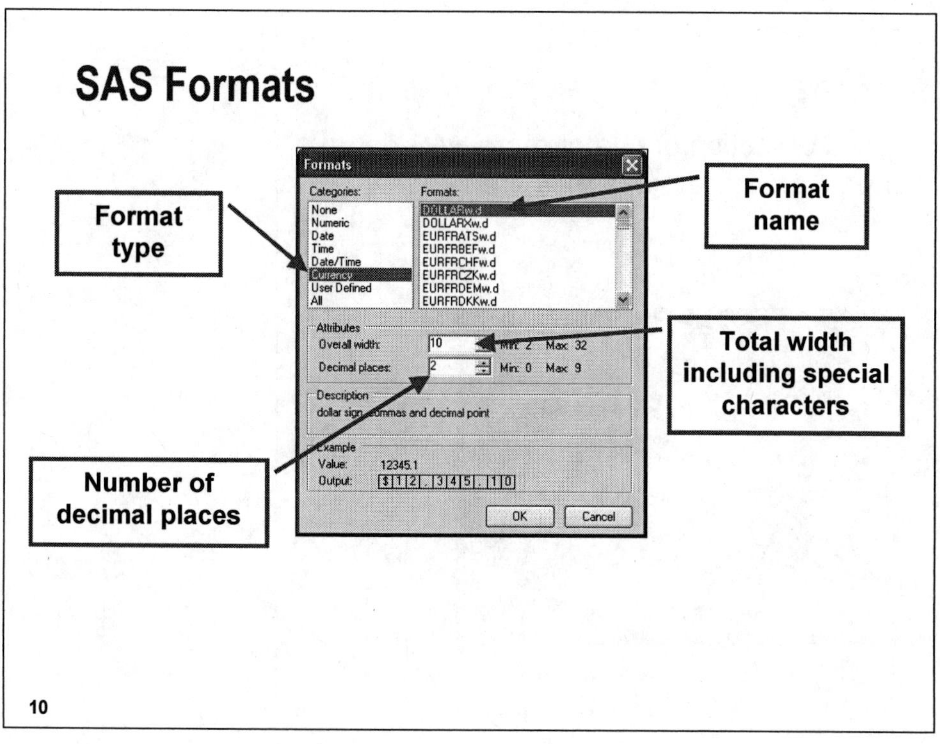

10

SAS Functions

SAS functions

- perform manipulations or calculations on character or numeric data and return a value
- are grouped by task.

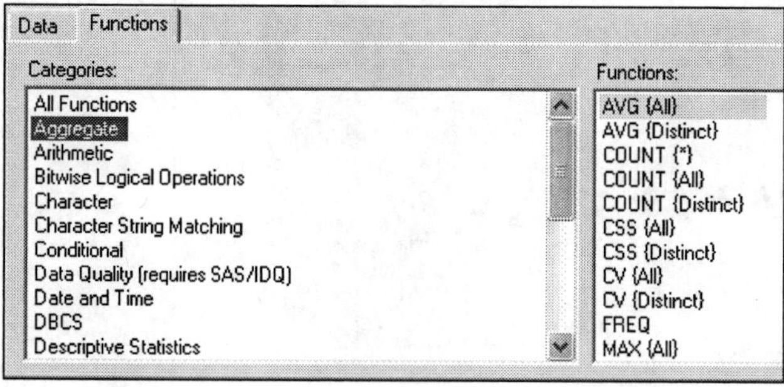

11

SAS Data Libraries

A SAS data library is a collection of one or more SAS data sets considered to be a group because they are stored in the same physical location.

SAS Data Library

12

SAS Data Libraries

A SAS data library can be thought of as a drawer in a filing cabinet and a SAS data set as one of the file folders in the drawer.

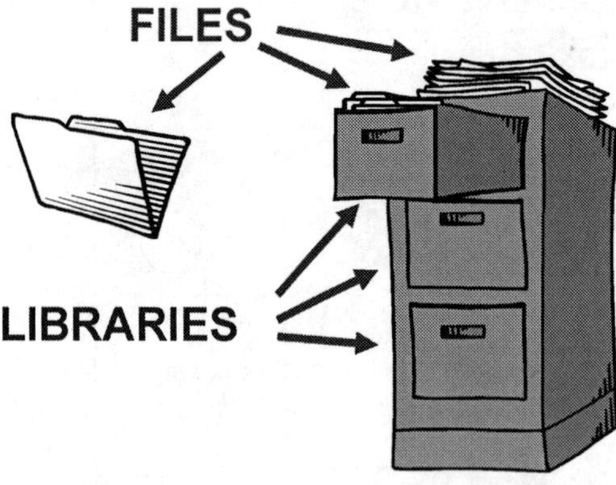

13 ...

SAS Data Libraries

There are a few data libraries created automatically by SAS. You reference a library by using an alias or nickname known as a **libref**.

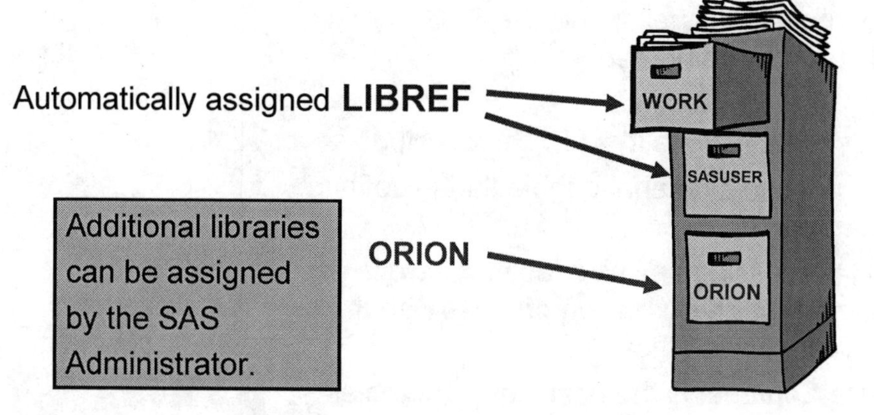

14

SAS Data Libraries

After a library has been defined, a data set in that physical storage location is referenced using a two-level name.

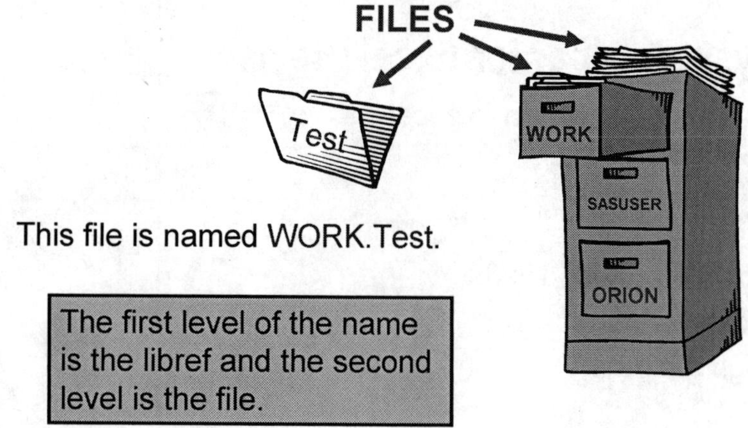

15

3.2 Using SAS Data Sources with Microsoft Excel

SAS Data Sources and Microsoft Excel

The SAS Add-In for Microsoft Office allows you to access any SAS Data Source that is available to the SAS Server or is stored locally on your computer.

The add-in extends the functionality of Excel to include

- accessing any relational database table that is defined as a SAS Data Source.
- accessing and processing any size table. There is no limit on the number of rows you can process with the SAS Add-In for Microsoft Office.
- using SAS Data Sources as the basis for pivot tables.

17

You must have proper authority and the appropriate SAS/ACCESS product(s) to access relational database tables.

SAS Data Analysis Toolbar for Excel (Review)

The SAS Data Analysis toolbar provides access to options for working with SAS data.

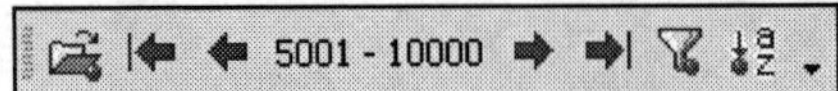

The tasks that can be performed include

- opening a SAS data source
- navigating through the data
- using a filter
- sorting the data.

✎ All of the features available from the SAS Data Analysis toolbar can also be accessed from the SAS menu.

18

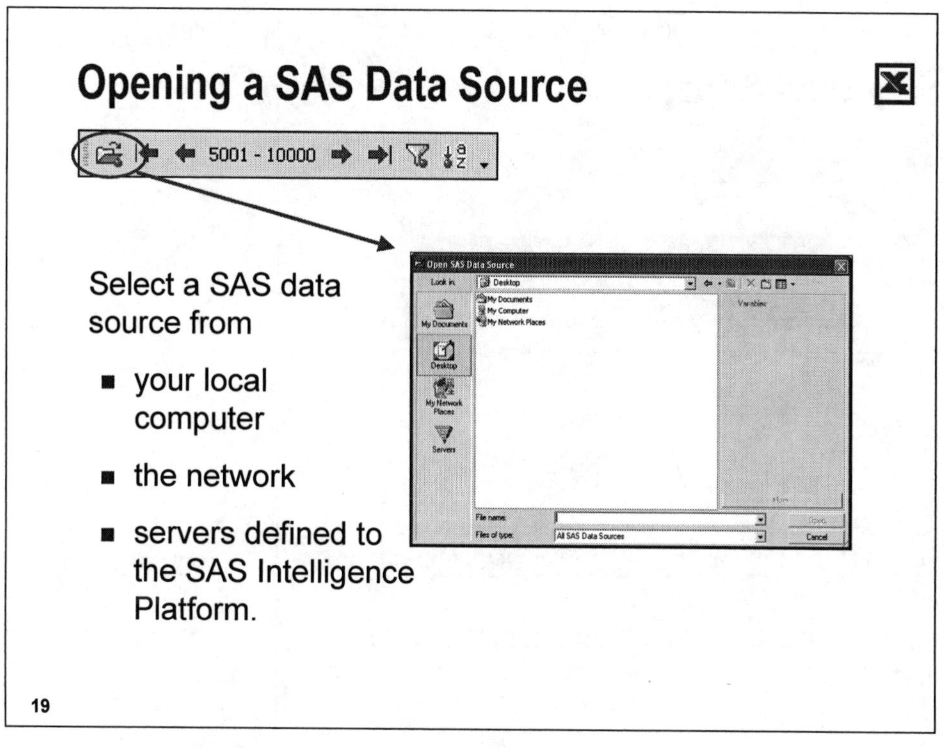

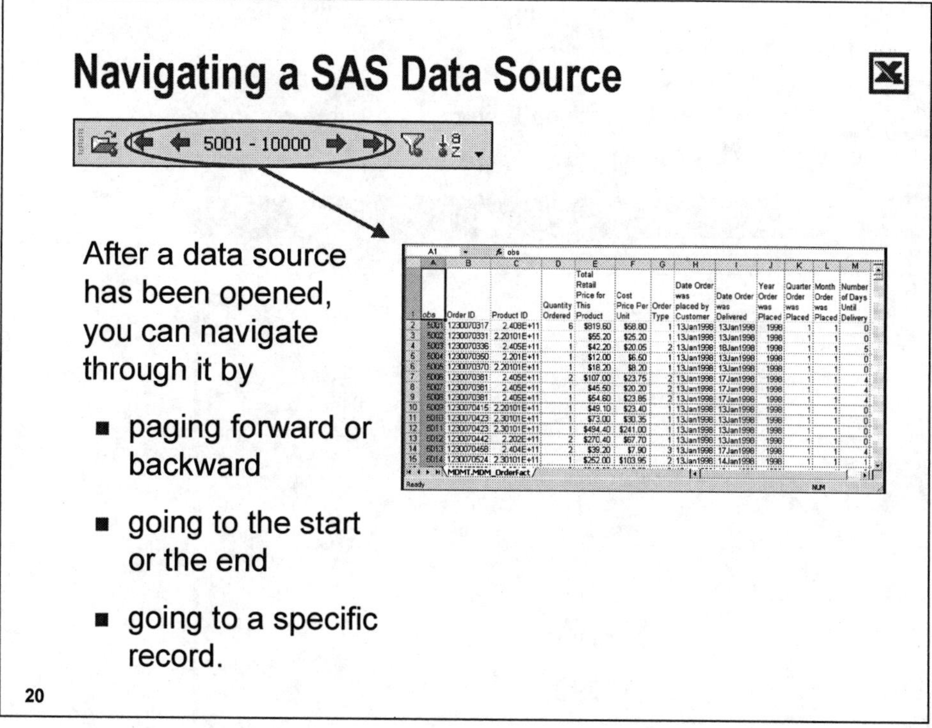

Although Microsoft Excel allows only a maximum of 65,536 rows to be displayed at one time, the underlying SAS Data Source may contain more rows.

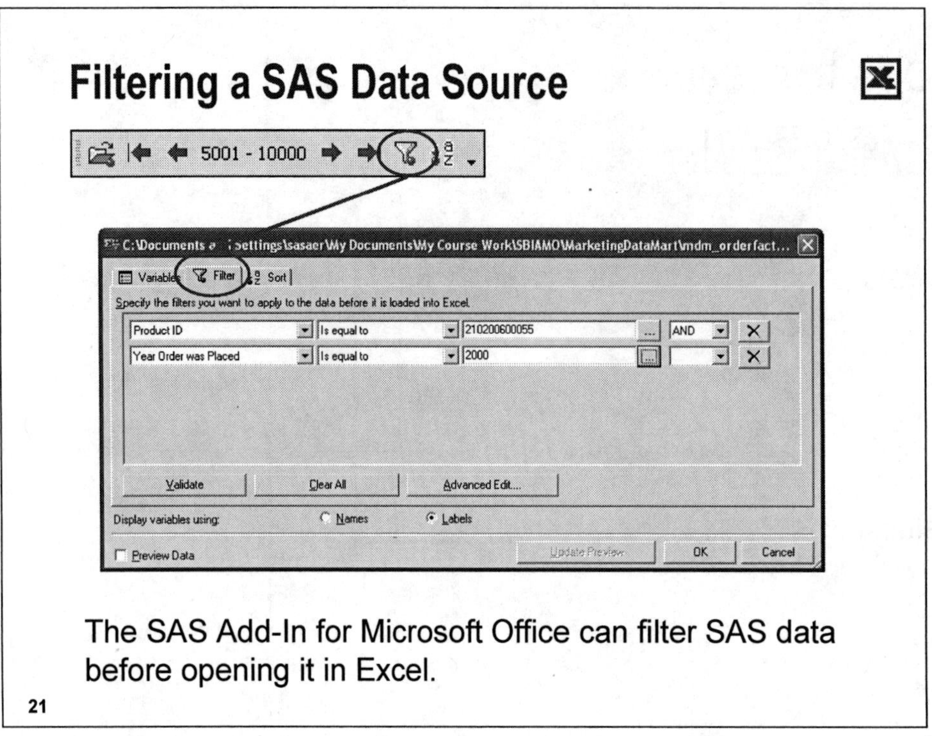

Filtering and sorting generate Structured Query Language (SQL) code behind the scenes, which is processed by the SAS Workspace Server.

Selecting Advanced Edit... opens an Expression Editor window for creating more advanced filtering expressions, including the use of SAS functions.

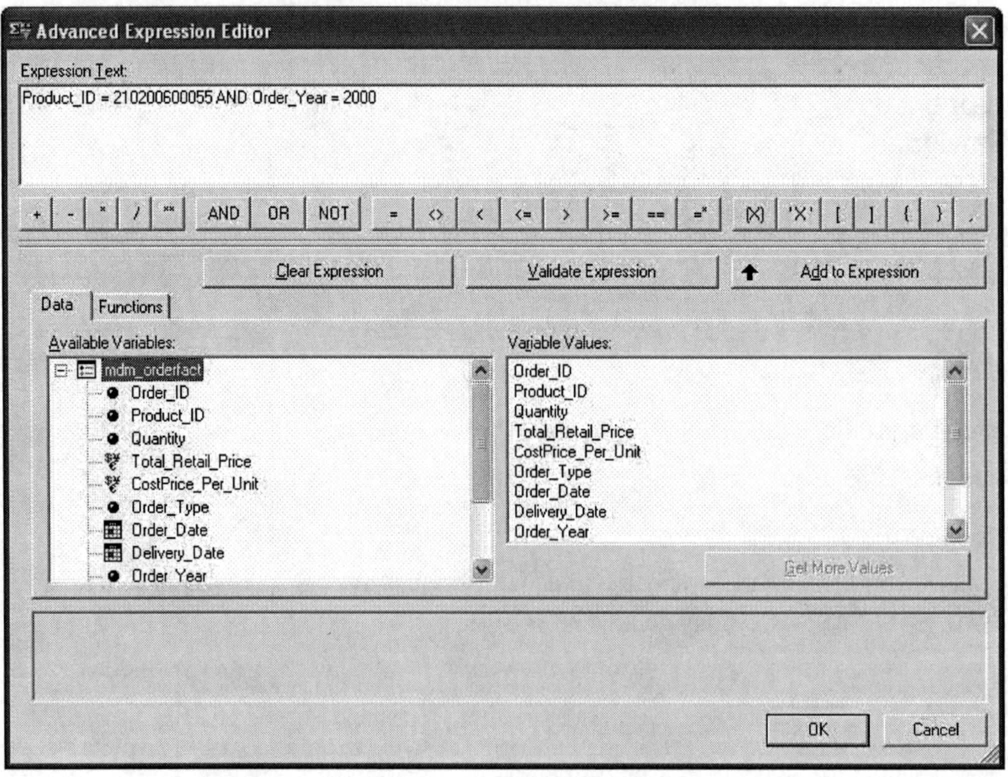

Common Comparison Operators

Symbol	Definition
=	Is equal to
<>	Is not equal to
>	Is greater than
<	Is less than
>=	Is greater or equal to
<=	Is less or equal to

22

Logical Operators

Logical operators include

AND if **both** expressions are true, then the compound expression is true

```
JobCode='FLTAT' and Salary > 50000
```

OR if **either** expression is true, then the compound expression is true

```
JobCode='PILOT' or Salary > 50000
```

NOT can be combined with other operators to **reverse the logic** of a comparison.

```
JobCode not = 'PILOT'
```

23

Special Operators

Special operators include

Is Between Values (Incl) selects observations in which the value of the variable falls within a range of values, inclusively.

```
Salary between 50000 and 70000
```

Is Between Values (Excl) selects observations in which the value of the variable falls outside a range of values.

```
Salary not between 50000 and 70000
```

24

Special Operators

The **Contains** operator selects observations that contain a specified substring.

```
Name contains 'SMITH'
```

Selects names like SMITH and SYM-SMITH.

The **Sounds Like (=*)** operator selects observations that contain spelling variations of the word specified.

```
Name =* 'SMITH'
```

Selects names like SMYTHE and SMITT.

25

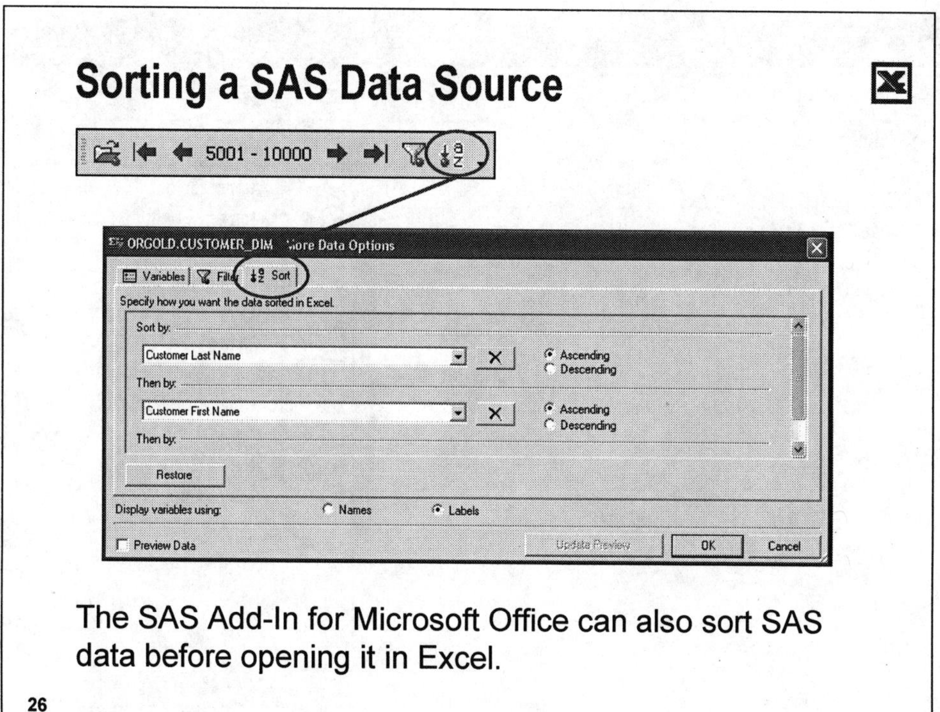

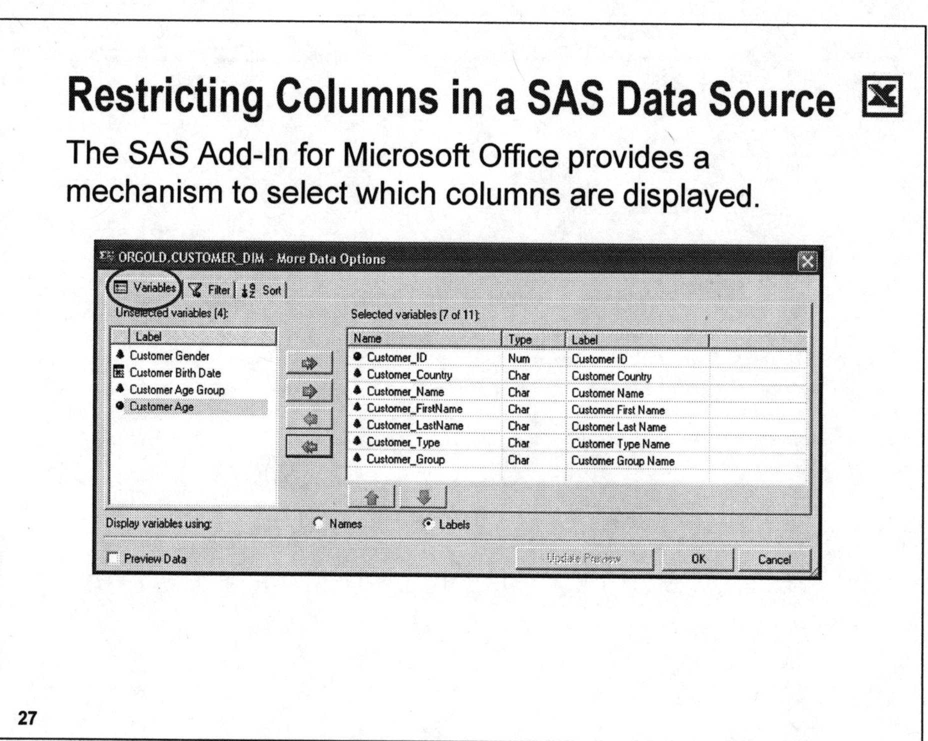

You can also select columns in the Open SAS Data Source window.

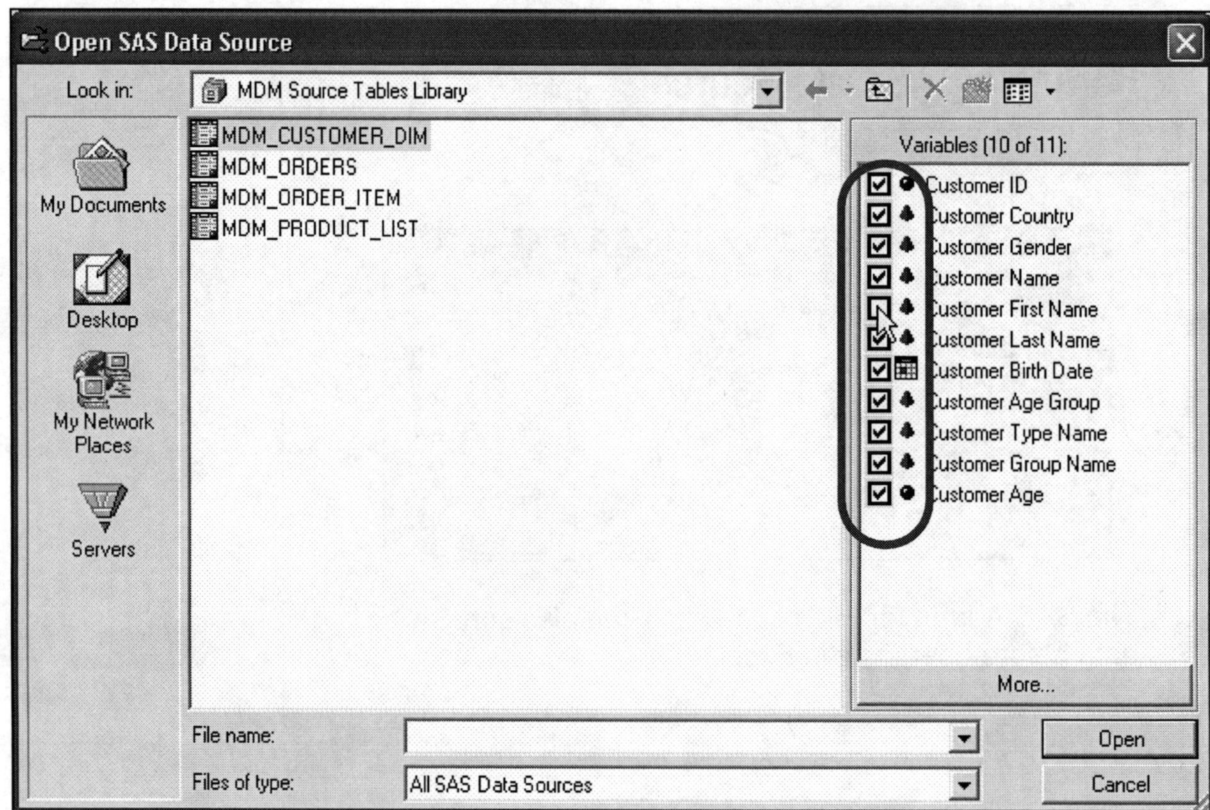
Open SAS Data Source
Look in:
MDM Source Tables Library
MDM_CUSTOMER_DIM
MDM_ORDERS
MDM_ORDER_ITEM
MDM_PRODUCT_LIST
My Documents
Desktop
My Network Places
Servers
Variables (10 of 11):
Customer ID
Customer Country
Customer Gender
Customer Name
Customer First Name
Customer Last Name
Customer Birth Date
Customer Age Group
Customer Type Name
Customer Group Name
Customer Age
More...
File name:
Files of type:
All SAS Data Sources
Open
Cancel

Working with SAS Data Sources in Microsoft Excel

For this demonstration, you will use the SAS Data Analysis toolbar to

- filter the data with an order number of 3
- filter the data for orders placed during year 2002
- sort the data in descending order by date ordered
- select the columns necessary for the report.

Output (partial listing):

Microsoft Excel - MDMS.MDM_ORDERS

	A	B	C	D	E
1	obs	Order ID	Customer ID	Date Order was placed by Customer	Date Order was Delivered
2	1	1244337136	31171	31Dec2002	04Jan2003
3	2	1244333825	15883	31Dec2002	01Jan2003
4	3	1244336615	32057	31Dec2002	05Jan2003
5	4	1244336610	26145	31Dec2002	04Jan2003
6	5	1244334701	59256	31Dec2002	03Jan2003
7	6	1244333486	8591	31Dec2002	06Jan2003
8	7	1244334124	55920	31Dec2002	04Jan2003
9	8	1244334730	73887	31Dec2002	04Jan2003
10	9	1244335957	73539	31Dec2002	01Jan2003
11	10	1244333974	19965	31Dec2002	05Jan2003
12	11	1244334702	60085	31Dec2002	03Jan2003
13	12	1244334601	39642	31Dec2002	01Jan2003
14	13	1244333558	26712	31Dec2002	05Jan2003
15	14	1244337607	62563	31Dec2002	03Jan2003

MDMS.MDM_ORDERS

Ready

Navigating a SAS Data Source

The SAS Data Analysis toolbar can be used to add data, navigate through the data, apply a filter, sort the data, and restrict which columns to display.

The SAS Data Analysis toolbar is available in Microsoft Excel only.

1. Return to the previous session of Microsoft Excel and open a new data source.

    a. Select **SAS** ⇨ **Open SAS Data Source** from the pull-down menus or select [icon] on the SAS Data Analysis toolbar.

    b. In the Open SAS Data Source window, select **Servers** from the shortcut bar.

    c. Choose **SASMain** and select [Open] (or double-click SASMain).

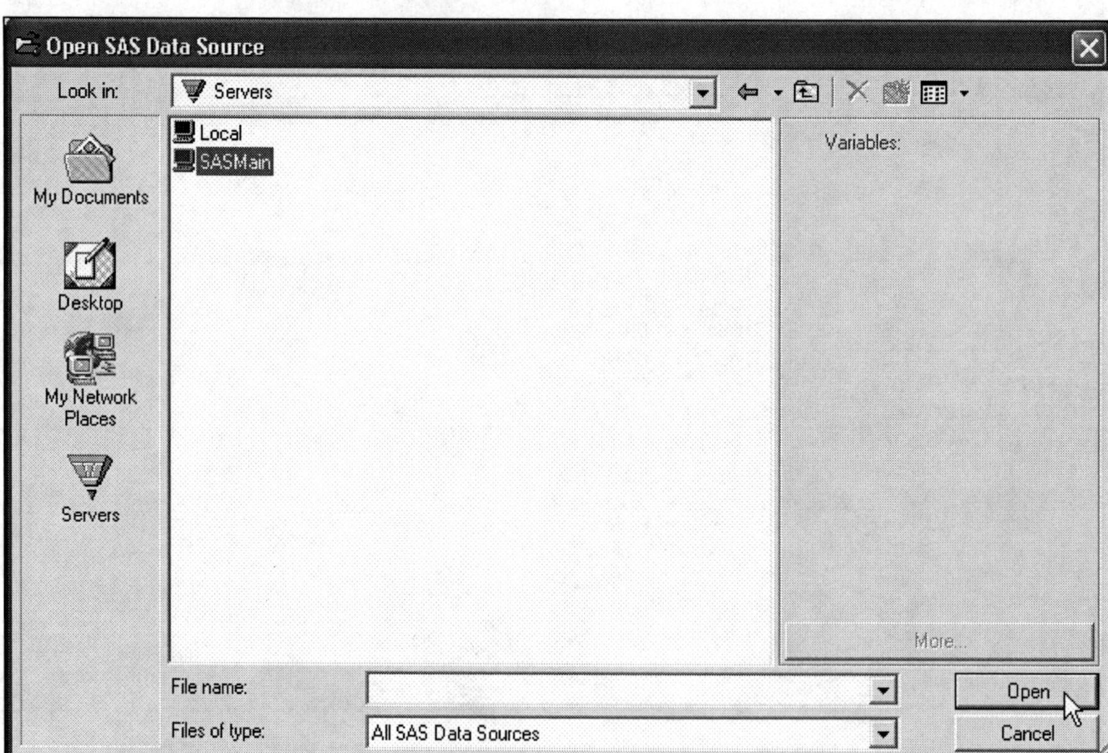

d. Select **MDM Source Tables Library** and then choose Open (or double-click MDM Source Tables Library).

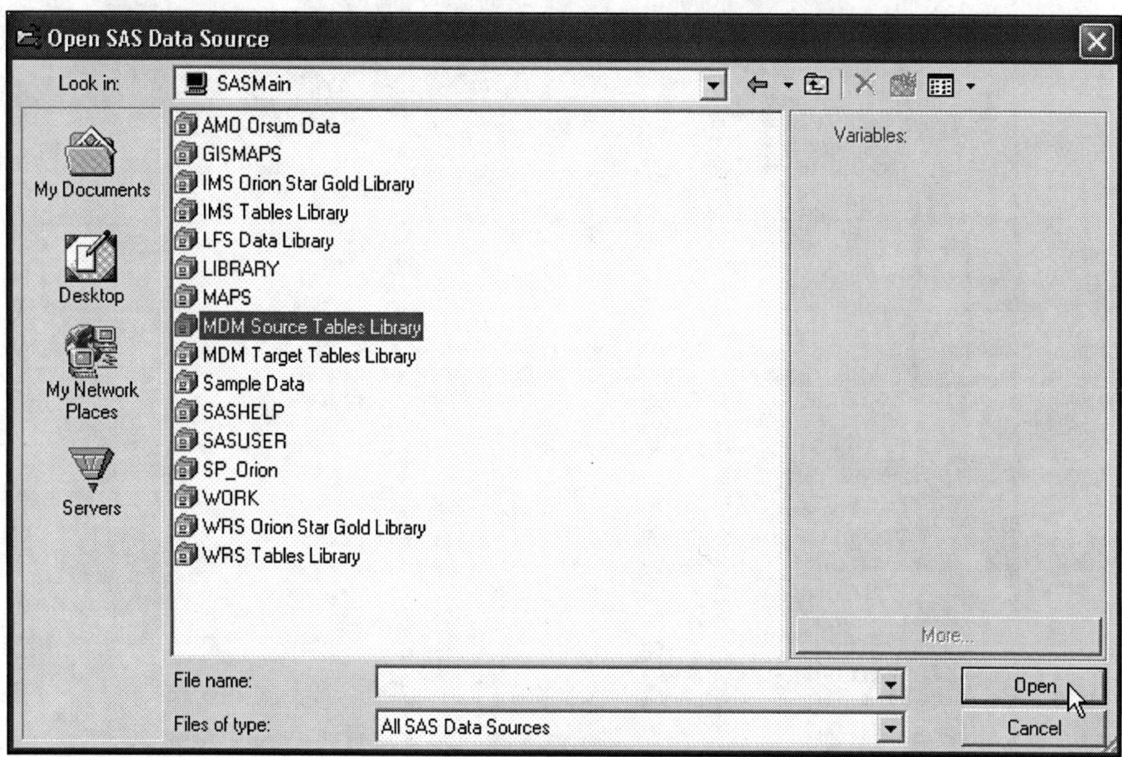

e. Select **MDM_ORDERS**, then choose Open (or double-click MDM_ORDERS).

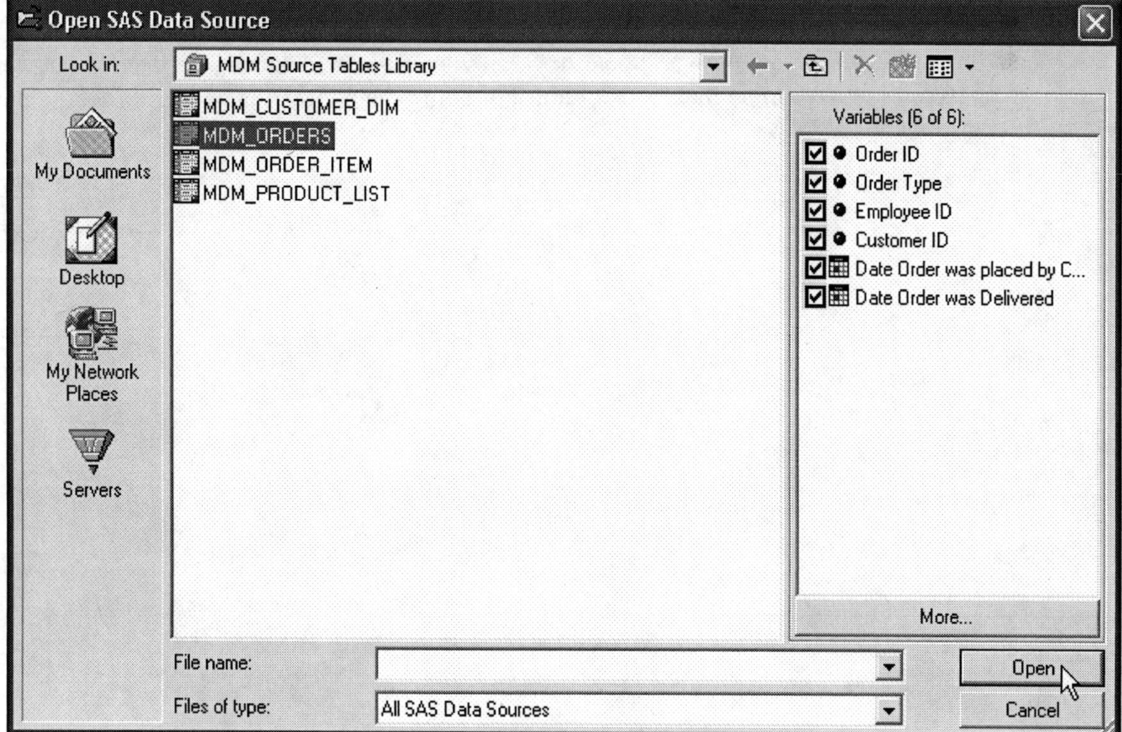

f. The data from the server is retrieved into the worksheet.

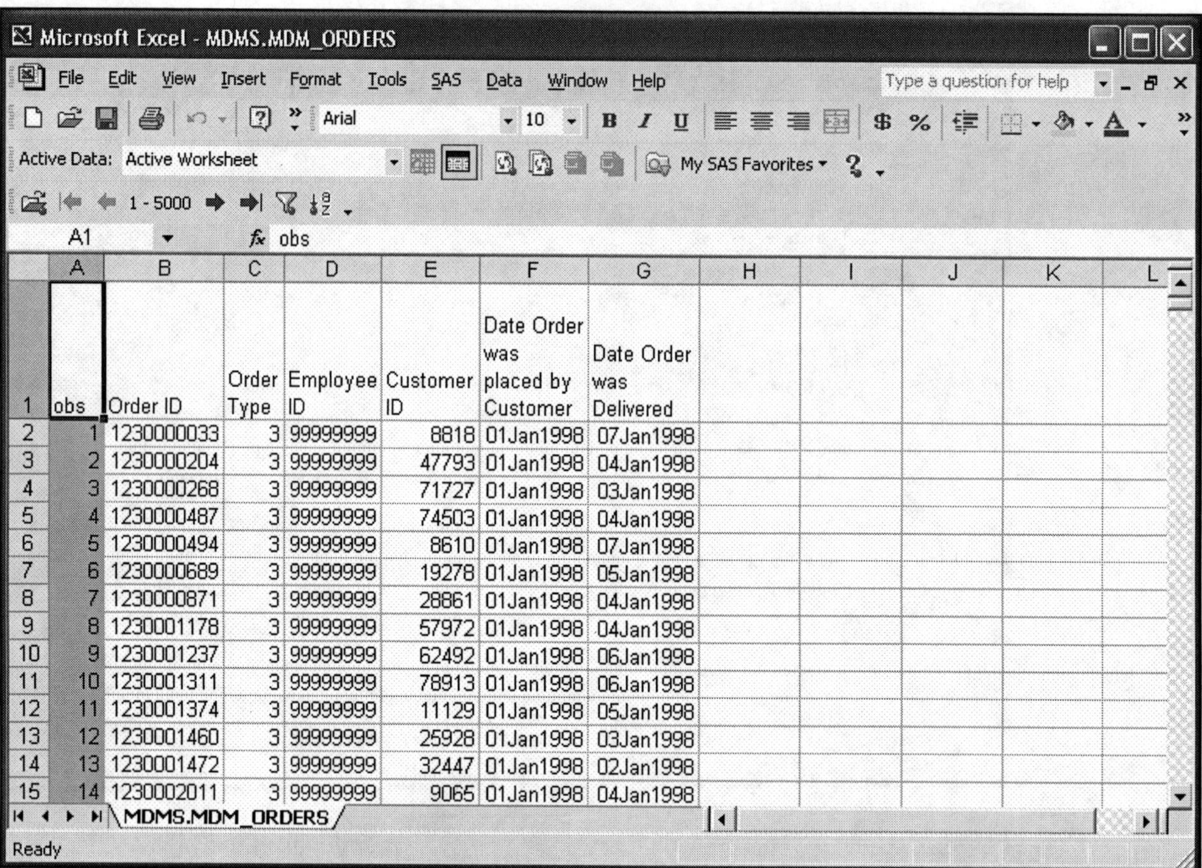

obs	Order ID	Order Type	Employee ID	Customer ID	Date Order was placed by Customer	Date Order was Delivered
1	1230000033	3	99999999	8818	01Jan1998	07Jan1998
2	1230000204	3	99999999	47793	01Jan1998	04Jan1998
3	1230000268	3	99999999	71727	01Jan1998	03Jan1998
4	1230000487	3	99999999	74503	01Jan1998	04Jan1998
5	1230000494	3	99999999	8610	01Jan1998	07Jan1998
6	1230000689	3	99999999	19278	01Jan1998	05Jan1998
7	1230000871	3	99999999	28861	01Jan1998	04Jan1998
8	1230001178	3	99999999	57972	01Jan1998	04Jan1998
9	1230001237	3	99999999	62492	01Jan1998	06Jan1998
10	1230001311	3	99999999	78913	01Jan1998	06Jan1998
11	1230001374	3	99999999	11129	01Jan1998	05Jan1998
12	1230001460	3	99999999	25928	01Jan1998	03Jan1998
13	1230001472	3	99999999	32447	01Jan1998	02Jan1998
14	1230002011	3	99999999	9065	01Jan1998	04Jan1998

Excel limits the number of rows available in a worksheet to 65,536 and the columns to 256. By adding data sources to your workbook via SAS, you can open data sources that are larger than 65,536 rows or have more than 256 columns, or both. The add-in has options to set the number of rows to view.

2. Click on the range of records (1-5000) from the SAS Data Analysis toolbar to change the starting point (or select **SAS** ⇨ **Navigate SAS Data Source** ⇨ **Go To Record**).

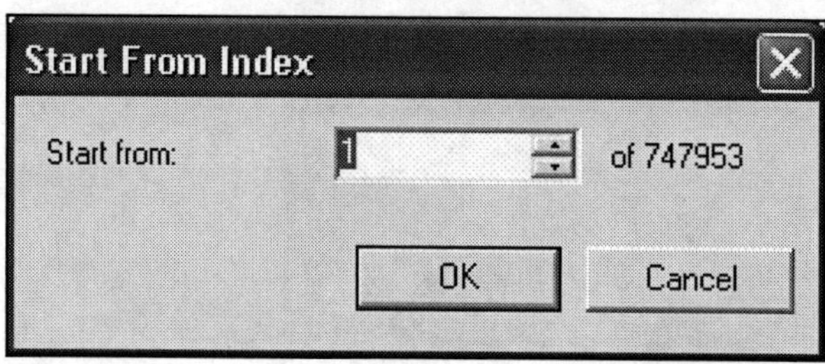

3. Type in a value of **70000**, then click OK.

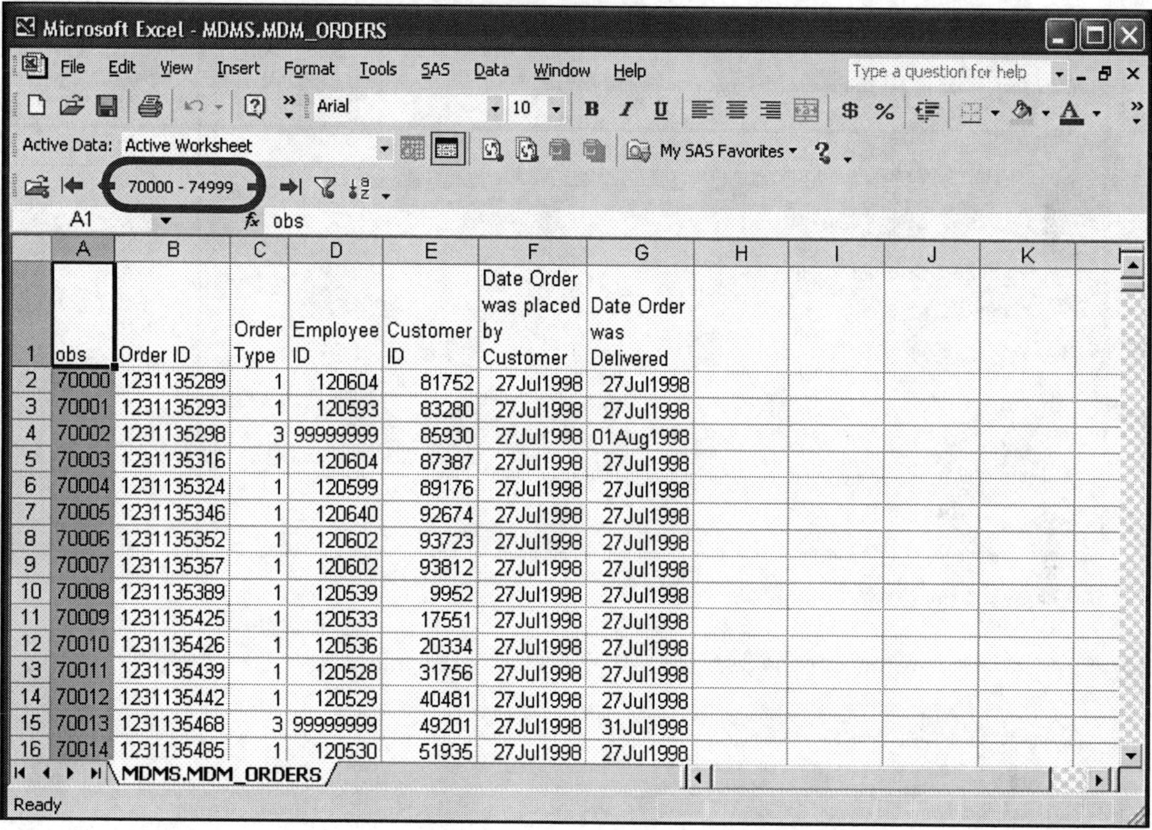

	A	B	C	D	E	F	G
1	obs	Order ID	Order Type	Employee ID	Customer ID	Date Order was placed by Customer	Date Order was Delivered
2	70000	1231135289	1	120604	81752	27Jul1998	27Jul1998
3	70001	1231135293	1	120593	83280	27Jul1998	27Jul1998
4	70002	1231135298	3	99999999	85930	27Jul1998	01Aug1998
5	70003	1231135316	1	120604	87387	27Jul1998	27Jul1998
6	70004	1231135324	1	120599	89176	27Jul1998	27Jul1998
7	70005	1231135346	1	120640	92674	27Jul1998	27Jul1998
8	70006	1231135352	1	120602	93723	27Jul1998	27Jul1998
9	70007	1231135357	1	120602	93812	27Jul1998	27Jul1998
10	70008	1231135389	1	120539	9952	27Jul1998	27Jul1998
11	70009	1231135425	1	120533	17551	27Jul1998	27Jul1998
12	70010	1231135426	1	120536	20334	27Jul1998	27Jul1998
13	70011	1231135439	1	120528	31756	27Jul1998	27Jul1998
14	70012	1231135442	1	120529	40481	27Jul1998	27Jul1998
15	70013	1231135468	3	99999999	49201	27Jul1998	31Jul1998
16	70014	1231135485	1	120530	51935	27Jul1998	27Jul1998

The worksheet now displays records from 70000-74999.

The default number of rows that is displayed can be changed in the SAS Options window on the Data tab:

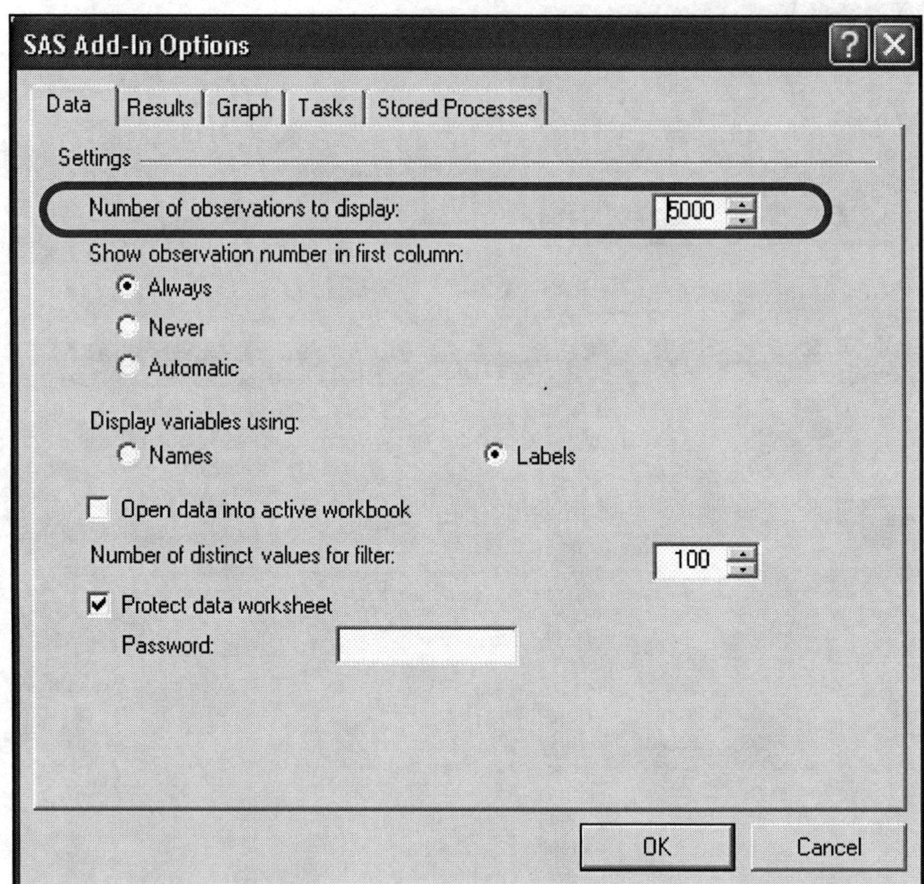

5000 rows is the default value.

The arrow tools on the SAS Data Analysis toolbar enable you to scroll through the data:

The arrows with the bars next to them take you all the way to the beginning or end of the data. The single arrows scroll by the number of rows listed in the options window.

4. Select (or **SAS** ⇨ **Navigate SAS Data Source** ⇨ **Go to End**).
5. Select (or **SAS** ⇨ **Navigate SAS Data Source** ⇨ **Go to Start**).

Using a Filter to Subset SAS Data in Excel

1. Filter the data for year 2002 to display only those orders that have an order type of 3.

   a. Select [Filter] on the SAS Data Analysis toolbar (or select **SAS** ⇨ **Filter SAS Data Source**).

   b. Build the first piece of the filter to subset the year.

      1) Select [▼] in the first box and select the desired column name **Order Type**.

      2) Select [▼] in the second box and specify the filter criteria **Is equal to**.

      3) Select [...] in the third box, select the value **3** and select [OK].

      4) Select [▼] in the last box and specify a condition (**AND**) in order to create a combination filter.

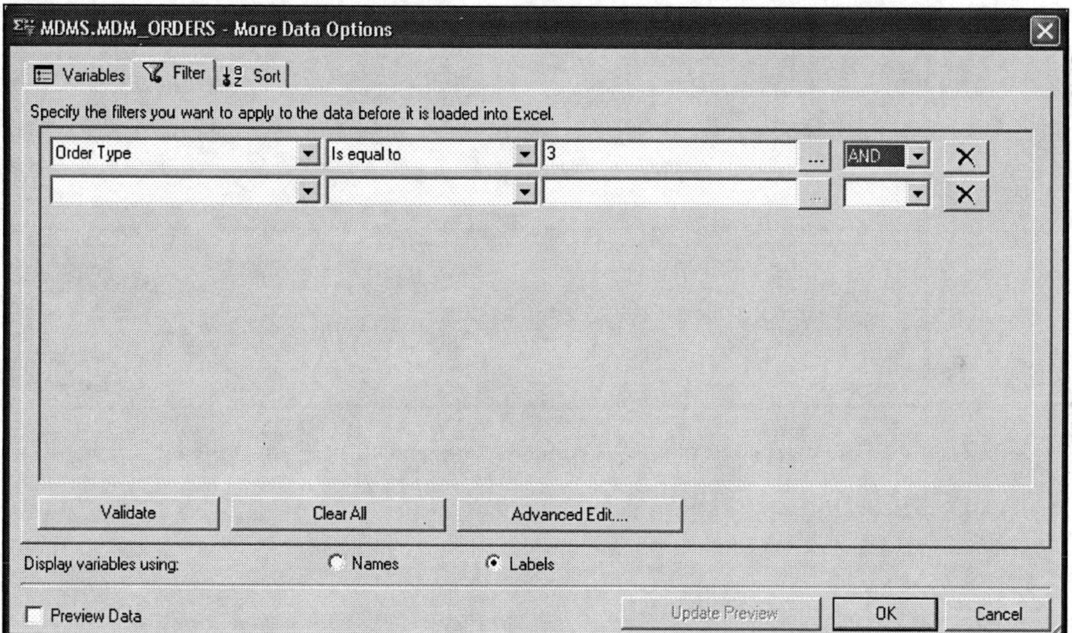

c. Build the final piece of the filter to subset for orders placed during the year 2002.

1) Select **Advanced Edit....** to bring up the Advanced Expression Editor window. The first piece of the filter is displayed.

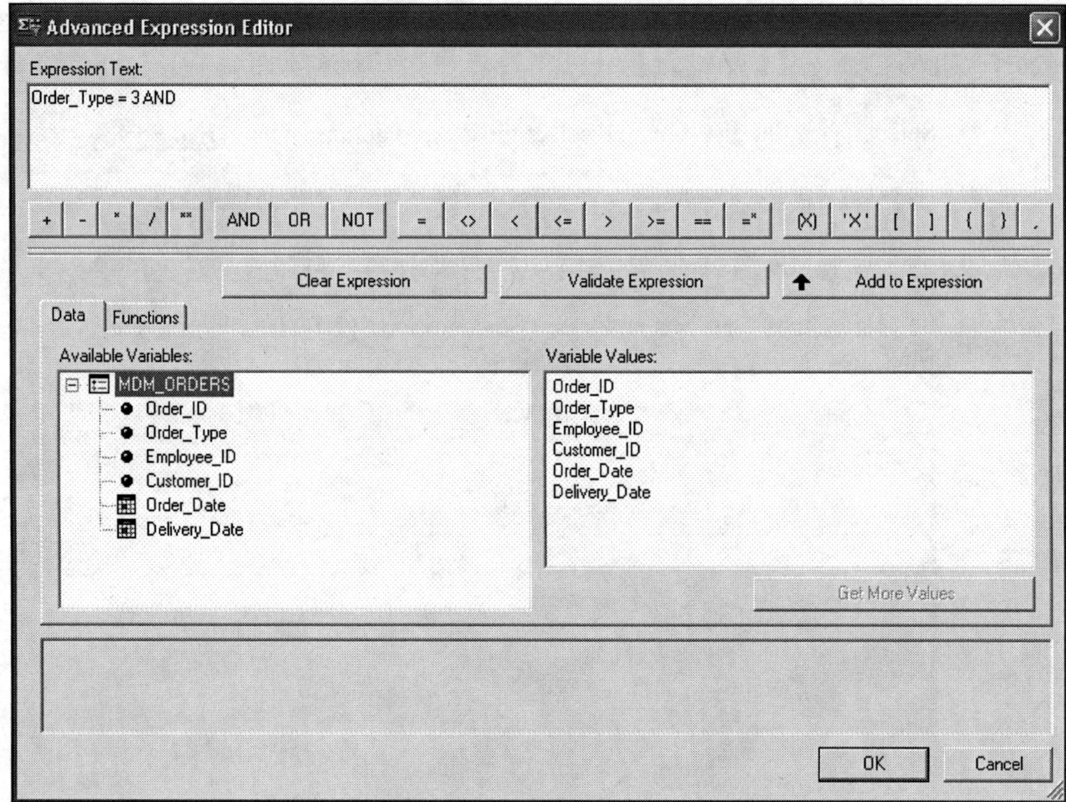

2) Place the cursor after the AND operator and select the **Functions** tab.

3) Select **Date and Time** in the Categories pane.

4) To add the YEAR function to the expression, double-click **YEAR** in the Functions pane.

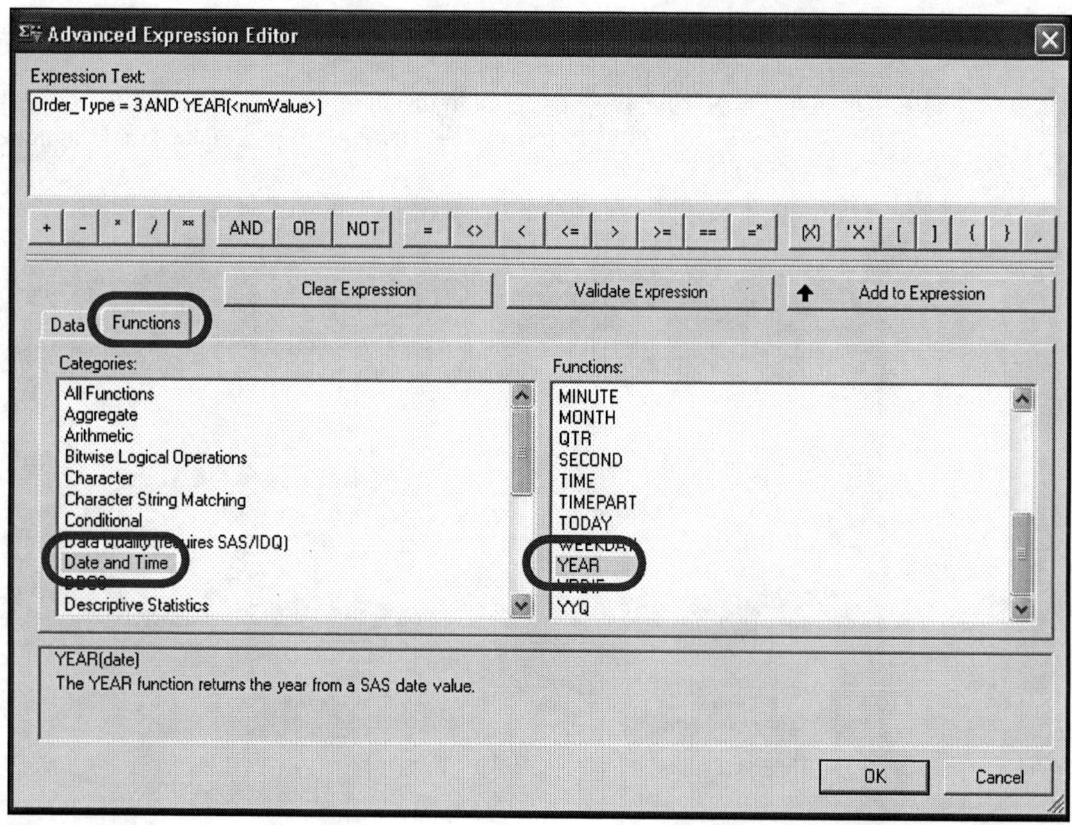

Help for a function is displayed at the bottom of the Advanced Expression Editor window.

5) Replace the <numValue> part of the expression with the appropriate column name.

a) Select the **Data** tab.

b) Highlight the **<numValue>** expression inside of the parenthesis of the DAY function in the Expression Text window. (Hint: When highlighting, make sure to include the brackets <>.)

c) Double-click **Order_Date** in the Available Variables pane.

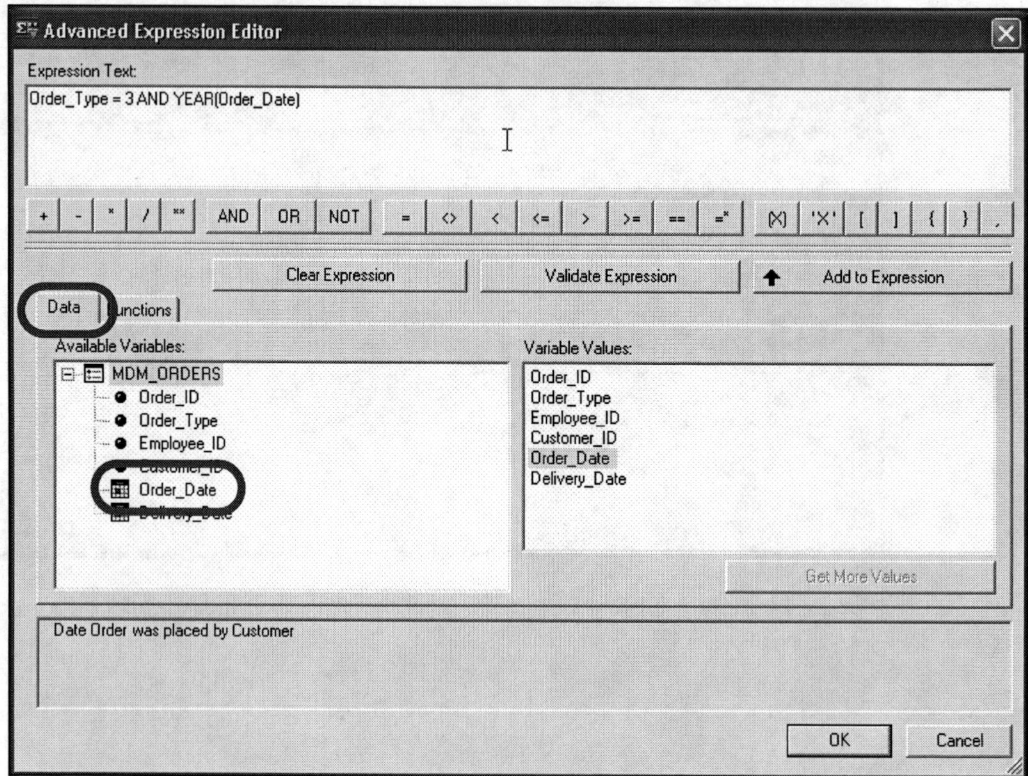

6) Move the cursor to the end of the expression in the Expression Text window and add one space.

7) Select [=].

8) Type in **2002**. The final expression should appear as seen here.

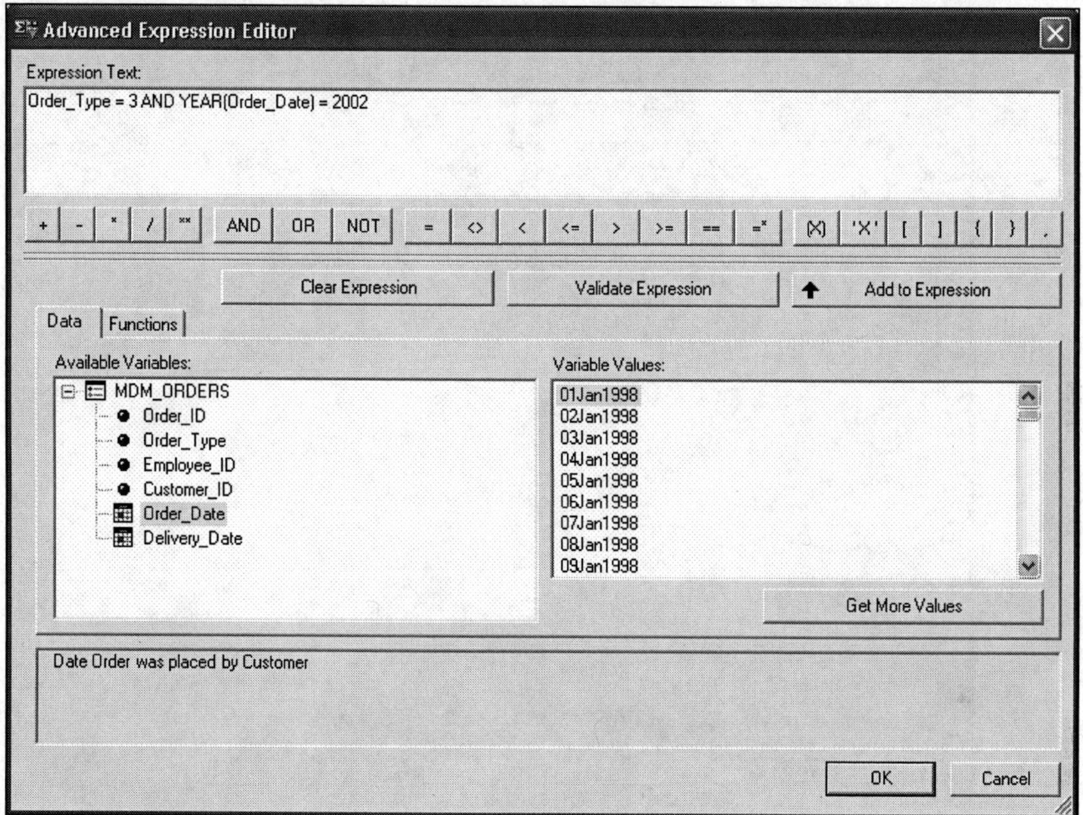

d. Select [Validate Expression] to validate the filter.

e. Select OK to close the validation window.

f. Select OK to close the Advanced Expression Editor window.

g. Select the **Preview Data** check box to preview the first 10 of 21,929 result records.

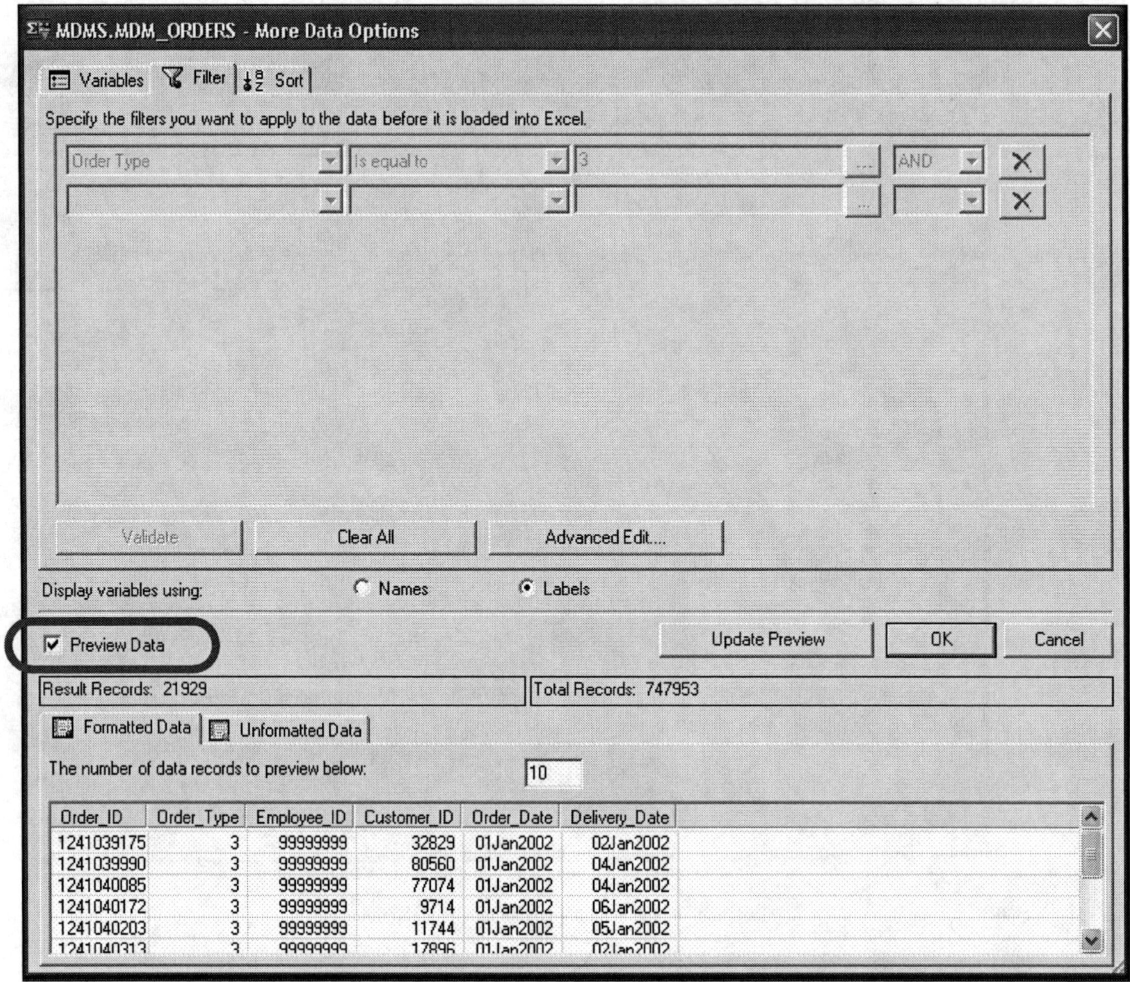

The formatted values are surfaced in this window. Unformatted values are available by selecting the **Unformatted Data** tab.

h. Deselect the **Preview Data** check box and select OK to close the Advanced Expression Builder window.

i. Select OK to close the More Data Options window and apply the filter to the data.

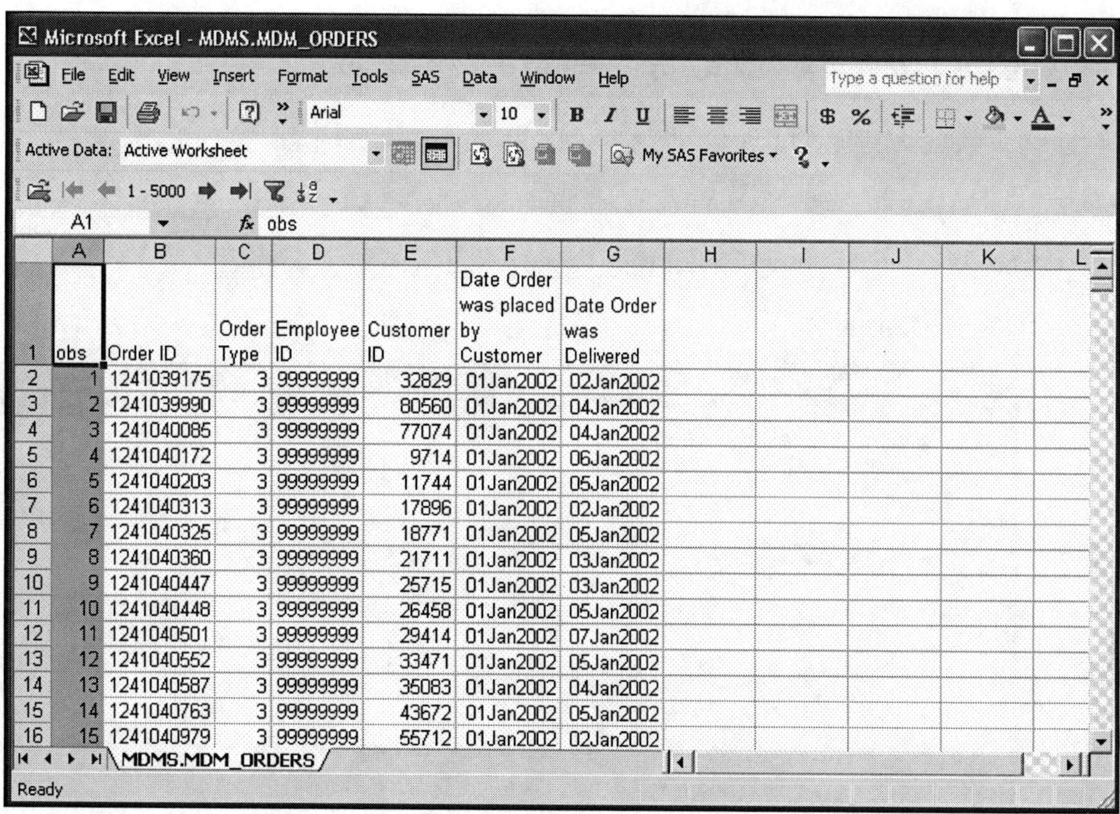

	A	B	C	D	E	F	G
1	obs	Order ID	Order Type	Employee ID	Customer ID	Date Order was placed by Customer	Date Order was Delivered
2	1	1241039175	3	99999999	32829	01Jan2002	02Jan2002
3	2	1241039990	3	99999999	80560	01Jan2002	04Jan2002
4	3	1241040085	3	99999999	77074	01Jan2002	04Jan2002
5	4	1241040172	3	99999999	9714	01Jan2002	06Jan2002
6	5	1241040203	3	99999999	11744	01Jan2002	05Jan2002
7	6	1241040313	3	99999999	17896	01Jan2002	02Jan2002
8	7	1241040325	3	99999999	18771	01Jan2002	05Jan2002
9	8	1241040360	3	99999999	21711	01Jan2002	03Jan2002
10	9	1241040447	3	99999999	25715	01Jan2002	03Jan2002
11	10	1241040448	3	99999999	26458	01Jan2002	05Jan2002
12	11	1241040501	3	99999999	29414	01Jan2002	07Jan2002
13	12	1241040552	3	99999999	33471	01Jan2002	05Jan2002
14	13	1241040587	3	99999999	35083	01Jan2002	04Jan2002
15	14	1241040763	3	99999999	43672	01Jan2002	05Jan2002
16	15	1241040979	3	99999999	55712	01Jan2002	02Jan2002

The data is filtered on the SAS Workspace Server and returned to Excel. The worksheet now displays 21,929 records that match the filter criteria.

Sorting SAS Data in Excel by Specifying a Sort Criteria

1. Sort the data by date in reverse order starting with the end of the year.

   a. Select [sort icon] on the SAS Data Analysis toolbar (or select **SAS** ⇨ **Sort SAS Data Source**).

   b. Select [▼] in the box and select **Date Order was placed by Customer**.

   c. Select **Descending**.

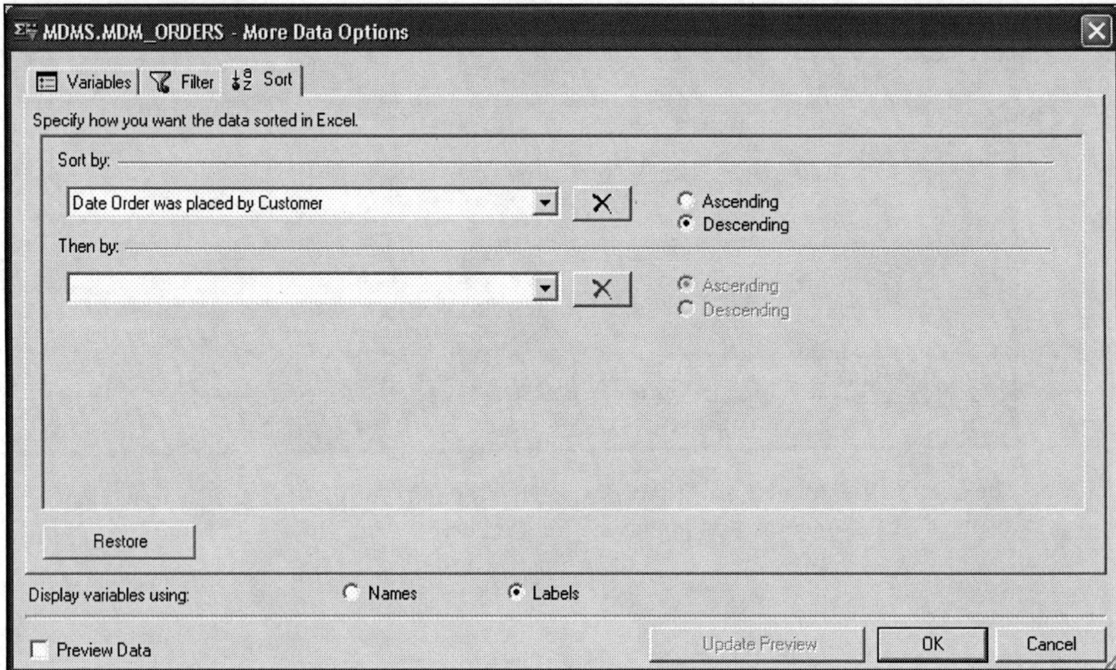

d. Select OK to close the More Data Options window and sort the data.

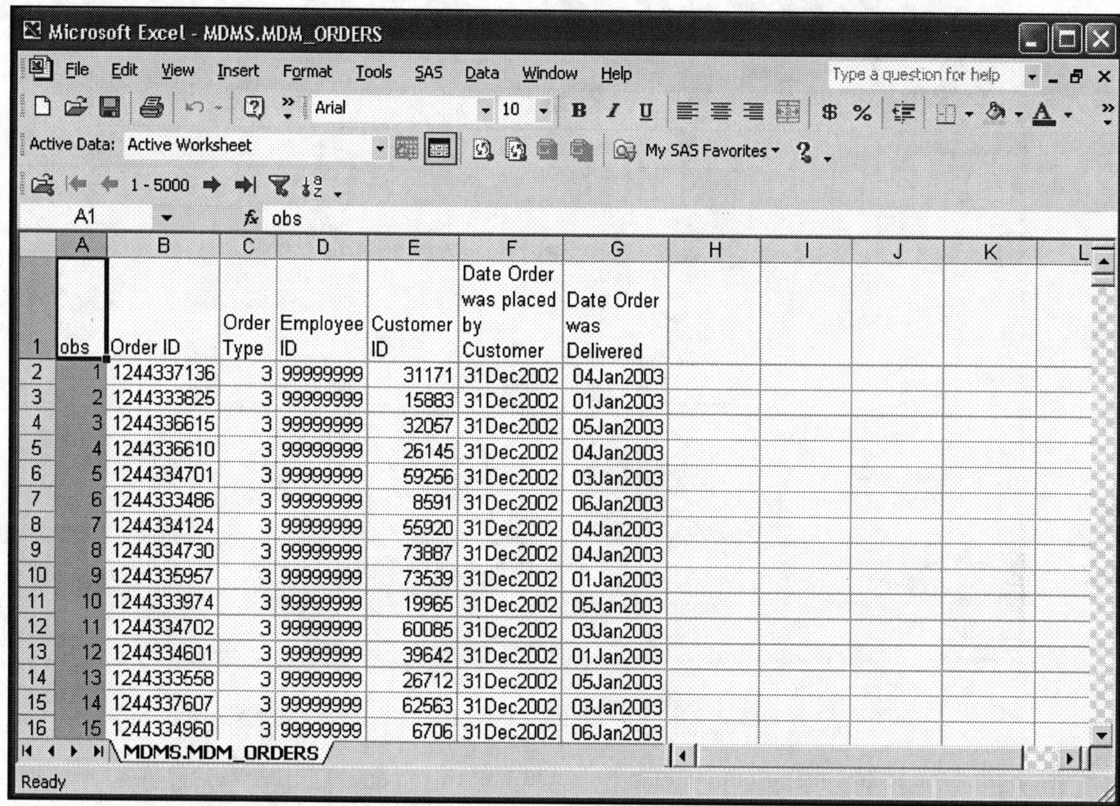

obs	Order ID	Order Type	Employee ID	Customer ID	Date Order was placed by Customer	Date Order was Delivered
1	1244337136	3	99999999	31171	31Dec2002	04Jan2003
2	1244333825	3	99999999	15883	31Dec2002	01Jan2003
3	1244336615	3	99999999	32057	31Dec2002	05Jan2003
4	1244336610	3	99999999	26145	31Dec2002	04Jan2003
5	1244334701	3	99999999	59256	31Dec2002	03Jan2003
6	1244333486	3	99999999	8591	31Dec2002	06Jan2003
7	1244334124	3	99999999	55920	31Dec2002	04Jan2003
8	1244334730	3	99999999	73887	31Dec2002	04Jan2003
9	1244335957	3	99999999	73539	31Dec2002	01Jan2003
10	1244333974	3	99999999	19965	31Dec2002	05Jan2003
11	1244334702	3	99999999	60085	31Dec2002	03Jan2003
12	1244334601	3	99999999	39642	31Dec2002	01Jan2003
13	1244333558	3	99999999	26712	31Dec2002	05Jan2003
14	1244337607	3	99999999	62563	31Dec2002	03Jan2003
15	1244334960	3	99999999	6706	31Dec2002	06Jan2003

The data is sorted on the SAS Workspace Server and returned to the worksheet.

Restricting SAS Data in Excel by Unselecting Columns

1. Display selected columns in Excel.

   a. Select the sort icon on the SAS Data Analysis toolbar (or select **SAS** ⇨ **Sort SAS Data Source**).

b. Select the **Variables** tab.

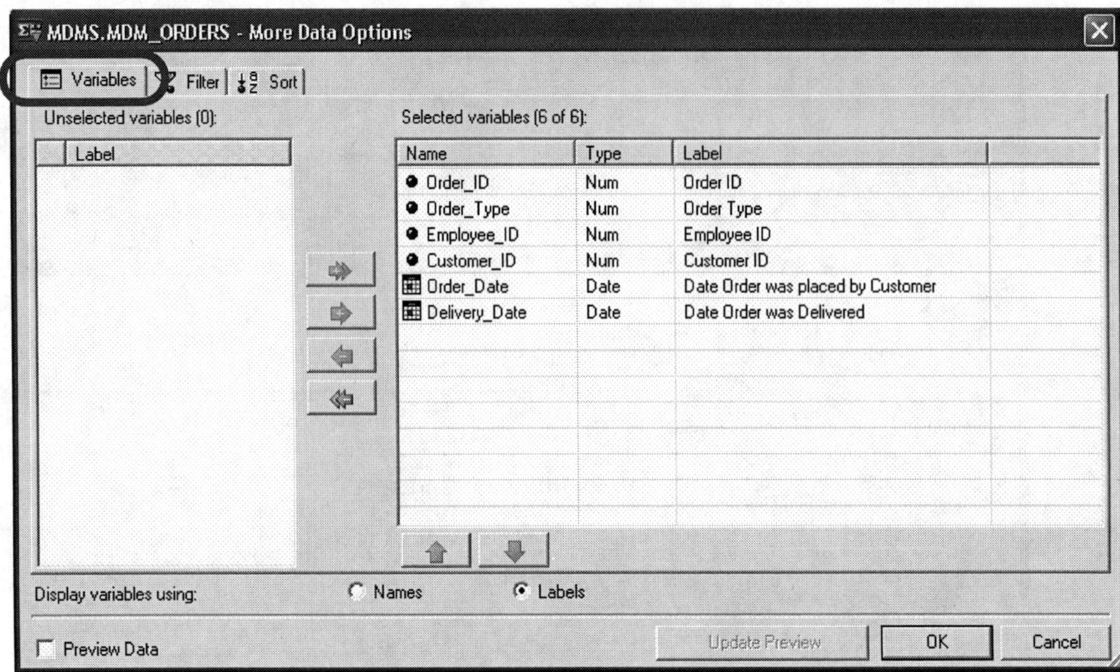

Use and to change the order of the column display in Excel.

c. Select the following columns in the Selected Variables pane: **Employee_ID** and **Order_Type**. (Use the Ctrl key to select more than one column at a time.)

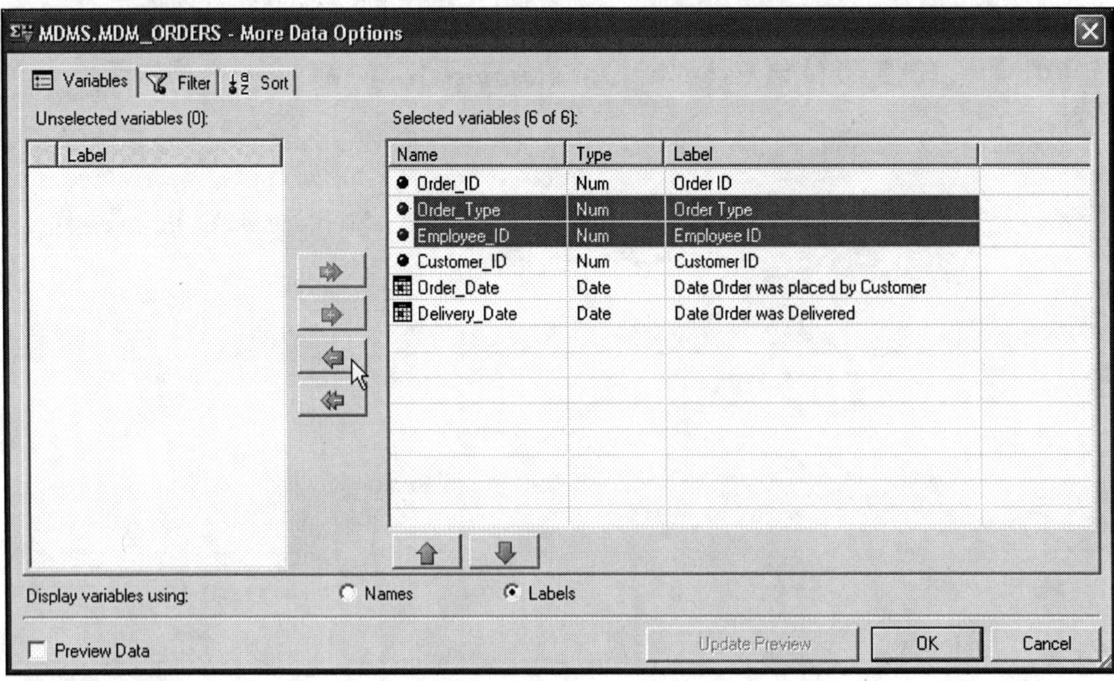

d. Select to move the selected columns to the Unselected Variables pane.

e. Select OK to close the More Data Options window and restrict the columns.

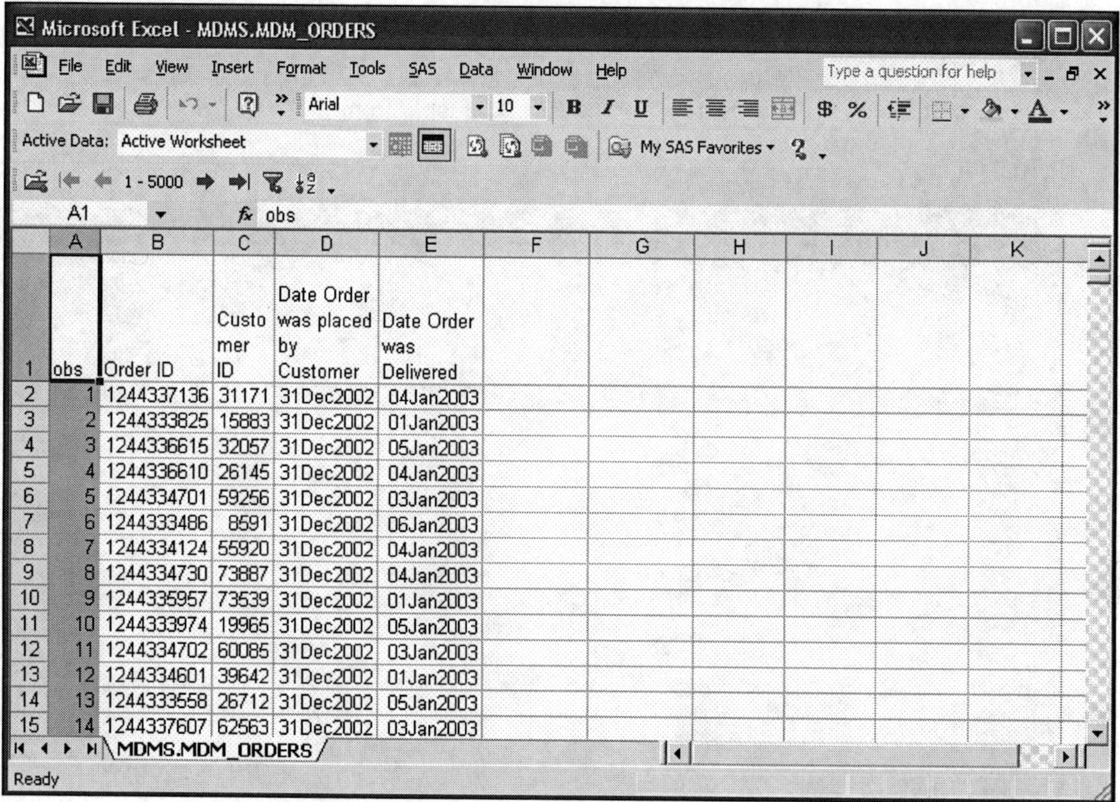

3.3 Exercises

1. Accessing SAS Data

In Microsoft Excel, open the **`MDM_CUSTOMER_DIM`** table from the MDM Source Tables Library.

Partial Output

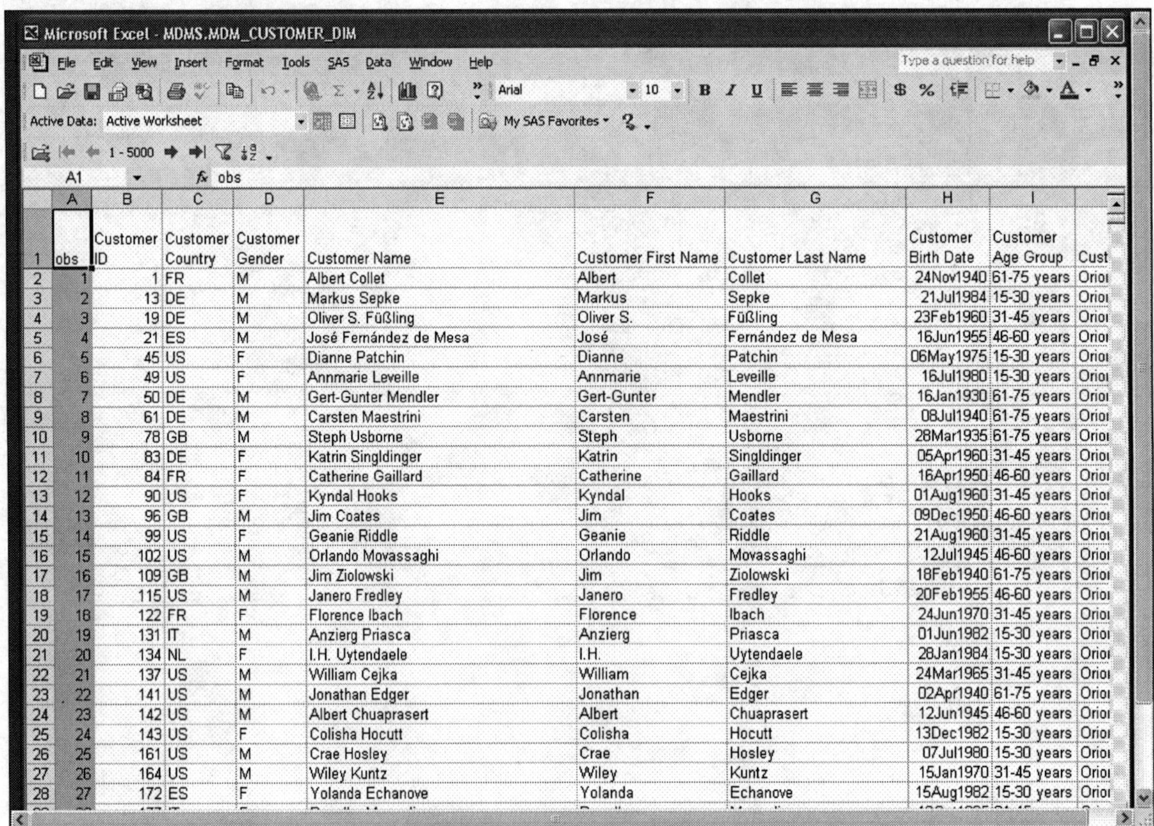

	A	B	C	D	E	F	G	H	I	
1	obs	Customer ID	Customer Country	Customer Gender	Customer Name	Customer First Name	Customer Last Name	Customer Birth Date	Customer Age Group	Cust
2	1	1	FR	M	Albert Collet	Albert	Collet	24Nov1940	61-75 years	Orioı
3	2	13	DE	M	Markus Sepke	Markus	Sepke	21Jul1984	15-30 years	Orioı
4	3	19	DE	M	Oliver S. Füßling	Oliver S.	Füßling	23Feb1960	31-45 years	Orioı
5	4	21	ES	M	José Fernández de Mesa	José	Fernández de Mesa	16Jun1955	46-60 years	Orioı
6	5	45	US	F	Dianne Patchin	Dianne	Patchin	06May1975	15-30 years	Orioı
7	6	49	US	F	Annmarie Leveille	Annmarie	Leveille	16Jul1980	15-30 years	Orioı
8	7	50	DE	M	Gert-Gunter Mendler	Gert-Gunter	Mendler	16Jan1930	61-75 years	Orioı
9	8	61	DE	M	Carsten Maestrini	Carsten	Maestrini	08Jul1940	61-75 years	Orioı
10	9	78	GB	M	Steph Usborne	Steph	Usborne	28Mar1935	61-75 years	Orioı
11	10	83	DE	F	Katrin Singldinger	Katrin	Singldinger	05Apr1960	31-45 years	Orioı
12	11	84	FR	F	Catherine Gaillard	Catherine	Gaillard	16Apr1950	46-60 years	Orioı
13	12	90	US	F	Kyndal Hooks	Kyndal	Hooks	01Aug1960	31-45 years	Orioı
14	13	96	GB	M	Jim Coates	Jim	Coates	09Dec1950	46-60 years	Orioı
15	14	99	US	F	Geanie Riddle	Geanie	Riddle	21Aug1960	31-45 years	Orioı
16	15	102	US	M	Orlando Movassaghi	Orlando	Movassaghi	12Jul1945	46-60 years	Orioı
17	16	109	GB	M	Jim Ziolowski	Jim	Ziolowski	18Feb1940	61-75 years	Orioı
18	17	115	US	M	Janero Fredley	Janero	Fredley	20Feb1955	46-60 years	Orioı
19	18	122	FR	F	Florence Ibach	Florence	Ibach	24Jun1970	31-45 years	Orioı
20	19	131	IT	M	Anzierg Priasca	Anzierg	Priasca	01Jun1982	15-30 years	Orioı
21	20	134	NL	F	I.H. Uytendaele	I.H.	Uytendaele	28Jan1984	15-30 years	Orioı
22	21	137	US	M	William Cejka	William	Cejka	24Mar1965	31-45 years	Orioı
23	22	141	US	M	Jonathan Edger	Jonathan	Edger	02Apr1940	61-75 years	Orioı
24	23	142	US	M	Albert Chuaprasert	Albert	Chuaprasert	12Jun1945	46-60 years	Orioı
25	24	143	US	F	Colisha Hocutt	Colisha	Hocutt	13Dec1982	15-30 years	Orioı
26	25	161	US	M	Crae Hosley	Crae	Hosley	07Jul1980	15-30 years	Orioı
27	26	164	US	M	Wiley Kuntz	Wiley	Kuntz	15Jan1970	31-45 years	Orioı
28	27	172	ES	F	Yolanda Echanove	Yolanda	Echanove	15Aug1982	15-30 years	Orioı

2. Filtering SAS Data

Use the Filter SAS Data Source tool to select observations with the following characteristics:

- U.S. customers
- younger than age 65
- having a February birthday.

Hint: To determine whether an individual has a February birthday, use the MONTH date and time function in the Advanced Edit Expression editor. Month values are returned as 1-12.

Partial Output

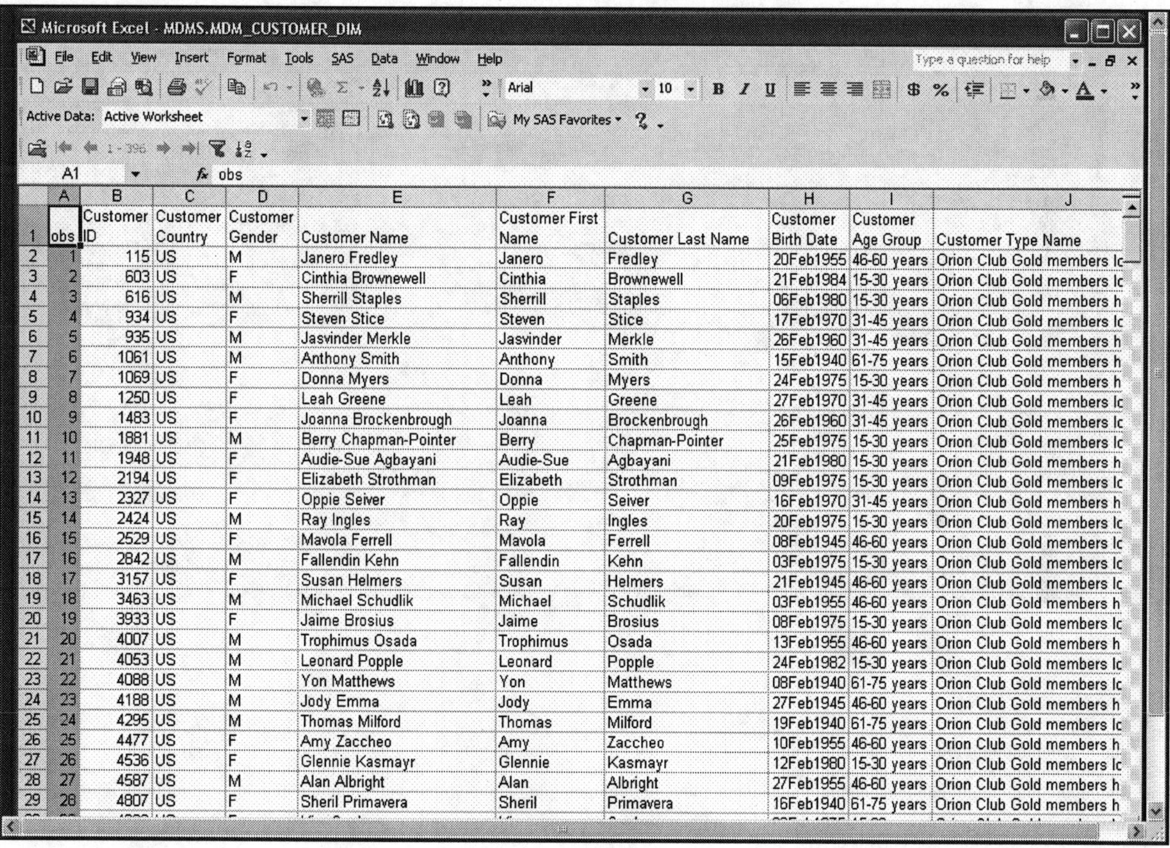

	obs	Customer ID	Customer Country	Customer Gender	Customer Name	Customer First Name	Customer Last Name	Customer Birth Date	Customer Age Group	Customer Type Name
2	1	115	US	M	Janero Fredley	Janero	Fredley	20Feb1955	46-60 years	Orion Club Gold members lc
3	2	603	US	F	Cinthia Brownewell	Cinthia	Brownewell	21Feb1984	15-30 years	Orion Club Gold members lc
4	3	616	US	M	Sherrill Staples	Sherrill	Staples	06Feb1980	15-30 years	Orion Club Gold members h
5	4	934	US	F	Steven Stice	Steven	Stice	17Feb1970	31-45 years	Orion Club Gold members lc
6	5	935	US	M	Jasvinder Merkle	Jasvinder	Merkle	26Feb1960	31-45 years	Orion Club Gold members h
7	6	1061	US	M	Anthony Smith	Anthony	Smith	15Feb1940	61-75 years	Orion Club Gold members h
8	7	1069	US	F	Donna Myers	Donna	Myers	24Feb1975	15-30 years	Orion Club Gold members h
9	8	1250	US	F	Leah Greene	Leah	Greene	27Feb1970	31-45 years	Orion Club Gold members lc
10	9	1483	US	F	Joanna Brockenbrough	Joanna	Brockenbrough	26Feb1960	31-45 years	Orion Club Gold members lc
11	10	1881	US	M	Berry Chapman-Pointer	Berry	Chapman-Pointer	25Feb1975	15-30 years	Orion Club Gold members lc
12	11	1948	US	F	Audie-Sue Agbayani	Audie-Sue	Agbayani	21Feb1980	15-30 years	Orion Club Gold members h
13	12	2194	US	F	Elizabeth Strothman	Elizabeth	Strothman	09Feb1975	15-30 years	Orion Club Gold members lc
14	13	2327	US	F	Oppie Seiver	Oppie	Seiver	16Feb1970	31-45 years	Orion Club Gold members h
15	14	2424	US	M	Ray Ingles	Ray	Ingles	20Feb1975	15-30 years	Orion Club Gold members lc
16	15	2529	US	F	Mavola Ferrell	Mavola	Ferrell	08Feb1945	46-60 years	Orion Club Gold members lc
17	16	2842	US	M	Fallendin Kehn	Fallendin	Kehn	03Feb1975	15-30 years	Orion Club Gold members lc
18	17	3157	US	F	Susan Helmers	Susan	Helmers	21Feb1945	46-60 years	Orion Club Gold members lc
19	18	3463	US	M	Michael Schudlik	Michael	Schudlik	03Feb1955	46-60 years	Orion Club Gold members h
20	19	3933	US	F	Jaime Brosius	Jaime	Brosius	08Feb1975	15-30 years	Orion Club Gold members lc
21	20	4007	US	M	Trophimus Osada	Trophimus	Osada	13Feb1955	46-60 years	Orion Club Gold members h
22	21	4053	US	M	Leonard Popple	Leonard	Popple	24Feb1982	15-30 years	Orion Club Gold members lc
23	22	4088	US	M	Yon Matthews	Yon	Matthews	08Feb1940	61-75 years	Orion Club Gold members lc
24	23	4188	US	M	Jody Emma	Jody	Emma	27Feb1945	46-60 years	Orion Club Gold members h
25	24	4295	US	M	Thomas Milford	Thomas	Milford	19Feb1940	61-75 years	Orion Club Gold members lc
26	25	4477	US	F	Amy Zaccheo	Amy	Zaccheo	10Feb1955	46-60 years	Orion Club Gold members h
27	26	4536	US	F	Glennie Kasmayr	Glennie	Kasmayr	12Feb1980	15-30 years	Orion Club Gold members lc
28	27	4587	US	M	Alan Albright	Alan	Albright	27Feb1955	46-60 years	Orion Club Gold members h
29	28	4807	US	F	Sheril Primavera	Sheril	Primavera	16Feb1940	61-75 years	Orion Club Gold members h

How many U.S. customers who meet the age requirement have a February birthday?

3. Sorting SAS Data

Sort the data by **Customer Last Name** and then **Customer First Name**.

Partial Output

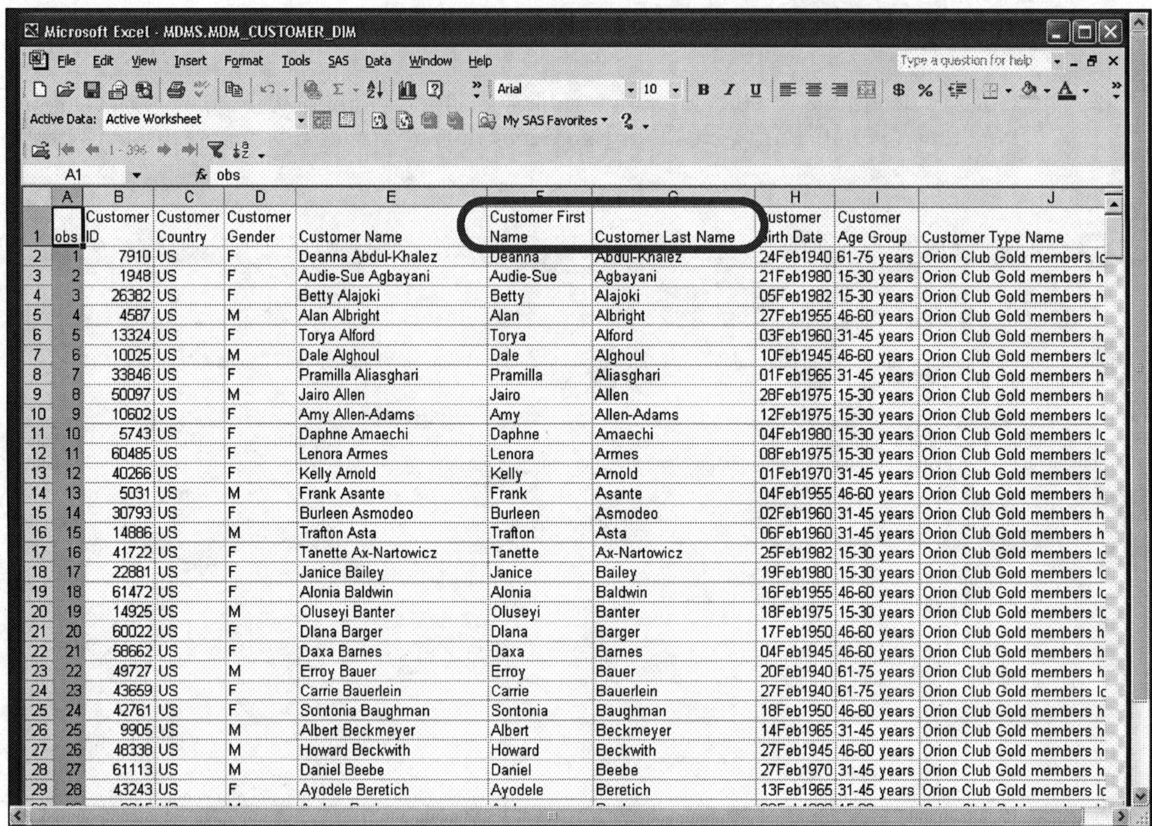

	A	B	C	D	E	F	G	H	I	J
1	obs	Customer ID	Customer Country	Customer Gender	Customer Name	Customer First Name	Customer Last Name	ustomer irth Date	Customer Age Group	Customer Type Name
2	1	7910	US	F	Deanna Abdul-Khalez	Deanna	Abdul-Khalez	24Feb1940	61-75 years	Orion Club Gold members lc
3	2	1948	US	F	Audie-Sue Agbayani	Audie-Sue	Agbayani	21Feb1980	15-30 years	Orion Club Gold members h
4	3	26382	US	F	Betty Alajoki	Betty	Alajoki	05Feb1982	15-30 years	Orion Club Gold members h
5	4	4587	US	M	Alan Albright	Alan	Albright	27Feb1955	46-60 years	Orion Club Gold members h
6	5	13324	US	F	Torya Alford	Torya	Alford	03Feb1960	31-45 years	Orion Club Gold members h
7	6	10025	US	M	Dale Alghoul	Dale	Alghoul	10Feb1945	46-60 years	Orion Club Gold members lc
8	7	33846	US	F	Pramilla Aliasghari	Pramilla	Aliasghari	01Feb1965	31-45 years	Orion Club Gold members h
9	8	50097	US	M	Jairo Allen	Jairo	Allen	28Feb1975	15-30 years	Orion Club Gold members h
10	9	10602	US	F	Amy Allen-Adams	Amy	Allen-Adams	12Feb1975	15-30 years	Orion Club Gold members lc
11	10	5743	US	F	Daphne Amaechi	Daphne	Amaechi	04Feb1980	15-30 years	Orion Club Gold members lc
12	11	60485	US	F	Lenora Armes	Lenora	Armes	08Feb1975	15-30 years	Orion Club Gold members lc
13	12	40266	US	F	Kelly Arnold	Kelly	Arnold	01Feb1970	31-45 years	Orion Club Gold members lc
14	13	5031	US	M	Frank Asante	Frank	Asante	04Feb1955	46-60 years	Orion Club Gold members h
15	14	30793	US	F	Burleen Asmodeo	Burleen	Asmodeo	02Feb1960	31-45 years	Orion Club Gold members h
16	15	14886	US	M	Trafton Asta	Trafton	Asta	06Feb1960	31-45 years	Orion Club Gold members h
17	16	41722	US	F	Tanette Ax-Nartowicz	Tanette	Ax-Nartowicz	25Feb1982	15-30 years	Orion Club Gold members lc
18	17	22881	US	F	Janice Bailey	Janice	Bailey	19Feb1980	15-30 years	Orion Club Gold members lc
19	18	61472	US	F	Alonia Baldwin	Alonia	Baldwin	16Feb1955	46-60 years	Orion Club Gold members lc
20	19	14925	US	M	Oluseyi Banter	Oluseyi	Banter	18Feb1975	15-30 years	Orion Club Gold members lc
21	20	60022	US	F	Dlana Barger	Dlana	Barger	17Feb1950	46-60 years	Orion Club Gold members h
22	21	58662	US	F	Daxa Barnes	Daxa	Barnes	04Feb1945	46-60 years	Orion Club Gold members h
23	22	49727	US	M	Erroy Bauer	Erroy	Bauer	20Feb1940	61-75 years	Orion Club Gold members h
24	23	43659	US	F	Carrie Bauerlein	Carrie	Bauerlein	27Feb1940	61-75 years	Orion Club Gold members lc
25	24	42761	US	F	Sontonia Baughman	Sontonia	Baughman	18Feb1950	46-60 years	Orion Club Gold members h
26	25	9905	US	M	Albert Beckmeyer	Albert	Beckmeyer	14Feb1965	31-45 years	Orion Club Gold members h
27	26	48338	US	M	Howard Beckwith	Howard	Beckwith	27Feb1945	46-60 years	Orion Club Gold members h
28	27	61113	US	M	Daniel Beebe	Daniel	Beebe	27Feb1970	31-45 years	Orion Club Gold members h
29	28	43243	US	F	Ayodele Beretich	Ayodele	Beretich	13Feb1965	31-45 years	Orion Club Gold members lc

4. Selecting and Ordering Columns

a. Limit and order the columns in the resulting data to **Customer_ID**, **Customer_Name**, **Customer_Type**, **Customer_Birthdate**, and **Customer_Gender**.

Partial Output

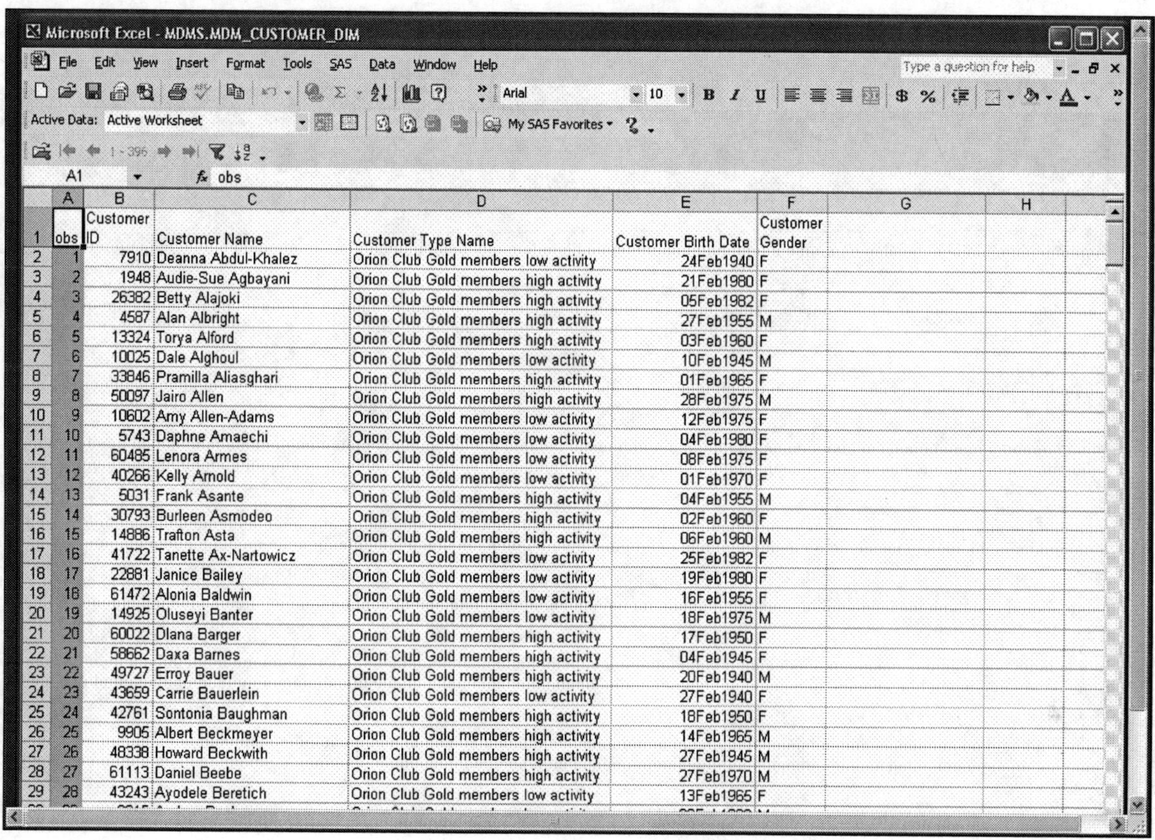

obs	Customer ID	Customer Name	Customer Type Name	Customer Birth Date	Customer Gender
1	7910	Deanna Abdul-Khalez	Orion Club Gold members low activity	24Feb1940	F
2	1948	Audie-Sue Agbayani	Orion Club Gold members high activity	21Feb1980	F
3	26382	Betty Alajoki	Orion Club Gold members high activity	05Feb1982	F
4	4587	Alan Albright	Orion Club Gold members high activity	27Feb1955	M
5	13324	Torya Alford	Orion Club Gold members high activity	03Feb1960	F
6	10025	Dale Alghoul	Orion Club Gold members low activity	10Feb1945	M
7	33846	Pramilla Aliasghari	Orion Club Gold members high activity	01Feb1965	F
8	50097	Jairo Allen	Orion Club Gold members high activity	28Feb1975	M
9	10602	Amy Allen-Adams	Orion Club Gold members low activity	12Feb1975	F
10	5743	Daphne Amaechi	Orion Club Gold members low activity	04Feb1980	F
11	60485	Lenora Armes	Orion Club Gold members low activity	08Feb1975	F
12	40266	Kelly Arnold	Orion Club Gold members low activity	01Feb1970	F
13	5031	Frank Asante	Orion Club Gold members high activity	04Feb1955	M
14	30793	Burleen Asmodeo	Orion Club Gold members high activity	02Feb1960	F
15	14886	Trafton Asta	Orion Club Gold members high activity	06Feb1960	M
16	41722	Tanette Ax-Nartowicz	Orion Club Gold members low activity	25Feb1982	F
17	22881	Janice Bailey	Orion Club Gold members low activity	19Feb1980	F
18	61472	Alonia Baldwin	Orion Club Gold members low activity	16Feb1955	F
19	14925	Oluseyi Banter	Orion Club Gold members low activity	18Feb1975	M
20	60022	Diana Barger	Orion Club Gold members high activity	17Feb1950	F
21	58662	Daxa Barnes	Orion Club Gold members high activity	04Feb1945	F
22	49727	Erroy Bauer	Orion Club Gold members high activity	20Feb1940	M
23	43659	Carrie Bauerlein	Orion Club Gold members low activity	27Feb1940	F
24	42761	Sontonia Baughman	Orion Club Gold members high activity	18Feb1950	F
25	9905	Albert Beckmeyer	Orion Club Gold members high activity	14Feb1965	M
26	48338	Howard Beckwith	Orion Club Gold members high activity	27Feb1945	M
27	61113	Daniel Beebe	Orion Club Gold members high activity	27Feb1970	M
28	43243	Ayodele Beretich	Orion Club Gold members low activity	13Feb1965	F

5. Filtering SAS Data

a. In Excel, use the **`MDM_ORDERS`** table in the MDM Source Tables Library and the Filter SAS Data Source tool to select the type 3 orders that were placed by customer number 89485 in the second quarter of the year 2000.

b. Limit the columns displayed to **`Order_ID`** and **`Order_Date`**.

Output

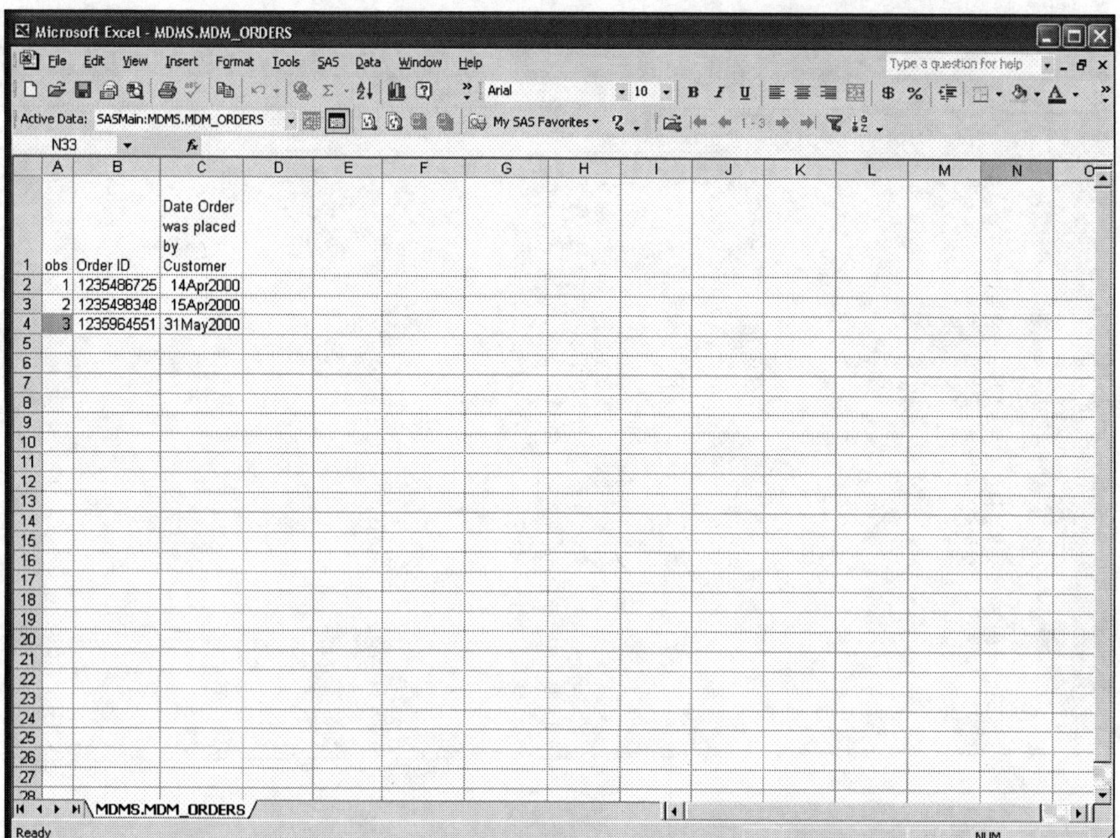

obs	Order ID	Date Order was placed by Customer
1	1235486725	14Apr2000
2	1235498348	15Apr2000
3	1235964551	31May2000

6. **Filtering and Formating SAS Data (Optional)**

   a. Use the **`MDM_ORDER_ITEMS`** table in the MDM Source Tables Library and the Filter SAS Data Source tool to select the order items with a 50% or higher discount of the total retail price.

   b. Limit the columns displayed to **`Product ID`**, **`Total Retail Price for this Product`**, **`Cost Price Per Unit`**, and **`Discount in percent of Normal Retail Price`**.

   c. Use Microsoft Excel's conditional formatting to highlight the 60% discounted items and expand the **`Product ID`** to 12 digits.

   Hint: Use **Format** ⇨ **Conditional Formatting…** to highlight discounts of **`.6`**.

Partial output

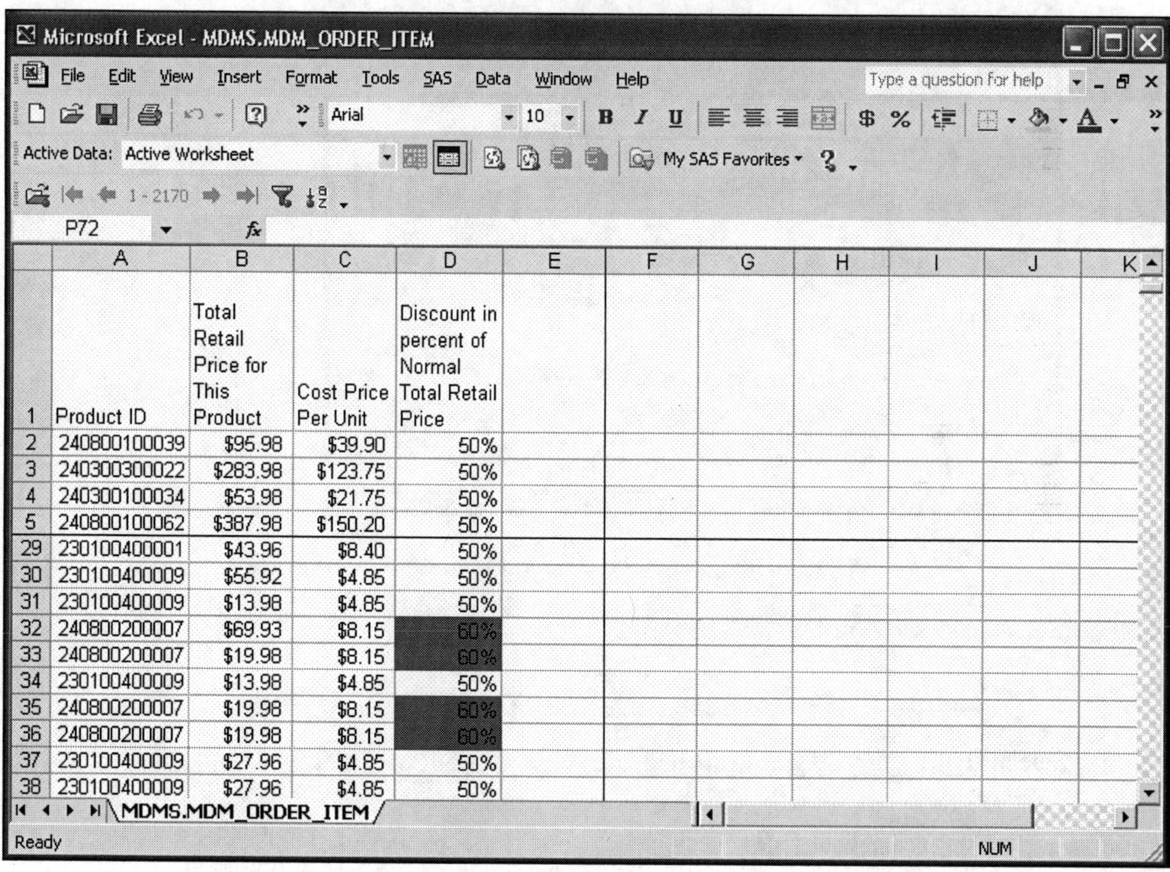

	A	B	C	D
1	Product ID	Total Retail Price for This Product	Cost Price Per Unit	Discount in percent of Normal Total Retail Price
2	240800100039	$95.98	$39.90	50%
3	240300300022	$283.98	$123.75	50%
4	240300100034	$53.98	$21.75	50%
5	240800100062	$387.98	$150.20	50%
29	230100400001	$43.96	$8.40	50%
30	230100400009	$55.92	$4.85	50%
31	230100400009	$13.98	$4.85	50%
32	240800200007	$69.93	$8.15	60%
33	240800200007	$19.98	$8.15	60%
34	230100400009	$13.98	$4.85	50%
35	240800200007	$19.98	$8.15	60%
36	240800200007	$19.98	$8.15	60%
37	230100400009	$27.96	$4.85	50%
38	230100400009	$27.96	$4.85	50%

3.4 Solutions to Exercises

1. Accessing SAS Data

a. Invoke Microsoft Excel by selecting **Start** ⇨ **Programs** ⇨ **Microsoft Office** ⇨ **Microsoft Excel**.

b. Select **SAS** ⇨ **Open SAS Data Source** from the pull-down menus, or select on the SAS Data Analysis toolbar.

c. In the Open SAS Data Source window, select **Servers** from the shortcut bar.

d. If prompted, enter the user name and password provided by the instructor.

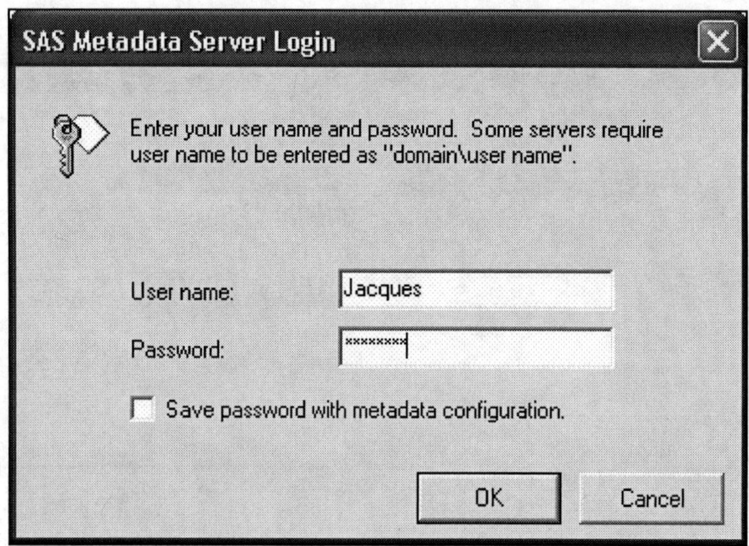

The values shown above may be different than those used in class.

Select .

e. Select **SASMain**, then choose Open (or double-click SASMain).

f. Select **MDM Source Tables Library**, then choose Open (or double-click Source Tables Library).

g. Select **MDM_CUSTOMER_DIM**, then choose Open (or double-click `MDM_CUSTOMER_DIM`). The data from the server is retrieved into the worksheet.

2. **Filtering SAS Data**

   a. Select the Filter icon [Filter] on the SAS Data Analysis toolbar (or select **SAS** ⇨ **Filter SAS Data Source**).

   b. Using the drop-down menus, select **Customer Country**, **Is equal to**, and **US**. Select [AND] and specify **Customer Age**, **Is less than**, and type `65`.

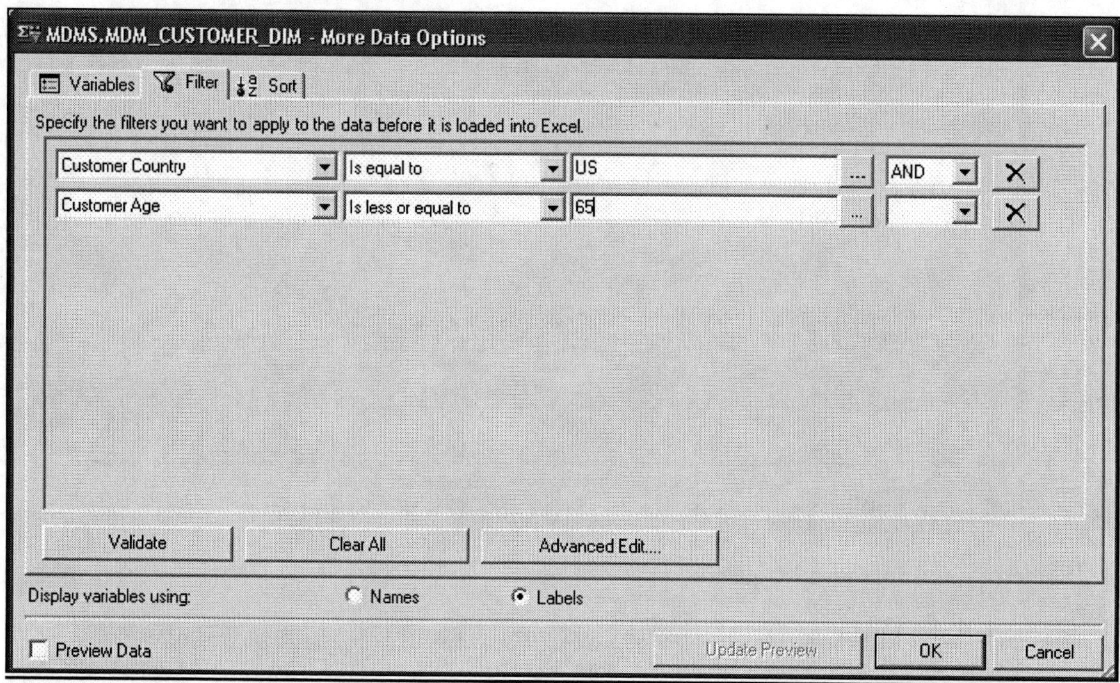

   c. Select [Advanced Edit....] to open the Advanced Expression editor. Select [AND], then use the Function tab to select the **MONTH** function (under the Date and Time function category) and the Data tab to select **Customer_Birthdate** as the <numValue>. Add the = operator and the numeric constant `65` until the entire expression reads

      Customer_Age < 65 AND Customer_Country = 'US' AND MONTH(Customer_BirthDate) = 2

   d. Select [OK] to close the Advanced Expression editor window.

   e. Select [OK] to close the More Data Options window and apply the specified filter.

   How many U.S. customers who meet the age requirement have a February birthday? **396**

3. **Sorting SAS Data**

   a. Select the Sort icon [Sort] on the SAS Data Analysis toolbar (or select **SAS** ⇨ **Sort SAS Data Source**).

b. Select **Customer_Last Name** as the variable to sort by and then by **Customer_First Name**.

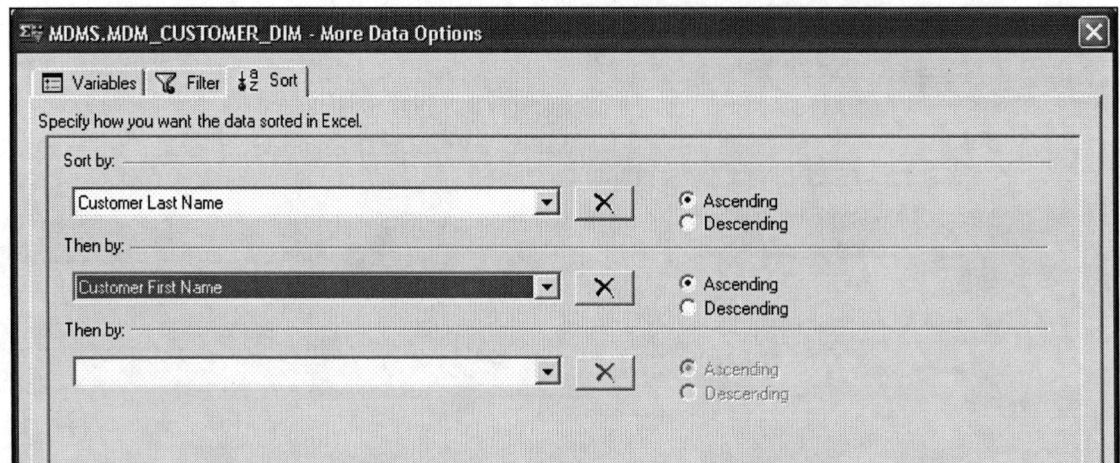

c. Select [OK] to close the More Data Options window and sort the data.

4. **Selecting and Ordering Columns**

   a. Select the **Variables** tab, and select **Customer_Country**, **Customer_FirstName**, **Customer_LastName**, **Customer_Age_Group**, **Customer_Group**, and **Customer_Age** to move to the Unselected variables pane by selecting [⇦].

   Use [⇧] and [⇩] to move the variables into the appropriate order.

5. **Filtering SAS Data**

   a. In Excel, use the **MDM_ORDERS** table in the MDM Source Tables Library and the Filter SAS Data Source tool to select the type 3 orders that were placed by customer number 89485 in the second quarter of the year 2000.

      1) Select **SAS** ⇨ **Open SAS Data Source** from the pull-down menus, or select [icon] on the SAS Data Analysis toolbar.

      2) In the Open SAS Data Source window, select **Servers** from the shortcut bar.

      3) Choose **SASMain**. Select [Open] (or double-click SASMain).

      4) Select **MDM Source Tables Library**, then choose [Open] (or double-click Source Tables Library).

      5) Select **MDM_Orders**, then choose [Open] (or double-click MDM_Orders). The data from the server is retrieved into the worksheet.

6) Select the filter icon on the SAS Data Analysis toolbar (or select **SAS** ⇨ **Filter SAS Data Source**).

7) Using the drop-down menus, specify an expression of Customer ID Is equal to 89485 AND Order Type Is equal to 3.

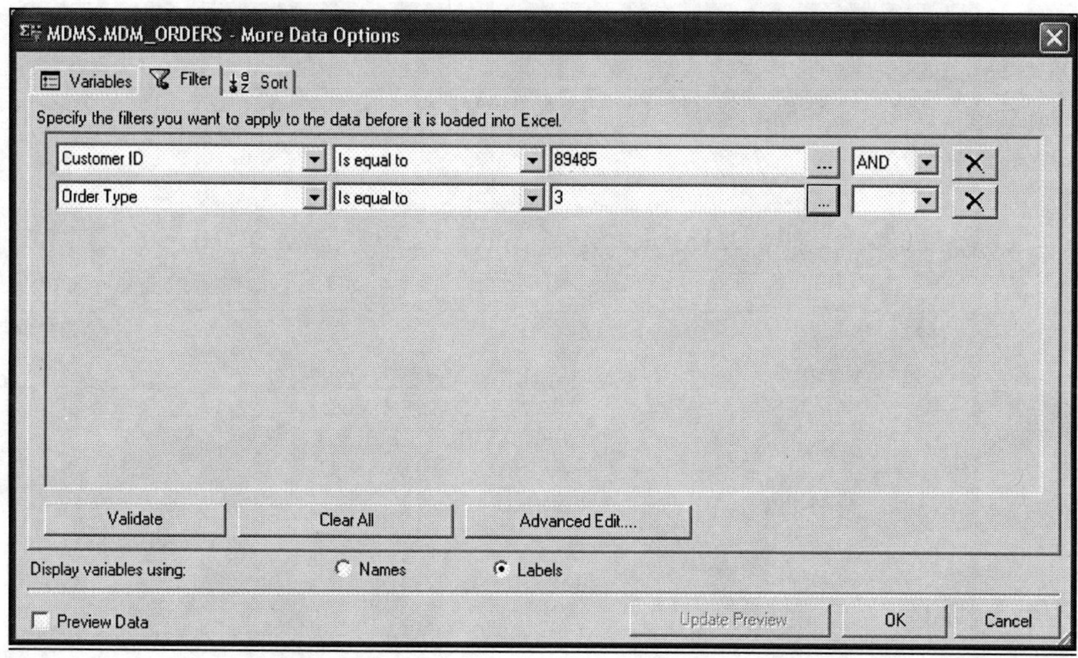

8) Select Advanced Edit.... to open the Advanced Expression editor. Select AND, then use the Function tab to select the YEAR function (under the Date and Time function category). Delete <numValue>. Use the Data tab to select **Order_Date** as the argument within the parentheses. Add the = operator and numeric constant until the entire expression reads

```
Customer_ID = 89485 AND Order_Type = 3  AND YEAR(Order_Date) = 2000
```

9) Select AND, then use the Function tab to select the QTR function (under the Date and Time function category). Delete the <numValue> and use the Data tab to select **Order_Date** as the argument. Add the = operator and numeric constant until the entire expression reads

Customer_ID = 89485 AND Order_Type = 3 AND YEAR(Order_Date) = 2000 AND QTR(Order_Date) = 2

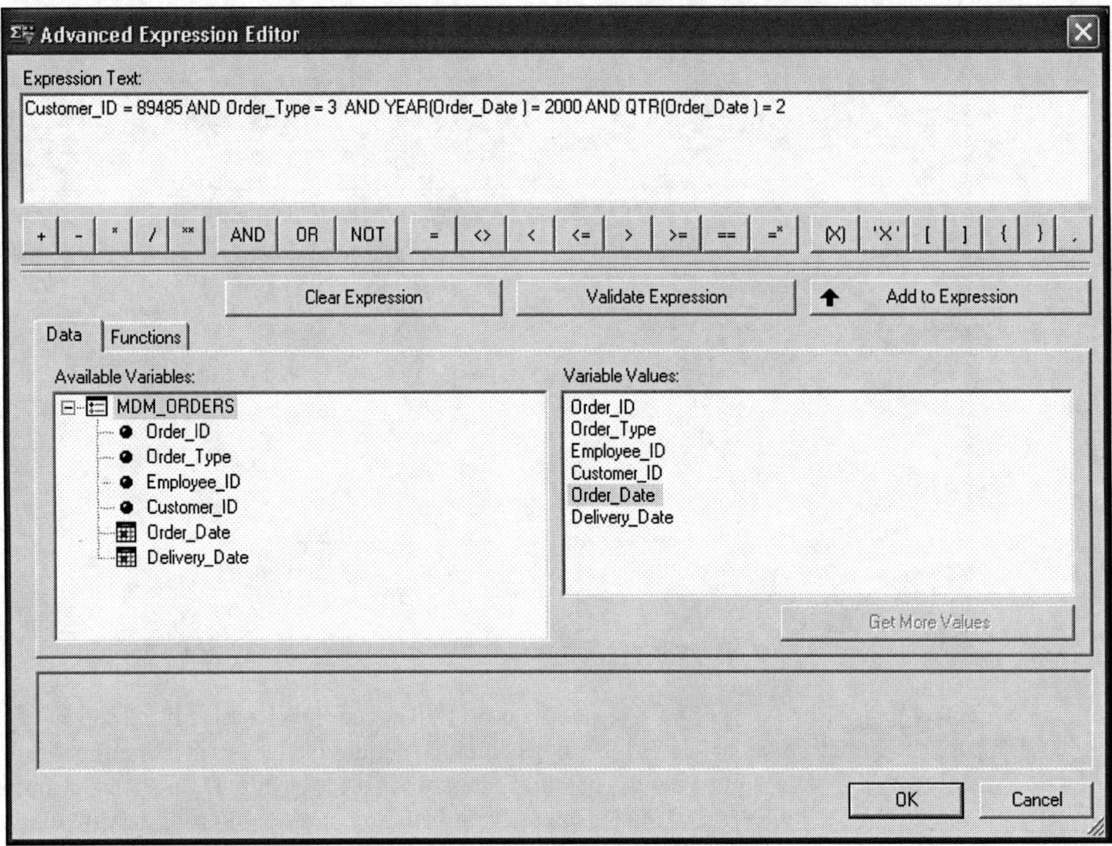

10) Select OK to close the Advanced Expression editor window.

b. Limit the columns displayed to **`Order_ID`** and **`Order_Date`**.

1) Select the **Variables** tab, and select **Order_Type**, **Employee_ID**, **Customer_ID**, and **Delivery_Date** and move them to the Unselected variables pane by selecting ⇦.

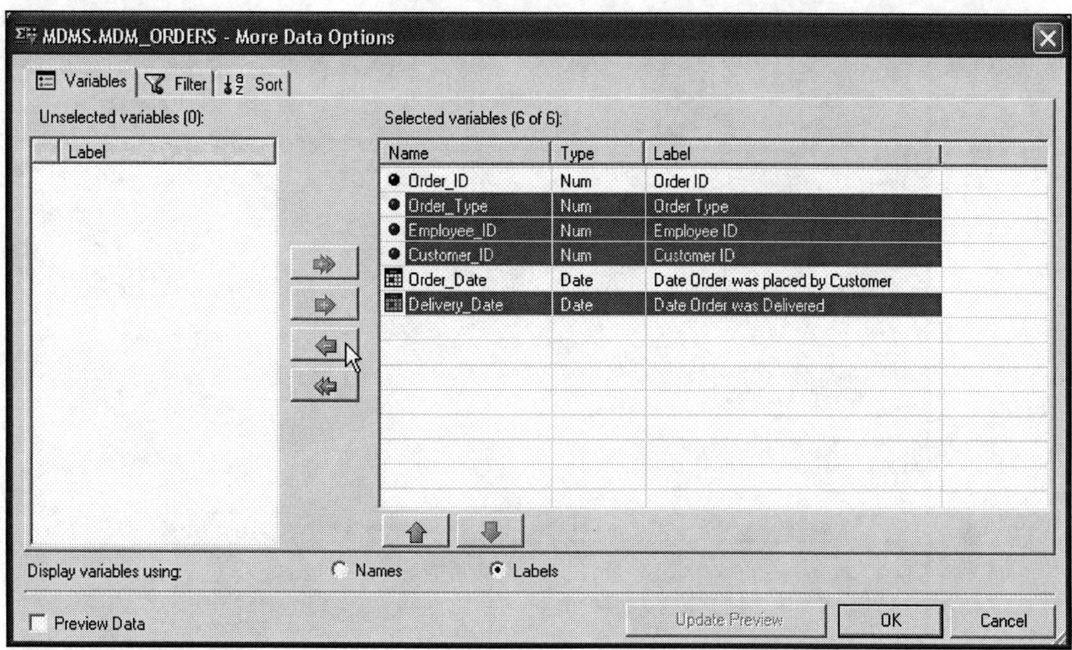

2) Select OK to close the More Data Options window and apply the specified filter.

6. **Filtering and Formatting SAS Data**

a. In Excel, use the **MDM_ORDER_ITEMS** table and the Filter SAS Data Source tool to select the order items with a discount of 50% or greater.

1) Select **SAS** ⇨ **Open SAS Data Source** from the pull-down menus, or select [icon] on the SAS Data Analysis toolbar.

2) In the Open SAS Data Source window, select **Servers** from the shortcut bar.

3) Choose **SASMain**. Select Open (or double-click SASMain).

4) Select **MDM Source Tables Library**, then choose Open (or double-click Source Tables Library).

5) Select **MDM_Orders**, then choose Open (or double-click MDM_Order_Items). The data from the server is retrieved into the worksheet.

6) Select the filter icon [icon] on the SAS Data Analysis toolbar (or select **SAS** ⇨ **Filter SAS Data Source**).

7) Using the drop-down menus, select **Discount in percent of Normal Total Retail Price** and **Is greater or equal** for the operator. Use the [...] button to select **50%** and select [OK].

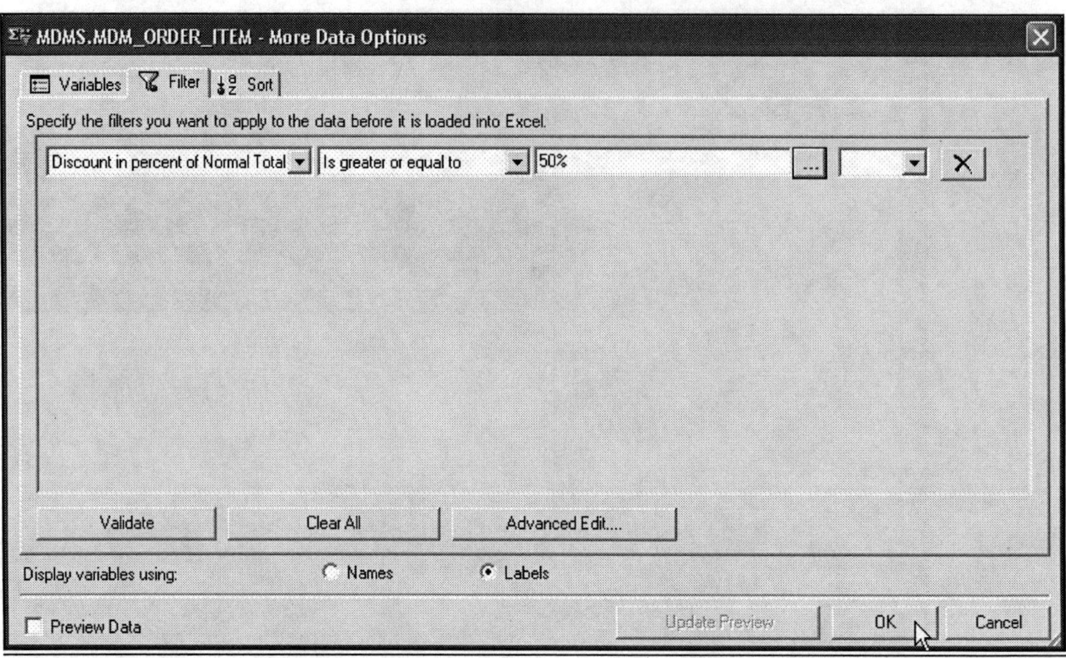

b. Select the **Variables** tab, and select **Order_Item_Num**, **Order_ID**, and **Quantity** to move to the Unselected variables pane by selecting [⇦]. Select [OK].

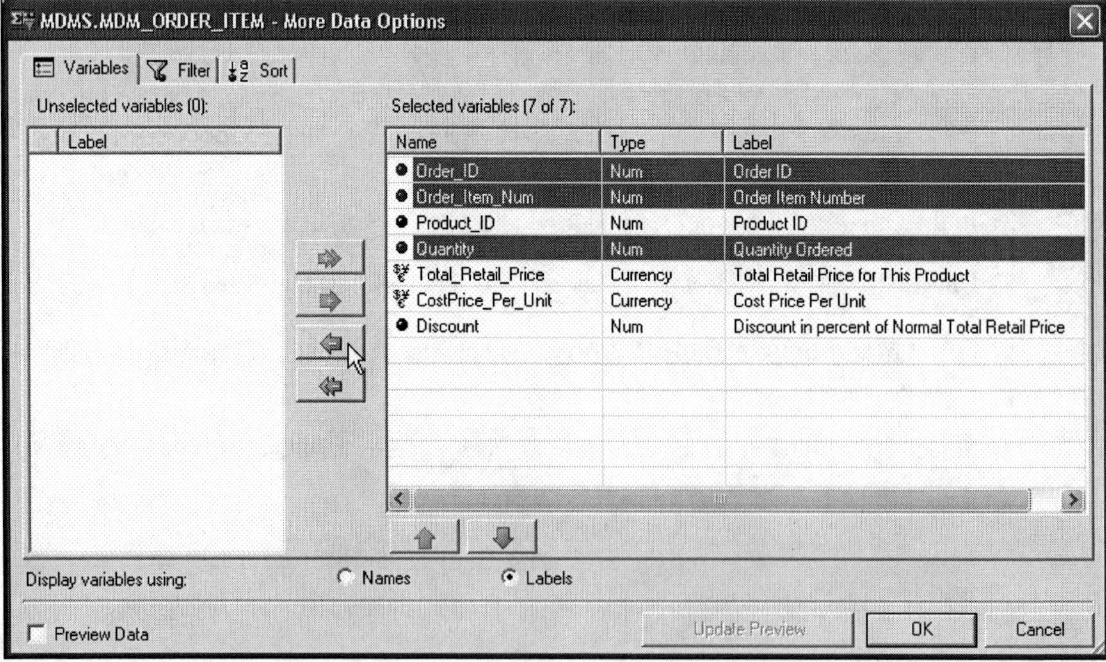

c. Use Excel's conditional formatting to highlight the items with discounts of 60%. Format the `Product ID` so that it is displayed as 12 digits with no decimal places.

1) In Excel, select **Discount in percent of Total Retail Price** by selecting the column heading.

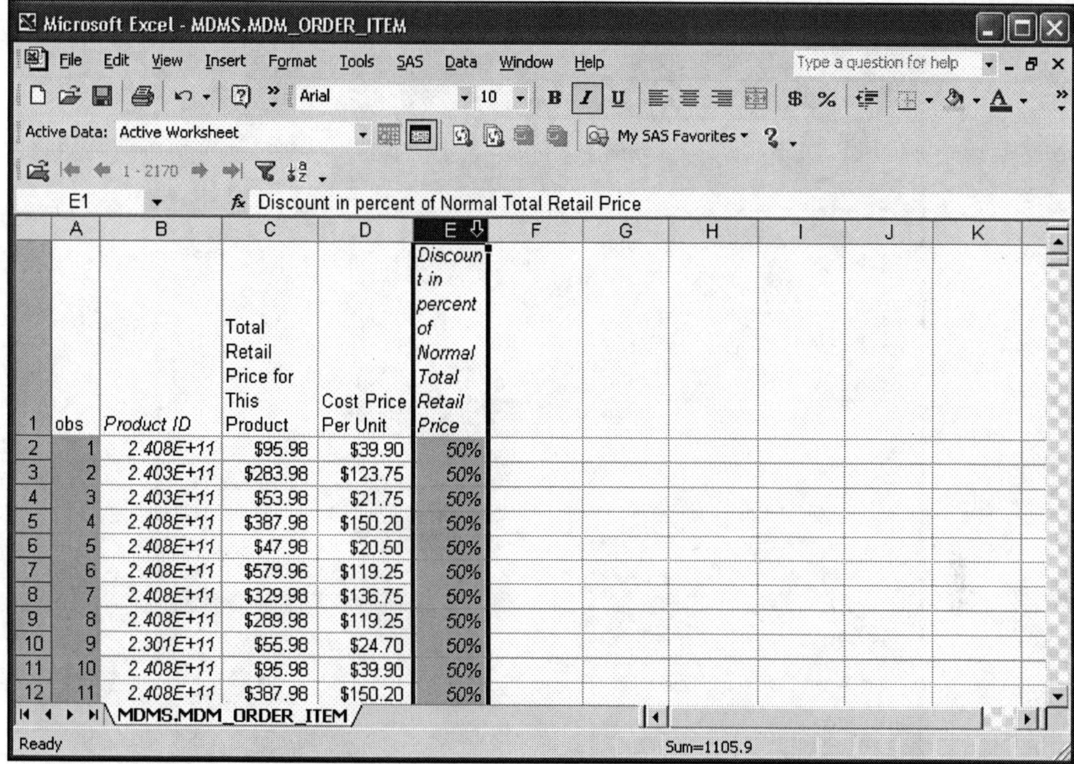

2) Select **Format** ⇨ **Conditional Formatting…** . Use the drop-down menus to select **Cell Value Is** and the operator **equal to**, and type in `.6`.

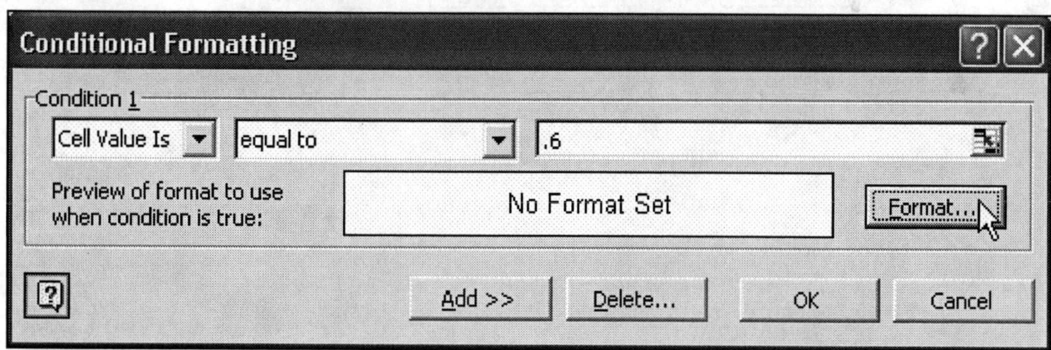

3) Select **Format...** and choose a color. Select **OK** and select **OK** to exit the Conditional Formatting window.

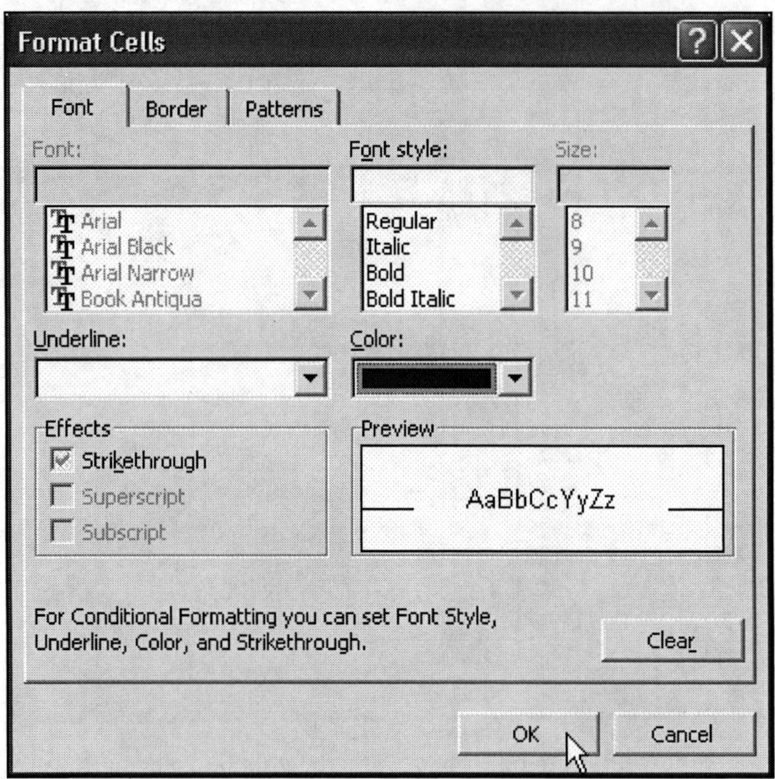

4) Select **Product ID**. Select **Format** ⇨ **Cells** ⇨ **Number** tab.

5) Select **Number** and change the number of decimal places to 0. Select OK to close the Format Cells window.

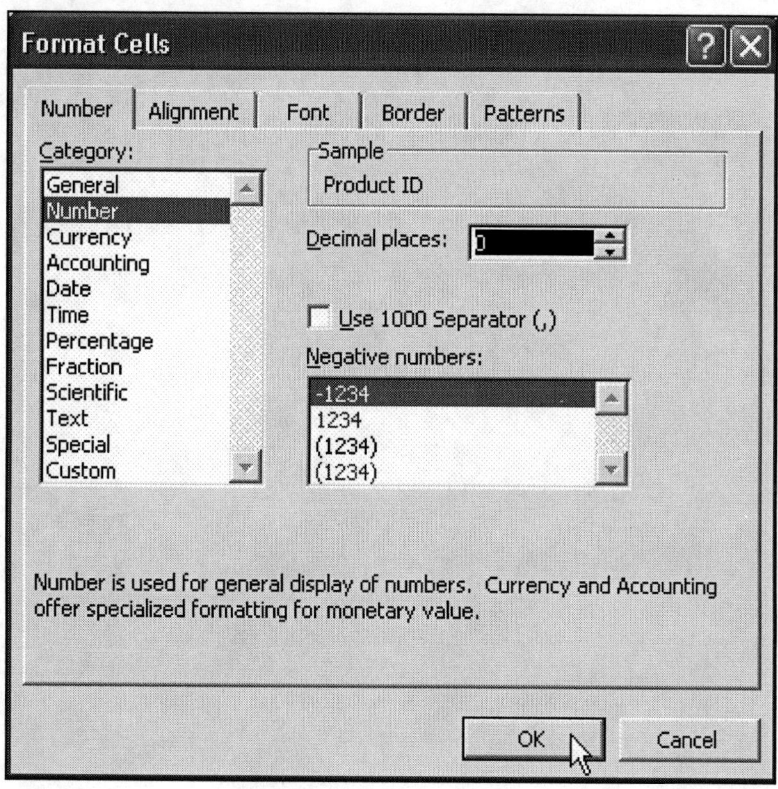

Chapter 4 Inserting SAS Results into Microsoft Office

4.1 An Overview of Stored Processes

Executing Stored Processes from within Microsoft Office

The SAS Add-In for Microsoft Office contains features that extend Microsoft Office by enabling you to execute stored processes dynamically and embed the results in Microsoft Word documents and Microsoft Excel spreadsheets.

SAS programming knowledge is not necessary to execute a stored process.

3

What Is a SAS Stored Process? 

A **stored process**

- is a SAS program that is stored on a server and described by metadata
- can be executed within a Web page, by Microsoft Word or Excel, and many of the clients in the SAS®9 Business Intelligence Architecture
- is similar in concept to programs run by SAS/IntrNet, but more versatile because of the underlying metadata and security support

4

Stored processes can be hosted by two types of servers, SAS Stored Process Servers and SAS Workspace Servers. The two servers are similar but have different capabilities. While the SAS Workspace Server has some security advantages, the SAS Stored Process Server is dedicated to executing stored processes and implements several features not available on SAS Workspace Servers, such as streaming output back to the SAS Add-In for Microsoft Office.

How Does a Stored Process Execute?

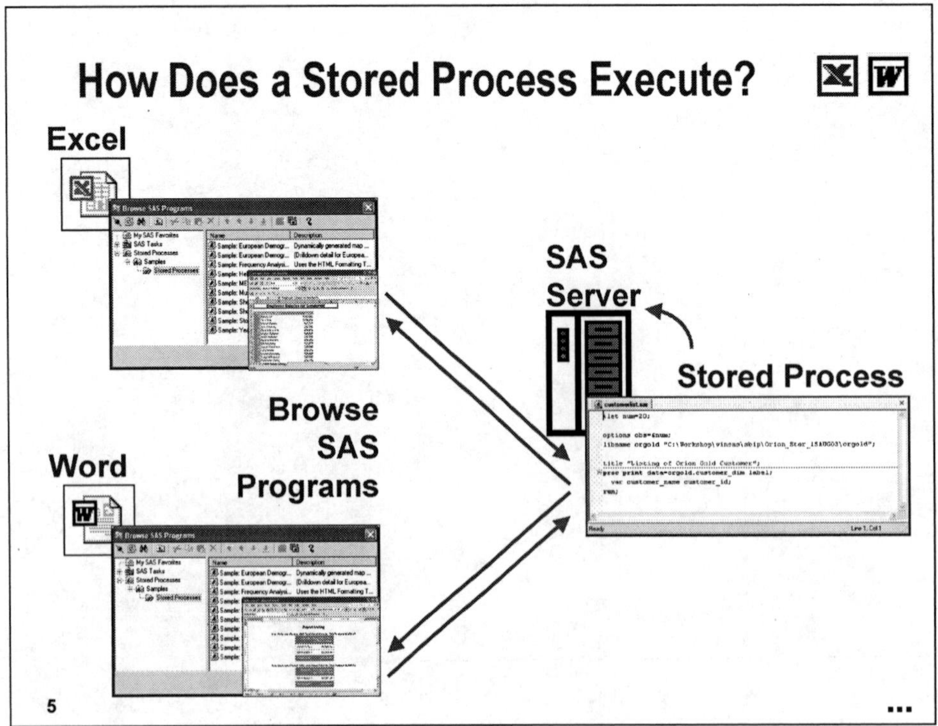

5

Why Use a SAS Stored Process?

- Stored process code is not embedded into client applications.
- Stored process programs ensure security and application integrity because the code is contained on a server.
- Stored process code can be maintained centrally and managed from the server.
- Stored process programs are always the latest version available for every client application.
- Stored process programs can be invoked from Web browsers and desktop applications.
- Running a stored process does not require the user to understand the underlying code.

6

Instead of embedding the SAS code into client applications, you can maintain and manage this code centrally from the server. This gives you the ability to change your SAS programs and at the same time ensure that every client who invokes a stored process will always get the latest version available.

What Can a Stored Process Do?

Because a stored process is a SAS program, it can create new data sets, files, and report output in a variety of formats.

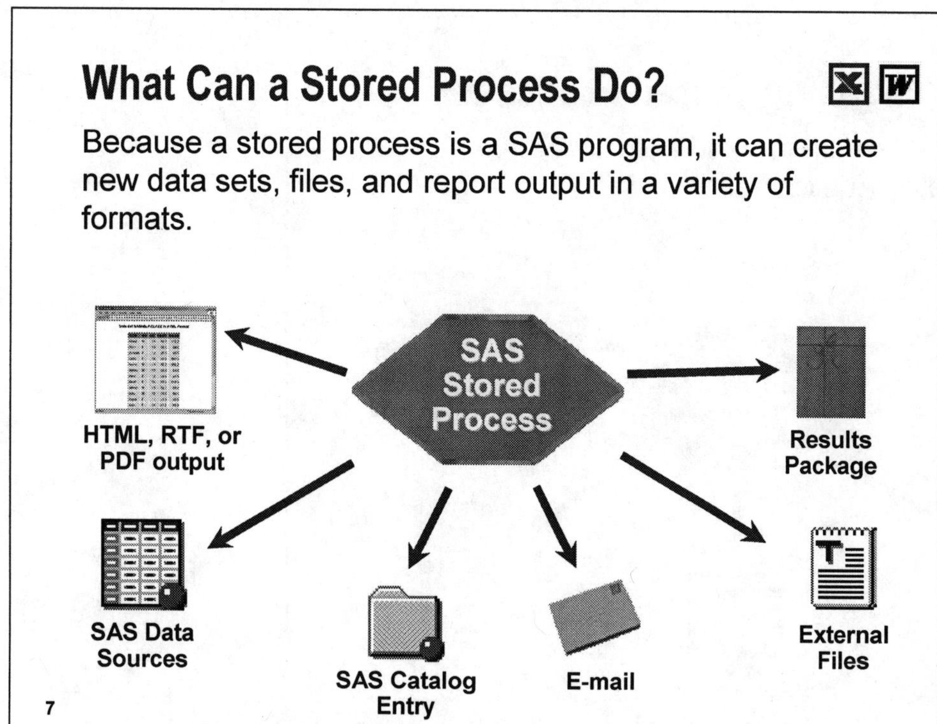

7

Results packages are collections of information such as reports, tables, binary files, HTML files, SAS data sets, and text files.

Stored Process Feedback

When a stored process is executed, the server automatically generates feedback in the background.

This information

- is called the SAS log
- is useful for debugging
- can be displayed in a separate window.

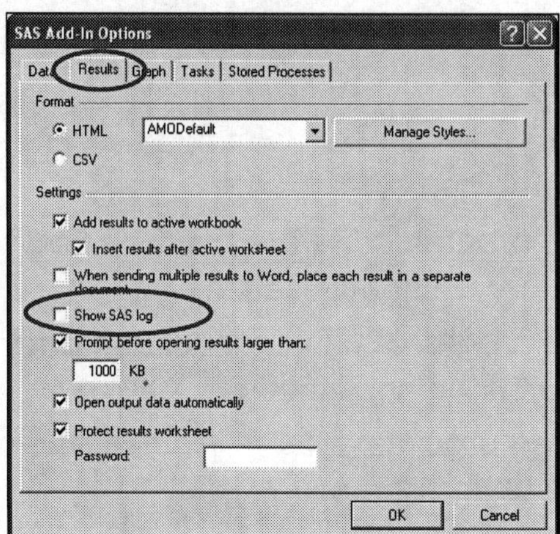

8

You can also select **Show SAS log** on the Results tab in Microsoft Word.

SAS tasks also produce SAS logs.

Methods for Invoking Stored Processes

Stored processes can be invoked from several of the SAS®9 Intelligence Applications.

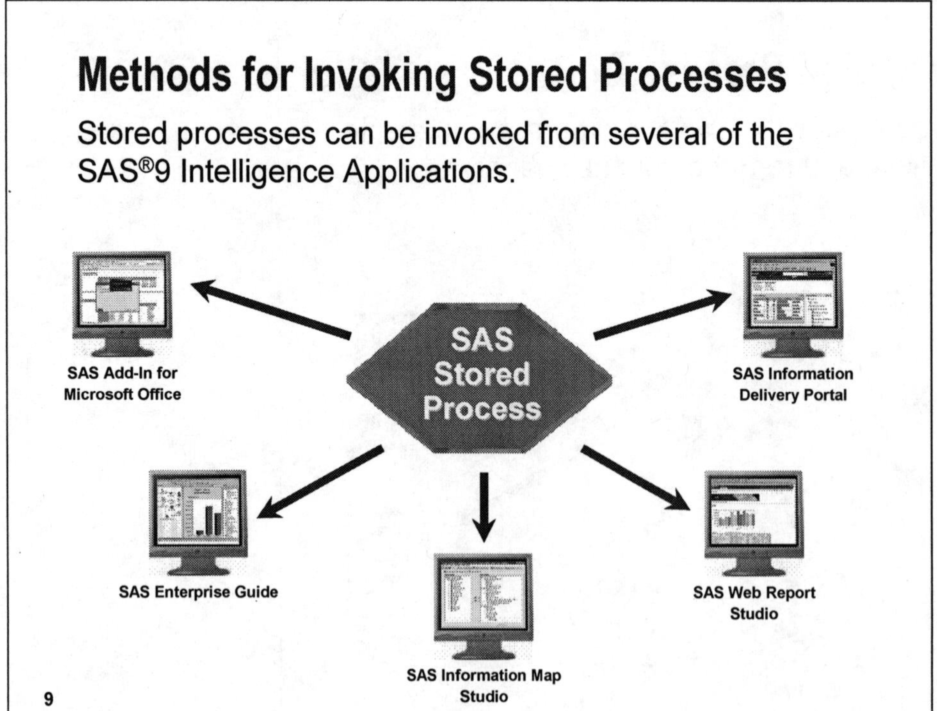

9

Creating Stored Processes

Stored processes can be created using

- SAS Enterprise Guide
- SAS ETL Studio
- the SAS program editor
- any text editor.

Once created, the stored process must be

- stored in a special location
- registered in the metadata repository to define the name of the stored process and associated parameters.

> Stored processes are designed to work within the context of the SAS Business Intelligence Platform architecture.

10

Beginning with version 3, SAS Enterprise Guide is the preferred method for creating stored processes because it provides the ability to create, register, and test stored processes from within one interface.

Running Stored Processes

For this demonstration, you will

- run a stored process from Microsoft Excel to create a salary report based on gender
- work with My SAS Favorites to create shortcuts.

Run a Stored Process from Excel

1. Select [icon] on the SAS Analysis Tools toolbar (or select **SAS** ⇨ **Browse SAS Programs** from the pull-down menus).

   a. If not already expanded, in the left pane of the Browse SAS Programs window select [+] beside **Stored Processes** to expand the folder listing.

   b. Select **Marketing Data Mart** in the left pane to see a listing of the available stored processes.

   c. Select **MDM Salary Listing**, then [Run].

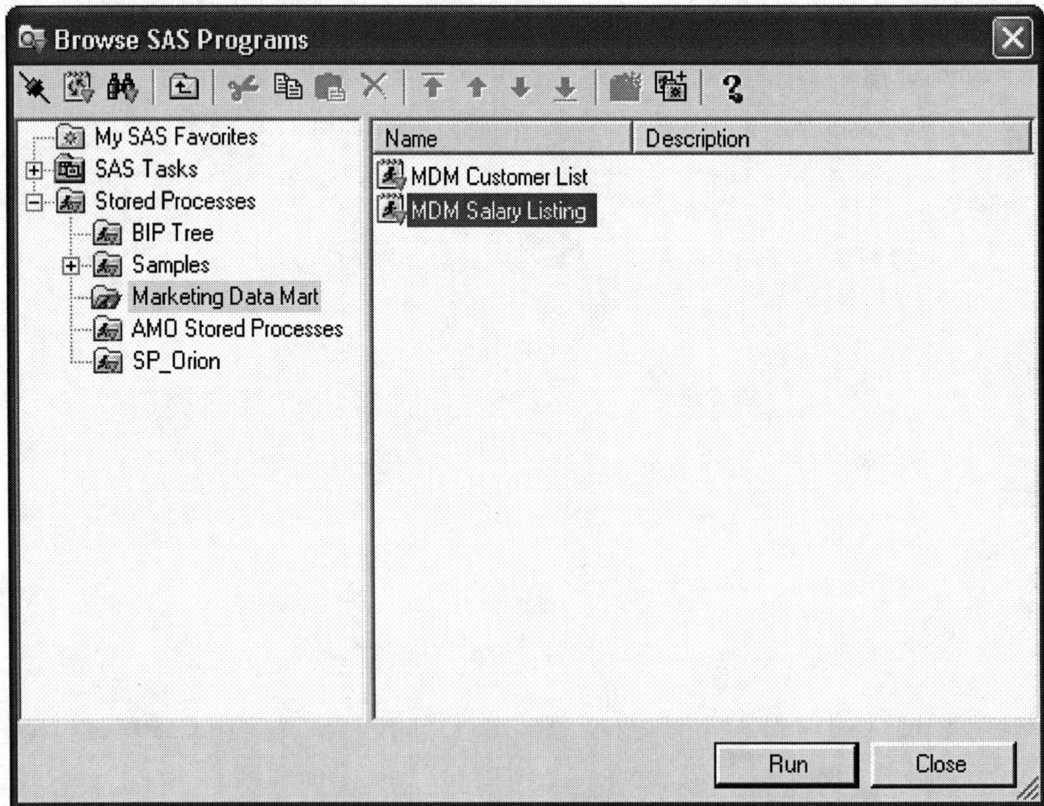

d. Because this stored process has a parameter, you are prompted to enter a value. Select **F** when the MDM Salary Listing window is displayed.

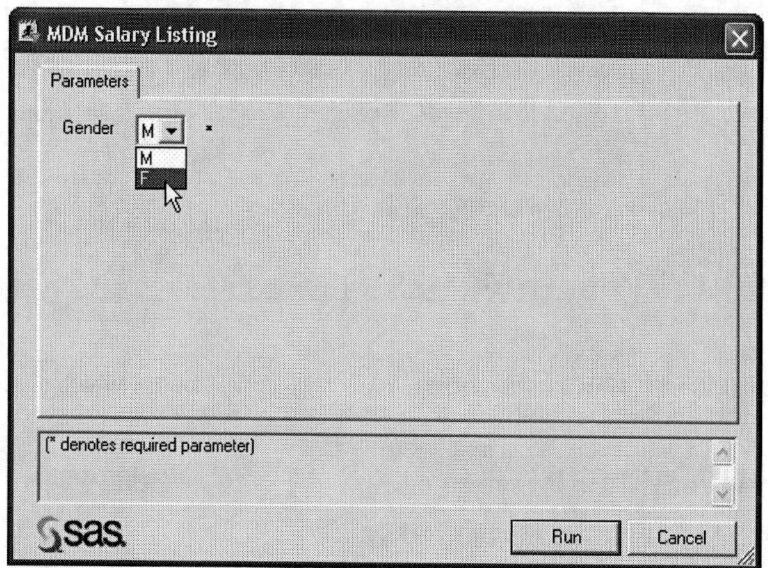

> The asterisk next to the `Gender` field indicates that it is required.

e. Select Run.

The program results are streamed back to an Excel worksheet.

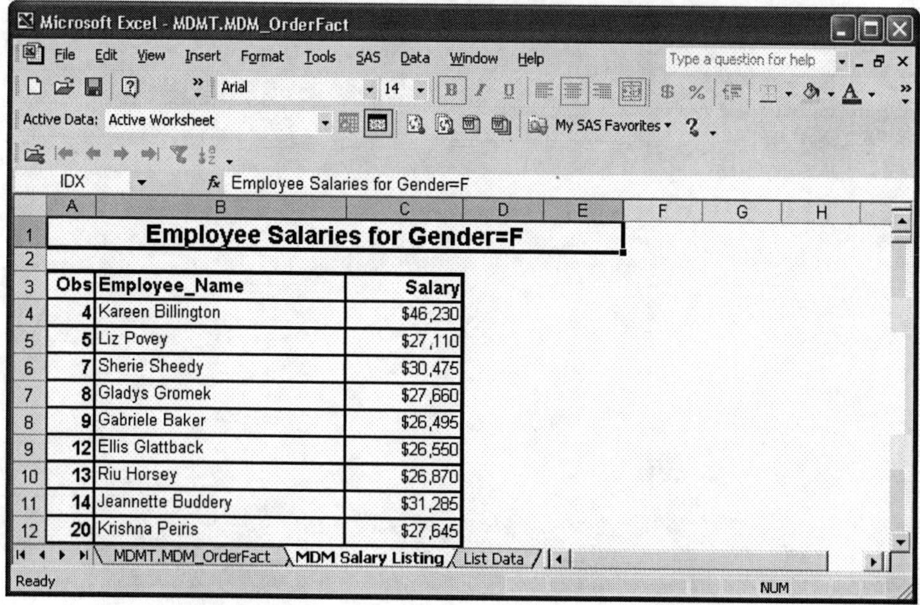

Employee Salaries for Gender=F

Obs	Employee_Name	Salary
4	Kareen Billington	$46,230
5	Liz Povey	$27,110
7	Sherie Sheedy	$30,475
8	Gladys Gromek	$27,660
9	Gabriele Baker	$26,495
12	Ellis Glattback	$26,550
13	Riu Horsey	$26,870
14	Jeannette Buddery	$31,285
20	Krishna Peiris	$27,645

The results are displayed in a read-only worksheet, so the values cannot be updated. To edit the worksheet, select **Tools** ⇨ **Protection** ⇨ **Unprotect Sheet…**.

> If you always want the sheet unprotected, you can select **SAS** ⇨ **Options** and then deselect the **Protect data worksheet** check box on the Results tab.

Managing Favorites

The Browse SAS Programs dialog box contains a special folder labeled My SAS Favorites. This folder contains a list of shortcuts to a user's favorite or most often selected stored processes or SAS tasks. Items can be added to this list by right-clicking on either a stored process or SAS task and then adding it to Favorites. Also, items added to My SAS Favorites then become available from a pull-down menu on the SAS Analysis Tools toolbar.

✎ My SAS Favorites is available in both Microsoft Excel and Word.

1. Select [icon] on the SAS Analysis Tools toolbar (or select **SAS** ⇨ **Browse SAS Programs** from the pull-down menus).

   a. If not already expanded, in the left pane of the Browse SAS Programs window select [+] beside **Stored Processes** to expand the folder listing.

   b. Select **Marketing Data Mart** in the left pane to see a listing of the available stored processes.

   c. Right-click **MDM Salary Listing**, then **Add to Favorites**.

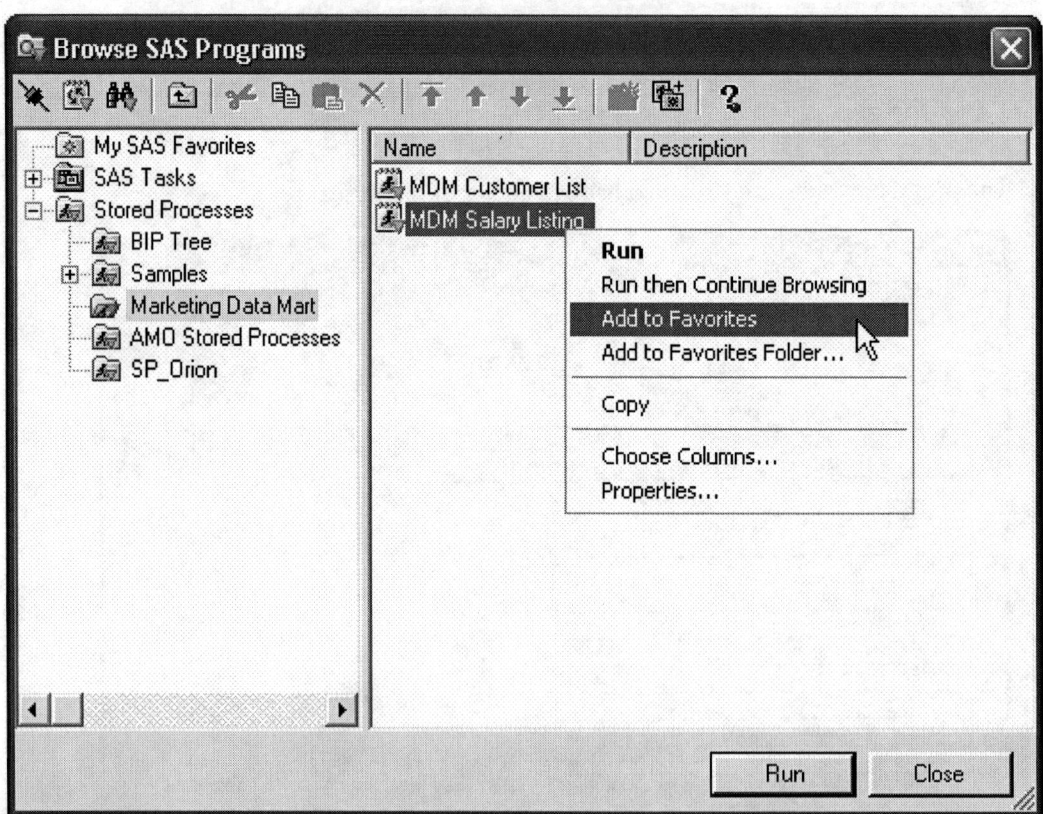

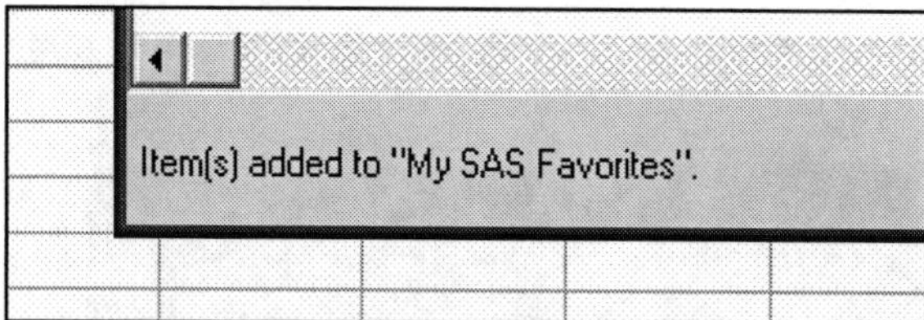

The stored process has now been added as a favorite.

d. Select **My SAS Favorites** in the left pane of the Browse SAS Programs window.

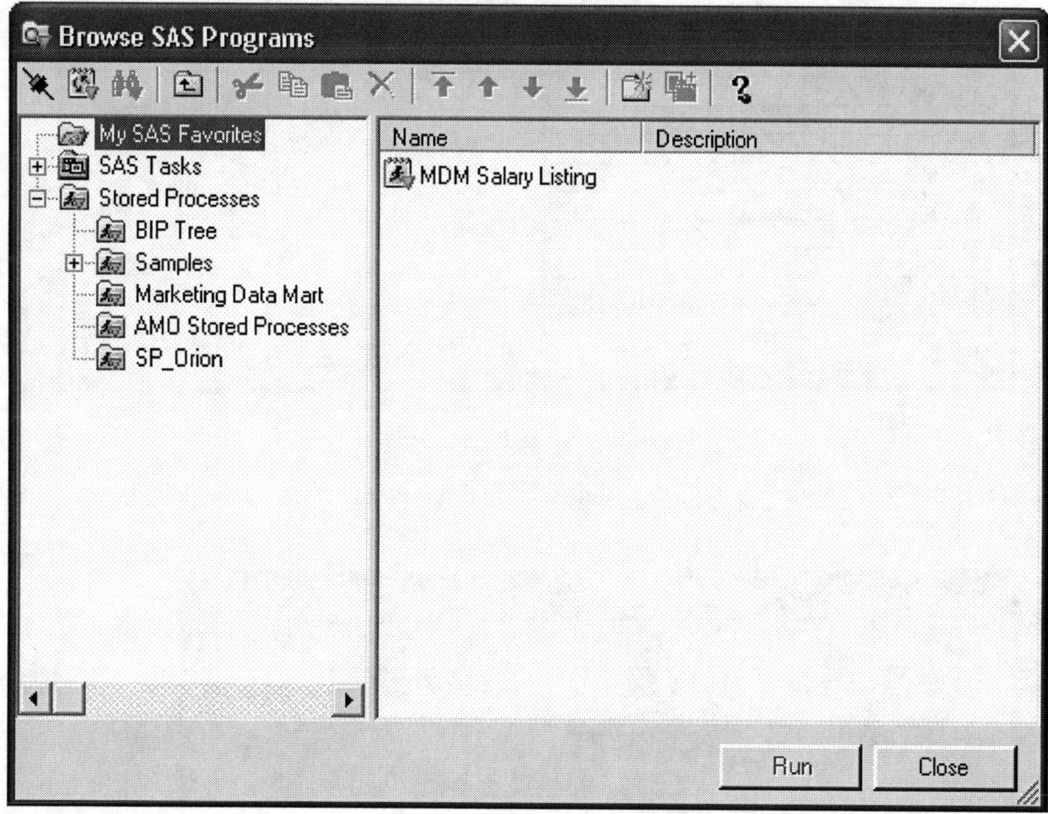

e. Close the Browse SAS Programs window by selecting Close.

f. Select **My SAS Favorites** from the SAS Analysis Tools toolbar. Note that the newly added favorite is on the list:

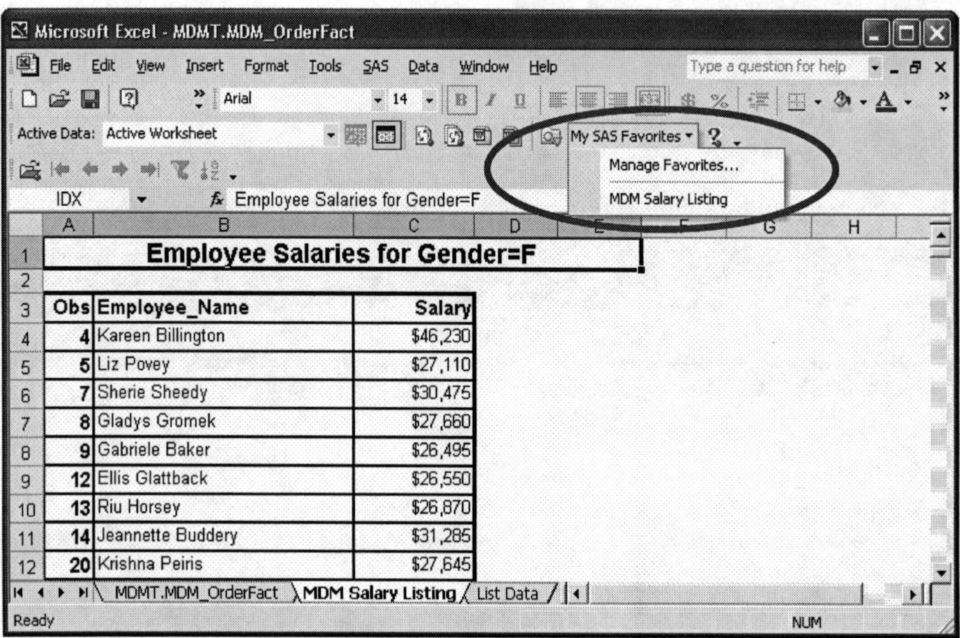

g. Organize favorites by selecting **Manage Favorites…**.

h. Select the **New Favorites Folder…** icon and type `For AMO Class` as the name of the new folder.

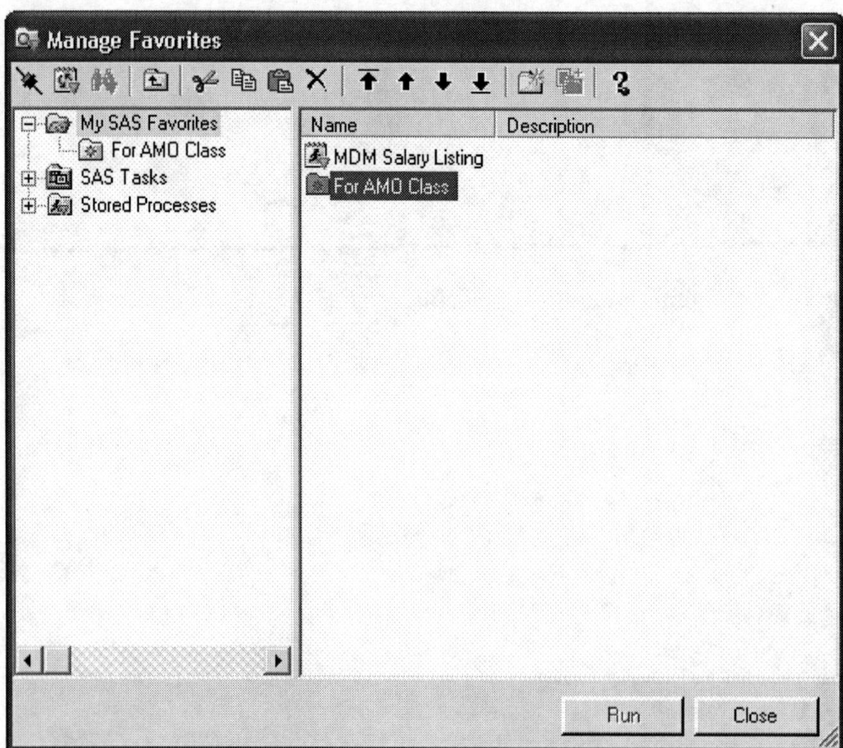

i. Drag **MDM Salary Listing** and drop it into the new folder **For AMO Class**.

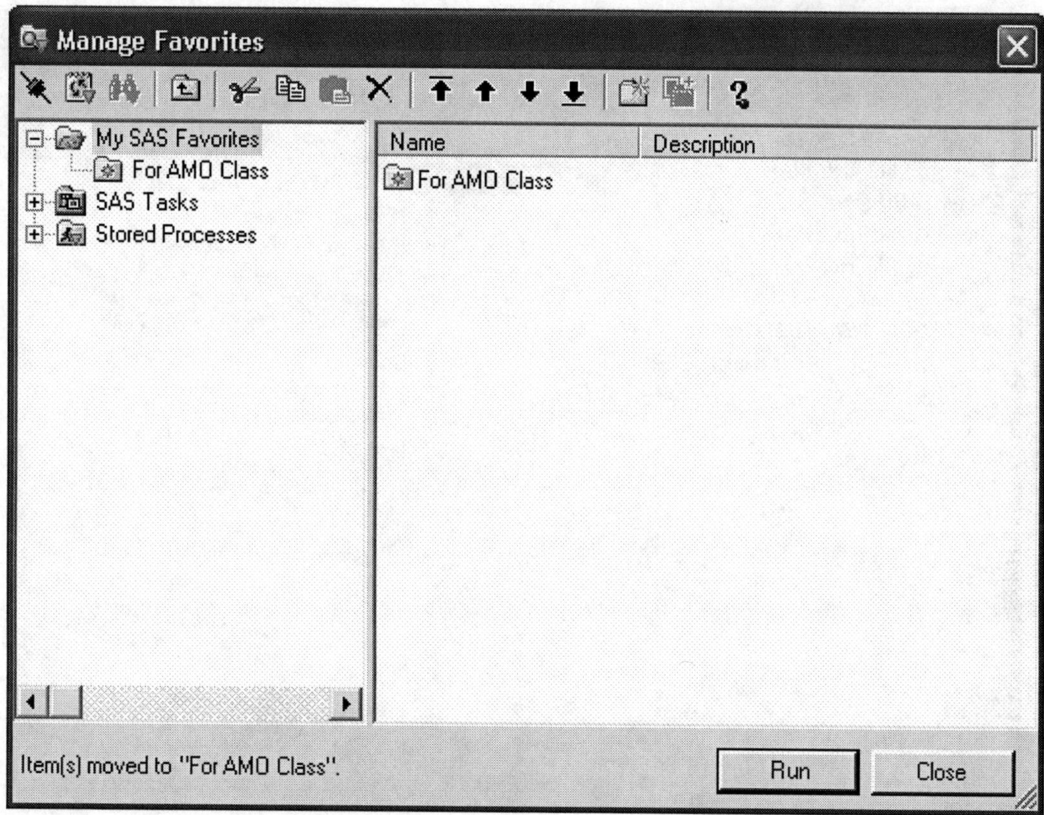

j. If not already expanded, in the left pane of the Browse SAS Programs window select ⊞ beside **Stored Processes** to expand the folder listing.

k. Select **AMO Stored Processes** in the left pane to see a listing of the available stored processes.

l. Right-click **AMO Sales Forecast**, then **Add to Favorites Folder…**.

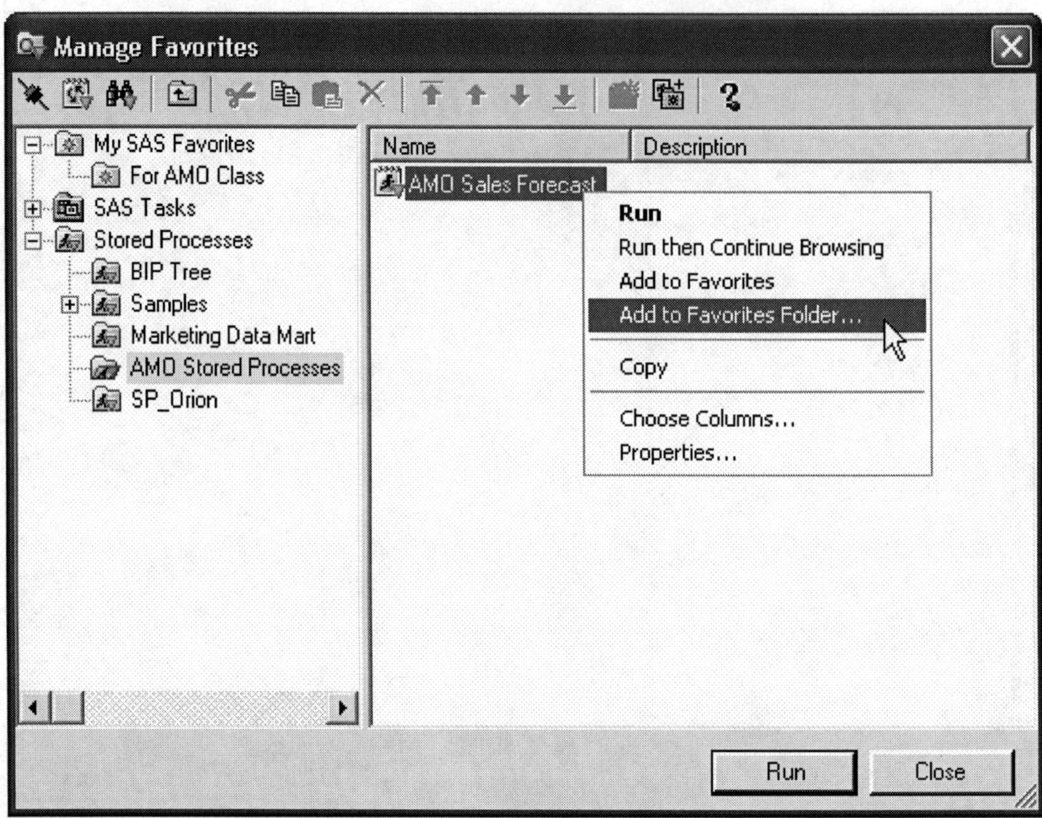

m. Select **For AMO Class**.

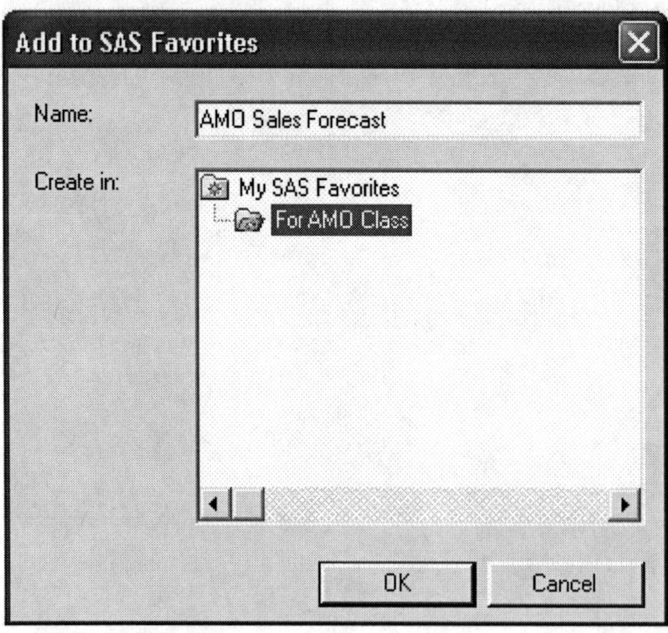

n. Select OK.

o. Select Close to close the Manage Favorites window.

p. Select **My SAS Favorites** from the SAS Analysis Tools toolbar. Note that the newly added folder is on the list:

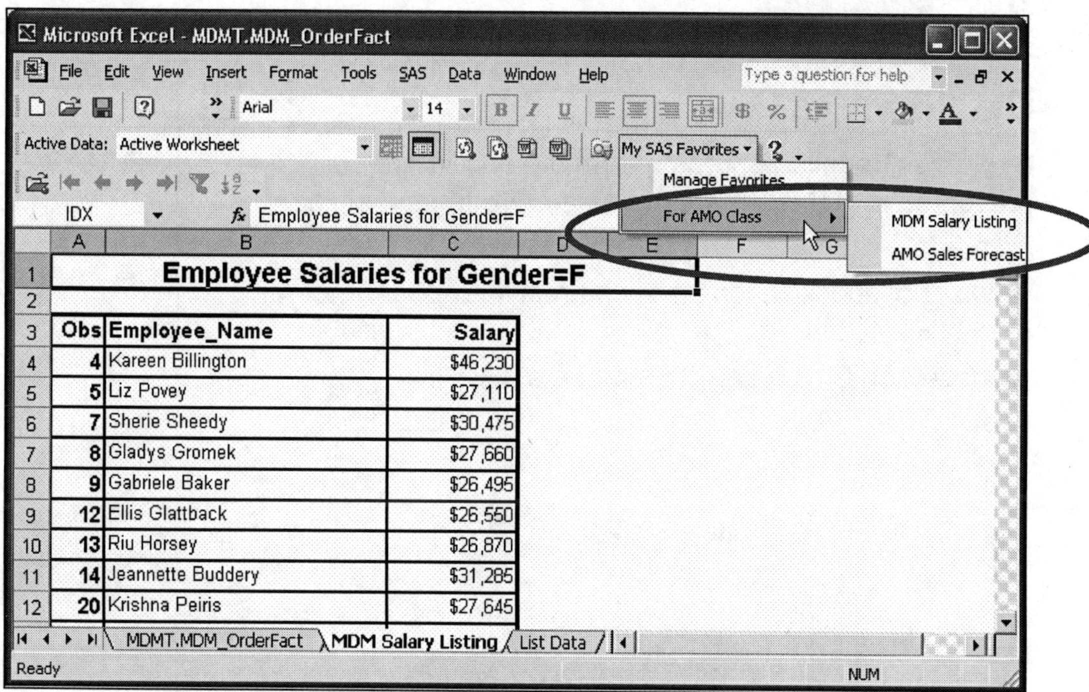

4.2 Customizing the Output Style

Output Styles

By default, results generated from the add-in are presented in HTML format and use a predefined style.

A *style* is

- a set of specifications that controls the appearance of the HTML output
- based on Cascading Style Sheets (CSS).

Employee Salaries for Gender=M

Obs	Employee_Name	Salary
1	Patrick Lu	$163,040
2	Tom Zhou	$108,255
3	Wilson Dawes	$87,975

13

The default HTML style for the SAS Add-In for Microsoft Office is AMODefault for Microsoft Excel and sasweb for Microsoft Word.

A *Cascading Style Sheet* (CSS) is a file that contains instructions on how to display content in HTML documents. A CSS can control almost every aspect of a page's layout, including text font and styles, color, margins, and images.

Output Styles

The SAS Add-In for Microsoft Office provides a variety of predefined styles that can be applied to output.

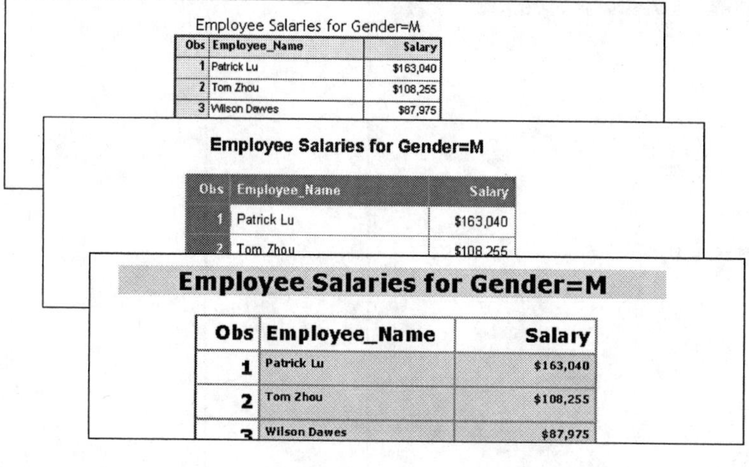

14

The Style Manager

The Style Manager can be used to change the default style and add, delete, or edit existing styles.

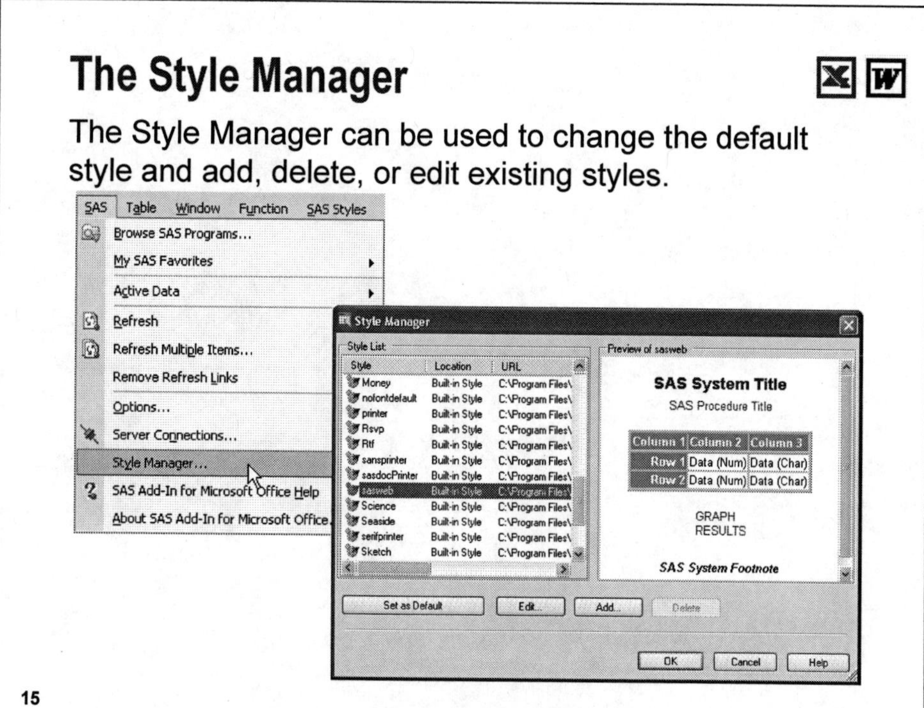

15

The Style Editor

The Style Editor is used to modify the attributes of an existing style or create a new style.

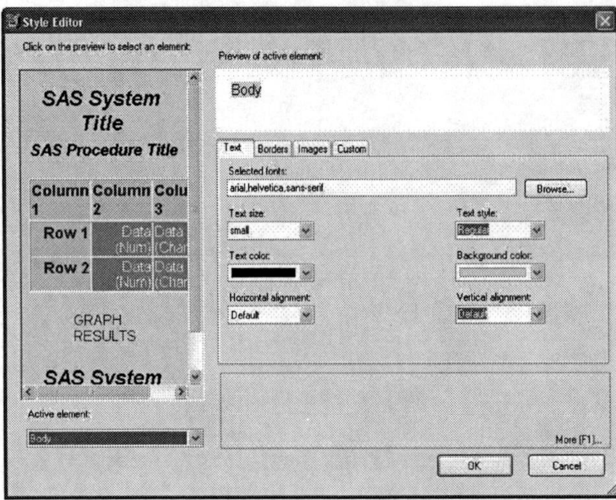

16

Applying a New Style with a Stored Process

For this demonstration, you will

- execute a stored process from Microsoft Word to create a sales forecasting report
- customize results with the Style Manager.

Run a Stored Process from Microsoft Word

1. Invoke Microsoft Word by selecting **Start** ⇨ **All Programs** ⇨ **Microsoft Office** ⇨ **Microsoft Word**.

   a. Select **File** ⇨ **Page Setup…**.

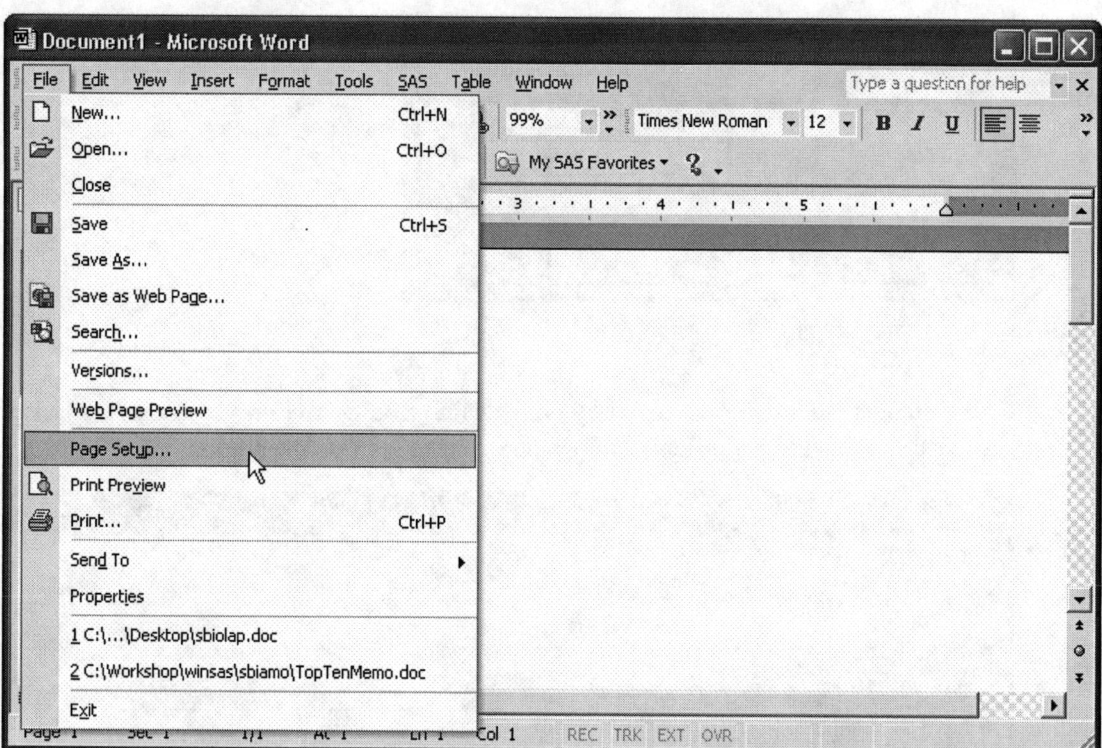

b. Select **Landscape**.

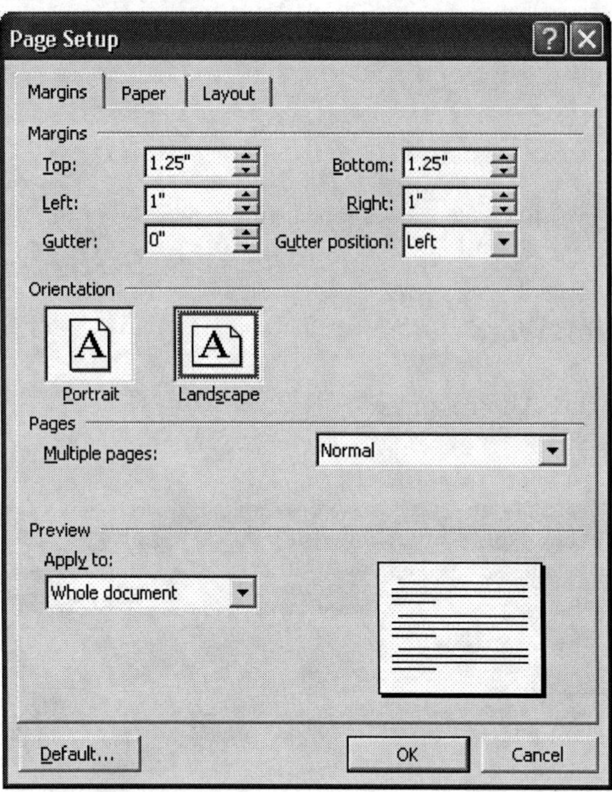

c. Select OK.

d. Create an opening line for the report by typing `The most current forecasting report:`. Press the **Enter** key to allow the report to start on the second line of the document.

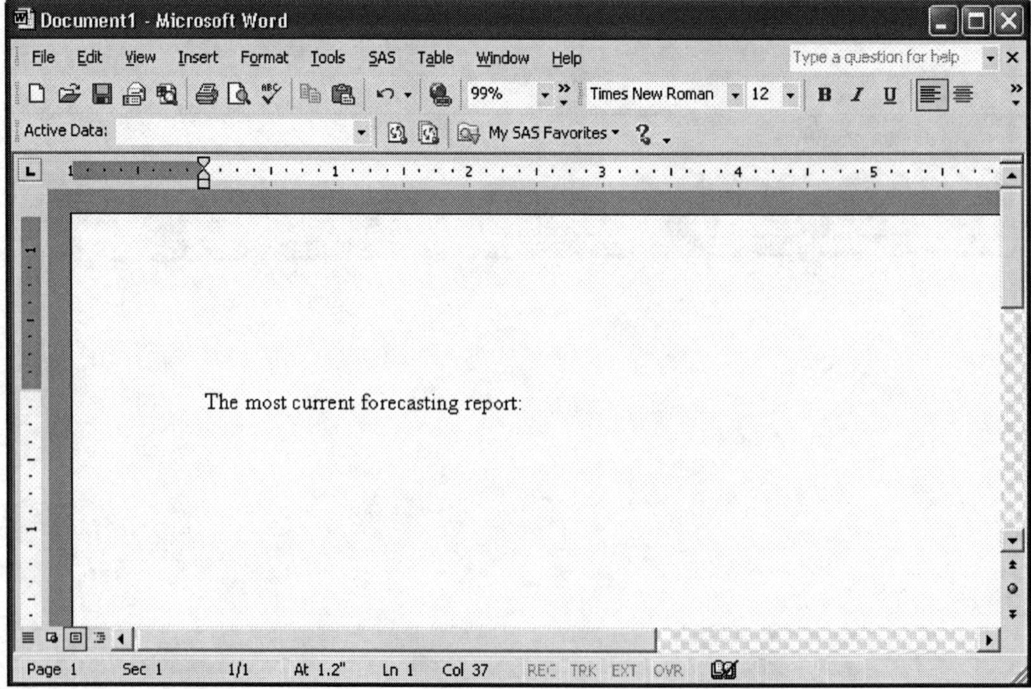

e. Select **My SAS Favorites** from the SAS Analysis Tools toolbar.

f. Select **For AMO Class** ⇨ **AMO Sales Forecast**.

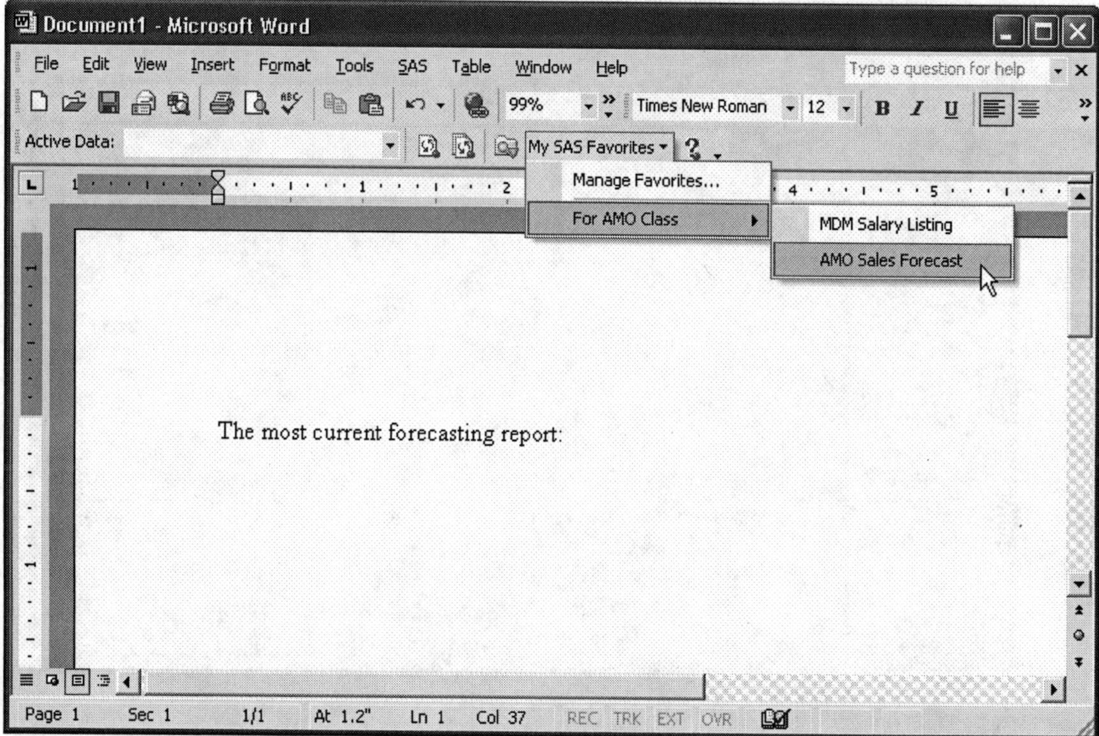

g. If prompted, enter the user name and password provided by the instructor.

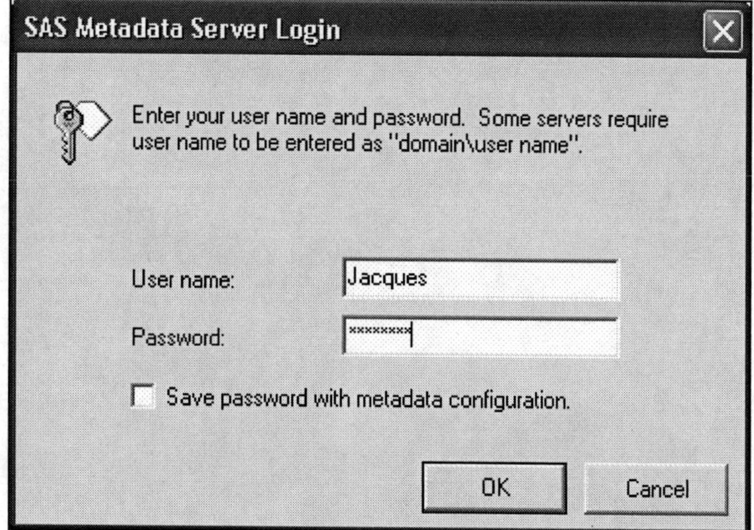

✎ The values shown above may be different than those used in class.

Select OK.

h. Keep the default values in the AMO Sales Forecast window.

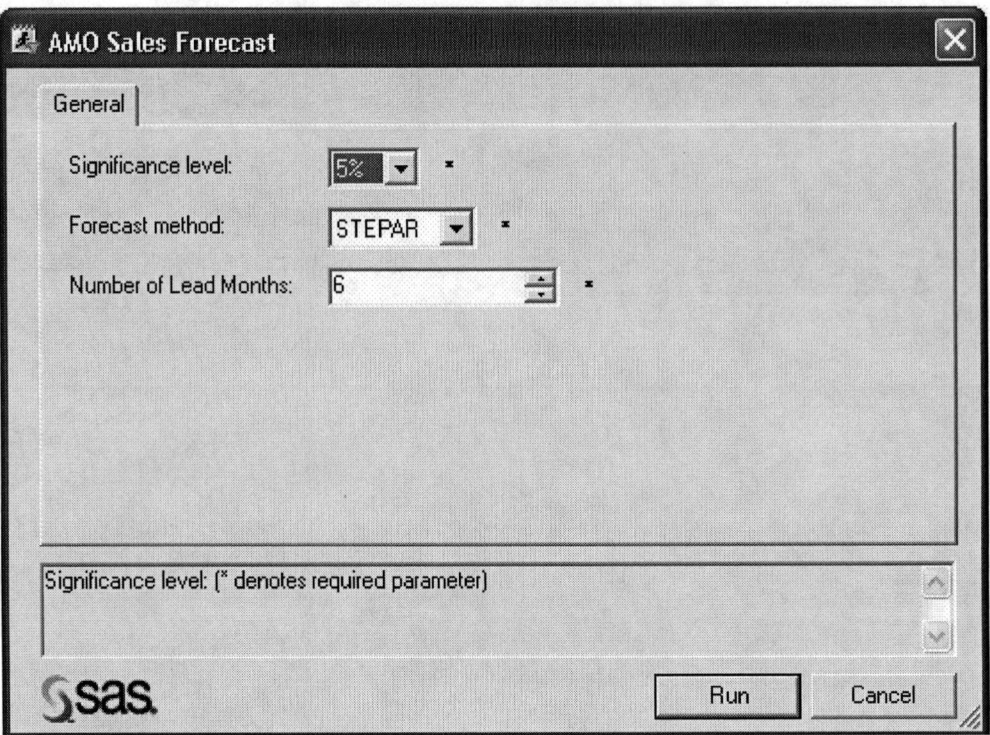

i. Select Run.

The output from the stored process is streamed back to a Word document in the HTML style that is defined in the stored process.

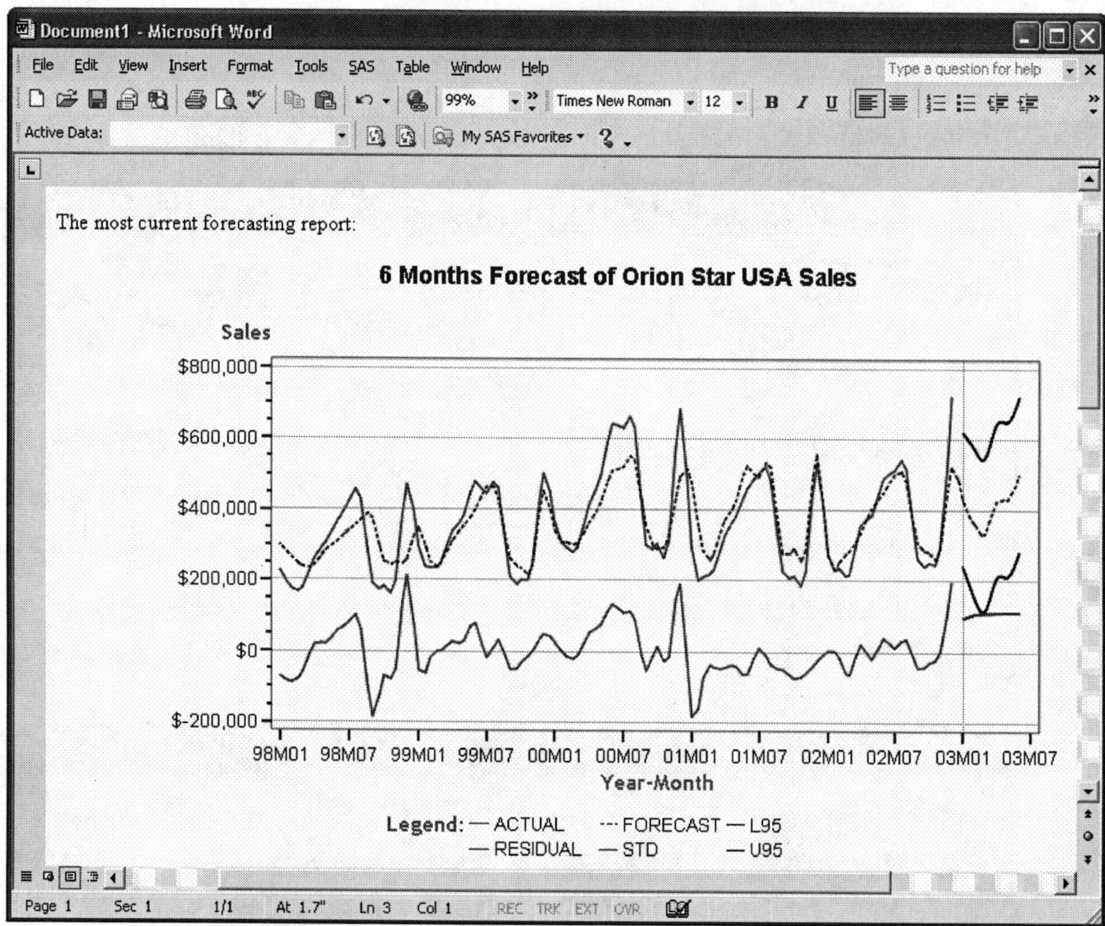

To make changes to the ActiveX graph, double-click the graph to open the Properties window:

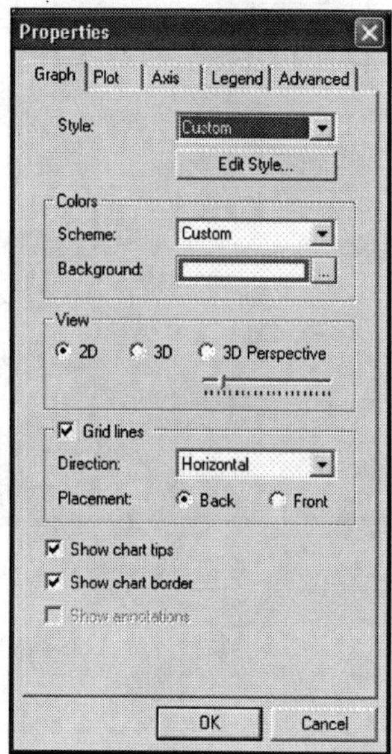

Customizing Results

1. To create a customized style sheet, select **SAS** ⇨ **Style Manager…** from the menu bar to enter the Style Manager window.

   a. An informational dialog box appears that describes color and image limitations when using styles.

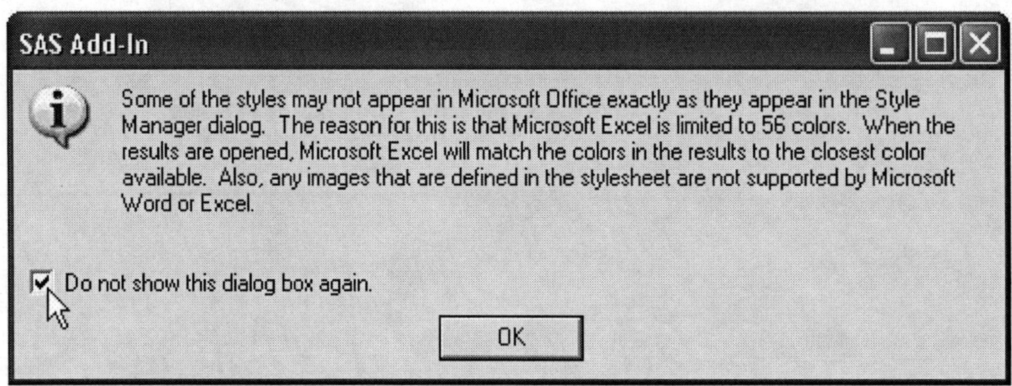

   Select the **Do not show this dialog box again.** check box and select OK.

   b. Select Add... to create a new customized style.

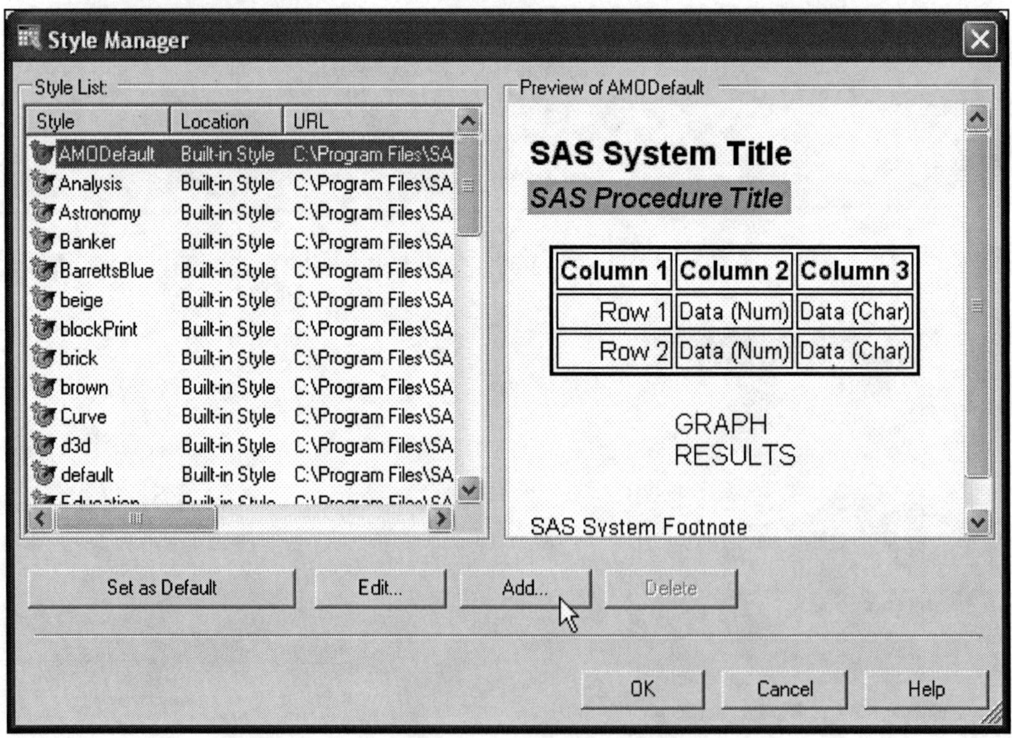

✎ The Style Manager is also available in Microsoft Excel.

c. Select **Add new based on existing style**. Type **`AMO Class`** in the `Style name` field. Select **AMODefault** in the `Based on` field and select OK.

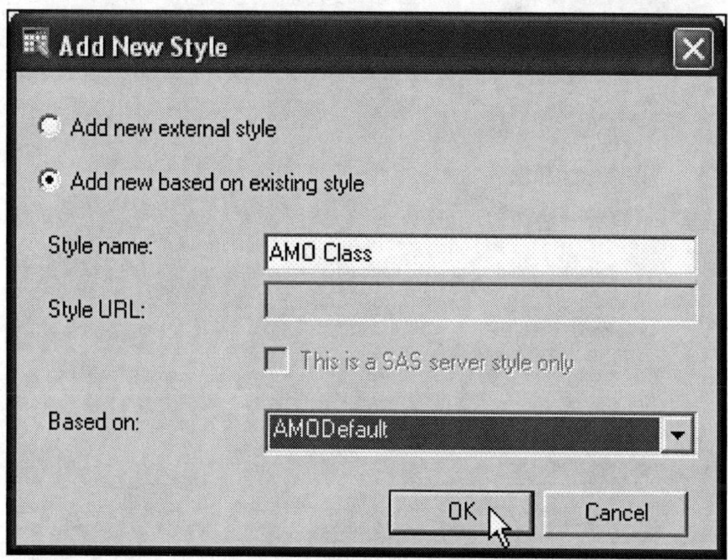

d. A style called AMO Class is added to the list of available files. To edit the style, highlight **AMO Class** in the Style List pane and select Edit....

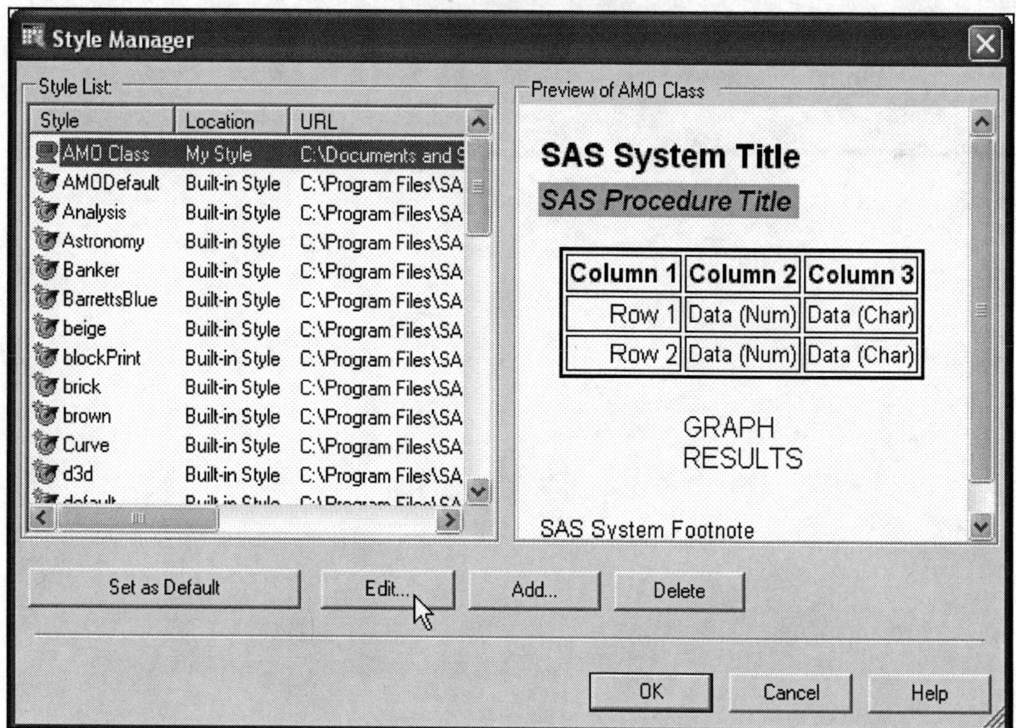

e. The Style Editor window opens automatically to enable you to customize the AMO Class style. To change the size and color of the SAS System Title in the style, select the title in the Preview pane and verify that System Title is listed in the `Active element` field.

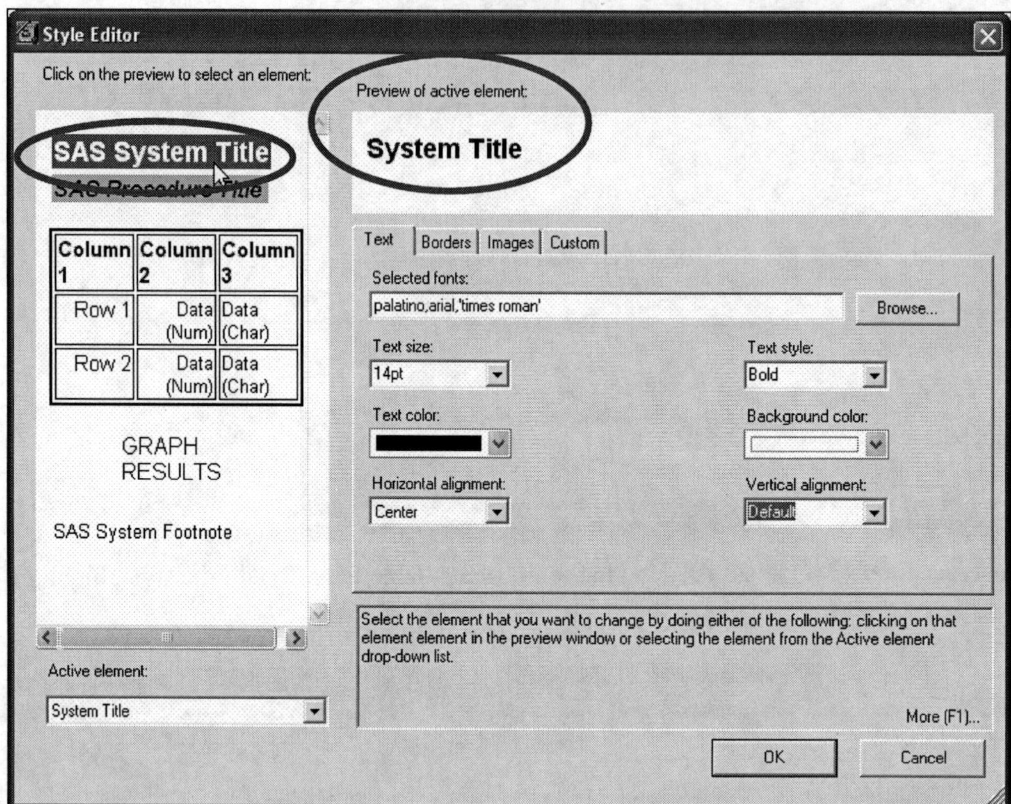

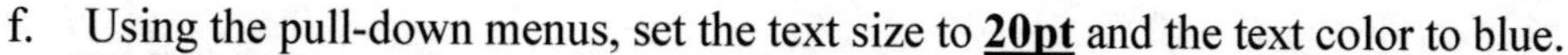

f. Using the pull-down menus, set the text size to **20pt** and the text color to blue.

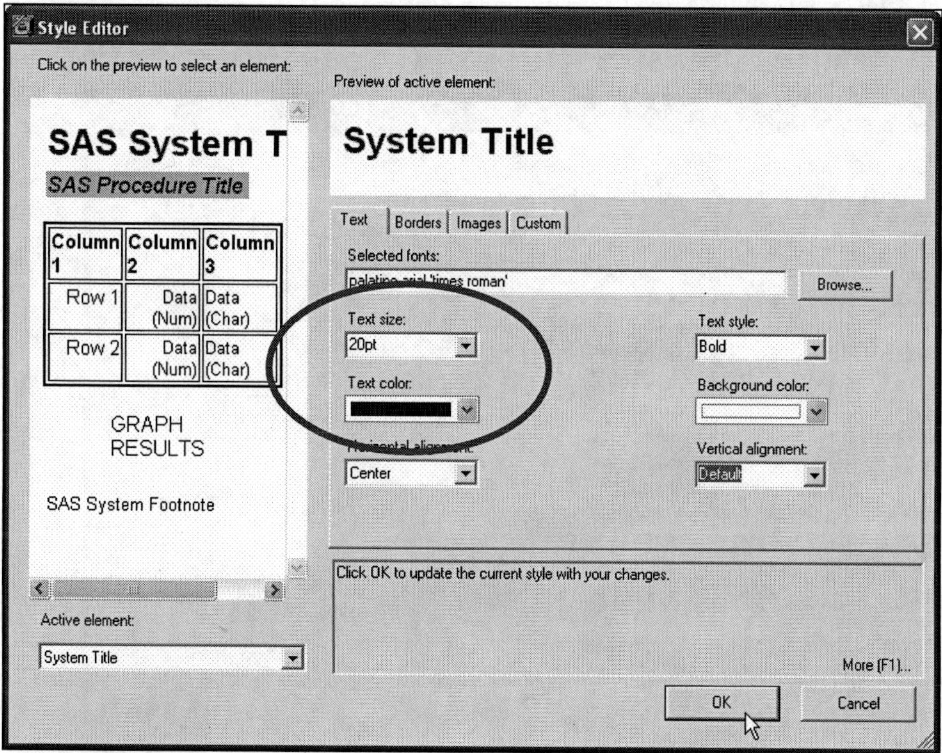

g. Select OK to save the changes to the AMO Class style.

h. To make the new style the default for all add-in output created in the future in Microsoft Word, highlight **AMO Class** in the Style List pane and select **Set as Default**. Select OK when you are finished.

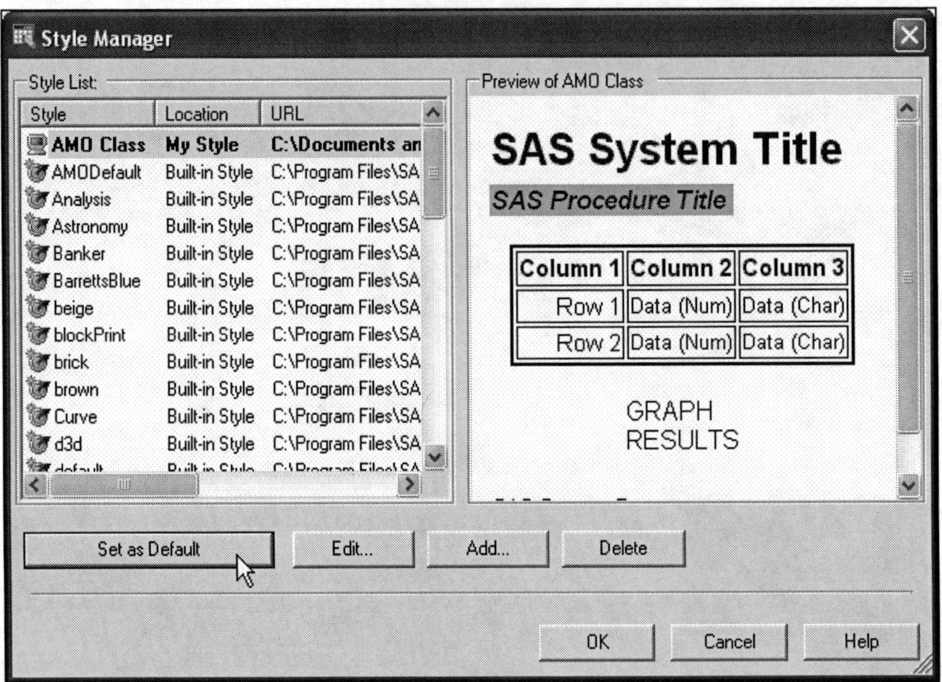

You may also set the default HTML style by selecting **SAS** ⇨ **Options** and then navigating to the Results tab. The default style for Microsoft Word may be different than the default style for Microsoft Excel.

Styles created in the Style Manager are available to both Microsoft Word and Microsoft Excel.

2. In order to see the new style, refresh the report.

   a. Left-click inside the body of the document to place the cursor inside the results you want to refresh.

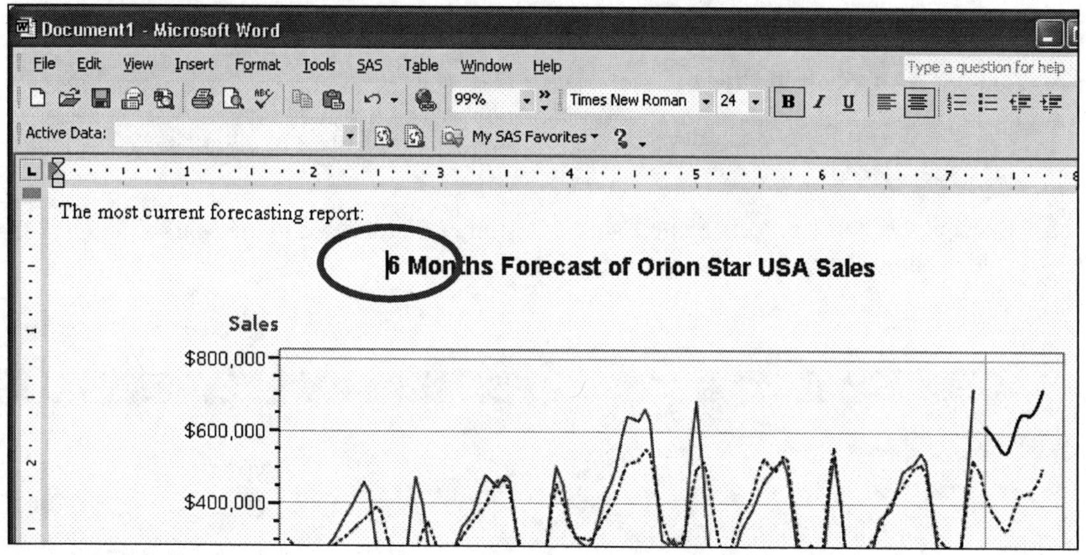

   b. Select [icon] on the SAS Analysis Tools toolbar (or select **SAS** ⇨ **Refresh** from the pull-down menus) to rerun the report.

   c. Keep the default parameter values in the AMO Sales Forecast window that is displayed.

   d. Select Run.

   The output from the stored process is streamed back with the new style.

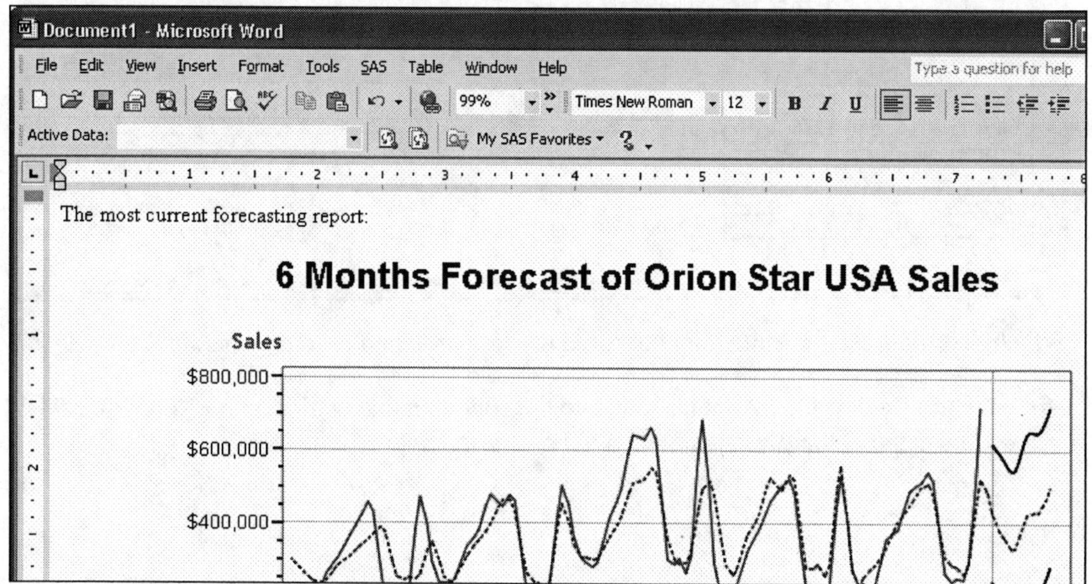

   Close Word by selecting **File** ⇨ **Exit**, and do not save the changes.

Exercises

1. Working with a Stored Process

a. Start Microsoft Excel and select the appropriate SAS Add-In Option to display the SAS log when task and stored process output is generated.

b. Execute the stored process named MDM Customer List located in the Marketing Data Mart folder. Limit the results to **20** records.

Output

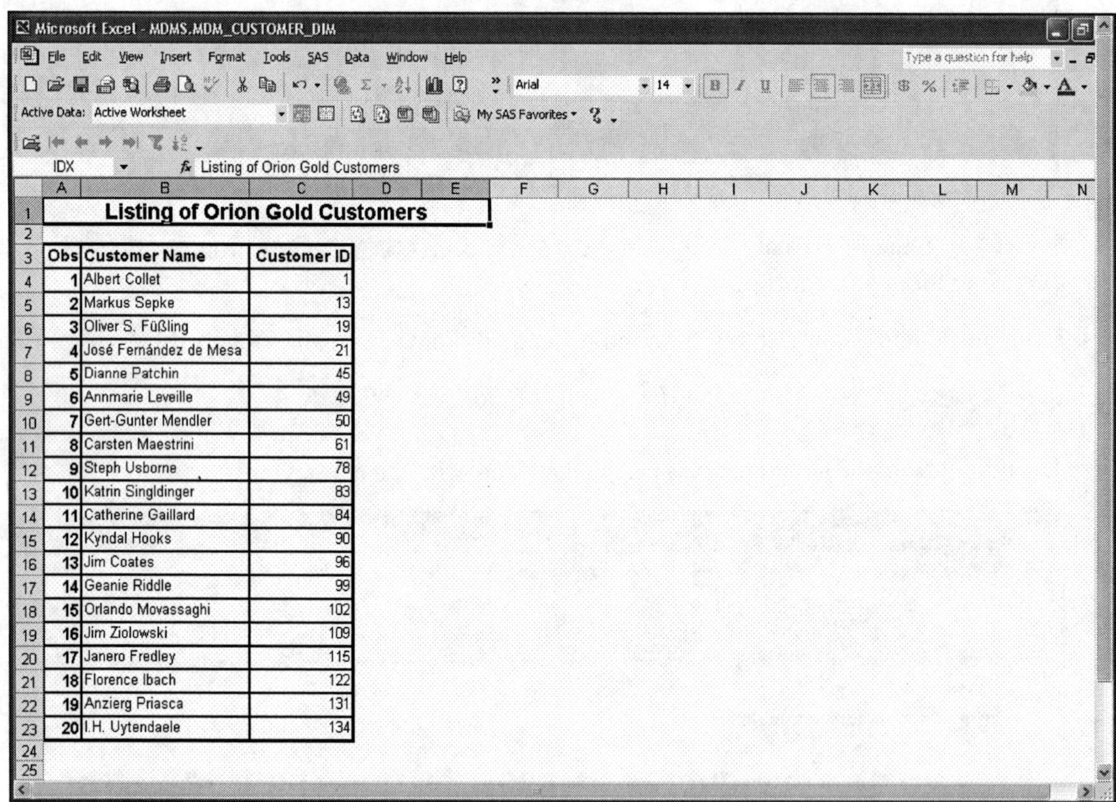

Listing of Orion Gold Customers

Obs	Customer Name	Customer ID
1	Albert Collet	1
2	Markus Sepke	13
3	Oliver S. Füßling	19
4	José Fernández de Mesa	21
5	Dianne Patchin	45
6	Annmarie Leveille	49
7	Gert-Gunter Mendler	50
8	Carsten Maestrini	61
9	Steph Usborne	78
10	Katrin Singldinger	83
11	Catherine Gaillard	84
12	Kyndal Hooks	90
13	Jim Coates	96
14	Geanie Riddle	99
15	Orlando Movassaghi	102
16	Jim Ziolowski	109
17	Janero Fredley	115
18	Florence Ibach	122
19	Anzierg Priasca	131
20	I.H. Uytendaele	134

Which SAS data set is specified in the stored process code and used to generate these results?

Hint: Review the SAS log and locate the code line that begins with PROC PRINT. What is the name of the file listed in the DATA= option?

c. Export the results to Microsoft Word.

Output

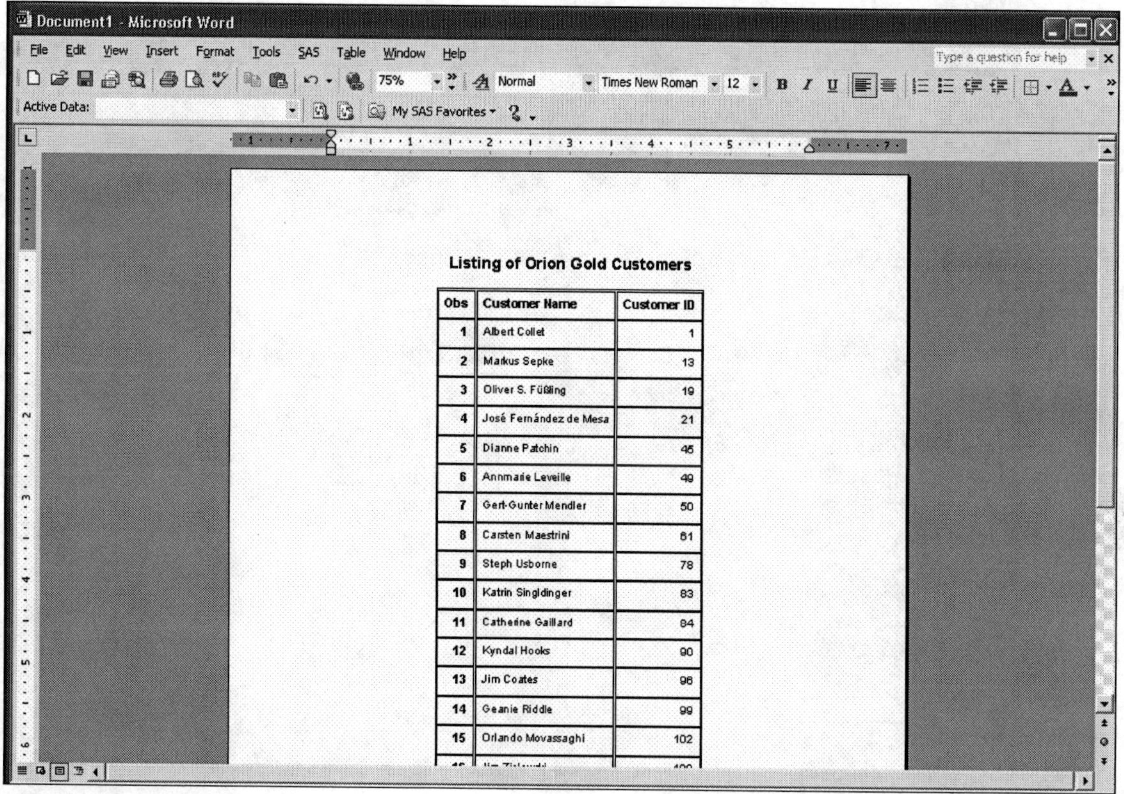

Obs	Customer Name	Customer ID
1	Albert Collet	1
2	Markus Sepke	13
3	Oliver S. Füßling	19
4	José Fernández de Mesa	21
5	Dianne Patchin	45
6	Annmarie Leveille	49
7	Gert-Gunter Mendler	50
8	Carsten Maestrini	61
9	Steph Usborne	78
10	Katrin Singldinger	83
11	Catherine Gaillard	84
12	Kyndal Hooks	90
13	Jim Coates	96
14	Geanie Riddle	99
15	Orlando Movassaghi	102

d. Add the stored process as a favorite.

2. **Working with the SAS Style Manager**

   a. From within Microsoft Word, create a new style called SASAddin based on the existing RTF style.

   b. Change the System Title to <u>**16pt**</u> font and **BOLD** with no italics.

c. Re-create the report from within Word using the SASAddin Style. Verify that the report was created successfully.

Output

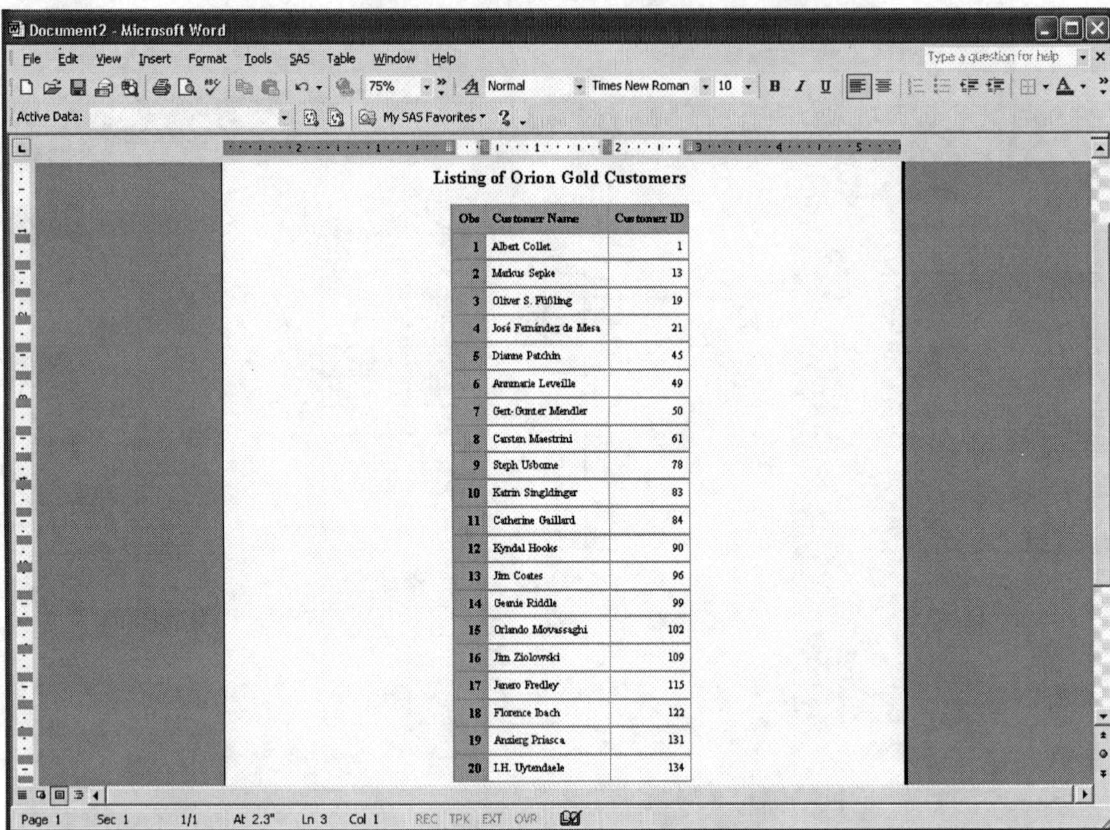
Listing of Orion Gold Customers

Obs	Customer Name	Customer ID
1	Albert Collet	1
2	Markus Sepke	13
3	Oliver S. Füßling	19
4	José Fernández de Mesa	21
5	Dianne Patchin	45
6	Annmarie Leveille	49
7	Gert-Gunter Mendler	50
8	Carsten Maestrini	61
9	Steph Usborne	78
10	Katrin Singldinger	83
11	Catherine Gaillard	84
12	Kyndal Hooks	90
13	Jim Coates	96
14	Geanie Riddle	99
15	Orlando Movassaghi	102
16	Jim Ziolowski	109
17	Janero Fredley	115
18	Florence Ibach	122
19	Anzierg Priasca	131
20	I.H. Uytendaele	134

3. Running a Stored Process in Microsoft Word

a. From within Microsoft Word, execute the stored process Orion Customer Counts in the Orion Star Sports and Outdoors folder.

b. Limit the graph to males in the 31-45 age range.

Output

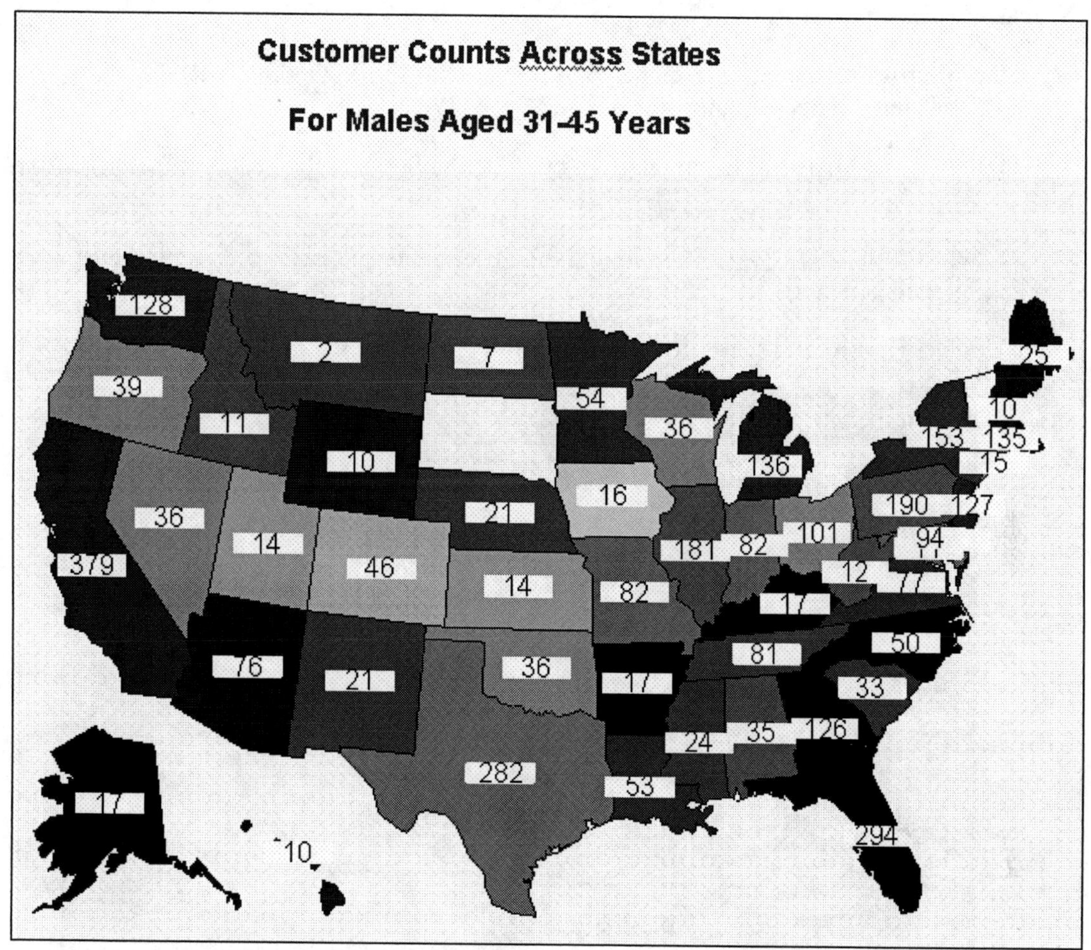

4. **Embedding Stored Process Results into a Microsoft Word Document (Optional)**

a. Orion Star management has requested a memo that highlights the company's top ten customers. Verify that the SAS Results option **Insert results into current document** is selected.

b. Execute the MDM Customer List stored process and embed the results into the existing memorandum located at S:\workshop\winsas\sbiamo\TopTenMemo.doc.

4.3 Solutions

1. Working with a Stored Process

a. Start Microsoft Excel and select the appropriate SAS Add-In Option to display the SAS log when task and stored process output is generated.

1) Invoke the Microsoft Excel program by selecting **Start** ⇨ **Programs** ⇨ **Microsoft Office** ⇨ **Microsoft Excel**.

2) Select **SAS** ⇨ **Options**. If prompted for a user name and password, enter the values provided by the instructor.

3) Select **Results** and select the option to **Show SAS Log**.

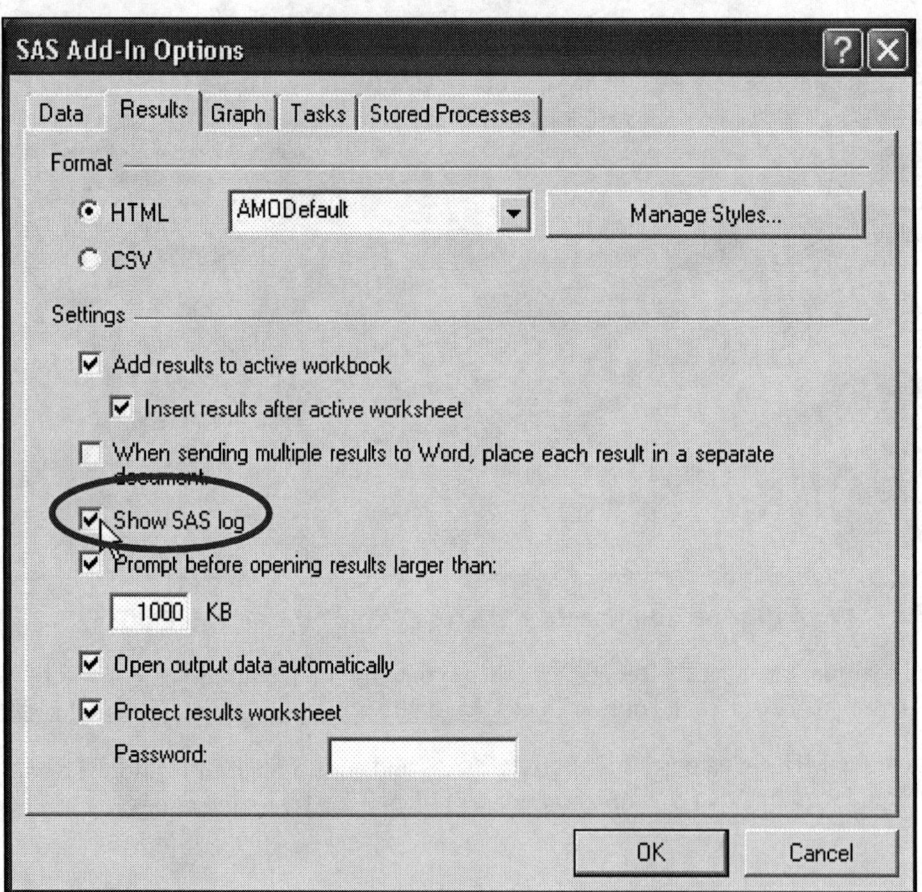

4) Select OK to exit the SAS Add-In Options window.

b. Execute the stored process named MDM Customer List located in the Marketing Data Mart folder. Limit the results to **20** records.

1) Select **SAS** ⇨ **Browse SAS Programs** from the pull-down menus.

2) Navigate to the Marketing Data Mart folder by expanding the tree (select **Stored Processes** ⇨ **Marketing Data Mart**).

3) Select **MDM Customer List**, then Run.

4) When prompted, limit the number of records processed to **20** and select Run.

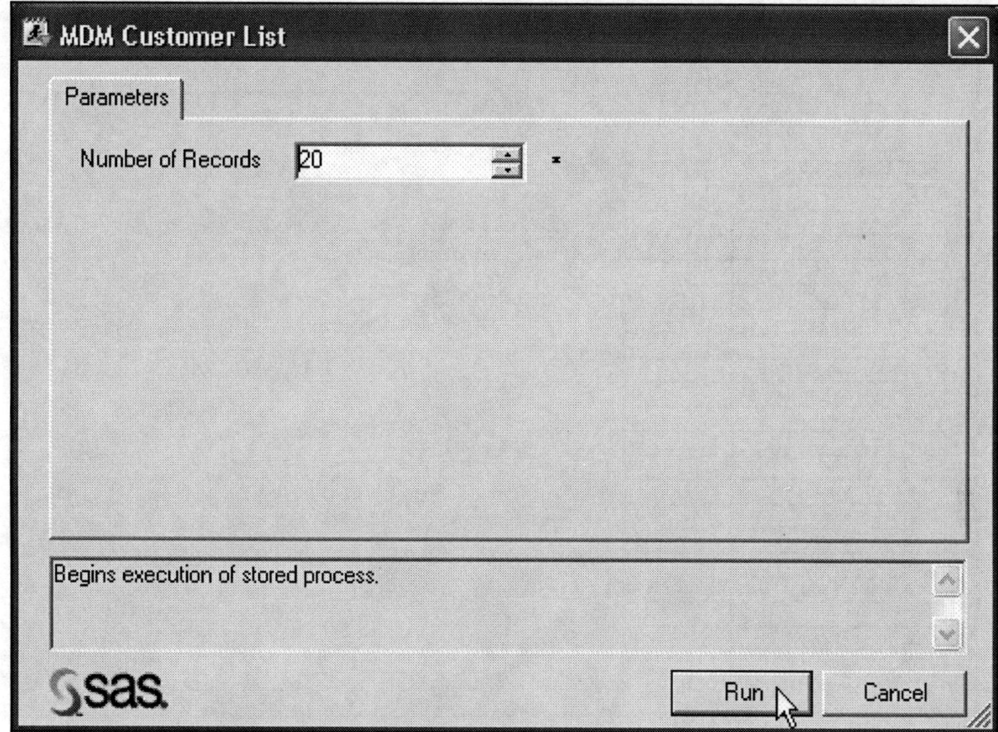

The program results are streamed back to a Microsoft Excel worksheet.

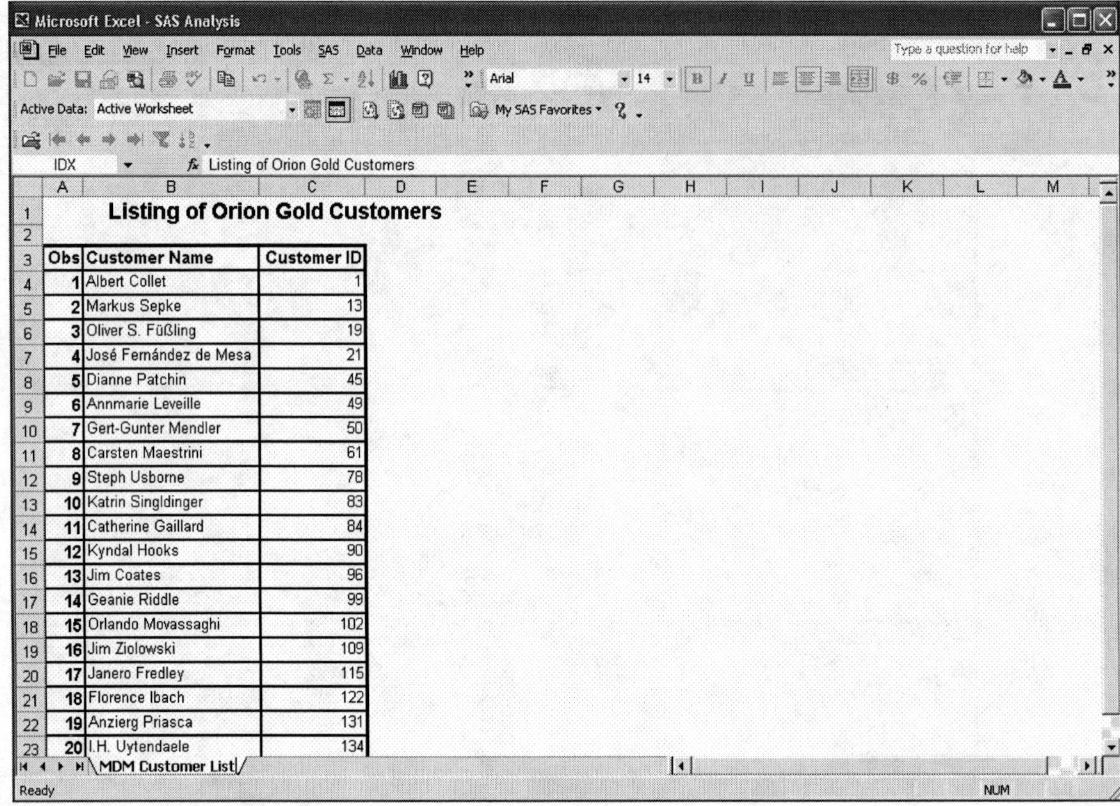

Listing of Orion Gold Customers

Obs	Customer Name	Customer ID
1	Albert Collet	1
2	Markus Sepke	13
3	Oliver S. Fü̈ßling	19
4	José Fernández de Mesa	21
5	Dianne Patchin	45
6	Annmarie Leveille	49
7	Gert-Gunter Mendler	50
8	Carsten Maestrini	61
9	Steph Usborne	78
10	Katrin Singldinger	83
11	Catherine Gaillard	84
12	Kyndal Hooks	90
13	Jim Coates	96
14	Geanie Riddle	99
15	Orlando Movassaghi	102
16	Jim Ziolowski	109
17	Janero Fredley	115
18	Florence Ibach	122
19	Anzierg Priasca	131
20	I.H. Uytendaele	134

To shut off the SAS log, select **SAS** ⇨ **Options** ⇨ **Results** and deselect the **Show SAS Log** option.

Which SAS data set is specified in the stored process code and used to generate these results?
`orgold.customer_dim`

c. Export the results to Microsoft Word.

1) Select **SAS** ⇨ **Send to Microsoft Word** (or choose the Send to Microsoft Word icon on the SAS Analysis Tools toolbar).

2) Accept the default of 20 records to process and select Run.

d. Add the stored process as a favorite.

1) Select **SAS** ⇨ **My SAS Favorites** ⇨ **Manage Favorites**… (or, from the SAS Analysis Tools toolbar, select **My SAS Favorites** ⇨ **Manage Favorites**…).

2) Right-click **MDM Customer List**.

3) Select **Add to Favorites**.

4) Close the Manage Favorites window by selecting Close.

5) Select **My SAS Favorites** from the toolbar. Note that the newly added favorite is on the list.

2. Working with the SAS Style Manager

a. From within Microsoft Word, create a new style called SASAddin based on the existing RTF style.

1) In Microsoft Word, select **SAS** ⇨ **Style Manager**.

2) Select Add... to add a new style.

3) Select **Add new based on existing**.

4) Enter `SASAddin` as the style name.

5) Use the drop-down menu and select **Rtf** as the Based on style. Select OK to open the Style Manager window.

b. Change the System Title to **16pt** font and **BOLD** with no italics.

1) Scroll down the Style List menu and select the **SASAddin** style.

2) Select Edit... to open the Style Editor.

3) Left-click on the System Title element in the preview pane (or use the drop-down menu) to select **System Title** as the Active Element.

4) Change the Text size to **16pt**.

5) Change the Text style to **Bold**.

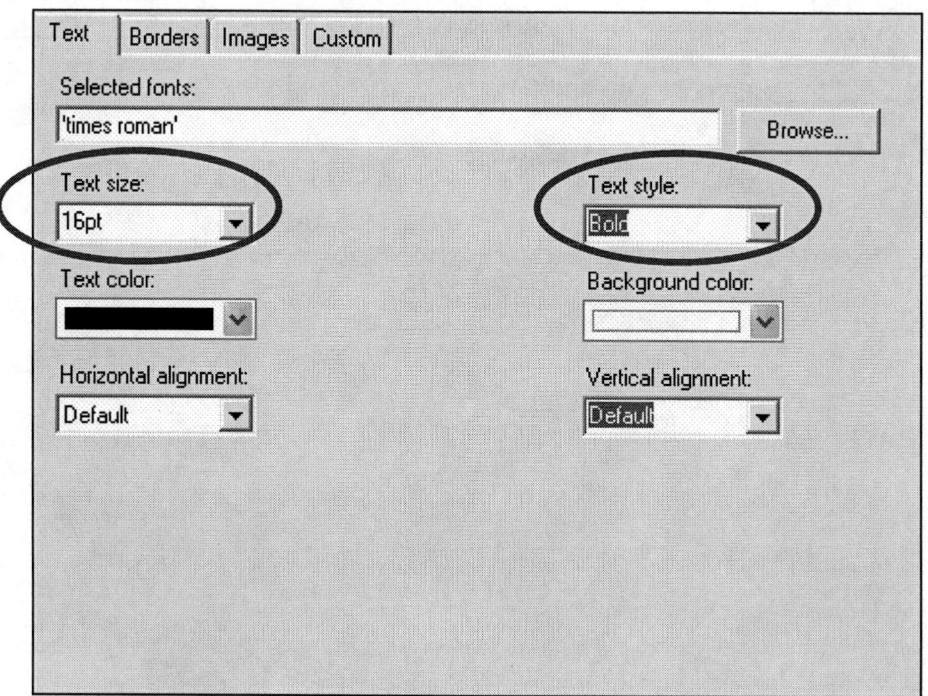

6) Select OK to close the Style Editor window.

c. Re-create the report from within Word using the SASAddin Style. Verify that the report was created successfully.

1) Select **SAS** ⇨ **Style Manager** ⇨ **SASAddin**.

2) Select [Set as Default] to make SASAddin the active style.

3) Select [OK] to close the Style Manager window.

4) Left-click inside the body of the document to place the cursor inside the results you want to refresh.

5) Select the Refresh button on the SAS Analysis Tools toolbar (or select **SAS** ⇨ **Refresh** from the pull-down menus) to rerun the report.

6) Do not change the parameter setting, and select [Run] to re-create the report.

3. **Running a Stored Process in Microsoft Word**

a. From within Microsoft Word, run the stored process Orion Customer Counts in the Orion Star Sports and Outdoors folder.

1) Invoke Microsoft Word by selecting **Start** ⇨ **Programs** ⇨ **Microsoft Office** ⇨ **Microsoft Word**.

2) Select **SAS** ⇨ **Browse SAS Programs**, or select the Browse button on the SAS Analysis Tools toolbar.

3) Expand the Stored Processes folder and select the **Orion Star Sports and Outdoors** folder.

4) Select **Orion Customer Counts** and select [Run].

b. Limit the graph to males in the 31-45 age range.

1) Select **M** for the Gender parameter and select **31-45 years** for the Age Group parameter.

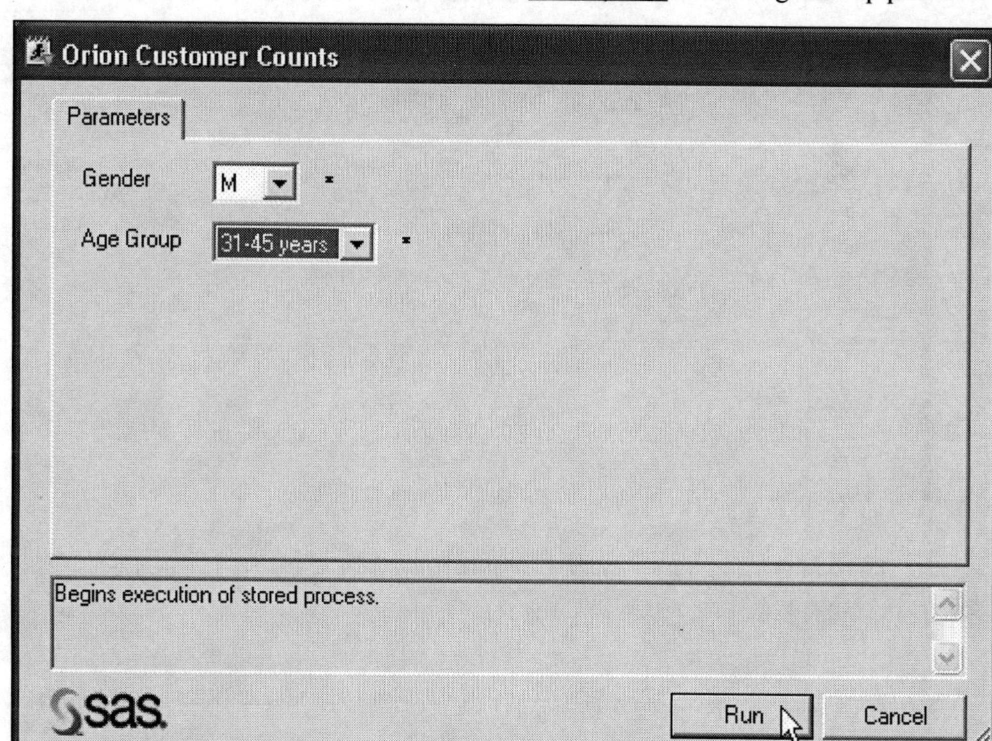

2) Select Run to generate the graph.

4. Embedding Stored Process Results into a Microsoft Word Document (Optional)

a. Verify that the SAS Results option **Insert results into current document** is selected.

1) From within Microsoft Word select **SAS** ⇨ **Options.**

2) On the Results tab, verify that the option **Insert results into current document** is selected.

b. Execute the MDM Customer List stored process and embed the results into the existing memorandum located at S:\workshop\winsas\sbiamo\TopTenMemo.doc.

1) Open an existing Microsoft Word file by selecting **File** ⇨ **Open** and then navigating to "S:\workshop\winsas\sbiamo".

2) Select **TopTenMemo.doc**.

3) Remove the text **<Insert Stored Process Results Here>** and leave the cursor in that area of the document.

4) Select **SAS** ⇨ **Browse SAS Programs** from the pull-down menus.

5) Navigate to the Marketing Data Mart folder by expanding the tree (select **Stored Processes** ⇨ **Marketing Data Mart**).

6) Select **MDM Customer List**, then Run.

7) When prompted, limit the number of records processed to **10** and select Run.

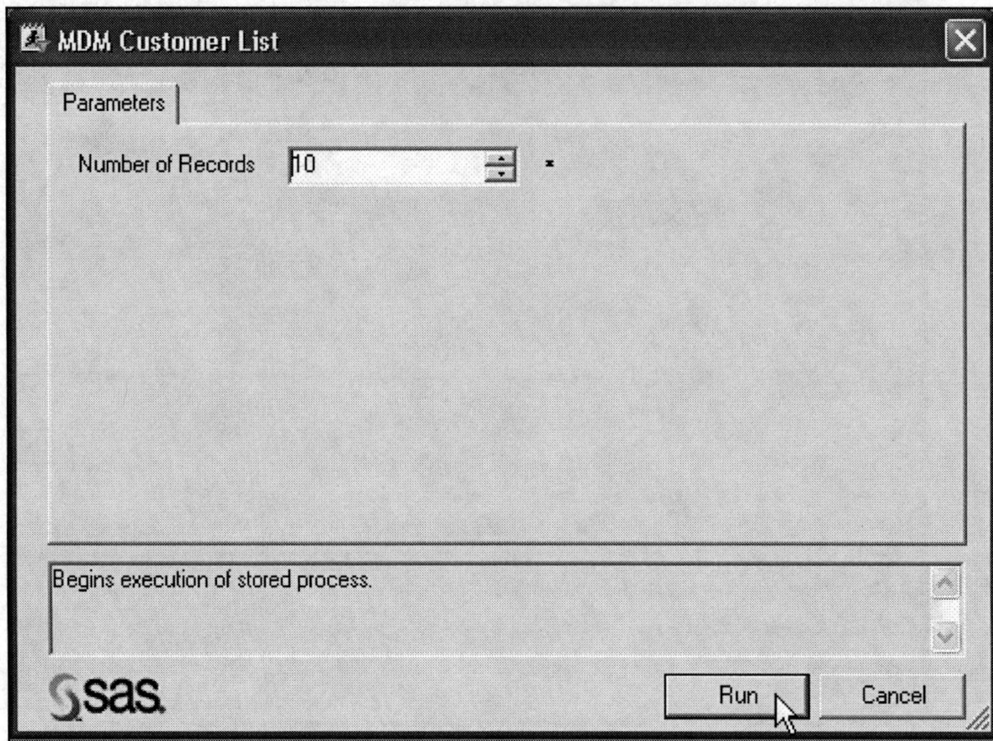

Chapter 5 Analyzing Data with SAS Tasks in Microsoft Office

5.1 Overview of SAS Tasks

Objectives

- State the definition of a SAS task.
- Access SAS tasks in Microsoft Office.
- State the function of the Selection pane in the SAS task dialog boxes.
- Review common features of many SAS tasks.

3

What Is a SAS Task?

A *task* is a specific type of analysis or report that you can perform against data.

A task is typically referenced by its description:

Bar Chart	Creates vertical, horizontal, or three-dimensional bar charts.
Correlations	Calculates a correlation coefficient between two numerical columns.
Summary Statistics	Summarizes data and computes descriptive statistics.
Transpose	Transposes data columns into data rows.

4

SAS tasks generate SAS code and formatted results. The tasks include SAS procedures that range from simple data listings to the most complex analytical procedures.

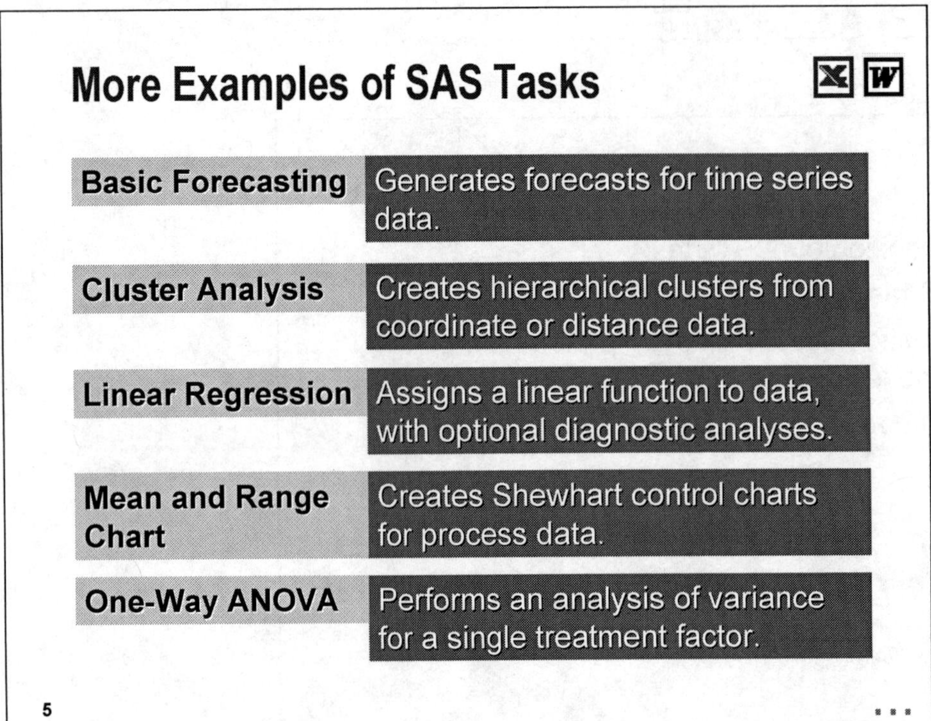

Some SAS tasks require licensing to additional SAS products such as SAS/GRAPH, SAS/STAT, SAS/QC, and SAS/ETS. A SAS task that does not have the appropriate product licensed will not produce the desired output when executed. Examination of the log file will reveal the missing component(s). To have the add-in display the SAS log, enable the option from the pull-down menus **SAS** ⇨ **Options**, and then select the **Results** tab.

Accessing SAS Tasks

Tasks can be selected through the SAS Menu or the SAS Analysis Tools toolbar. The Browse SAS Programs window displays tasks grouped by category.

Example categories include

- Survival Analysis
- ANOVA
- Data
- Describe
- Graph.

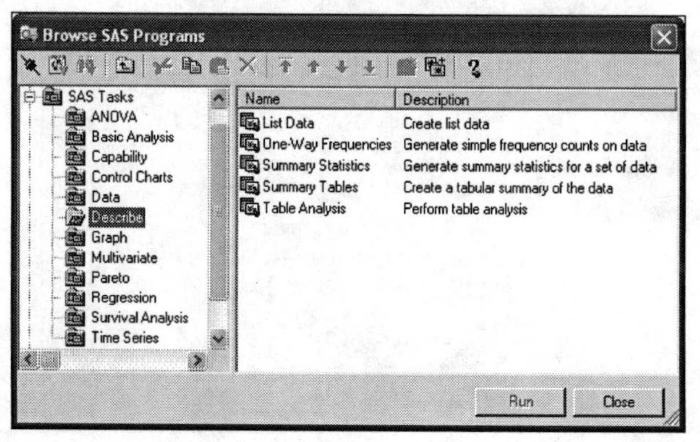

6

Select [icon], the Browse SAS Programs icon, on the SAS Analysis Tools toolbar, or **SAS** ⇨ **Browse SAS Program...** to get access to SAS tasks.

Active Data Sources

SAS tasks can be run against the following:

- a data source that is on your local computer
- a data source on a SAS Workspace Server
- data sources inside an Excel spreadsheet
- an Excel spreadsheet.

The default active data source is

- your current worksheet for Microsoft Excel
- blank (not selected) for Microsoft Word.

7

All sort and filter options that are specified will be applied when a task is run.

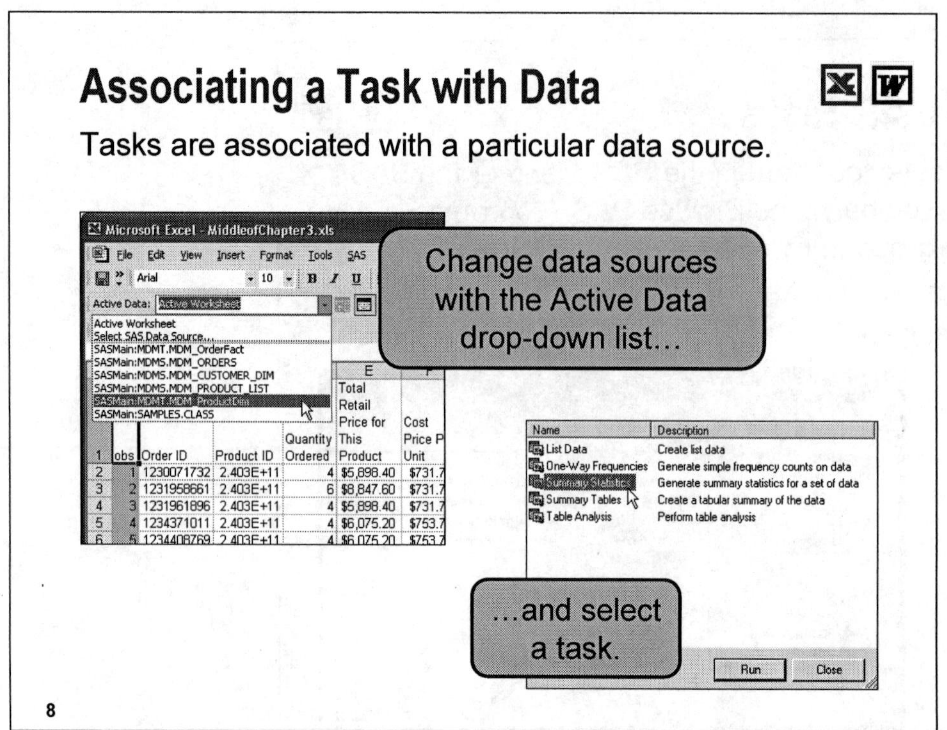

The Active Data drop-down list is part of the SAS Analysis Tools toolbar. To have SAS tasks always prompt you for a data source, enable the option from the pull-down menus **SAS** ⇨ **Options…** and then select **Tasks**.

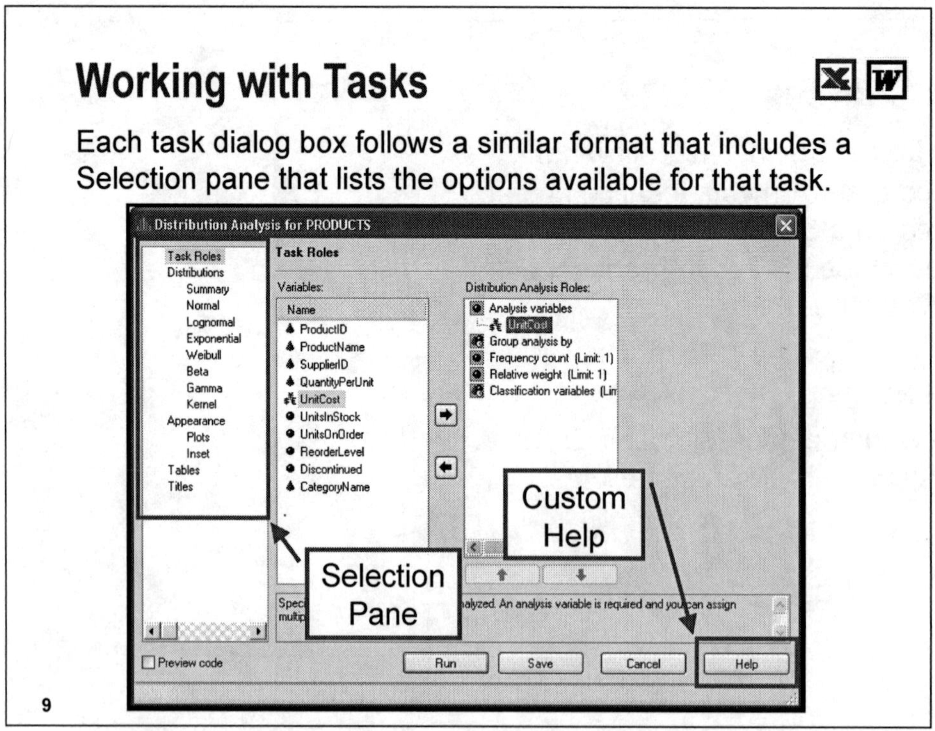

Mouse-over help is displayed automatically as the cursor hovers over any part of the task dialog box.

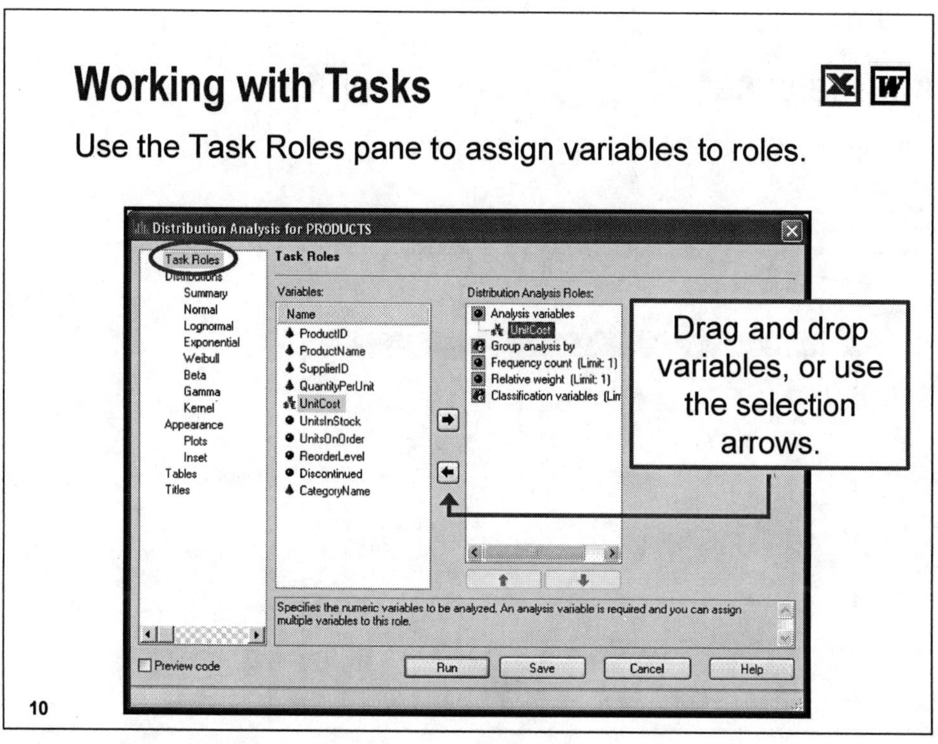
Working with Tasks
Use the Task Roles pane to assign variables to roles.
Distribution Analysis for PRODUCTS
Task Roles
Summary
Normal
Lognormal
Exponential
Weibull
Beta
Gamma
Kernel
Appearance
Plots
Inset
Tables
Titles
Task Roles
Variables:
Name
ProductID
ProductName
SupplierID
QuantityPerUnit
UnitCost
UnitsInStock
UnitsOnOrder
ReorderLevel
Discontinued
CategoryName
Distribution Analysis Roles:
Analysis variables
UnitCost
Group analysis by
Frequency count (Limit: 1)
Relative weight (Limit: 1)
Classification variables
Drag and drop variables, or use the selection arrows.
Specifies the numeric variables to be analyzed. An analysis variable is required and you can assign multiple variables to this role.
Preview code
Run
Save
Cancel
Help
10

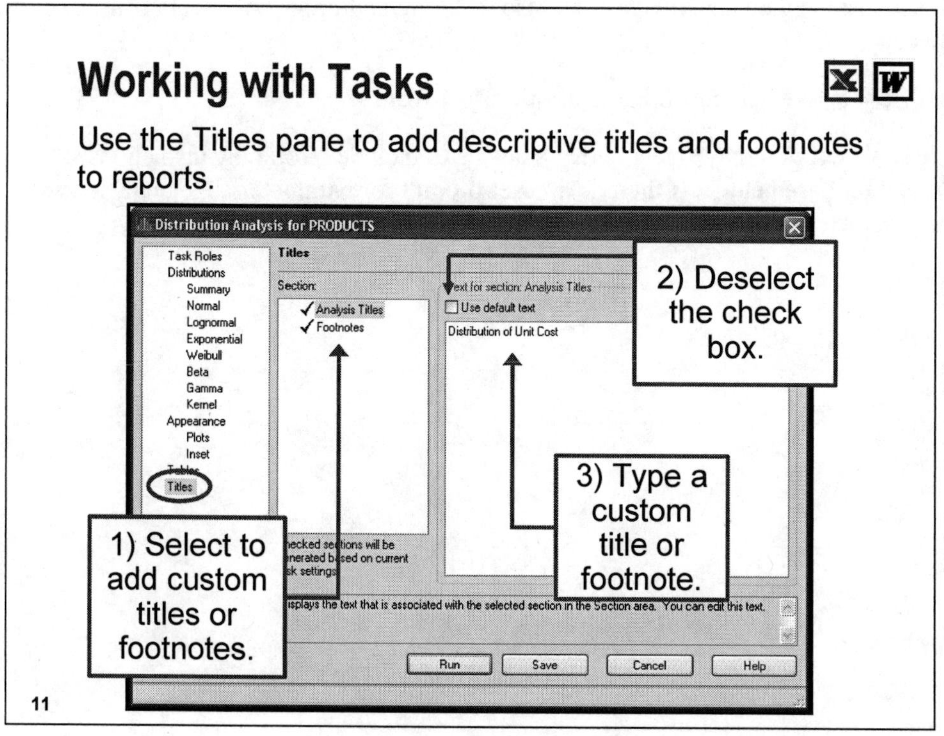
Working with Tasks
Use the Titles pane to add descriptive titles and footnotes to reports.
Distribution Analysis for PRODUCTS
Task Roles
Distributions
Summary
Normal
Lognormal
Exponential
Weibull
Beta
Gamma
Kernel
Appearance
Plots
Inset
Titles
Titles
Section:
Analysis Titles
Footnotes
Use default text
Distribution of Unit Cost
2) Deselect the check box.
3) Type a custom title or footnote.
1) Select to add custom titles or footnotes.
Run
Save
Cancel
Help
11

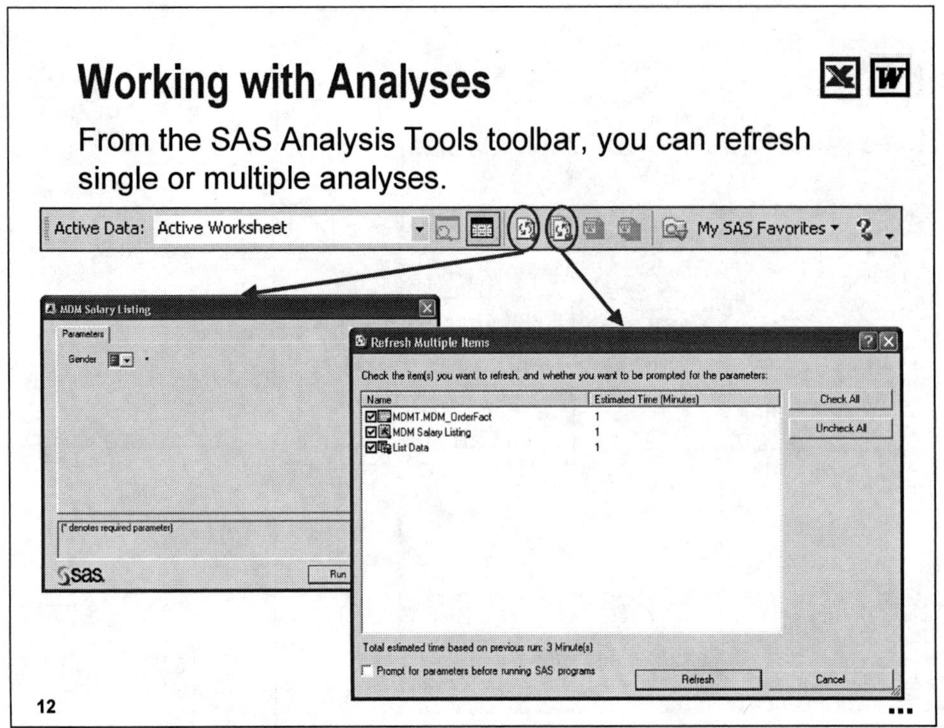

The result of a SAS task is considered an analysis result. Also, filtering and/or sorting a data source is considered an analysis result.

You may refresh analyses from both Microsoft Excel and Microsoft Word.

When refreshing multiple analyses, you may select which analysis to include. You may also choose whether the user is prompted for parameters. If there is no user prompt for parameters, the analyses will refresh with the previous parameter selections.

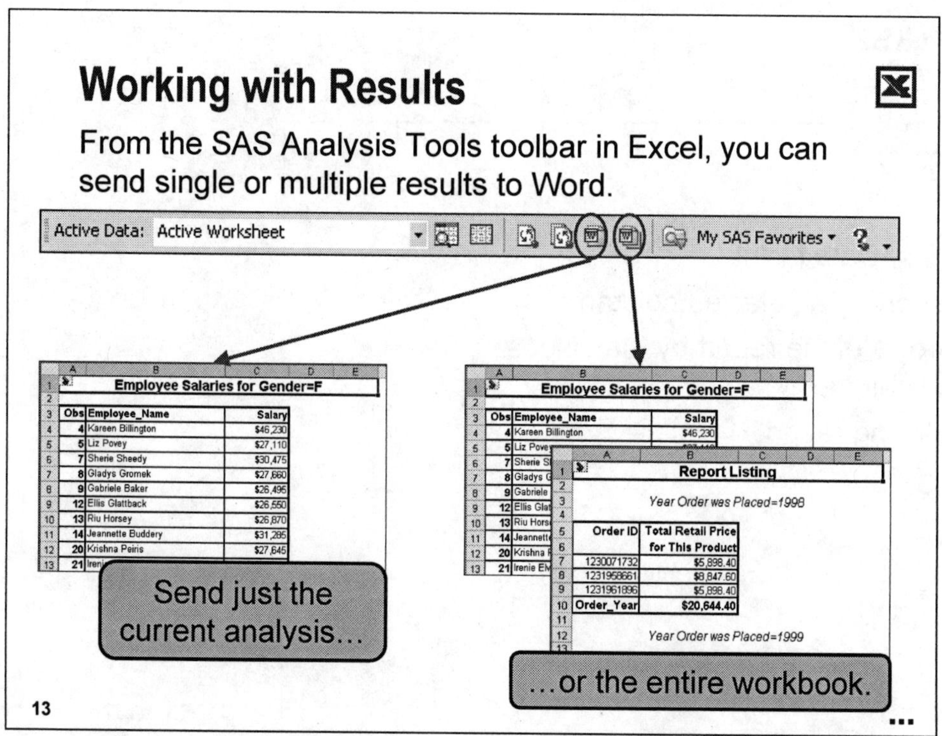

By default when you send multiple results to Microsoft Word, all results will be placed into a single document. To have each result placed into a separate document, enable the option from the pull-down menus **SAS** ⇨ **Options…** and then select **Results**.

Analyses that have been sent to Word but are based on an Excel spreadsheet data source (as opposed to a SAS data source) are not capable of being refreshed from within Microsoft Word. Word is unable to open and read an Excel spreadsheet data source.

5.2 List Data Task

Objectives

- Access the List Data task.
- Order the report by a selected column.
- Identify the rows of the report by the values of a selected column.
- Generate a listing report.

15

List Data Task

The List Data task displays rows of data in a SAS table or rows of an Excel spreadsheet.

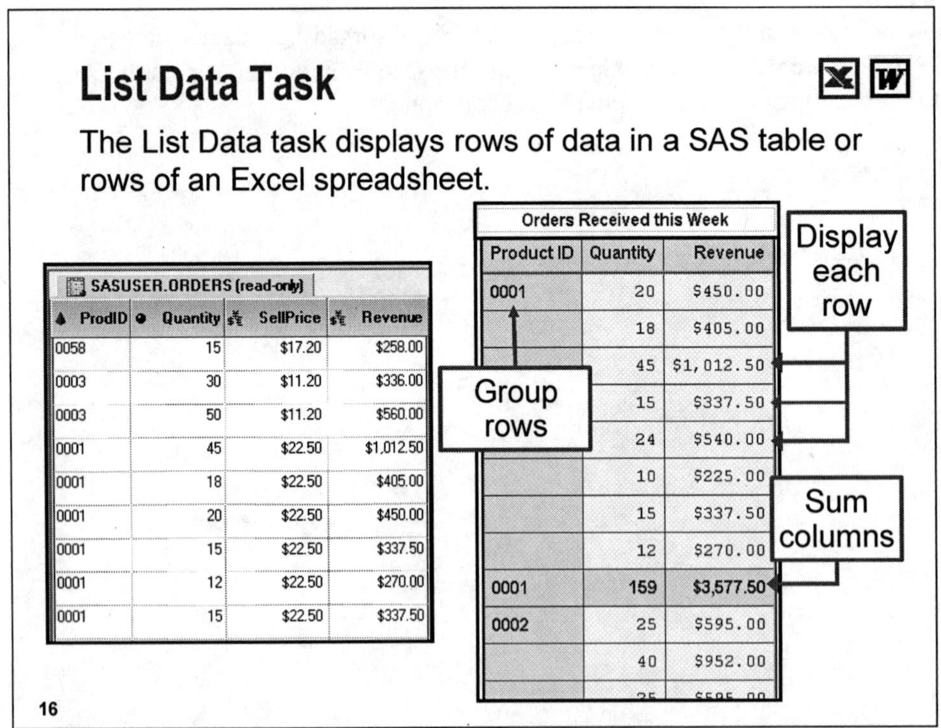

16

To access the List Data task, select **Describe** ⇨ **List Data** from the Browse SAS Programs dialog box.

List Data: Task Roles

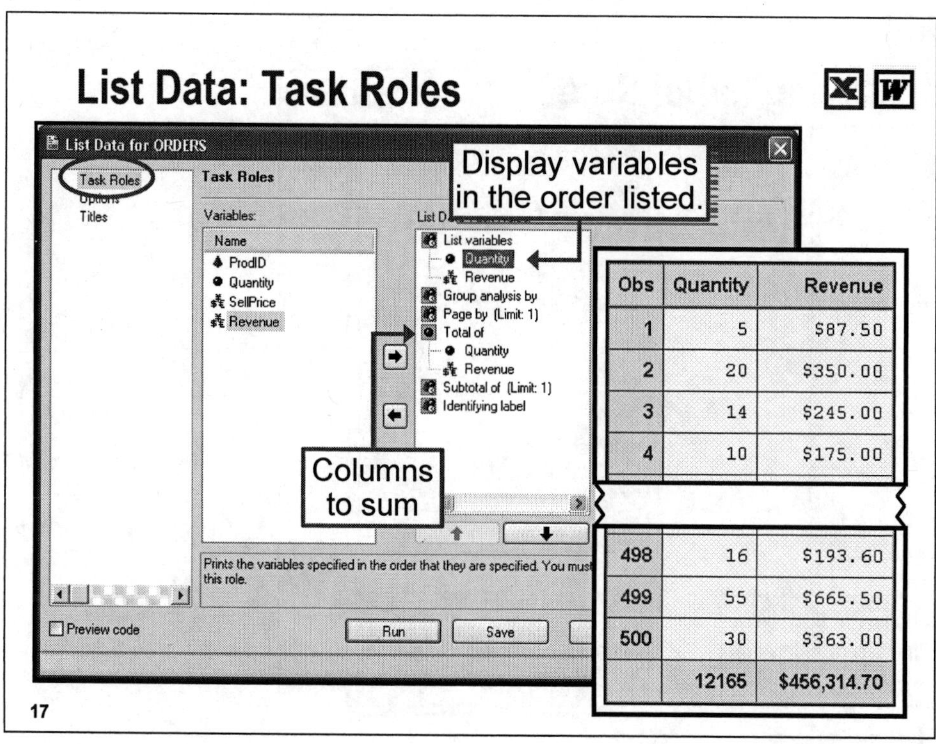

17

List Data: Group Analysis by Role

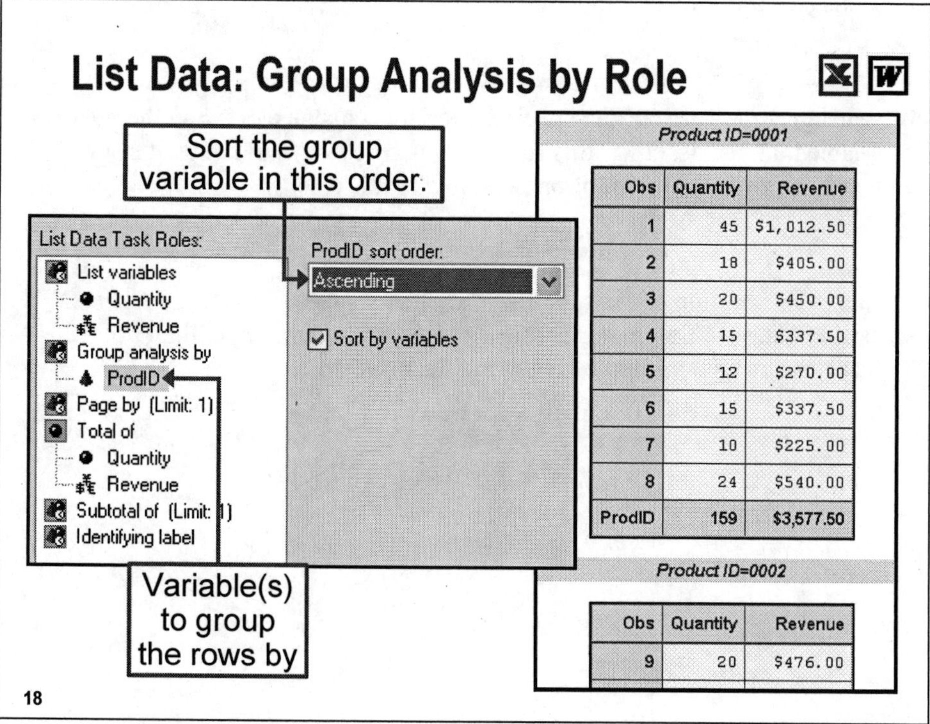

18

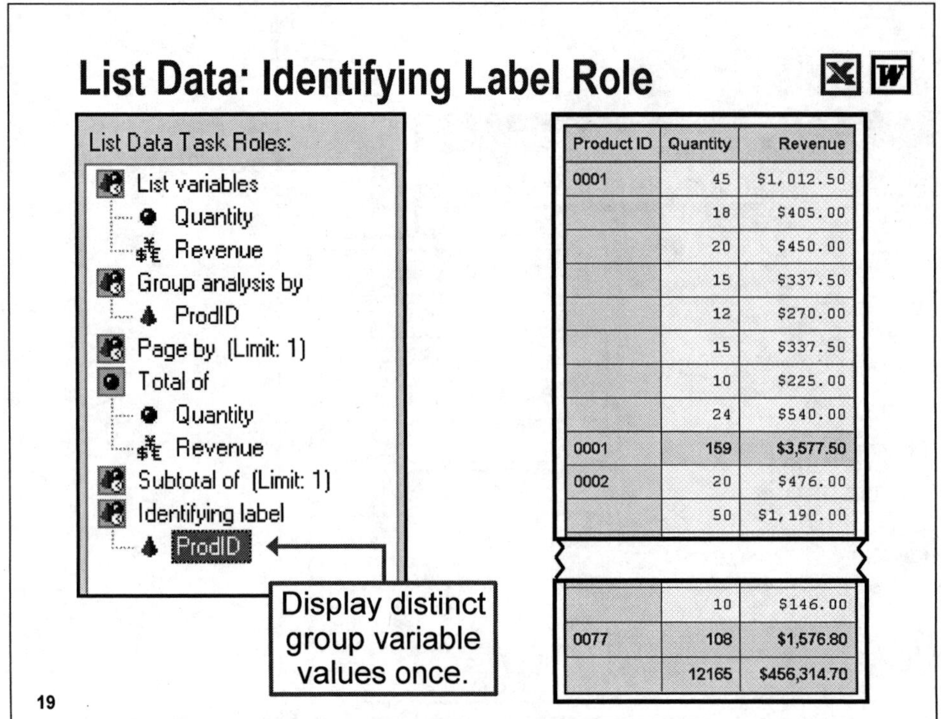

Additional roles available for this task are shown below:

Page by

displays a new table whenever the value of the specified variable changes, or when the next BY group begins. The variable that you assign to this role must also be a variable in the Group analysis by role. You can assign a maximum of one variable to this role.

Subtotal of

displays a subtotal whenever the value of the specified variable changes or when the next BY group begins. The variable that you assign to this role must also be a variable in the Group analysis by role. You can assign a maximum of one variable to this role.

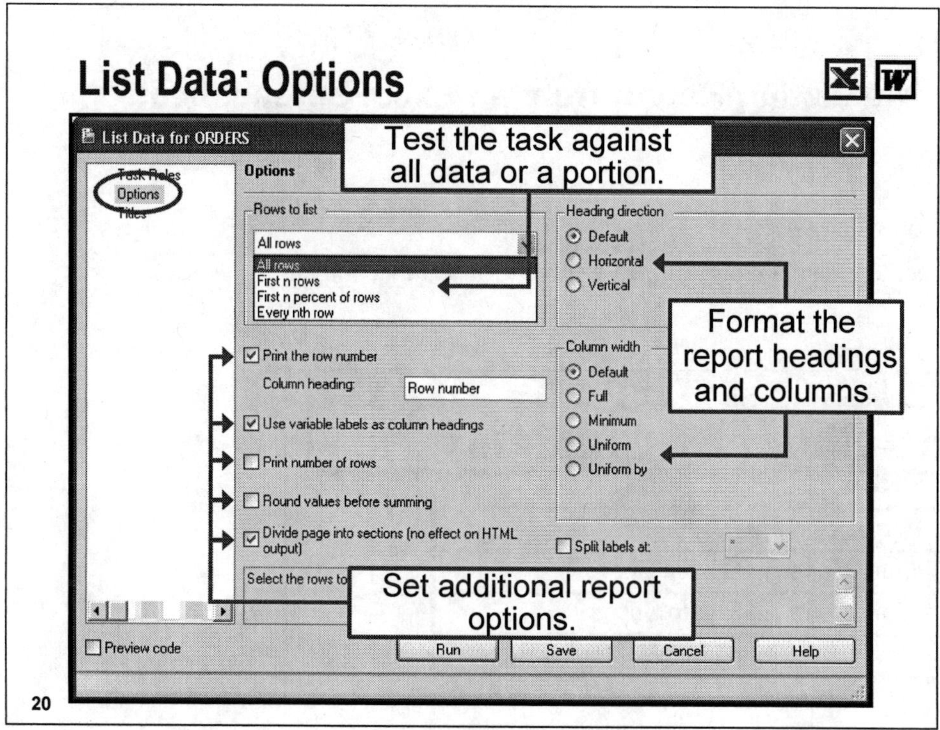

Descriptions of selected options are shown below:

Use variable labels as column headings

uses the variable label instead of the variable name as the column heading.

Print number of rows

reports the number of rows in the table at the end of the output, or the number of rows in each BY group at the end of each BY group's output.

Round values before summing

rounds each numeric value to the number of decimal places in its format, or to two decimal places if no format is specified.

Divide page into sections

causes the List Data task to put as many columns on each page as it can. If there are more columns than can fit across a page, the columns that do not fit are put in subsequent sections on the same page. This setting is ignored if HTML is the result format.

Heading direction

determines the directions of the column headings. Column headings can be printed horizontally or vertically, or SAS can determine the optimal arrangement for each column.

Split labels at

defines a split character. If the variable labels contain one of the split characters (*, !, @, #, $, %, ^, &, or +), the labels will be split at the split character(s).

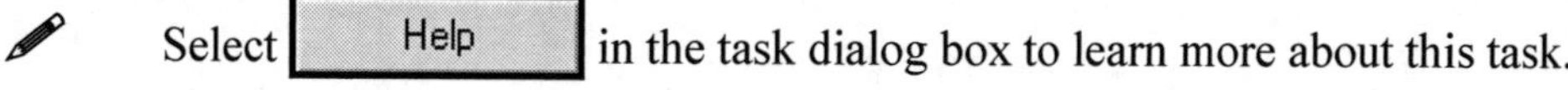

Select Help in the task dialog box to learn more about this task.

Creating a Listing Report from an Excel Spreadsheet

For this demonstration, you will

- use an Excel spreadsheet to create a report of men's shoes grouped by company.

Output (partial listing):

	A	B	C
1	**Men's Shoes by Company**		
2			
3	**Product Group**	**Product Name**	
4	**Eclipse Shoes**	4men Men's Air Golden Shoes	
5		4men Men's Air Presto Shoes	
6		Atmosphere Acma Men's Running Shoes	
7		Atmosphere Mic Plus.Men's Running Shoe	
8		Big Guy Men's Air 120 Soccer Shoes	
9		Big Guy Men's Air 45 Soccer Shoes	
10		Big Guy Men's Air 45 Trainer Shoes	
11		Big Guy Men's Air 90 Accel Shoes	
12		Big Guy Men's Air Ace 4 Plus Low-Tennis Shoe	
13		Big Guy Men's Air Align Shoes	
14		Big Guy Men's Air Aragon Shoes	
15		Big Guy Men's Air Arma Shoes	

Opening an Excel Spreadsheet Data Source

1. Select the **Open** icon from the Microsoft Excel toolbar (or select **File** ⇨ **Open…**).

2. Add the local Excel table **Products.xls**.

   a. Navigate to S:\workshop\winsas\sbiamo (or the location provided by the instructor) and select **Products.xls**.

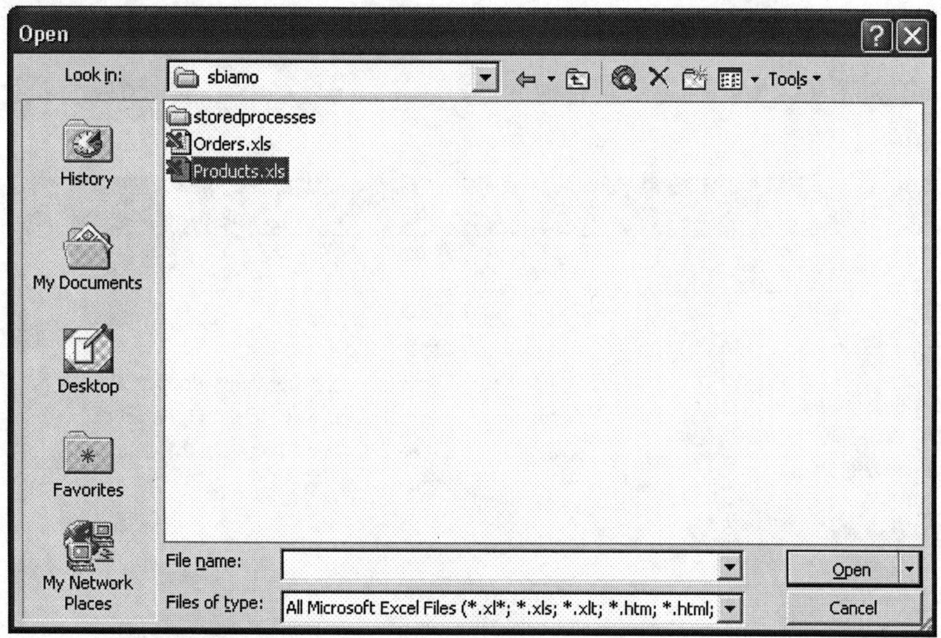

   b. Select Open.

3. If it is not selected, select the **Labels in First Row** icon from the SAS Data Analysis toolbar so that the labels in the first row will be used as the column names. (When selected, the icon appears as .)

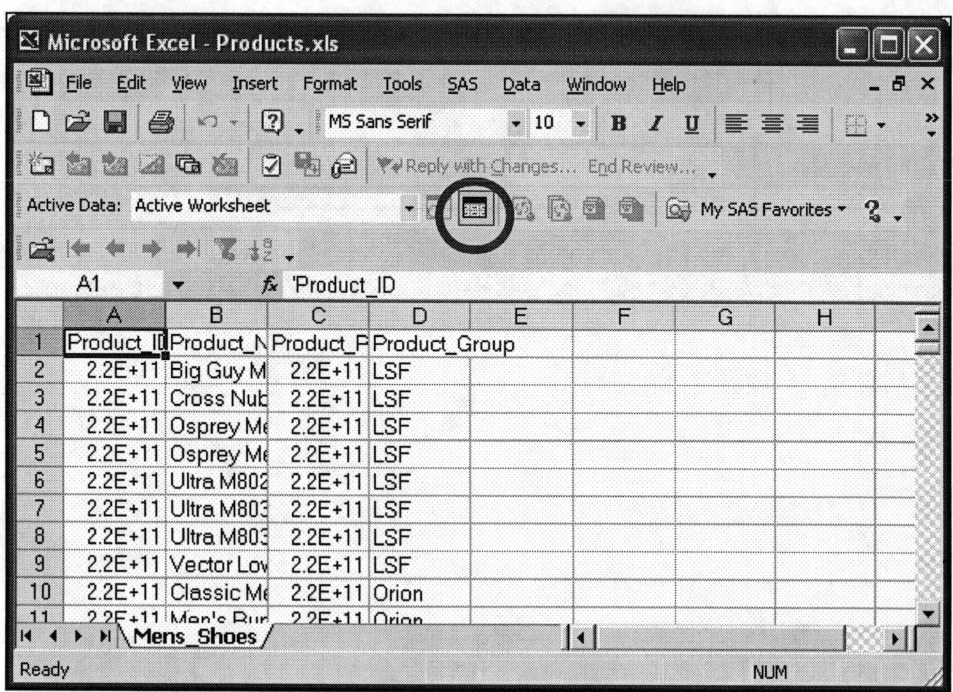

If the Excel spreadsheet does not contain labels in the first row, SAS tasks will give each column a generic name (Variable 1, Variable 2, and so on).

Running a List Data Task

1. Open the List Data task.

   a. Select [icon] on the SAS Analysis Tools toolbar (or select **SAS** ⇨ **Browse SAS Programs**).

   b. Expand the group **SAS Tasks** and select the folder **Describe** ⇨ **List Data** task. Then select Run.

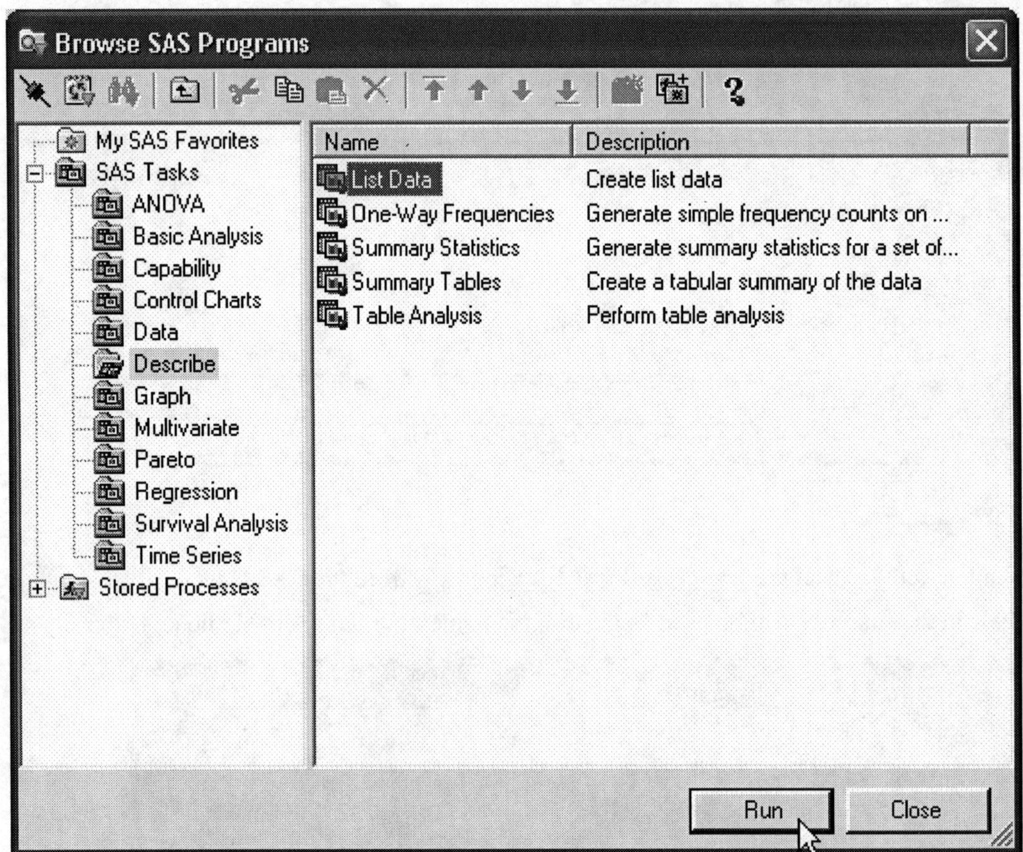

A List Data dialog box opens and enables you to select the columns that you want to see in the report and to specify a role for those columns. In this dialog box, you can also change output formatting options.

2. Drag the **Product_Name** column from the Variables pane to the List Data Task Roles pane. Drop the column in the List variables role. Columns placed in this role will be printed in the report in the order in which they are listed.

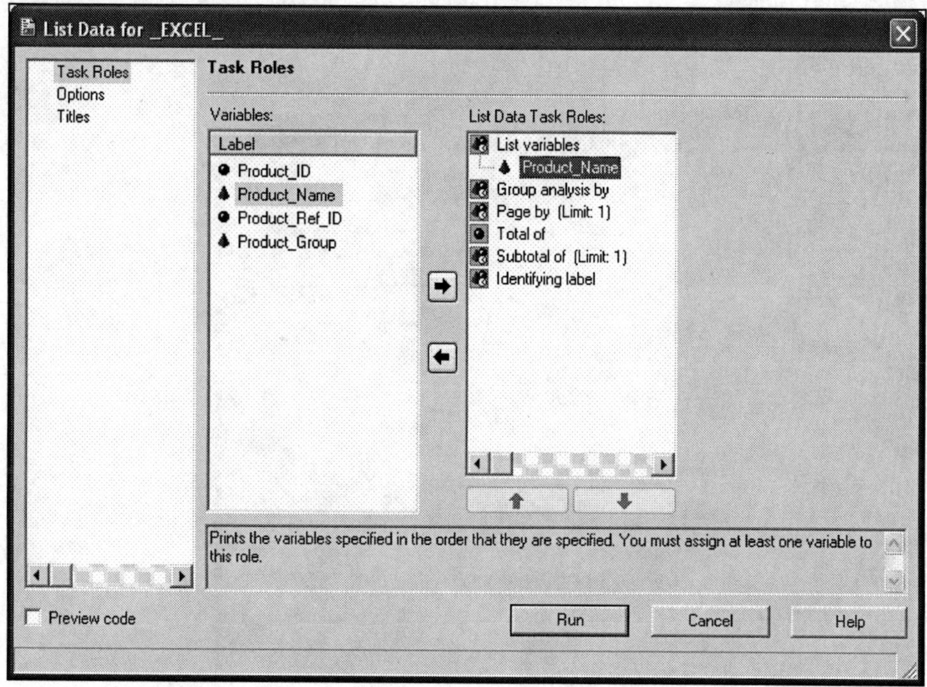

The ➡ button can also be used to assign variable(s) to roles.

3. Drag **Product_Group** to the Group analysis by role. Assigning a column to this role causes the table to be sorted and grouped by the specified column.

   To specify the sort order for a column in the Group analysis by role, select either **Ascending** or **Descending** from the sort order drop-down list. For this demonstration, retain the default value of ascending order for `Product_Group`.

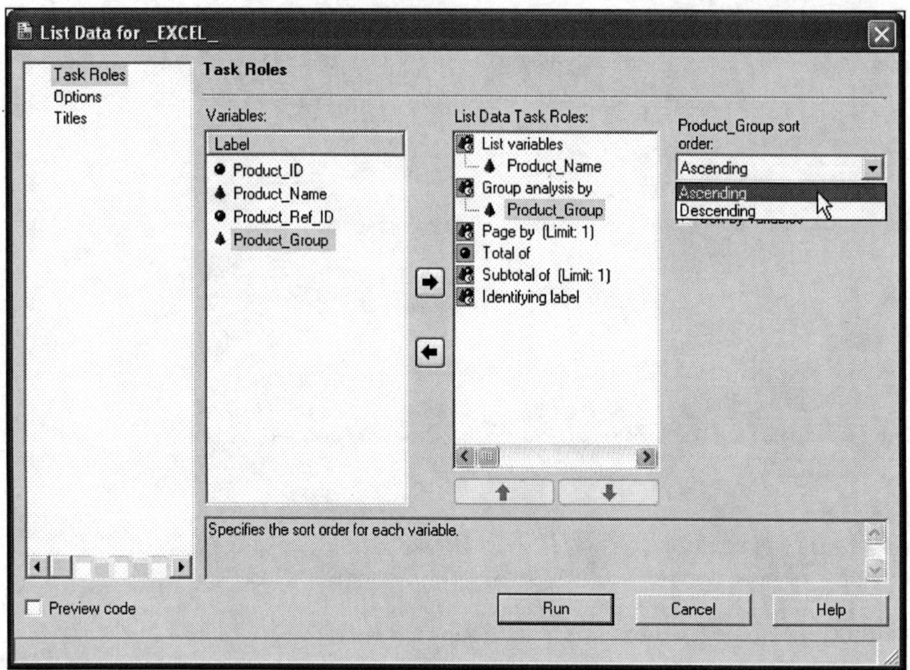

4. Drag **Product_Group** to the Identifying label role. By assigning `Product_Group` to this role, the values of `Product_Group` appear only on the first row of the group of data associated with a product value.

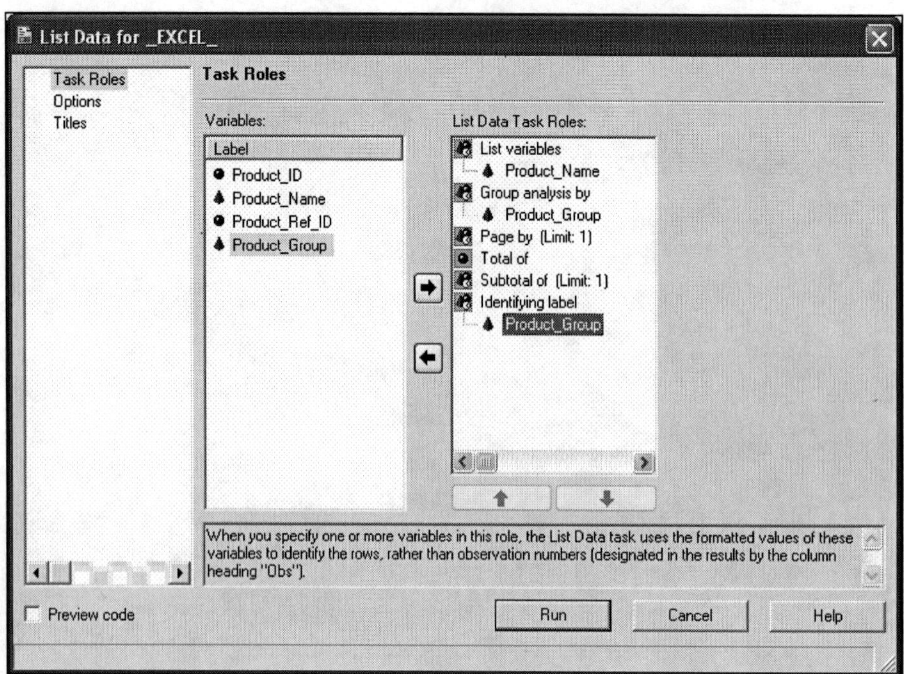

5. To specify a label to be used in this task for the column **`Product_Name`**, right-click on the column name in the List Data Task Roles pane. Select **Properties** from the pop-up menu.

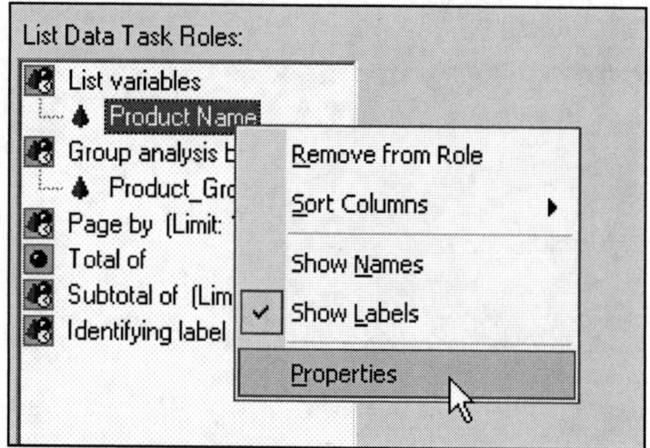

6. In the Properties dialog box, type **`Product Name`** in the `Label` field and select OK.

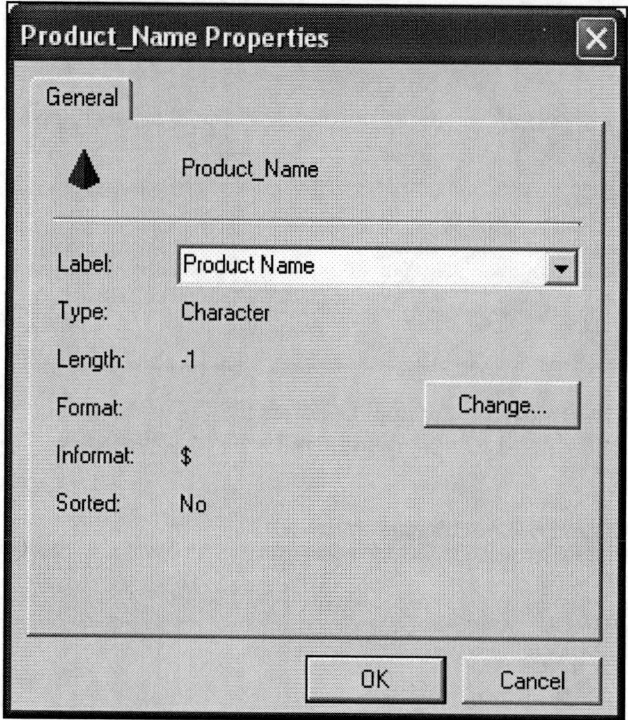

7. Similarly, create a label of **`Product Group`** for the `Product_Group` field.

8. You can choose to view either the name or label associated with each column. To display the label instead of the column name in the dialog box, right-click on the column's name in the List Data dialog box and select **Show Labels** from the pop-up menu.

9. To specify additional report options, select **Options** in the Selection pane.

10. To use the smallest possible column width for the listing report, select **Minimum** in the Column width pane. Also deselect the option **Print the row number**.

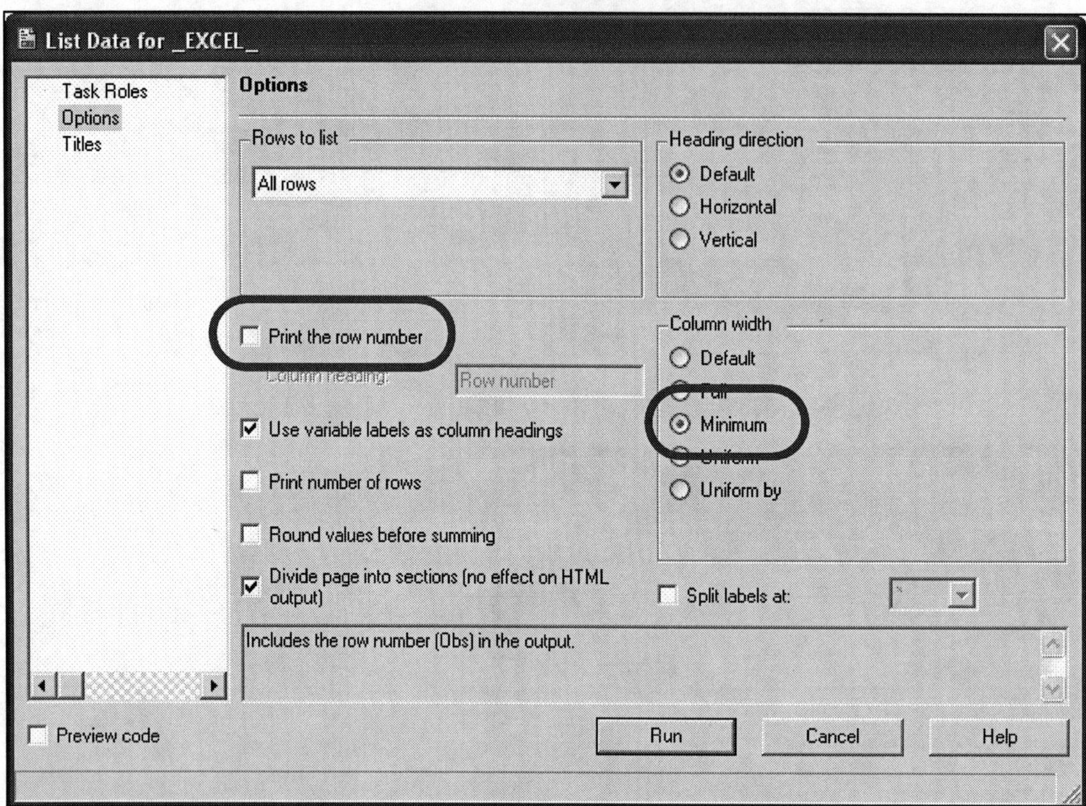

11. To specify a title for the report, select **Titles** in the Selection pane. Deselect the Use default text check box. In the `Text` field, delete the default title of Report Listing and type **`Men's Shoes by Company`**.

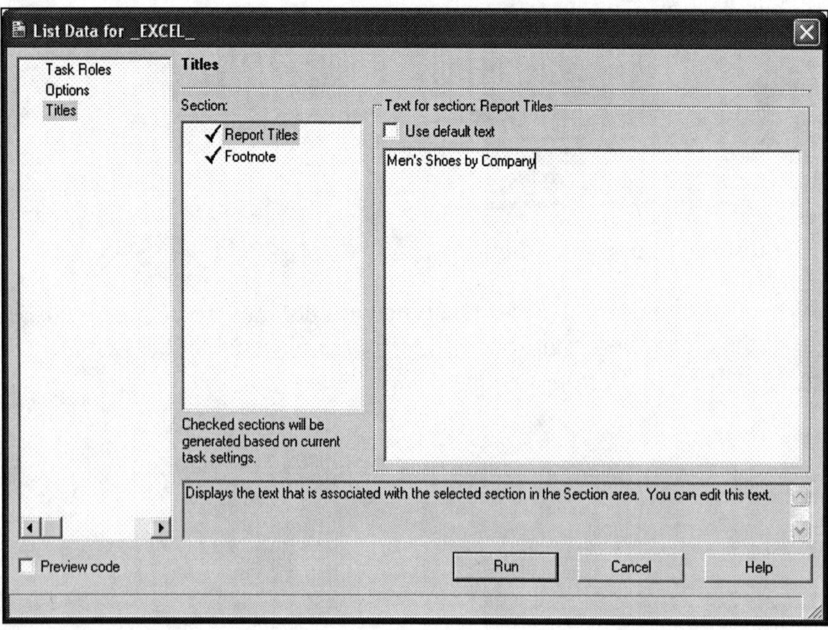

12. Select [Run] to generate the report.

	A	B	C
1	**Men's Shoes by Company**		
2			
3	**Product Group**	**Product Name**	
4	**Eclipse Shoes**	4men Men's Air Golden Shoes	
5		4men Men's Air Presto Shoes	
6		Atmosphere Acma Men's Running Shoes	
7		Atmosphere Mic Plus.Men's Running Shoe	
8		Big Guy Men's Air 120 Soccer Shoes	
9		Big Guy Men's Air 45 Soccer Shoes	
10		Big Guy Men's Air 45 Trainer Shoes	
11		Big Guy Men's Air 90 Accel Shoes	
12		Big Guy Men's Air Ace 4 Plus Low-Tennis Shoe	
13		Big Guy Men's Air Align Shoes	
14		Big Guy Men's Air Aragon Shoes	

5.3 One-Way Frequencies Task

Objectives

- Access the One-Way Frequencies task.
- Generate a one-way frequency table.

23

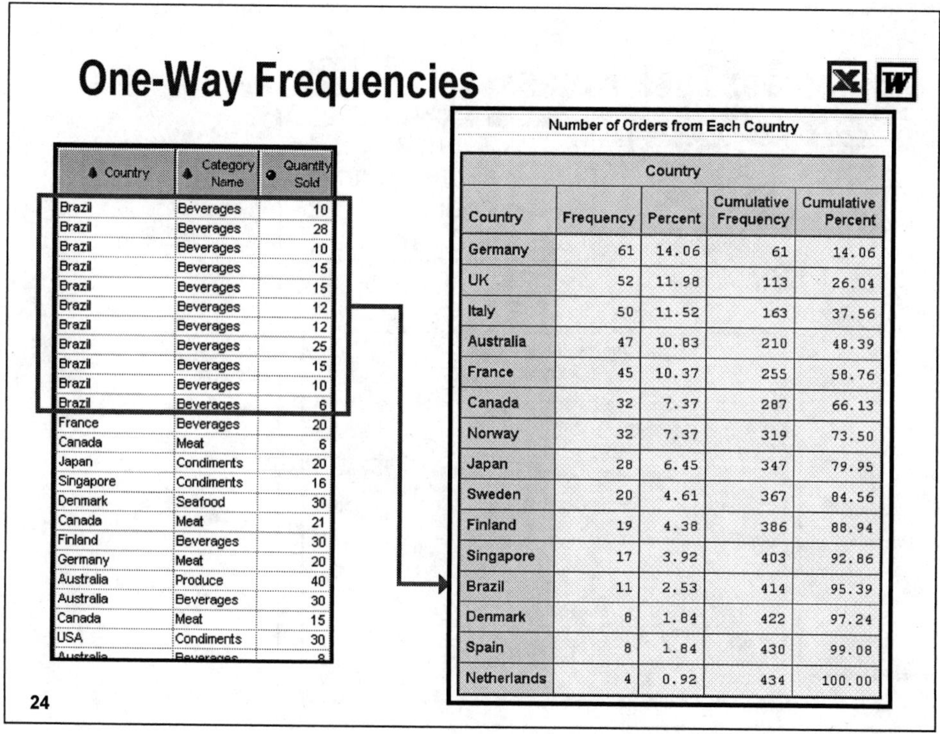

Country	Category Name	Quantity Sold
Brazil	Beverages	10
Brazil	Beverages	28
Brazil	Beverages	10
Brazil	Beverages	15
Brazil	Beverages	15
Brazil	Beverages	12
Brazil	Beverages	12
Brazil	Beverages	25
Brazil	Beverages	15
Brazil	Beverages	10
Brazil	Beverages	6
France	Beverages	20
Canada	Meat	6
Japan	Condiments	20
Singapore	Condiments	16
Denmark	Seafood	30
Canada	Meat	21
Finland	Beverages	30
Germany	Meat	20
Australia	Produce	40
Australia	Beverages	30
Canada	Meat	15
USA	Condiments	30

Number of Orders from Each Country

Country	Frequency	Percent	Cumulative Frequency	Cumulative Percent
Germany	61	14.06	61	14.06
UK	52	11.98	113	26.04
Italy	50	11.52	163	37.56
Australia	47	10.83	210	48.39
France	45	10.37	255	58.76
Canada	32	7.37	287	66.13
Norway	32	7.37	319	73.50
Japan	28	6.45	347	79.95
Sweden	20	4.61	367	84.56
Finland	19	4.38	386	88.94
Singapore	17	3.92	403	92.86
Brazil	11	2.53	414	95.39
Denmark	8	1.84	422	97.24
Spain	8	1.84	430	99.08
Netherlands	4	0.92	434	100.00

A one-way frequency table shows the distribution of a variable's values.

To access the One-Way Frequencies task, select **Describe** ⇨ **One-Way Frequencies** from the Browse SAS Programs dialog box.

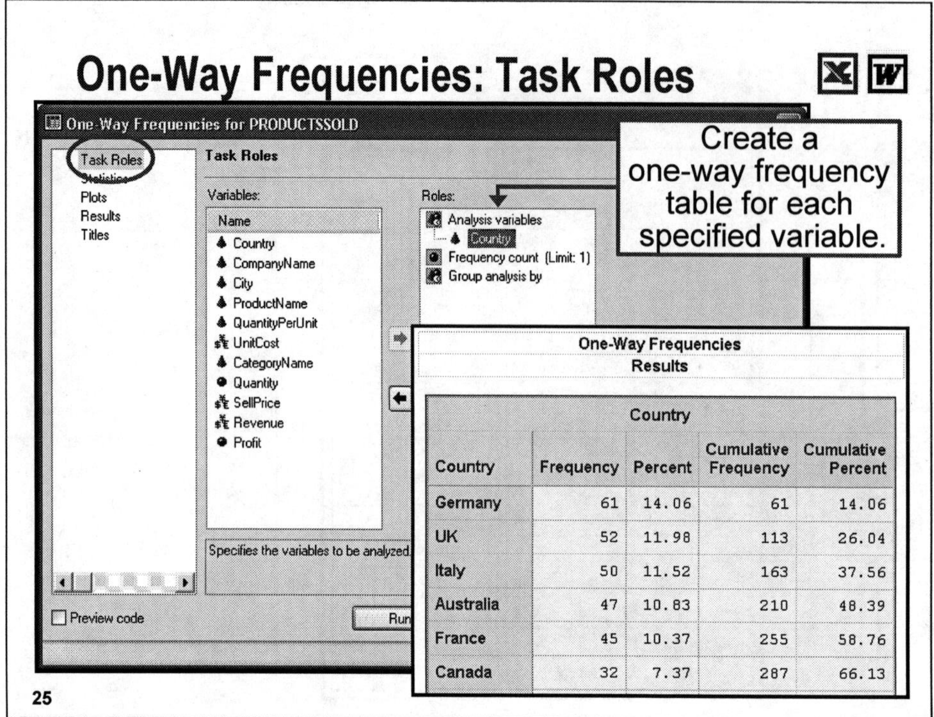

Country				
Country	Frequency	Percent	Cumulative Frequency	Cumulative Percent
Germany	61	14.06	61	14.06
UK	52	11.98	113	26.04
Italy	50	11.52	163	37.56
Australia	47	10.83	210	48.39
France	45	10.37	255	58.76
Canada	32	7.37	287	66.13

25

The One-Way Frequencies task produces a one-way frequency table for each variable included in the Analysis variables role.

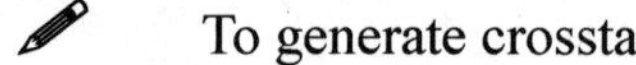 To generate crosstabulation tables, also known as contingency tables, use the Table Analysis.

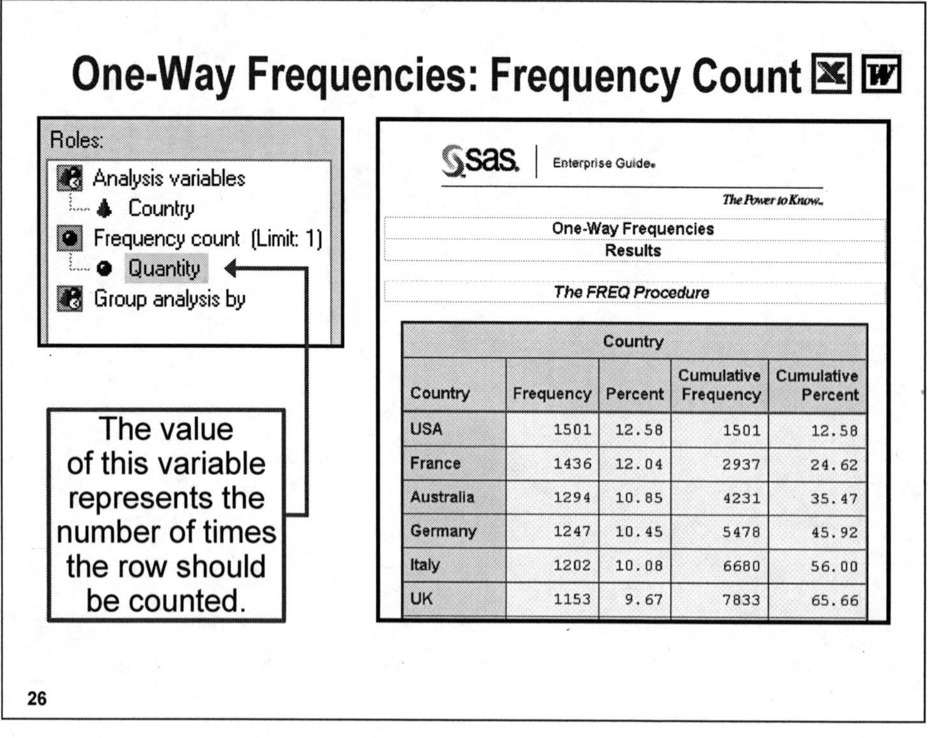

Country				
Country	Frequency	Percent	Cumulative Frequency	Cumulative Percent
USA	1501	12.58	1501	12.58
France	1436	12.04	2937	24.62
Australia	1294	10.85	4231	35.47
Germany	1247	10.45	5478	45.92
Italy	1202	10.08	6680	56.00
UK	1153	9.67	7833	65.66

26

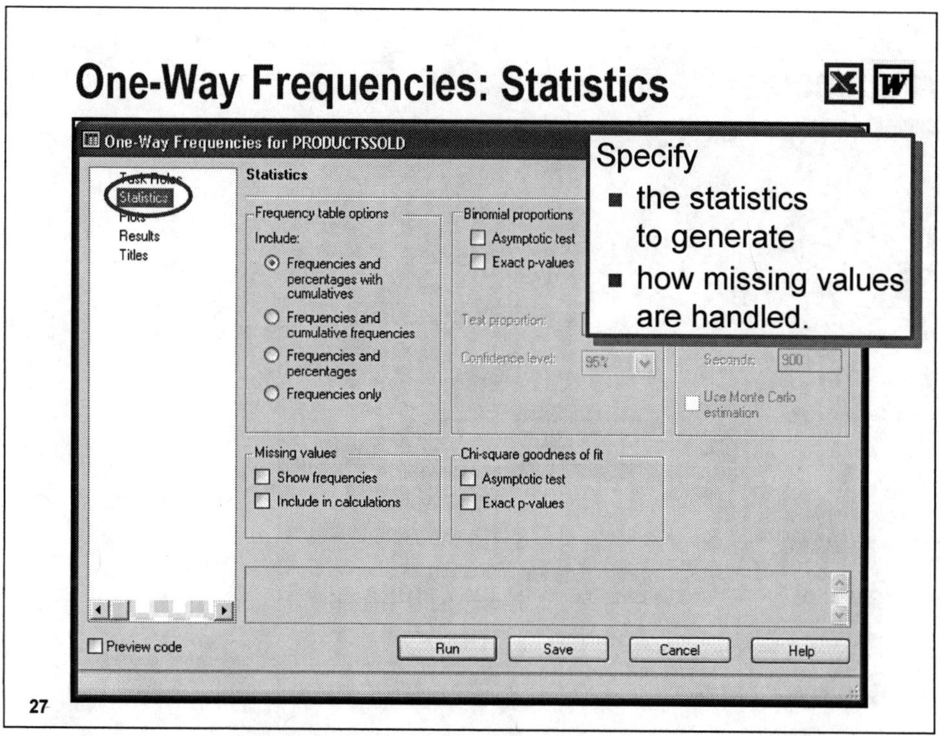
One-Way Frequencies: Statistics
One-Way Frequencies for PRODUCTSSOLD
Specify
the statistics to generate
how missing values are handled.
Statistics
Results
Titles
Frequency table options
Include:
Frequencies and percentages with cumulatives
Frequencies and cumulative frequencies
Frequencies and percentages
Frequencies only
Binomial proportions
Asymptotic test
Exact p-values
Missing values
Show frequencies
Include in calculations
Chi-square goodness of fit
Asymptotic test
Exact p-values
Preview code
Run
Save
Cancel
Help
27

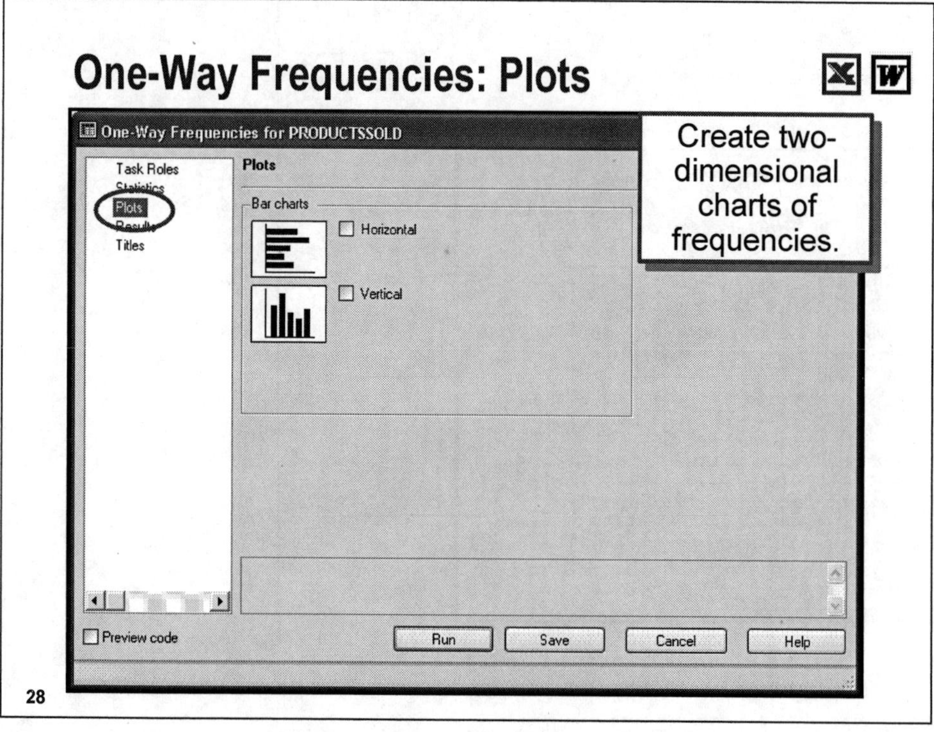
One-Way Frequencies: Plots
One-Way Frequencies for PRODUCTSSOLD
Create two-dimensional charts of frequencies.
Task Roles
Plots
Titles
Bar charts
Horizontal
Vertical
Preview code
Run
Save
Cancel
Help
28

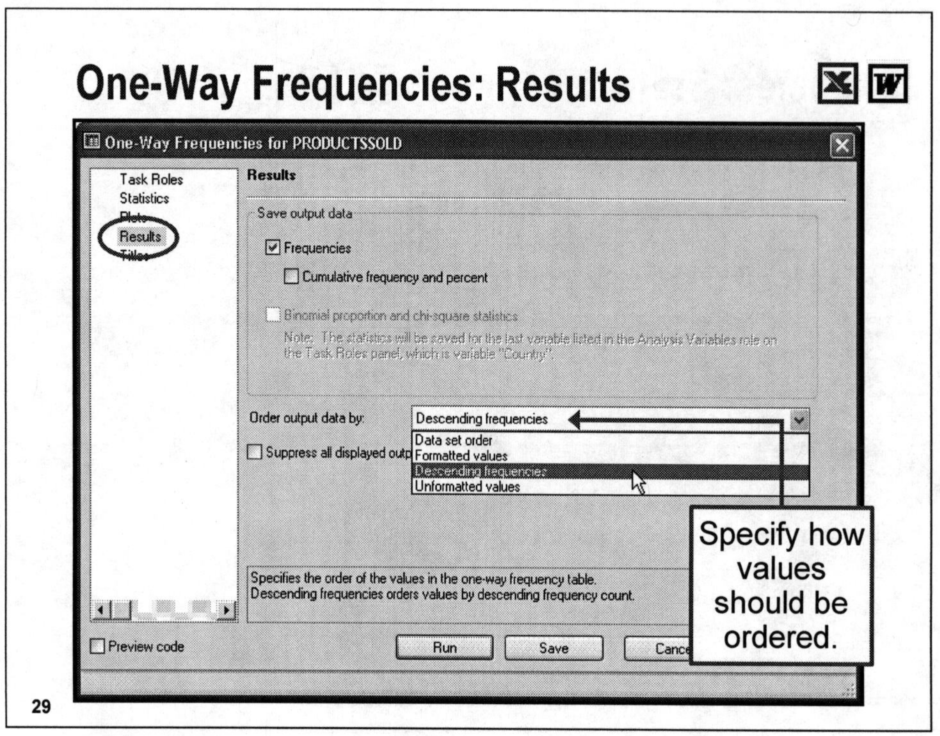

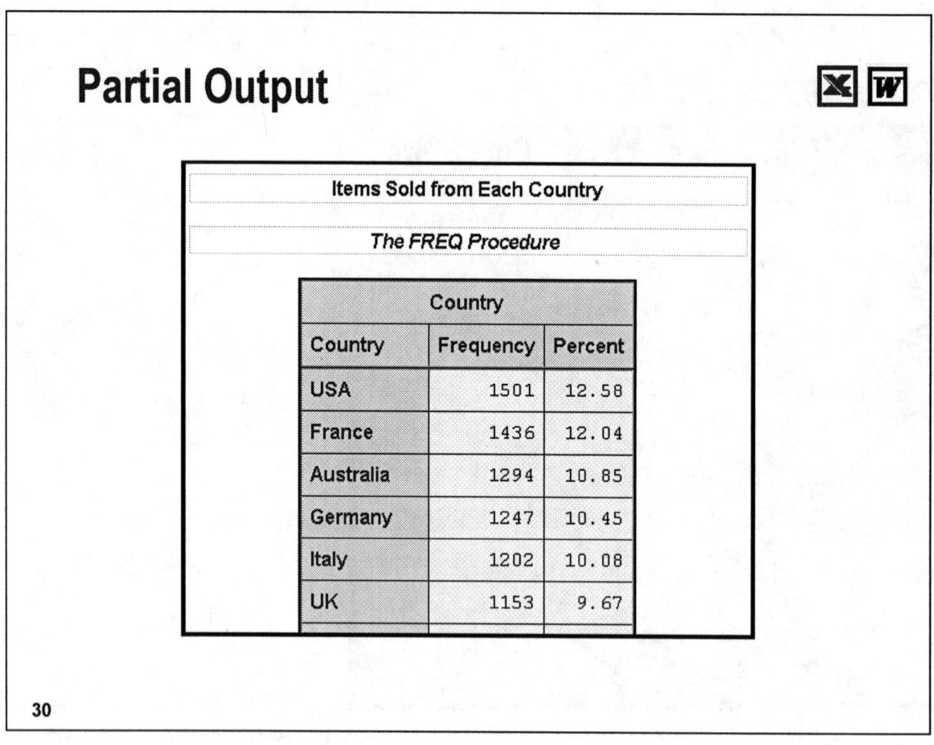

Items Sold from Each Country

The FREQ Procedure

Country		
Country	Frequency	Percent
USA	1501	12.58
France	1436	12.04
Australia	1294	10.85
Germany	1247	10.45
Italy	1202	10.08
UK	1153	9.67

Generating a One-Way Frequency Report

For this demonstration, you will

- use Microsoft Word to create a frequency report of the number of customers in each country.

Output (partial listing):

Frequency Distribution for Countries

Customer Country		
Customer_Country	Frequency	Percent
United States	5463	31.84
France	2221	12.95
Italy	2018	11.76
Germany	1968	11.47
Spain	1650	9.62
United Kingdom	1188	6.92

Setting the Active Data Source in Microsoft Word

1. Invoke Microsoft Word by selecting **Start** ⇨ **All Programs** ⇨ **Microsoft Office** ⇨ **Microsoft Word**.
2. Using the pull-down menu on the Active Data selection box, select **Select SAS Data Source…** from the SAS Analysis Tools toolbar (or select **SAS** ⇨ **Active Data** ⇨ **Select SAS Data Source…**).

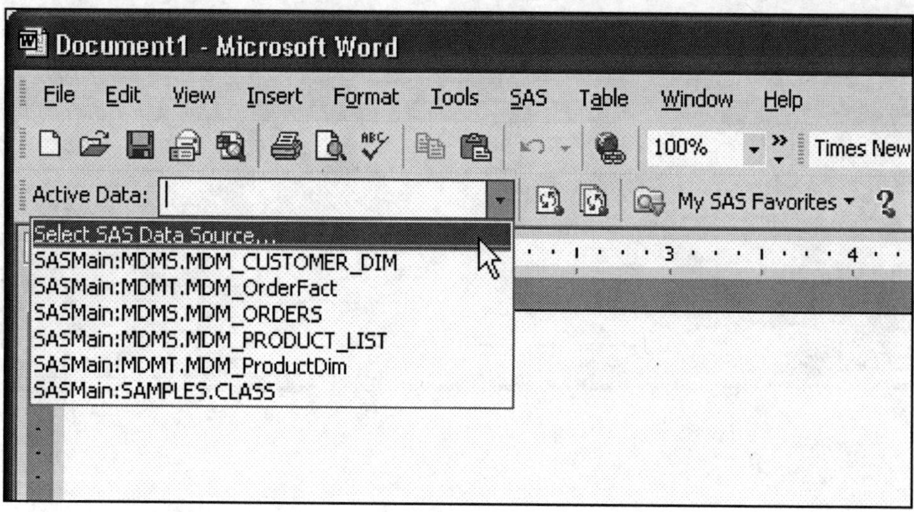

a. If prompted, enter the user name and password provided by the instructor.

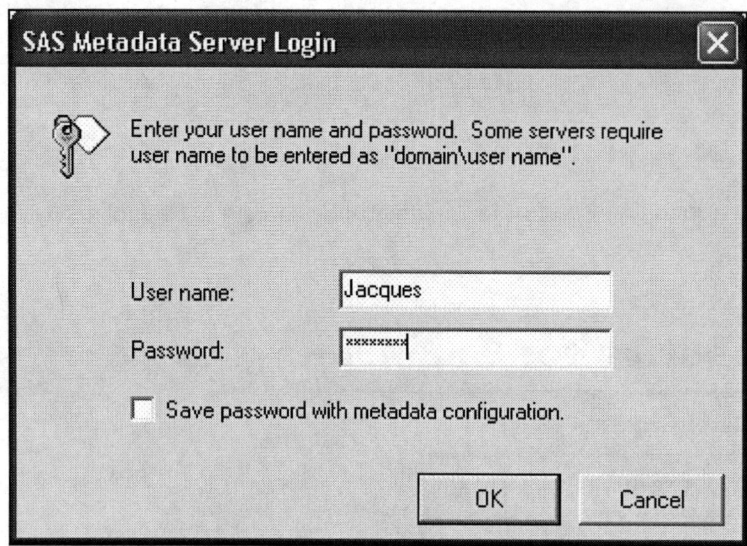

The values shown above may be different than those used in class.

b. Select OK.

3. In the Open SAS Data Source window, select **Servers** from the shortcut bar. Then, choose **SASMain** and select Open.

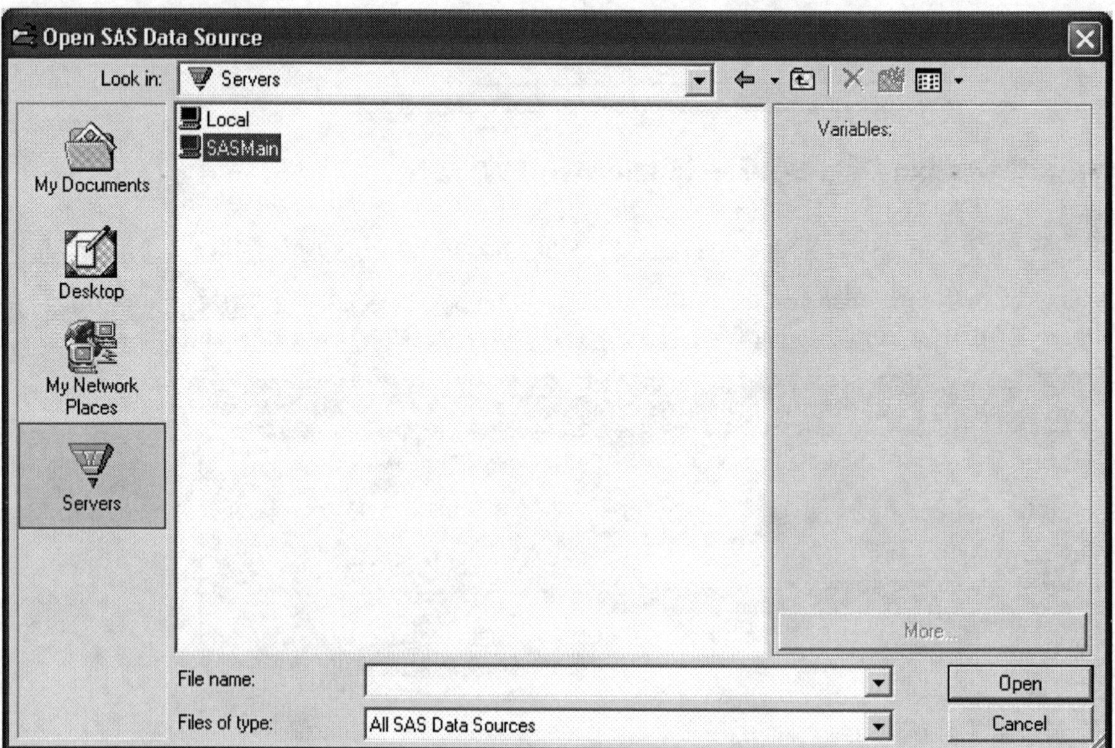

a. Choose **MDM Source Tables Library** and select Open.

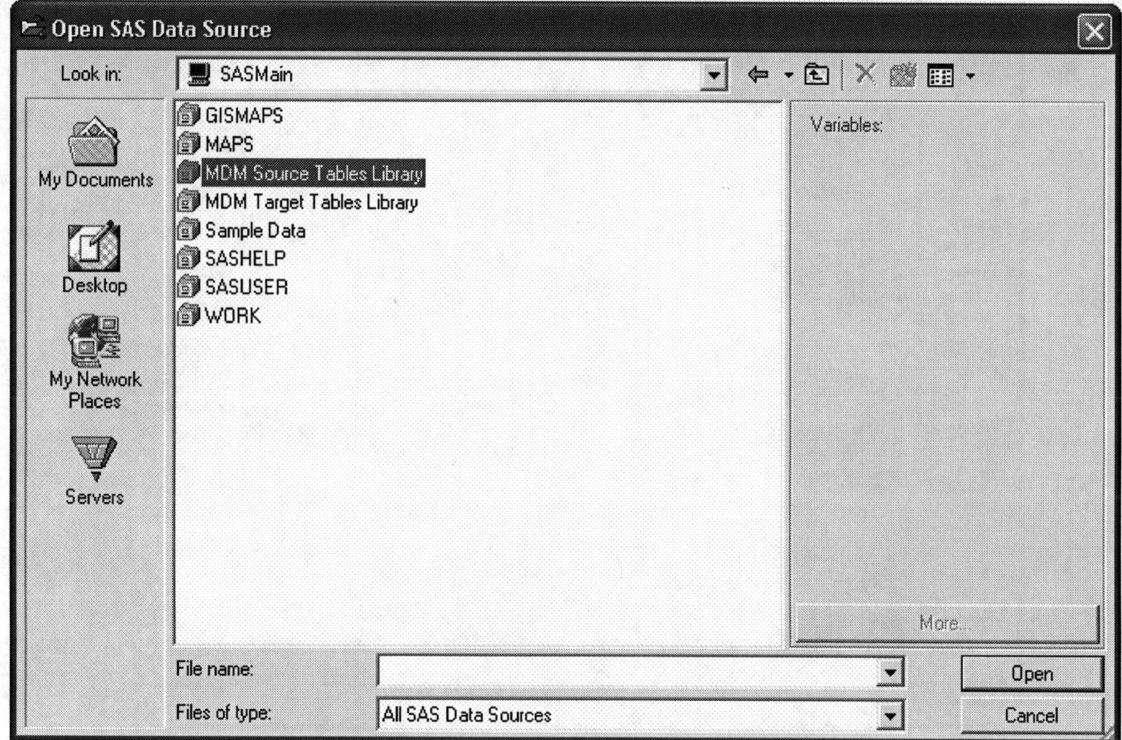

b. Select the **MDM_CUSTOMER_DIM** table, then choose Open.

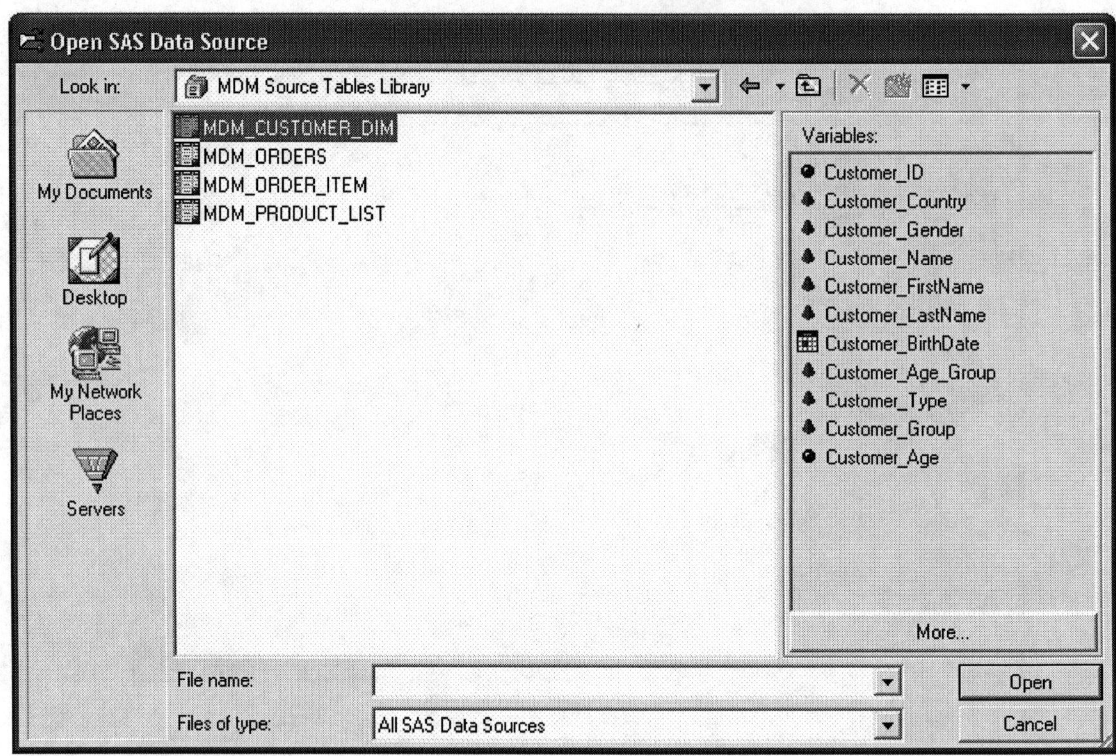

If you cannot read the entire name of a table, use the View Mode icon on the toolbar to change the view to Detail or List. You may deselect any columns that you choose not to include from the data source.

The SAS table is now the active data source in Microsoft Word.

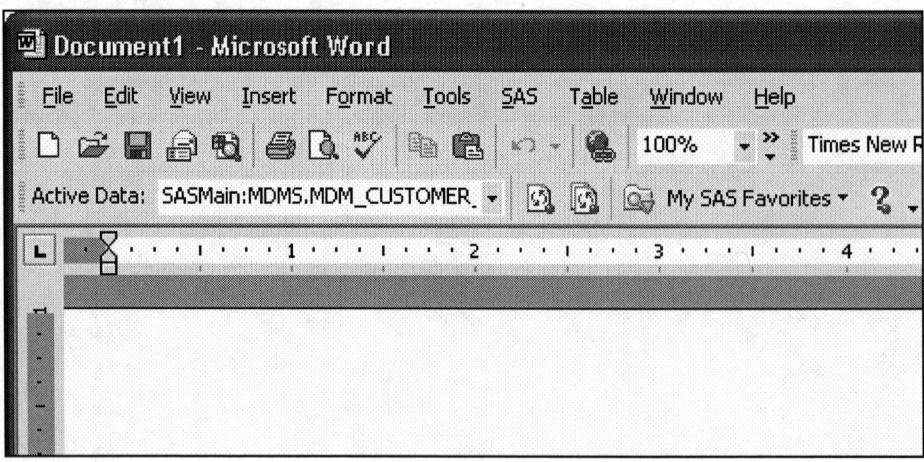

Running a One-Way Frequencies Task

1. Open the One-Way Frequencies task.

   a. Select [icon] on the SAS Analysis Tools toolbar (or select **SAS** ⇨ **Browse SAS Programs**).

   b. Expand the group **SAS Tasks** and select the folder **Describe** ⇨ **One-Way Frequencies**. Then select [Run].

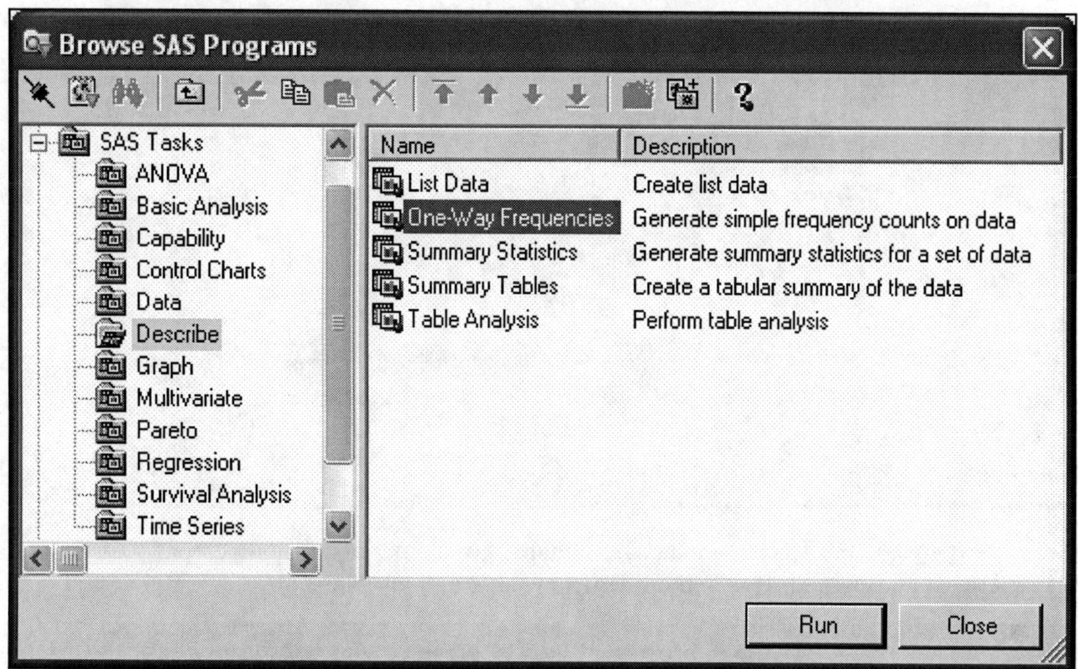

A One-Way Frequencies dialog box opens and enables you to select the columns that you want to see in the report and to specify a role for those columns. In this dialog box, you can also change output formatting options.

2. Drag the **Customer Country** column from the Variables pane and drop it on the Analysis variables role in the Roles pane.

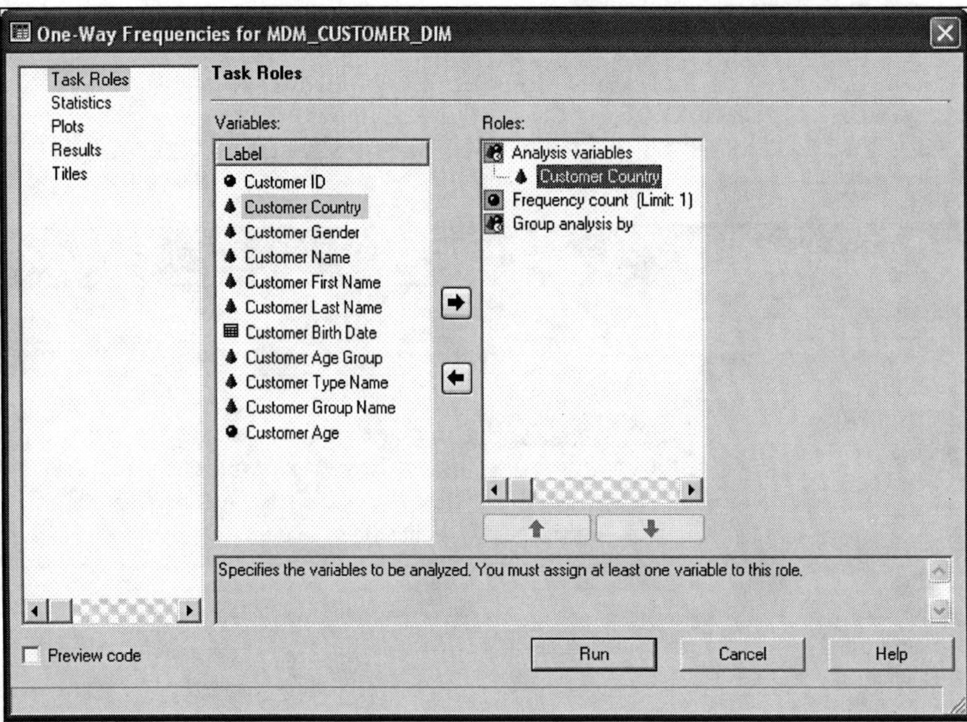

3. Select **Statistics** in the Selection pane. To include only the frequency and percent statistics, select **Frequencies and percentages** in the Frequency table options pane.

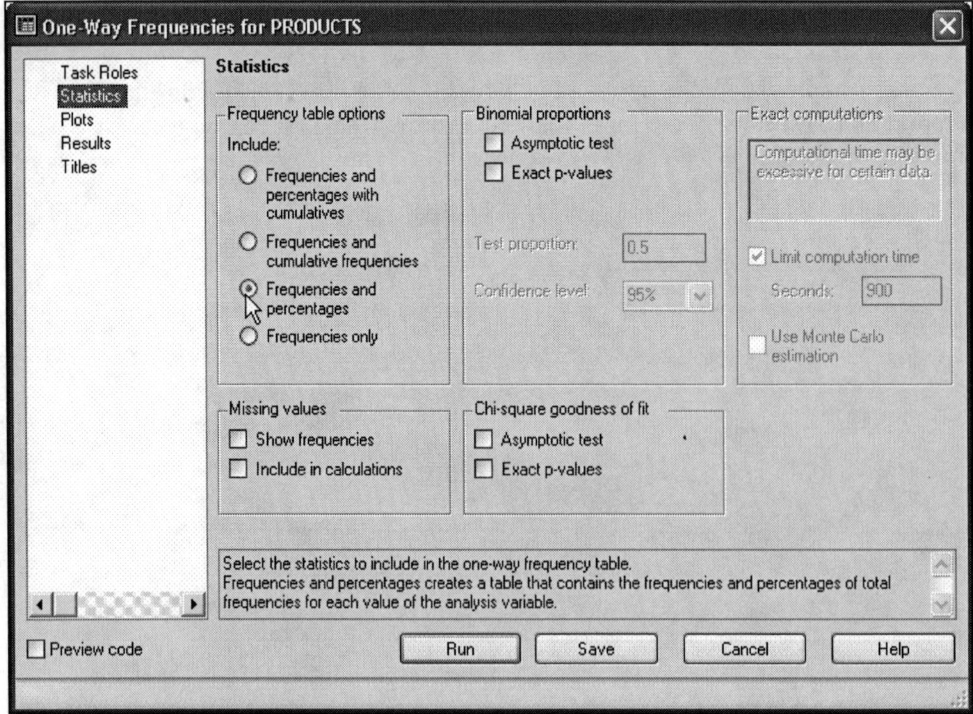

4. Select **Results** in the Selection pane. To have the report ordered with the highest count appearing first, select **Descending frequencies** in the Order output data by pane.

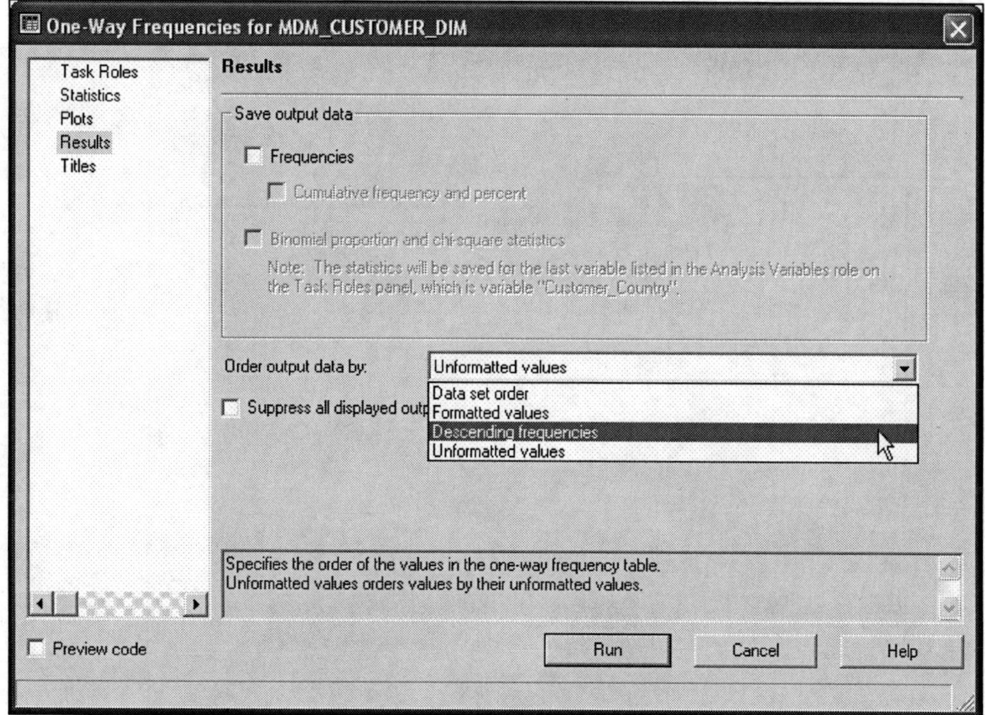

5. Select **Titles** in the Selection pane. To modify the title, first deselect the Use default text check box. In the `Text` field, delete the default title of One-Way Frequencies Results and type **`Frequency Distribution for Countries`**.

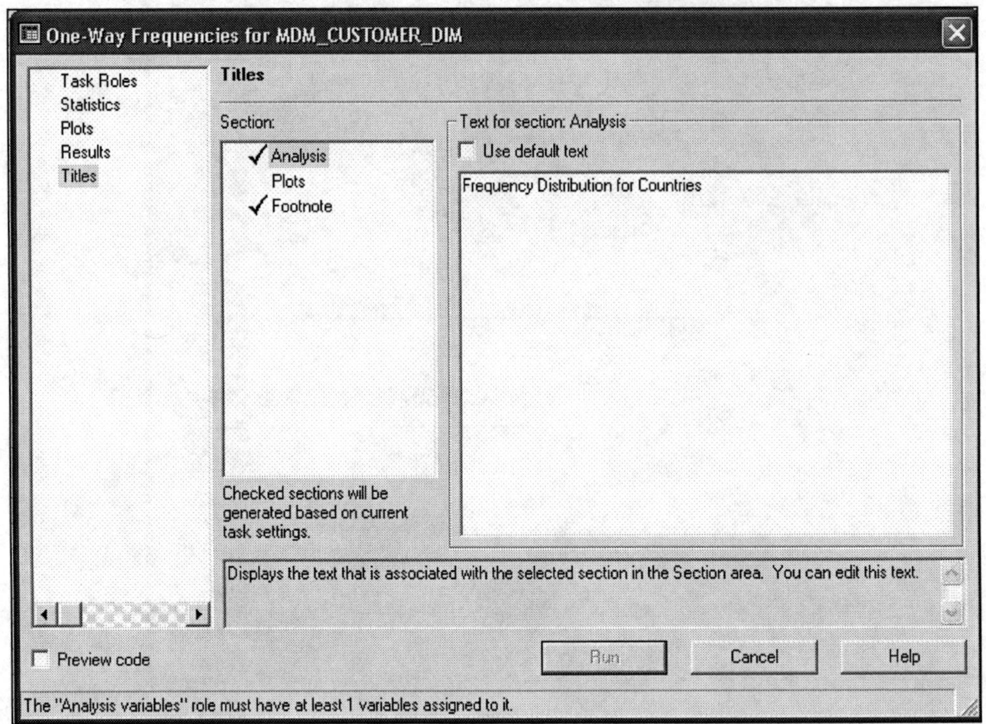

In the Titles window, when **Analysis** is selected in the Section pane, the Text area displays only your title text. In order to display the footnote text, you must select **Footnotes** in the Section pane.

6. Select Run to generate the report.

Frequency Distribution for Countries

The FREQ Procedure

Customer Country		
Customer_Country	Frequency	Percent
United States	5463	31.84
France	2221	12.95
Italy	2018	11.76
Germany	1968	11.47
Spain	1650	9.62
United Kingdom	1188	6.92

7. To remove the title The FREQ Procedure that is added to the output automatically, select **SAS** ⇨ **Options** and select the **Tasks** tab. Deselect **Include SAS procedure titles in results**. Select OK to close the Options window.

> The Tasks pane also includes an option that enables you to change or delete the default footnote.

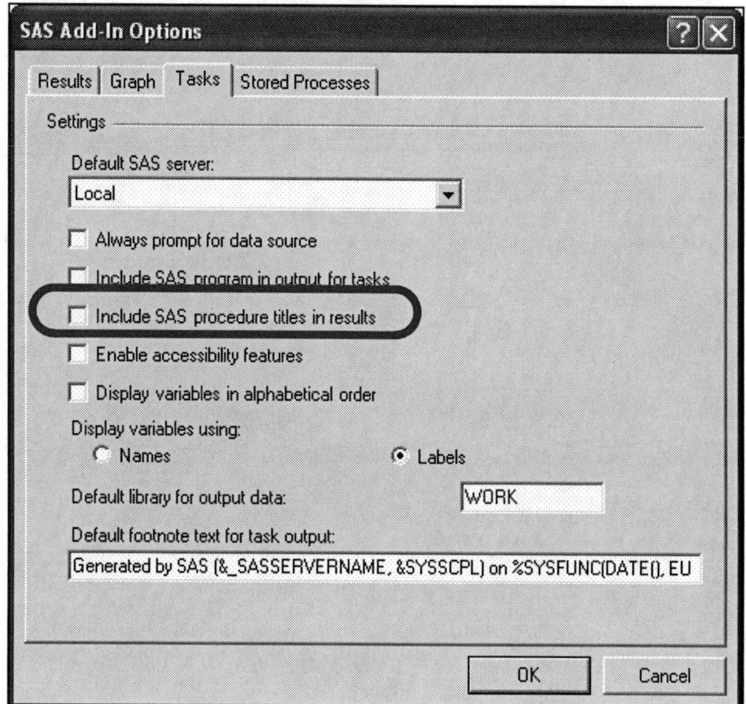

8. In order to see the report without the procedure title, refresh the report.

   a. Left-click inside the body of the document to place the cursor inside the results that you want to refresh.

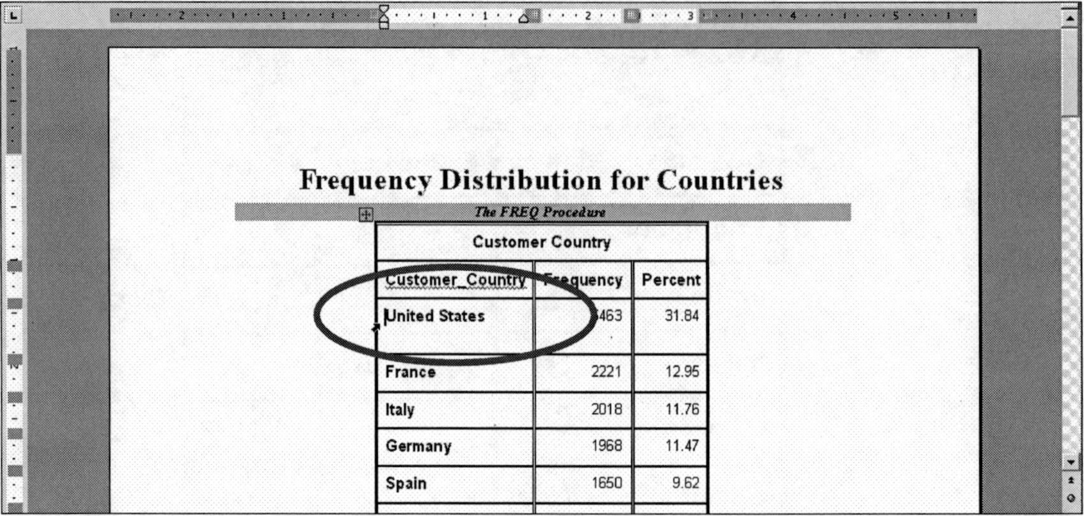

✏ You can also use Microsoft Word bookmarks to have the cursor located inside a report. Select **Insert** ⇨ **Bookmark...** from the Word pull-down menus. Find the bookmark associated with the report and select **Go To**.

Bookmarks are named in accordance with the task or stored process that ran to create the report. Each bookmark also has a unique number appended to the name that reflects the order in which the analyses where run.

   b. Select [icon] on the SAS Analysis Tools toolbar (or select **SAS** ⇨ **Refresh** from the pull-down menus) to rerun the report.

   c. Select [Run] and examine the results.

The updated report is streamed back to Word without the procedure title.

Frequency Distribution for Countries

Customer Country		
Customer_Country	**Frequency**	**Percent**
United States	5463	31.84
France	2221	12.95
Italy	2018	11.76
Germany	1968	11.47
Spain	1650	9.62
United Kingdom	1188	6.92
Netherlands	914	5.33

9. In Microsoft Word, select **File** ⇨ **Exit** and do not save the changes.

5.4 Exercises

1. Preparing a Data Source for SAS Tasks

a. Any order that takes over three weeks for delivery is considered a delayed delivery order. Open and filter a SAS data source to find out how many orders were delayed.

- In Microsoft Excel, deselect the SAS option **Include SAS procedure titles in results**.
- Open the **`MDM_OrderFact`** table from the MDM Target Tables library.
- Filter the data to select only those orders that took over 21 days to deliver.

How many orders took over 21 days to deliver?

Partial Output

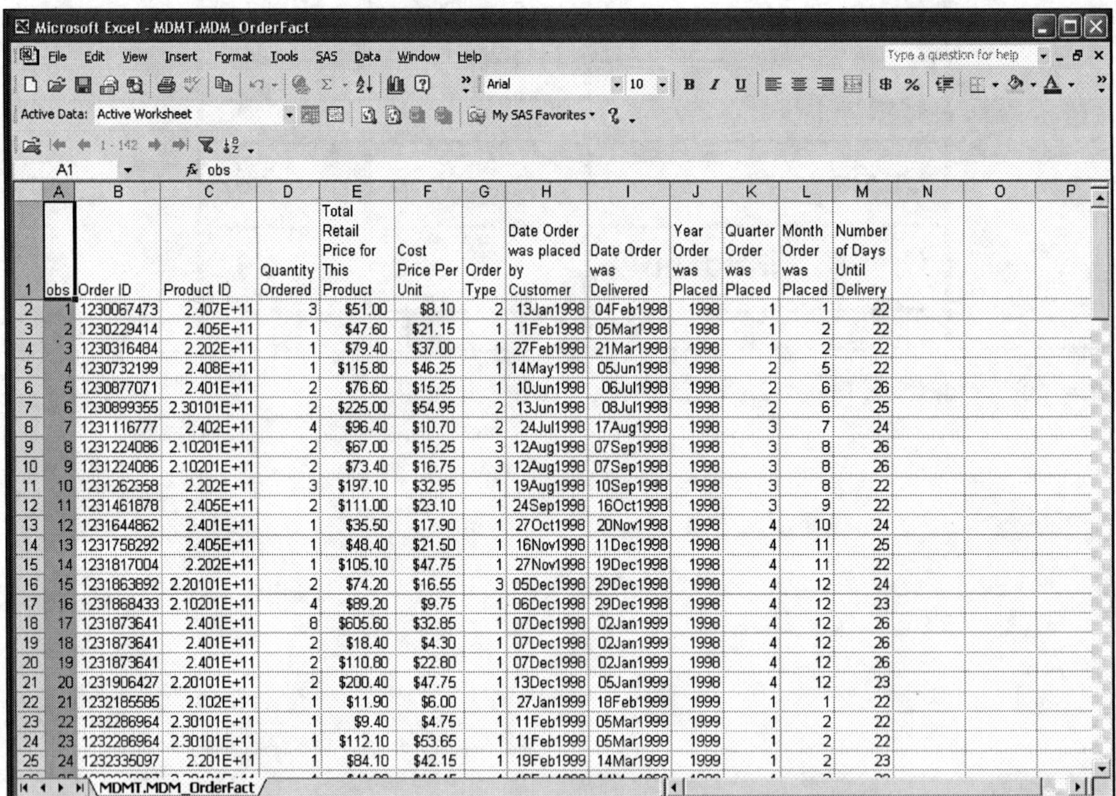

obs	Order ID	Product ID	Quantity Ordered	Total Retail Price for This Product	Cost Price Per Unit	Order Type	Date Order was placed by Customer	Date Order was Delivered	Year Order was Placed	Quarter Order was Placed	Month Order was Placed	Number of Days Until Delivery
1	1230067473	2.407E+11	3	$51.00	$8.10	2	13Jan1998	04Feb1998	1998	1	1	22
2	1230229414	2.405E+11	1	$47.60	$21.15	1	11Feb1998	05Mar1998	1998	1	2	22
3	1230316484	2.202E+11	1	$79.40	$37.00	1	27Feb1998	21Mar1998	1998	1	2	22
4	1230732199	2.408E+11	1	$115.80	$46.25	1	14May1998	05Jun1998	1998	2	5	22
5	1230877071	2.401E+11	2	$76.60	$15.25	1	10Jun1998	06Jul1998	1998	2	6	26
6	1230899355	2.30101E+11	2	$225.00	$54.95	2	13Jun1998	08Jul1998	1998	2	6	25
7	1231116777	2.402E+11	4	$96.40	$10.70	2	24Jul1998	17Aug1998	1998	3	7	24
8	1231224086	2.10201E+11	2	$67.00	$15.25	3	12Aug1998	07Sep1998	1998	3	8	26
9	1231224086	2.10201E+11	2	$73.40	$16.75	3	12Aug1998	07Sep1998	1998	3	8	26
10	1231262358	2.202E+11	3	$197.10	$32.95	1	19Aug1998	10Sep1998	1998	3	8	22
11	1231461878	2.405E+11	2	$111.00	$23.10	1	24Sep1998	16Oct1998	1998	3	9	22
12	1231644862	2.401E+11	1	$35.50	$17.90	1	27Oct1998	20Nov1998	1998	4	10	24
13	1231758292	2.405E+11	1	$48.40	$21.50	1	16Nov1998	11Dec1998	1998	4	11	25
14	1231817004	2.202E+11	1	$105.10	$47.75	1	27Nov1998	19Dec1998	1998	4	11	22
15	1231863892	2.20101E+11	2	$74.20	$16.55	3	05Dec1998	29Dec1998	1998	4	12	24
16	1231868433	2.10201E+11	4	$89.20	$9.75	1	06Dec1998	29Dec1998	1998	4	12	23
17	1231873641	2.401E+11	8	$605.60	$32.85	1	07Dec1998	02Jan1999	1998	4	12	26
18	1231873641	2.401E+11	2	$18.40	$4.30	1	07Dec1998	02Jan1999	1998	4	12	26
19	1231873641	2.401E+11	2	$110.80	$22.80	1	07Dec1998	02Jan1999	1998	4	12	26
20	1231906427	2.20101E+11	2	$200.40	$47.75	1	13Dec1998	05Jan1999	1998	4	12	23
21	1232185585	2.102E+11	1	$11.90	$6.00	1	27Jan1999	18Feb1999	1999	1	1	22
22	1232286964	2.30101E+11	1	$9.40	$4.75	1	11Feb1999	05Mar1999	1999	1	2	22
23	1232286964	2.30101E+11	1	$112.10	$53.65	1	11Feb1999	05Mar1999	1999	1	2	22
24	1232335097	2.201E+11	1	$84.10	$42.15	1	19Feb1999	14Mar1999	1999	1	2	23

2. Creating a Listing Report

a. Using the filtered **`MDM_OrderFact`** table from the previous exercise (verify that that **Active Worksheet** is selected in the Active Data window), create a listing report.

1) Specify that **`Order ID`**, **`Quantity Ordered`**, **`Order Type`**, and **`Number of Days until Delivery`** be displayed in the report.

2) Specify that the report be grouped by the **`Quarter`** the order was placed.

3) Specify the title of Delayed Deliveries by Quarter and no footnote.

4) Select the appropriate option to suppress the column that contains row numbers.

5) Select the appropriate option to display the number of rows printed in the report.

When you opened the **`MDM_OrderFact`** table in Excel, the values for **`Order Type`** were numeric. Why are they appearing as text in this listing report?

Partial Output

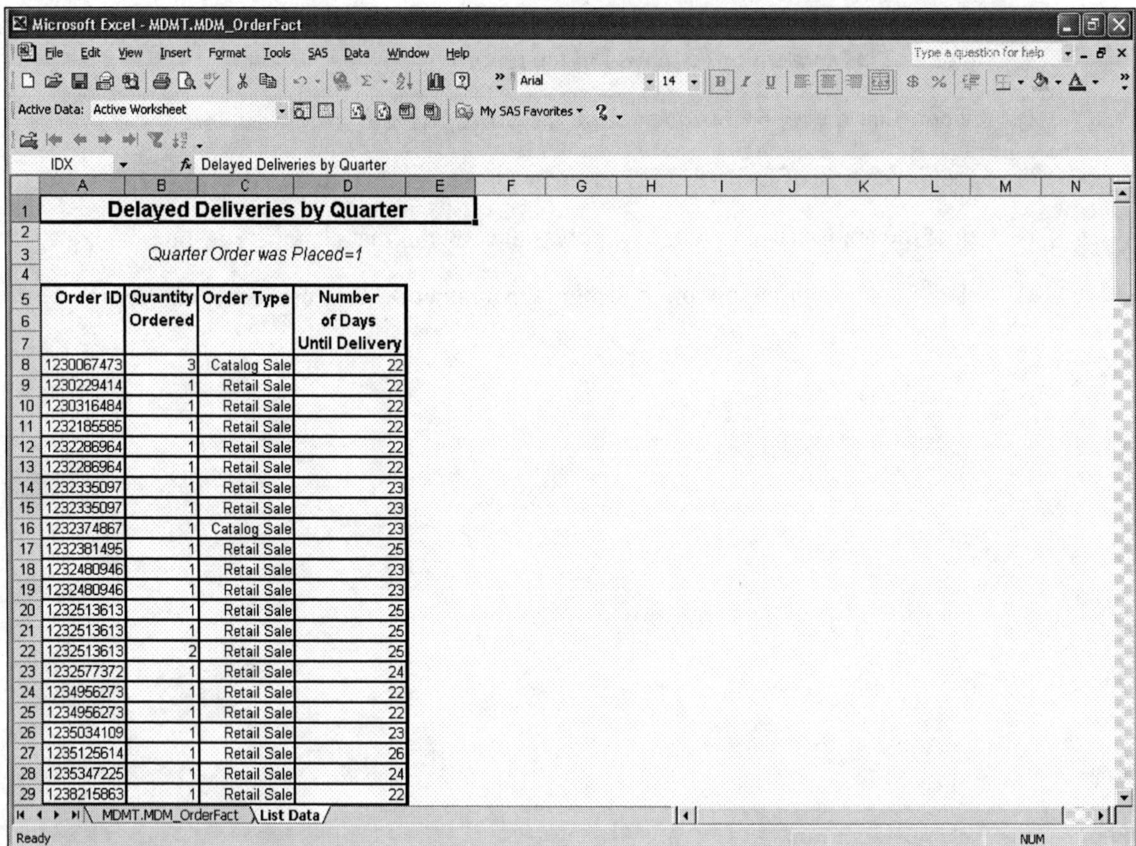

Delayed Deliveries by Quarter

Quarter Order was Placed=1

Order ID	Quantity Ordered	Order Type	Number of Days Until Delivery
1230067473	3	Catalog Sale	22
1230229414	1	Retail Sale	22
1230316484	1	Retail Sale	22
1232185585	1	Retail Sale	22
1232286964	1	Retail Sale	22
1232286964	1	Retail Sale	22
1232335097	1	Retail Sale	23
1232335097	1	Retail Sale	23
1232374867	1	Catalog Sale	23
1232381495	1	Retail Sale	25
1232480946	1	Retail Sale	23
1232480946	1	Retail Sale	23
1232513613	1	Retail Sale	25
1232513613	1	Retail Sale	25
1232513613	2	Retail Sale	25
1232577372	1	Retail Sale	24
1234956273	1	Retail Sale	22
1234956273	1	Retail Sale	22
1235034109	1	Retail Sale	23
1235125614	1	Retail Sale	26
1235347225	1	Retail Sale	24
1238215863	1	Retail Sale	22

3. Creating a Listing Report

a. Similar to the previous exercise, create a listing report using the filtered **`MDM_OrderFact`** data.

1) Specify that **`Order ID`**, **`Quantity Ordered`**, and **`Number of Days until Delivery`** be displayed in the report.

2) Specify that the report be grouped by the type of order placed.

3) Specify the title Delayed Deliveries by Order Type with no footnote.

4) Select the appropriate option to suppress the column that contains row numbers.

5) Select the appropriate option to display the number of rows printed in the report.

Partial Output

	A	B	C	D	E
1	**Delayed Deliveries by Order Type**				
2					
3	*Order Type=Retail Sale*				
4					
5	**Order ID**	**Quantity**	**Order Type**	**Number**	
6		**Ordered**		**of Days**	
7				**Until Delivery**	
8	1230229414	1	Retail Sale	22	
9	1230316484	1	Retail Sale	22	
10	1230732199	1	Retail Sale	22	
11	1230877071	2	Retail Sale	26	
12	1231262358	3	Retail Sale	22	
13	1231461878	2	Retail Sale	22	
14	1231644862	1	Retail Sale	24	
15	1231758292	1	Retail Sale	25	
16	1231817004	1	Retail Sale	22	
17	1231868433	4	Retail Sale	23	
18	1231873641	8	Retail Sale	26	
19	1231873641	2	Retail Sale	26	
20	1231873641	2	Retail Sale	26	

4. **Sending Multiple Results to Word**

   a. Verify that the SAS option **When sending multiple results to Word, place each result in a separate document** is deselected.

b. Send both of these listing reports to a single Microsoft Word document.

Partial Output

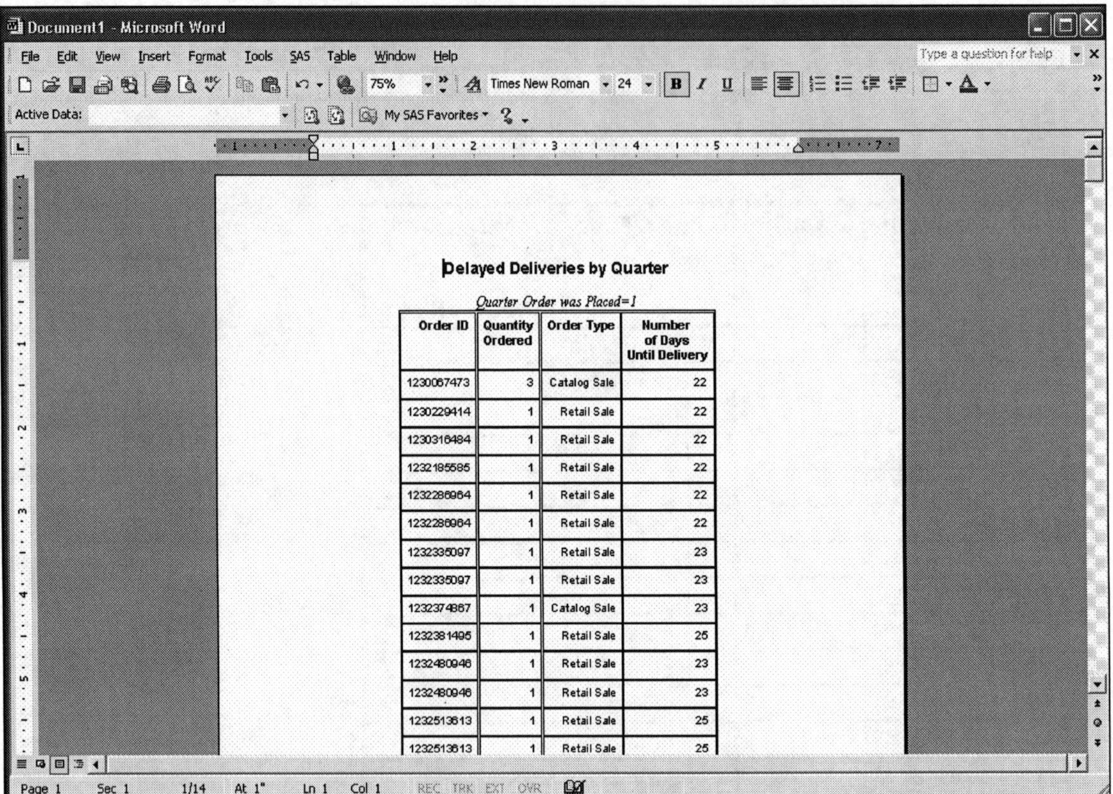

Delayed Deliveries by Quarter

Quarter Order was Placed=1

Order ID	Quantity Ordered	Order Type	Number of Days Until Delivery
1230067473	3	Catalog Sale	22
1230229414	1	Retail Sale	22
1230316484	1	Retail Sale	22
1232185585	1	Retail Sale	22
1232286964	1	Retail Sale	22
1232286964	1	Retail Sale	22
1232335097	1	Retail Sale	23
1232335097	1	Retail Sale	23
1232374867	1	Catalog Sale	23
1232381495	1	Retail Sale	25
1232480946	1	Retail Sale	23
1232480946	1	Retail Sale	23
1232513613	1	Retail Sale	25
1232513613	1	Retail Sale	25

5. Creating a One-Way Frequency Report

a. Using the filtered **`MDM_OrderFact`** table from the previous exercises, execute the One-Way Frequency task in Microsoft Excel to display the number of delayed deliveries by quarter.

1) Create a one-way frequency table based on the **`Quarter`** the order was placed.

2) Specify that only the frequencies and percentages are displayed.

3) Specify that a vertical bar chart be produced in addition to the frequency report.

4) For each output item, specify an appropriate title and no footnote.

Which quarter experienced the most delayed deliveries?

Output

Frequency of Delayed Orders by Quarter

Quarter Order was Placed		
Order_Qtr	Frequency	Percent
1	38	26.76
2	27	19.01
3	48	33.8
4	29	20.42

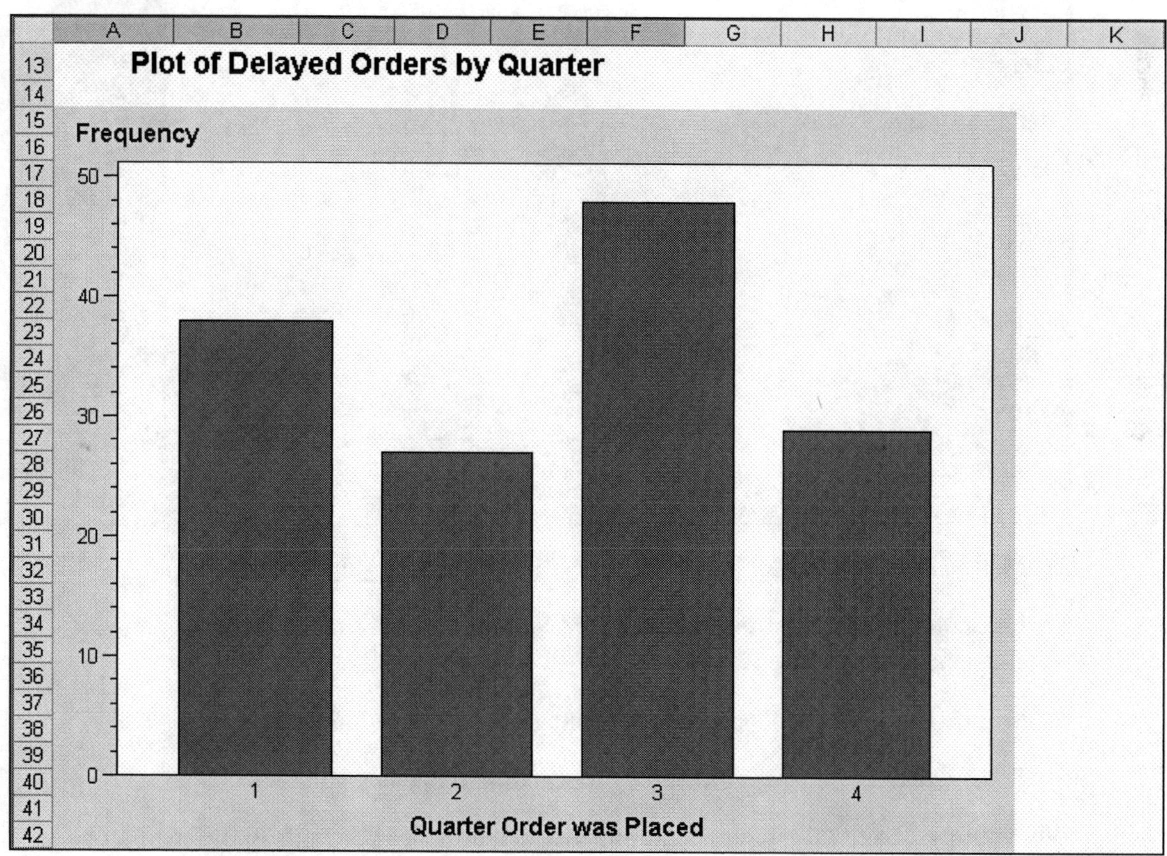

6. Running Tasks from Microsoft Word

a. You are interested in identifying your most important suppliers. Use the One-Way Frequency task to identify the number of products obtained from each supplier.

1) Specify that the SASAddin output style is used to create the following report from within Microsoft Word.

Partial Output

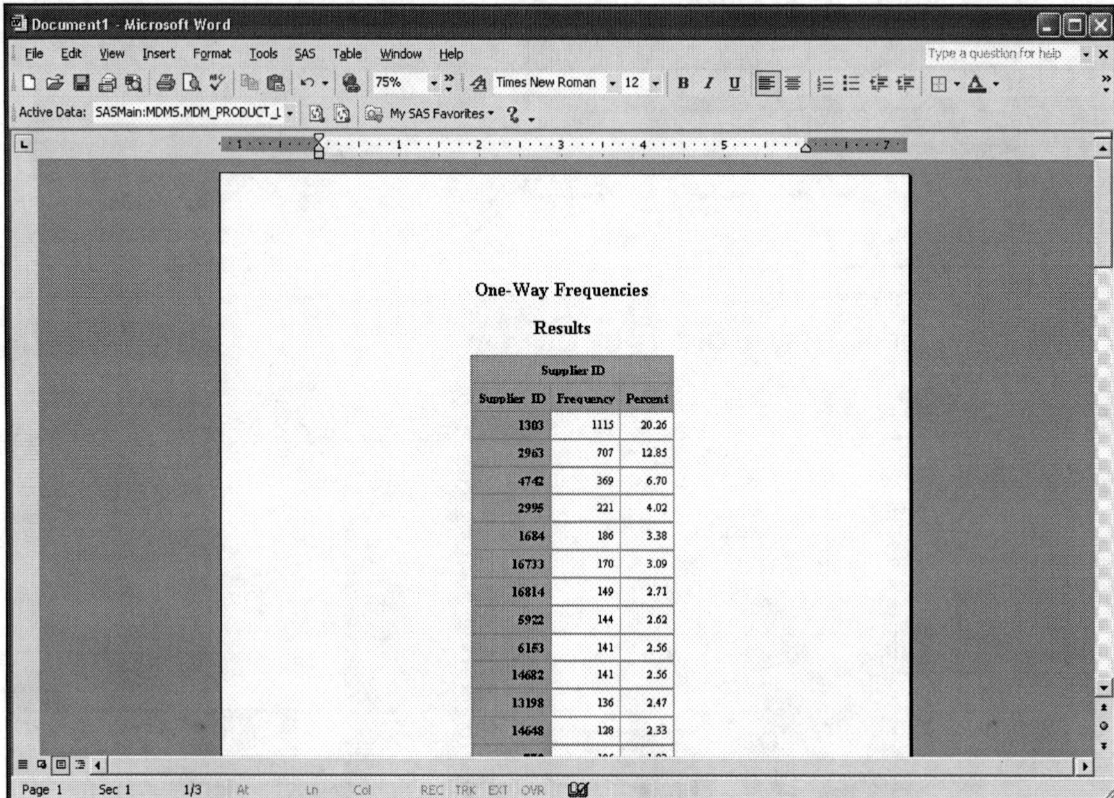

One-Way Frequencies

Results

Supplier ID		
Supplier ID	Frequency	Percent
1303	1115	20.26
2963	707	12.85
4742	369	6.70
2995	221	4.02
1684	186	3.38
16733	170	3.09
16814	149	2.71
5922	144	2.62
6153	141	2.56
14682	141	2.56
13198	136	2.47
14648	128	2.33

2) Make sure the option **Include SAS procedure titles in results** is deselected.

3) Use `MDM_Product_List` in the MDM Source Tables Library to create a one-way frequency table of `Supplier ID`.

4) Specify that only frequencies and percentages be displayed in the report.

5) Specify that the output be ordered by descending frequency values.

Which `Supplier ID` references the supplier that provides you with 30 different products?

b. Enhance the report by refreshing the output.

1) Specify that the sasweb output style is used.

2) Specify the title Number of Products from each Supplier with no footnote.

Partial Output

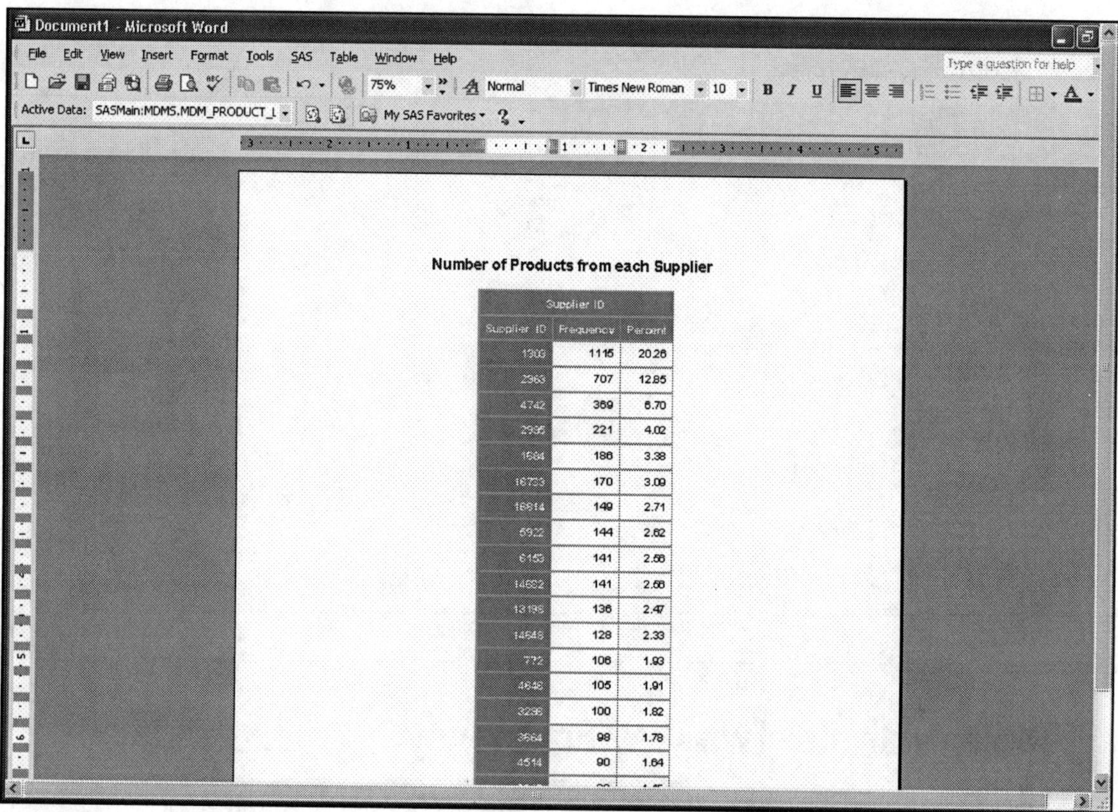

Number of Products from each Supplier

Supplier ID		
Supplier ID	Frequency	Percent
1303	1115	20.28
2963	707	12.85
4742	369	6.70
2995	221	4.02
1684	186	3.38
16733	170	3.09
16814	149	2.71
5922	144	2.62
6153	141	2.56
14682	141	2.56
13199	136	2.47
14648	128	2.33
772	106	1.93
4646	105	1.91
3298	100	1.82
3664	98	1.78
4514	90	1.64

5.5 Table Analysis Task

Objectives

- Use the Table Analysis task to generate a two-way frequency table.

34

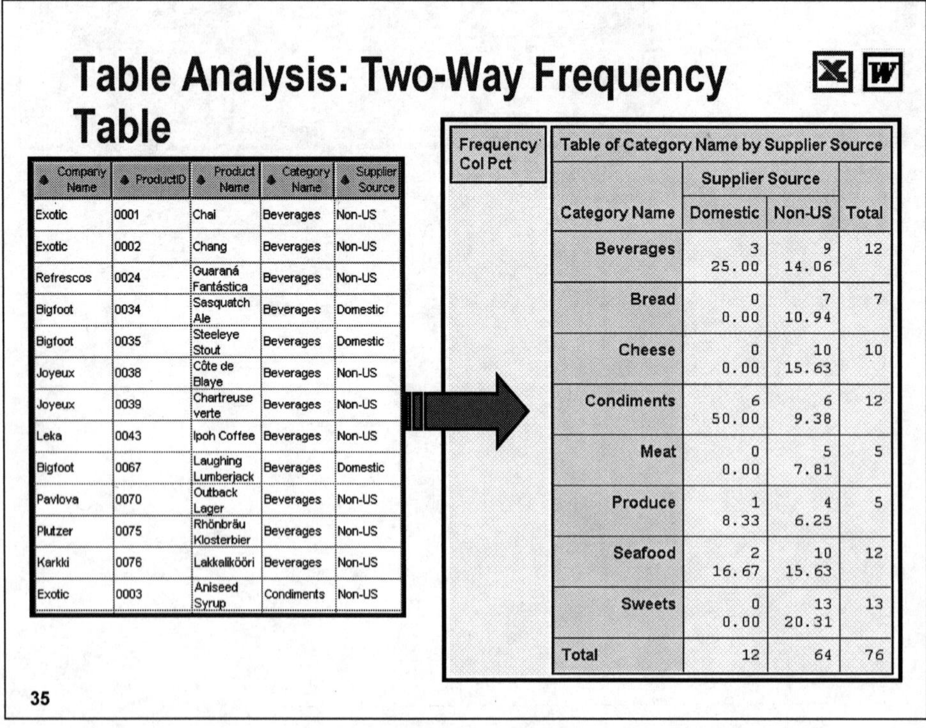

Company Name	ProductID	Product Name	Category Name	Supplier Source
Exotic	0001	Chai	Beverages	Non-US
Exotic	0002	Chang	Beverages	Non-US
Refrescos	0024	Guaraná Fantástica	Beverages	Non-US
Bigfoot	0034	Sasquatch Ale	Beverages	Domestic
Bigfoot	0035	Steeleye Stout	Beverages	Domestic
Joyeux	0038	Côte de Blaye	Beverages	Non-US
Joyeux	0039	Chartreuse verte	Beverages	Non-US
Leka	0043	Ipoh Coffee	Beverages	Non-US
Bigfoot	0067	Laughing Lumberjack	Beverages	Domestic
Pavlova	0070	Outback Lager	Beverages	Non-US
Plutzer	0075	Rhönbräu Klosterbier	Beverages	Non-US
Karkki	0076	Lakkalikööri	Beverages	Non-US
Exotic	0003	Aniseed Syrup	Condiments	Non-US

Frequency
Col Pct

Table of Category Name by Supplier Source			
	Supplier Source		
Category Name	Domestic	Non-US	Total
Beverages	3 25.00	9 14.06	12
Bread	0 0.00	7 10.94	7
Cheese	0 0.00	10 15.63	10
Condiments	6 50.00	6 9.38	12
Meat	0 0.00	5 7.81	5
Produce	1 8.33	4 6.25	5
Seafood	2 16.67	10 15.63	12
Sweets	0 0.00	13 20.31	13
Total	12	64	76

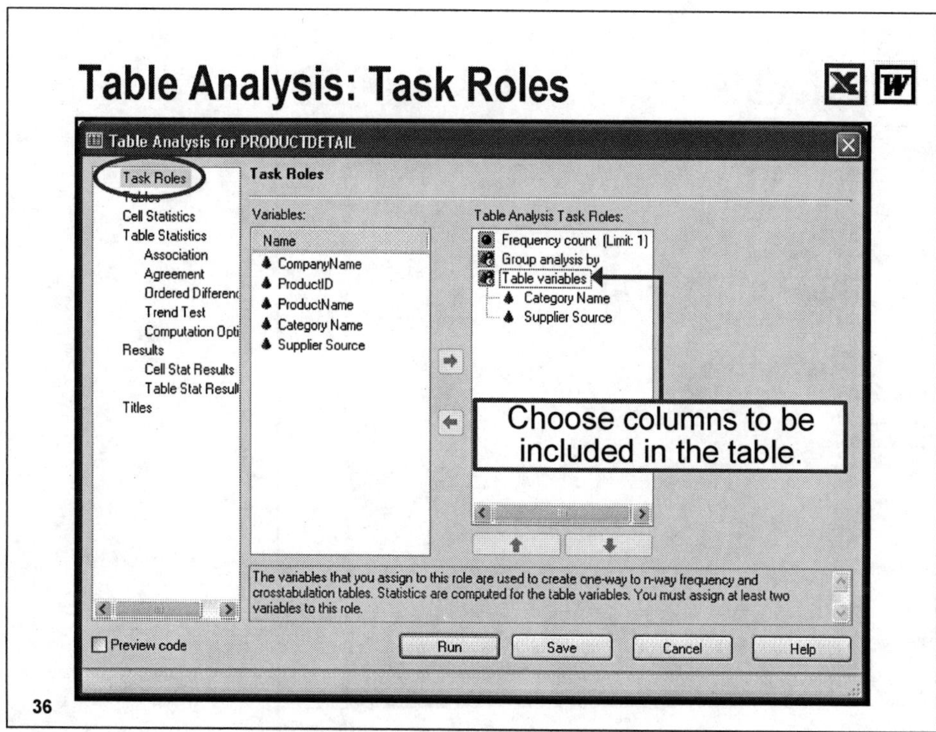

✎ Columns not placed into the Table variables role will not be available for table creation when constructing tables with the Tables option (as seen below).

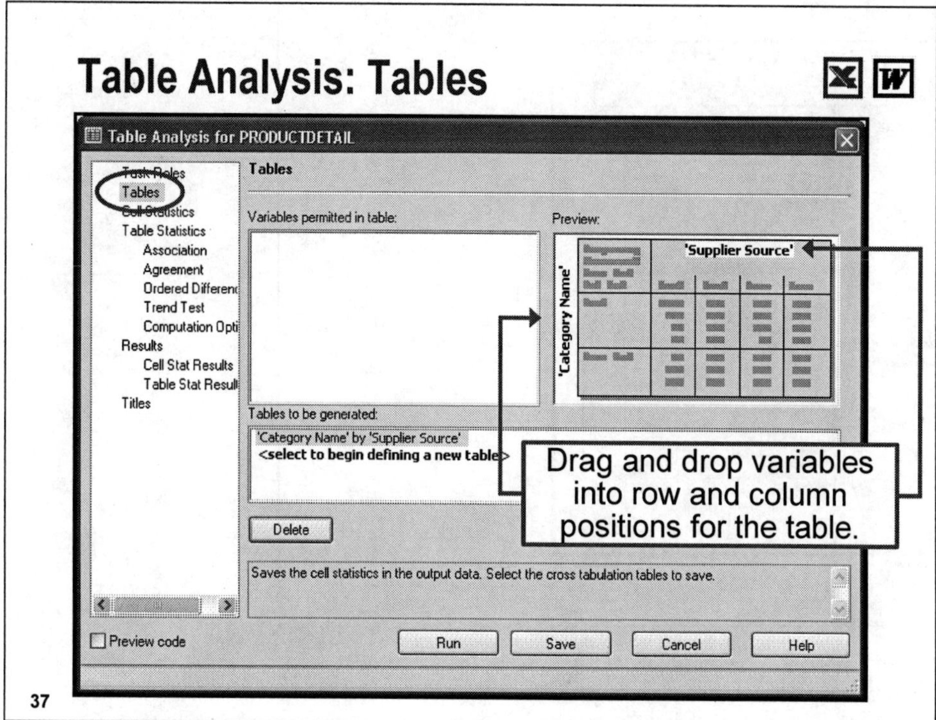

You can create multiple tables by selecting **< select to begin defining a new table >** in the Tables to be generated pane.

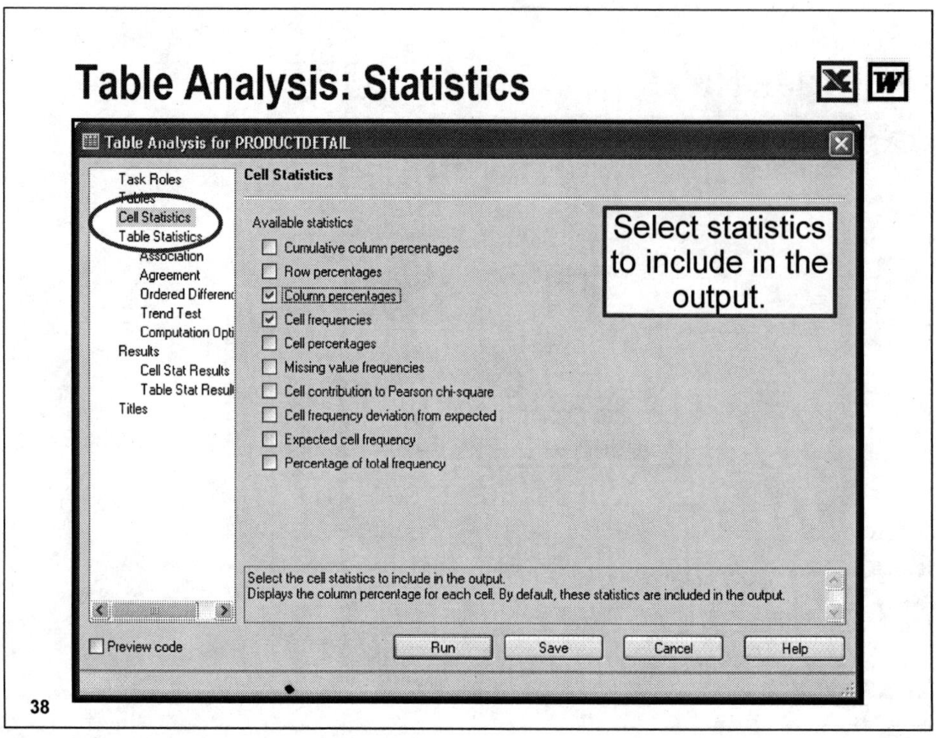

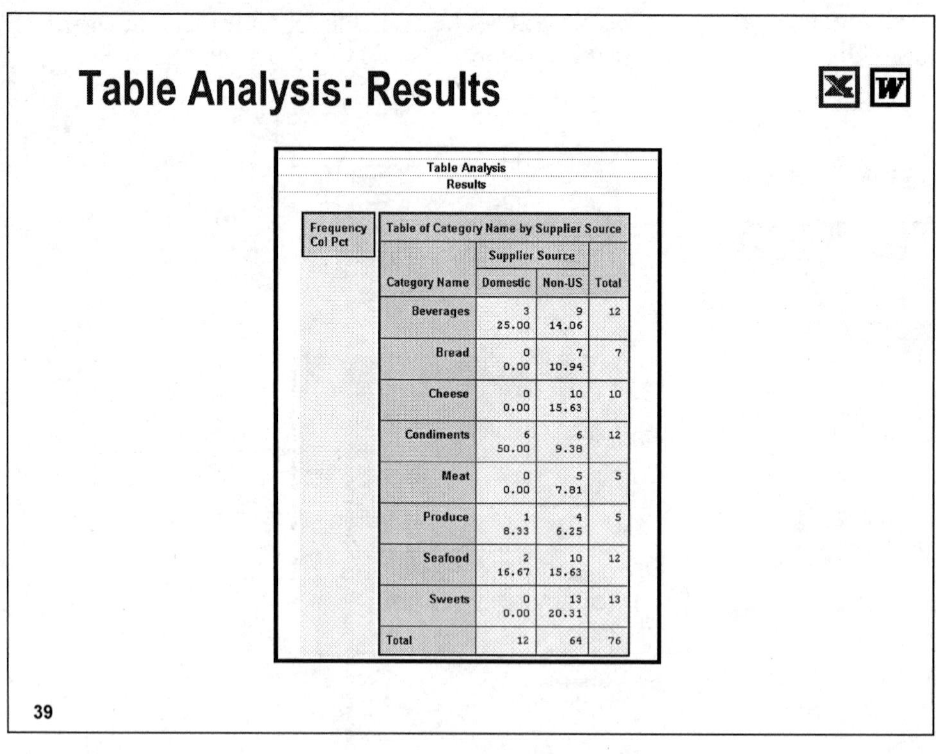

Table Analysis
Results

Frequency
Col Pct

Table of Category Name by Supplier Source

Category Name	Supplier Source: Domestic	Supplier Source: Non-US	Total
Beverages	3 25.00	9 14.06	12
Bread	0 0.00	7 10.94	7
Cheese	0 0.00	10 15.63	10
Condiments	6 50.00	6 9.38	12
Meat	0 0.00	5 7.81	5
Produce	1 8.33	4 6.25	5
Seafood	2 16.67	10 15.63	12
Sweets	0 0.00	13 20.31	13
Total	12	64	76

Creating a Two-Way Frequency Report

For this demonstration, you will

- create a two-way frequency report of `Customer Age Group` by `Customer Gender`.

Output:

Table Analysis

Results

The FREQ Procedure

Frequency Row Pct Col Pct	Table of Customer_Age_Group by Customer_Gender			
	Customer_Age_Group(Customer Age Group)	Customer_Gender(Customer Gender)		
		Female	Male	Total
	15-30 years	2487 45.22 32.07	3013 54.78 32.04	5500
	31-45 years	1867 45.56 24.08	2231 54.44 23.73	4098
	46-60 years	1793 44.23 23.12	2261 55.77 24.05	4054
	61-75 years	1607 45.85 20.72	1898 54.15 20.19	3505
	Total	7754	9403	17157

MDMT.MDM_OrderFact | Table Analysis | MDM Salary Listing

Setting the Active Data Source in Excel

1. Return to the `MDMT.MDM_OrderFact` worksheet tab in Excel.
2. Using the pull-down menu on the Active Data selection box, select **Select SAS Data Source…** from the SAS Analysis Tools toolbar (or select **SAS** ⇨ **Active Data** ⇨ **Select SAS Data Source…**).

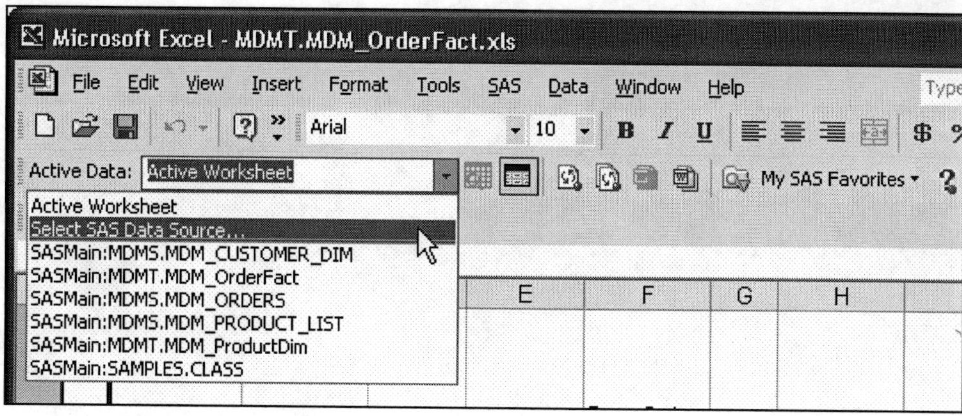

3. In the Open SAS Data Source window, select **Servers** from the shortcut bar. Then, choose **SASMain** and select Open.

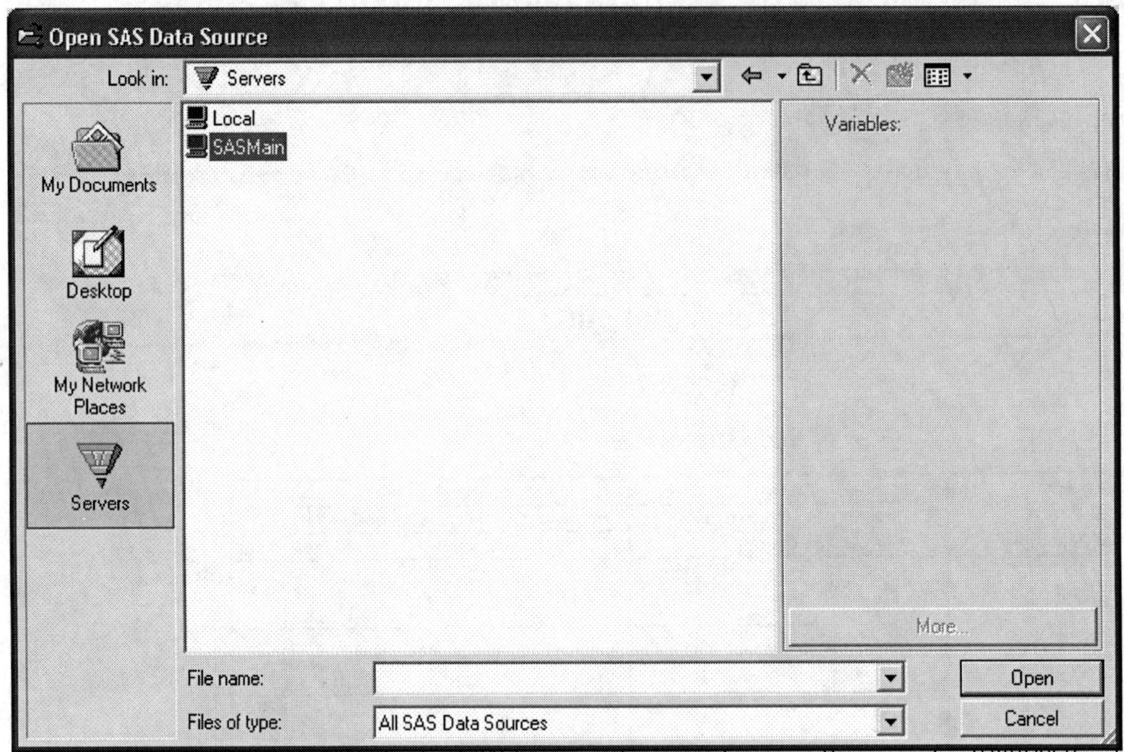

You can access data local to your machine or through a SAS server.

a. Choose **MDM Source Tables Library** and select Open.

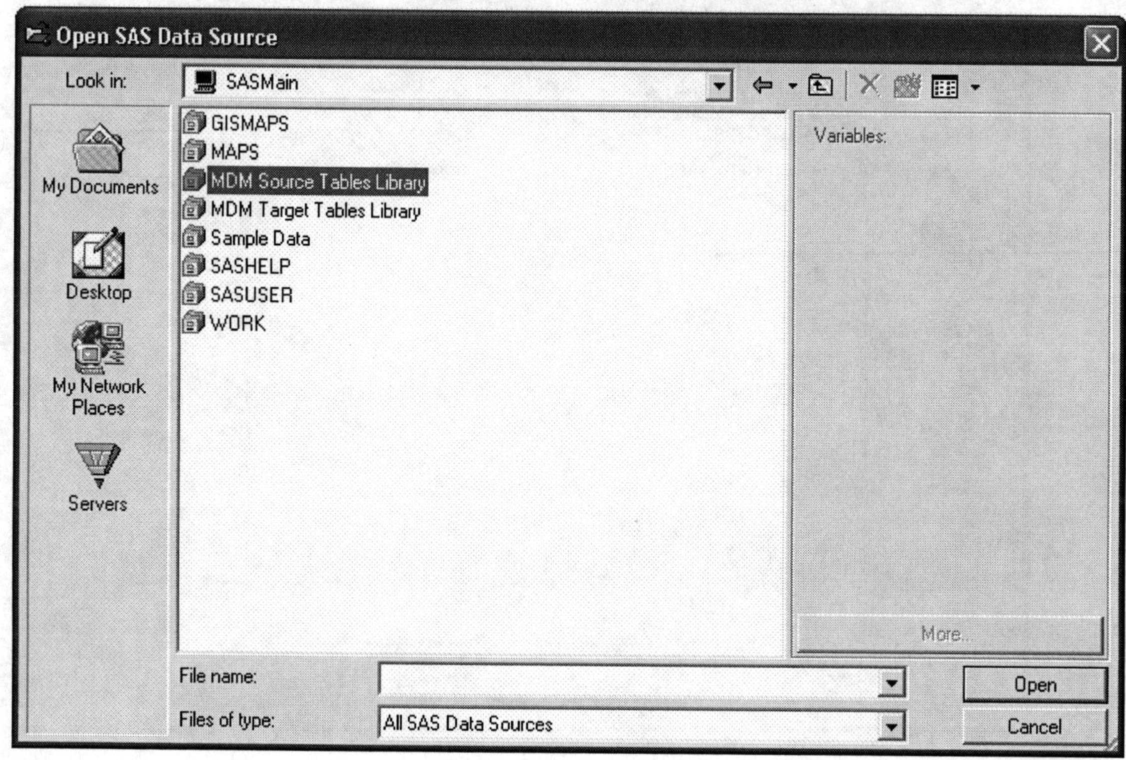

b. Select the **MDM_CUSTOMER_DIM** table and then choose Open.

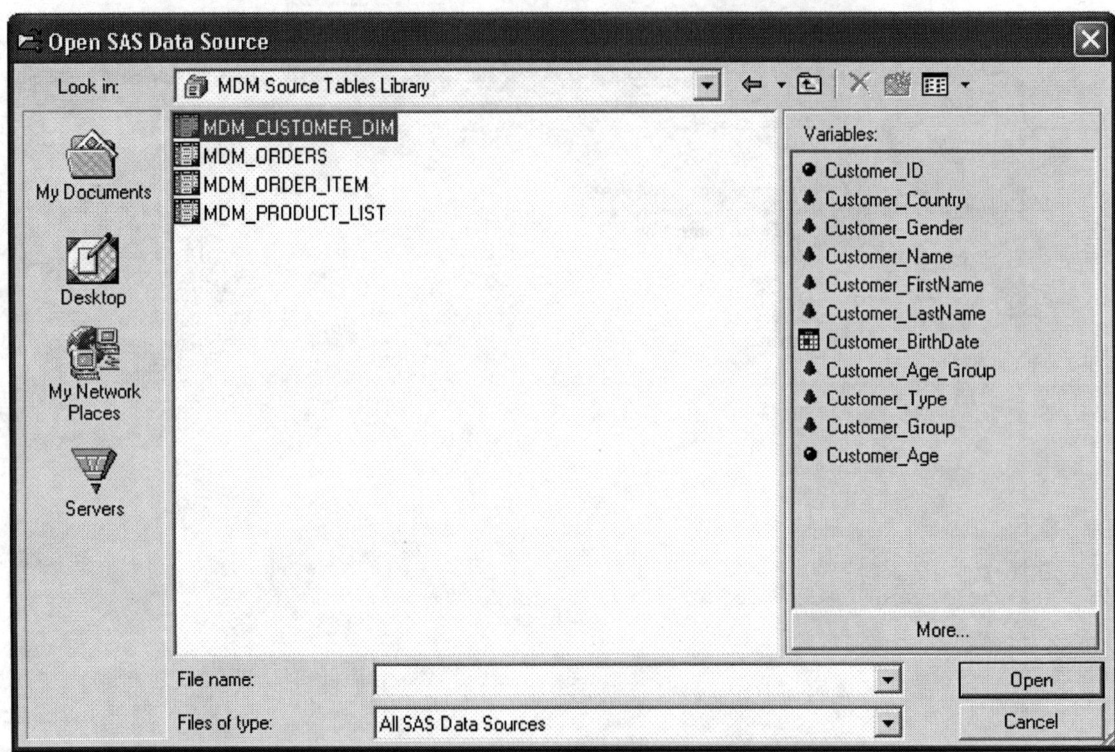

If you cannot read the entire name of a table, use the View Mode icon on the toolbar to change the view to Detail or List. You may deselect any columns that you choose not to include from the data source.

The SAS table is now the active data source in Microsoft Excel.

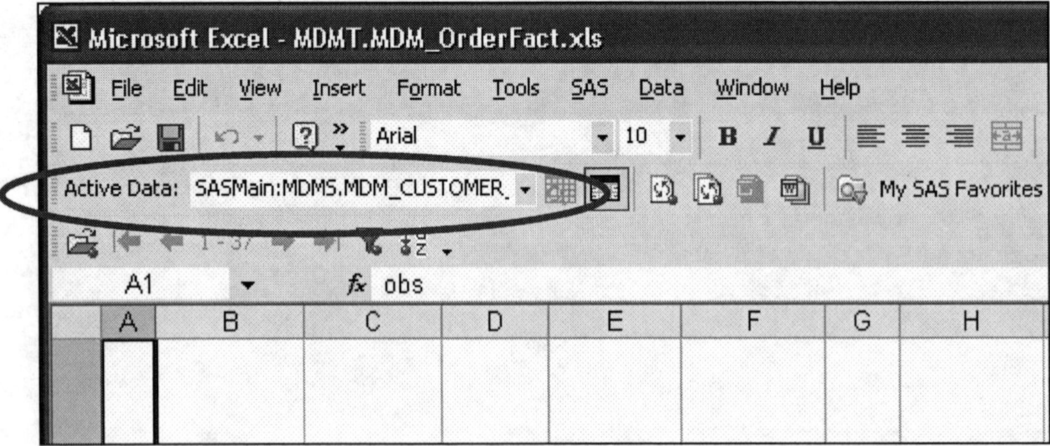

Adding a Task to Favorites

1. Select [icon] on the SAS Analysis Tools toolbar (or select **SAS** ⇨ **Browse SAS Programs** from the pull-down menus).

   a. If not already expanded, in the left pane of the Browse SAS Programs window select [+] beside **SAS Tasks** to expand the folder listing.

   b. Select **Describe** in the left pane to see a listing of the available tasks.

   c. Right-click **Table Analysis** ⇨ **Add to Favorites Folder…**.

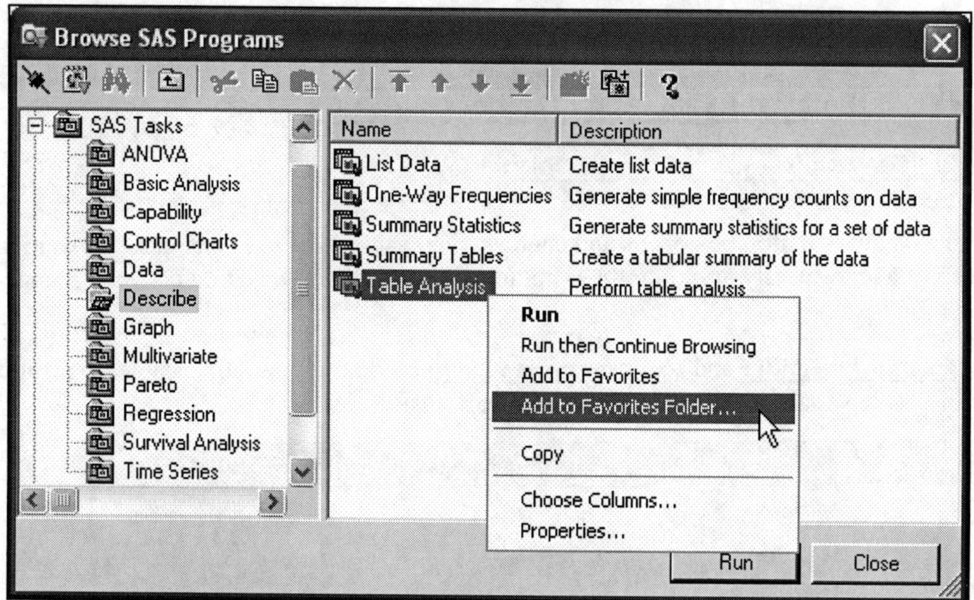

   d. Select **For AMO Class**, then [OK].

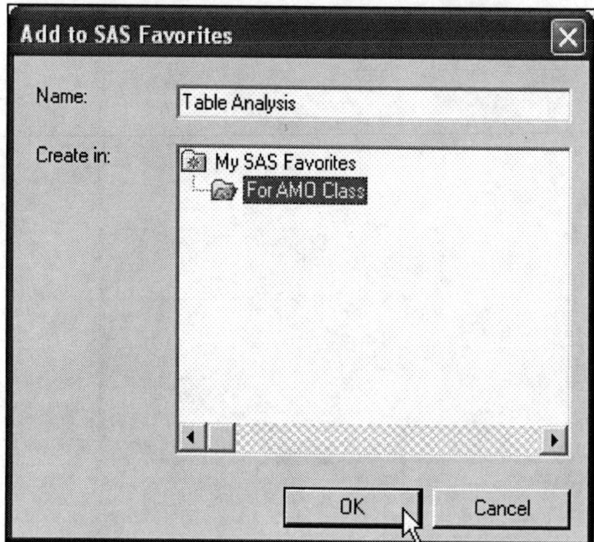

   e. Select [Close] to exit the Browse SAS Programs dialog box.

Running a Table Analysis Task

1. Open the Table Analysis task.

   a. Select **My SAS Favorites** ⇨ **For AMO Class** ⇨ **Table Analysis** from the SAS Analysis Tools toolbar.

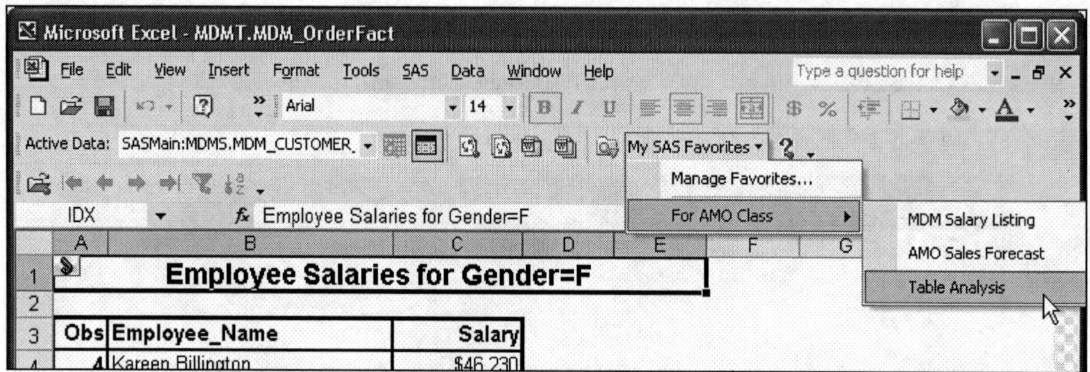

A Table Analysis dialog box opens and enables you to select the columns that you want to see in the report and to specify a role for those columns. In this dialog box, you can also change output formatting options.

2. Drag the **Customer Gender** and **Customer Age Group** columns from the Variables pane and drop them on the Table variables role in the Table Analysis Task Roles pane.

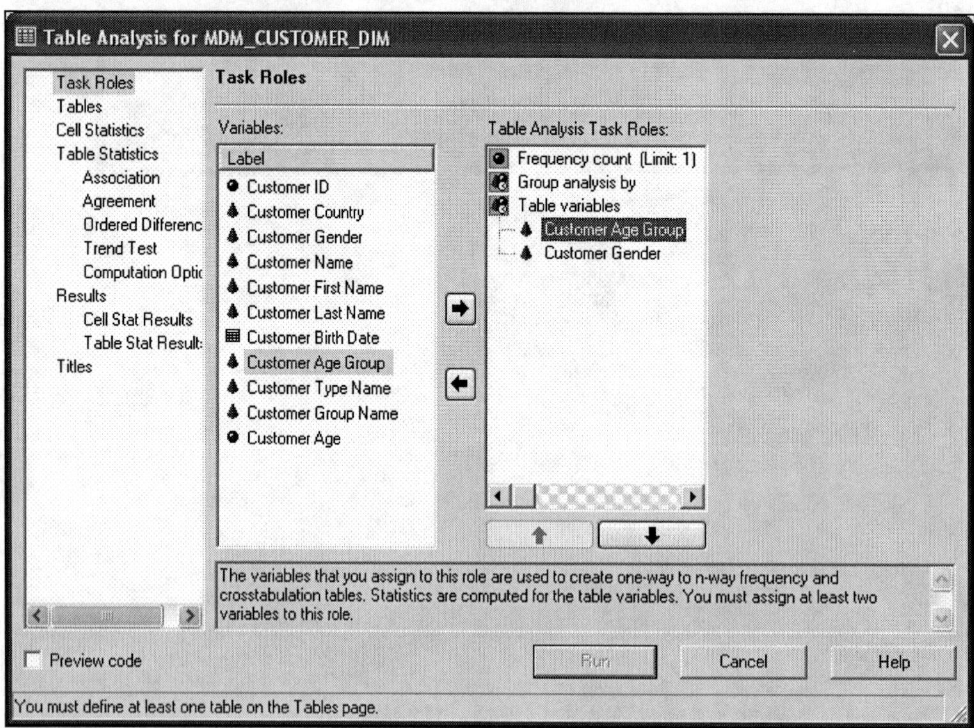

3. Select **Tables** in the Selection pane to define the structure of the table. Drag the **Customer Gender** column from the Variables permitted in table pane and drop it on <drag variables here> in the Preview pane. Drag the **Customer Age Group** column from the Variables permitted in table pane and drop it on the center of the table in the Preview pane.

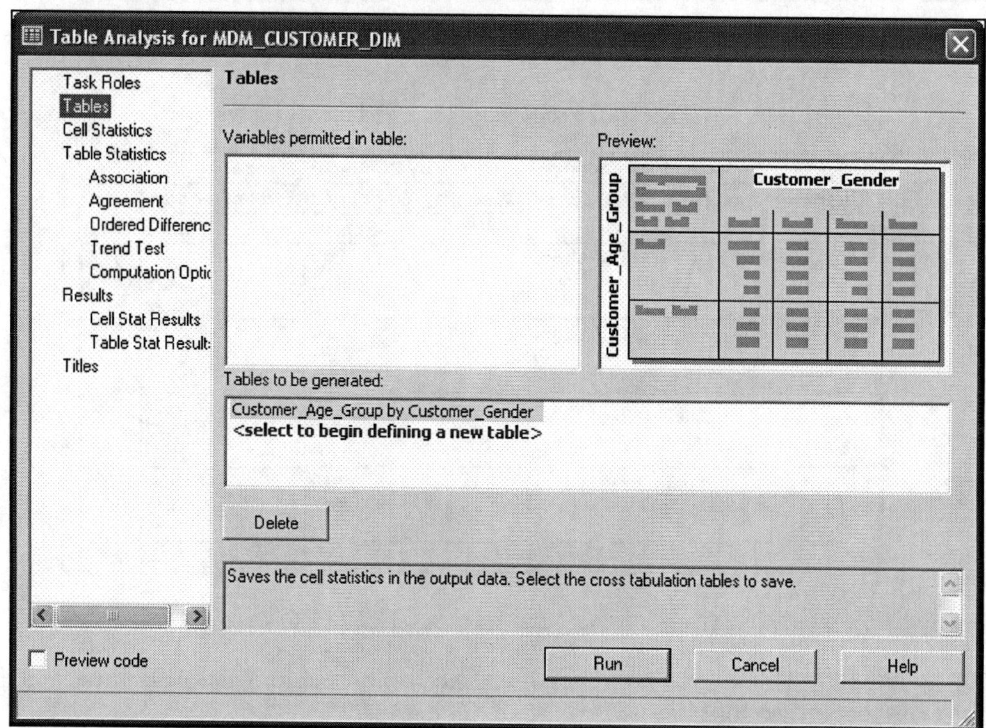

4. Select **Cell Statistics** in the Selection pane. Select the **Row percentages** check box.

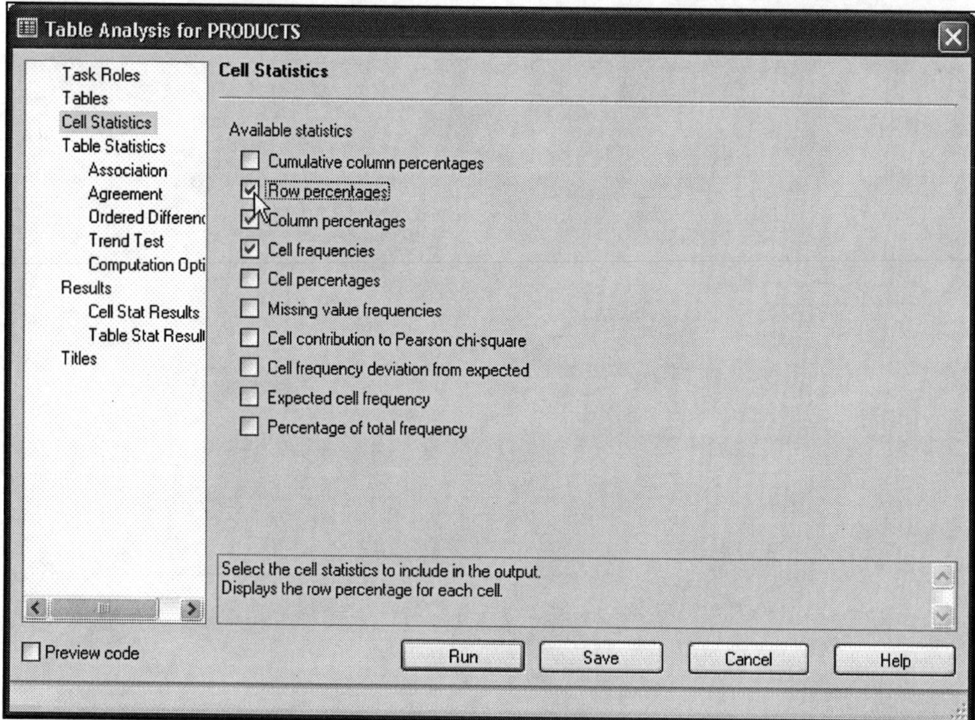

5. Select Run to generate the report.

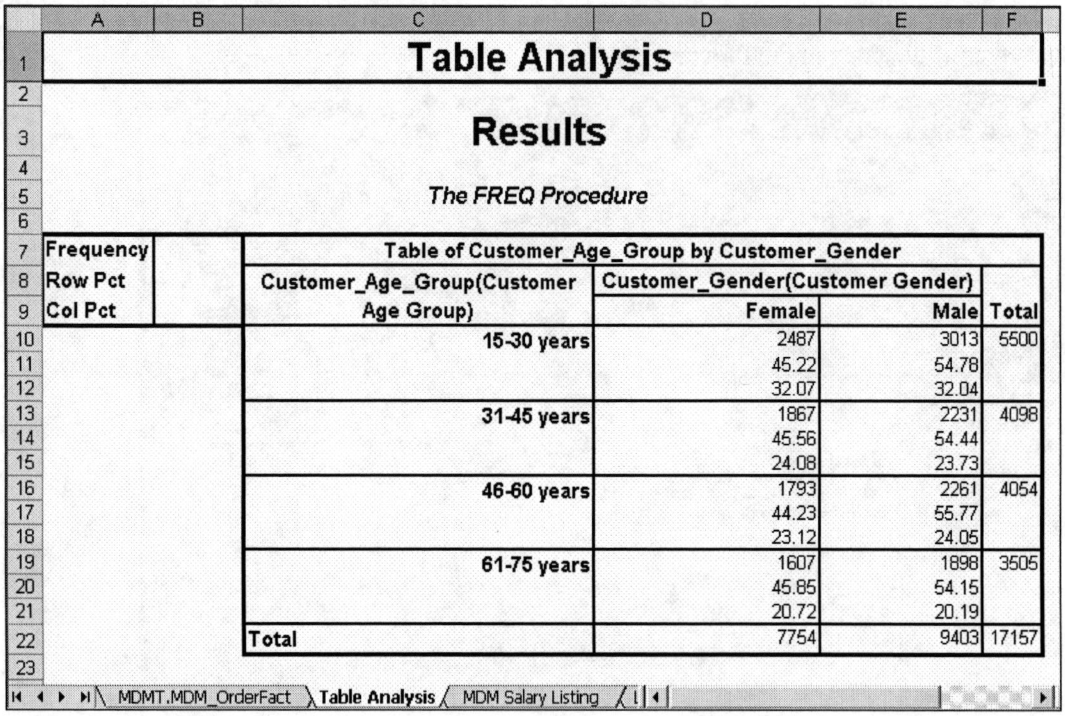

Table Analysis

Results

The FREQ Procedure

Frequency Row Pct Col Pct	Table of Customer_Age_Group by Customer_Gender			
	Customer_Age_Group(Customer Age Group)	Customer_Gender(Customer Gender)		
		Female	Male	Total
	15-30 years	2487 45.22 32.07	3013 54.78 32.04	5500
	31-45 years	1867 45.56 24.08	2231 54.44 23.73	4098
	46-60 years	1793 44.23 23.12	2261 55.77 24.05	4054
	61-75 years	1607 45.85 20.72	1898 54.15 20.19	3505
	Total	7754	9403	17157

MDMT.MDM_OrderFact | Table Analysis | MDM Salary Listing

The procedure title appears because the SAS options that are set for Microsoft Excel and the SAS options that are set for Microsoft Word are independent.

5.6 Summary Table Task

Objectives

- Access the Summary Tables task.
- Create a table of average and total cost and sales for the Orion companies.

42

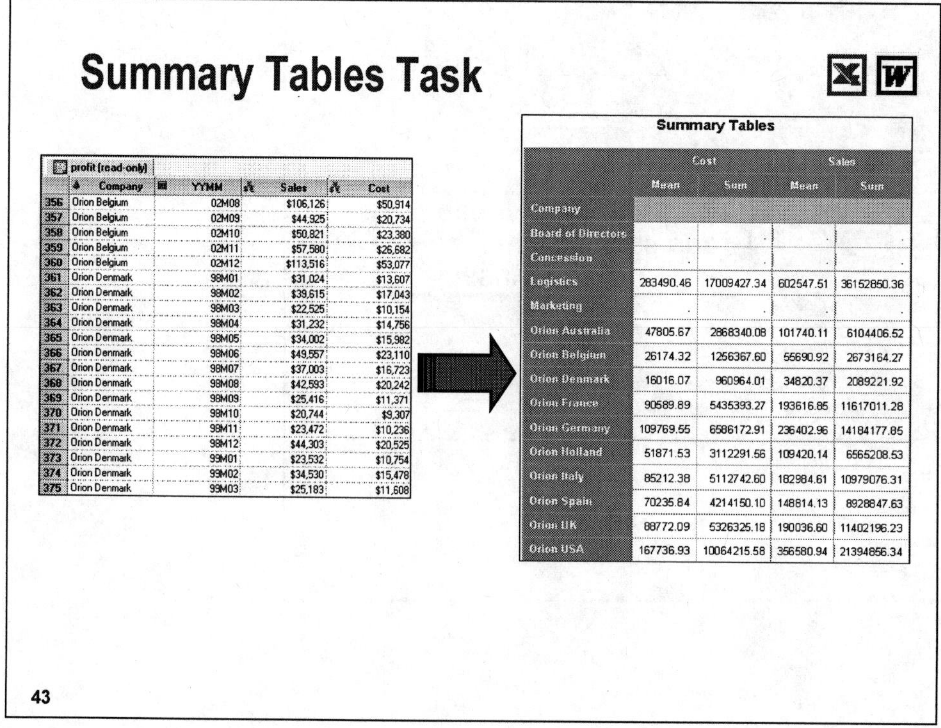

	Company	YYMM	Sales	Cost
356	Orion Belgium	02M08	$106,126	$50,914
357	Orion Belgium	02M09	$44,925	$20,734
358	Orion Belgium	02M10	$50,821	$23,380
359	Orion Belgium	02M11	$57,580	$26,682
360	Orion Belgium	02M12	$113,516	$53,077
361	Orion Denmark	98M01	$31,024	$13,607
362	Orion Denmark	98M02	$39,615	$17,043
363	Orion Denmark	98M03	$22,525	$10,154
364	Orion Denmark	98M04	$31,232	$14,756
365	Orion Denmark	98M05	$34,002	$15,982
366	Orion Denmark	98M06	$49,557	$23,110
367	Orion Denmark	98M07	$37,003	$16,723
368	Orion Denmark	98M08	$42,593	$20,242
369	Orion Denmark	98M09	$25,416	$11,371
370	Orion Denmark	98M10	$20,744	$9,307
371	Orion Denmark	98M11	$23,472	$10,236
372	Orion Denmark	98M12	$44,303	$20,525
373	Orion Denmark	99M01	$23,532	$10,754
374	Orion Denmark	99M02	$34,530	$15,478
375	Orion Denmark	99M03	$25,183	$11,608

Summary Tables

	Cost		Sales	
	Mean	Sum	Mean	Sum
Company				
Board of Directors	.	.	.	.
Concession	.	.	.	.
Logistics	283490.46	17009427.34	602547.51	36152850.36
Marketing	.	.	.	.
Orion Australia	47805.67	2868340.08	101740.11	6104406.52
Orion Belgium	26174.32	1256367.60	55690.92	2673164.27
Orion Denmark	16016.07	960964.01	34820.37	2089221.92
Orion France	90589.89	5435393.27	193616.85	11617011.28
Orion Germany	109769.55	6586172.91	236402.96	14184177.85
Orion Holland	51871.53	3112291.56	109420.14	6565208.53
Orion Italy	85212.38	5112742.60	182984.61	10979076.31
Orion Spain	70235.84	4214150.10	148814.13	8928847.63
Orion UK	88772.09	5326325.18	190036.60	11402196.23
Orion USA	167736.93	10064215.58	356580.94	21394856.34

To access the Summary Tables task, select **Describe** ⇨ **Summary Tables** from the Browse SAS Programs dialog box.

Summary Tables: Task Roles

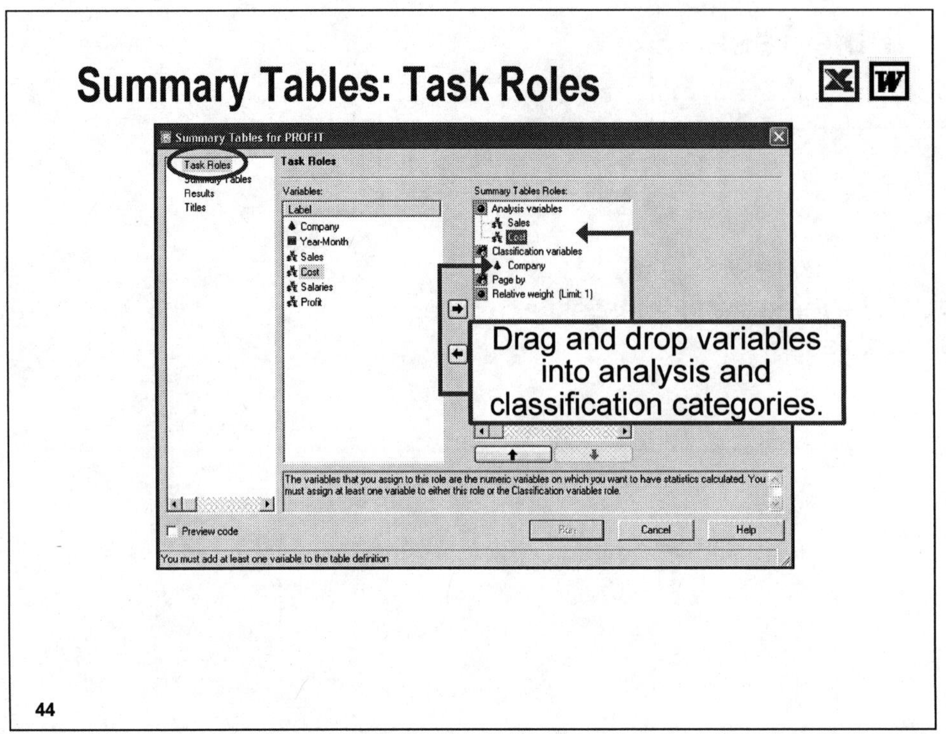

44

Summary Tables: Summary Tables

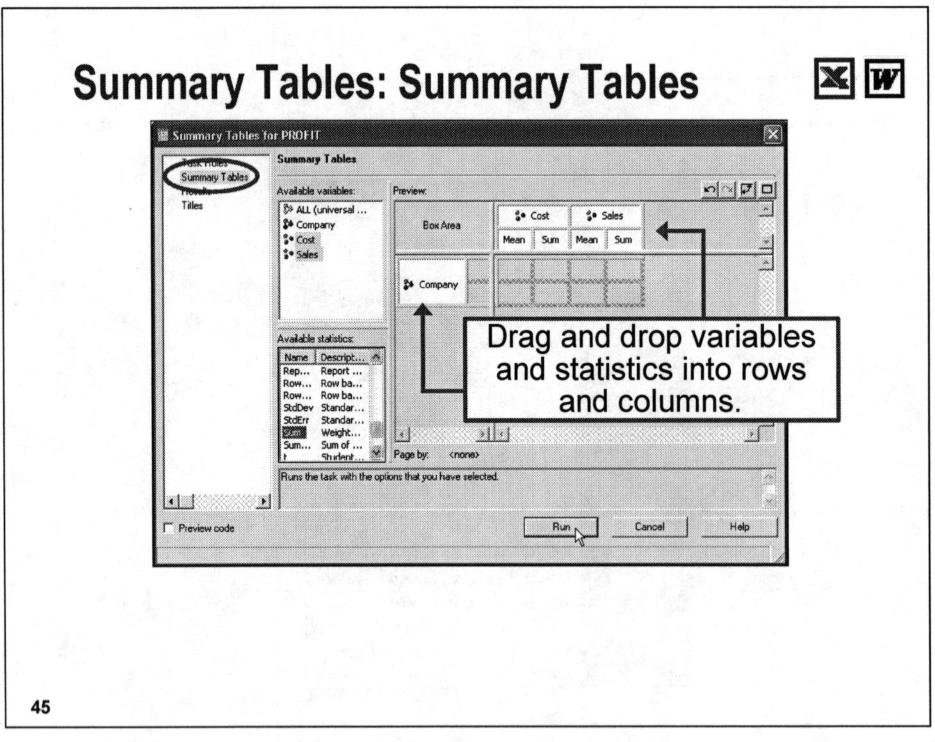

45

Summary Tables: Results

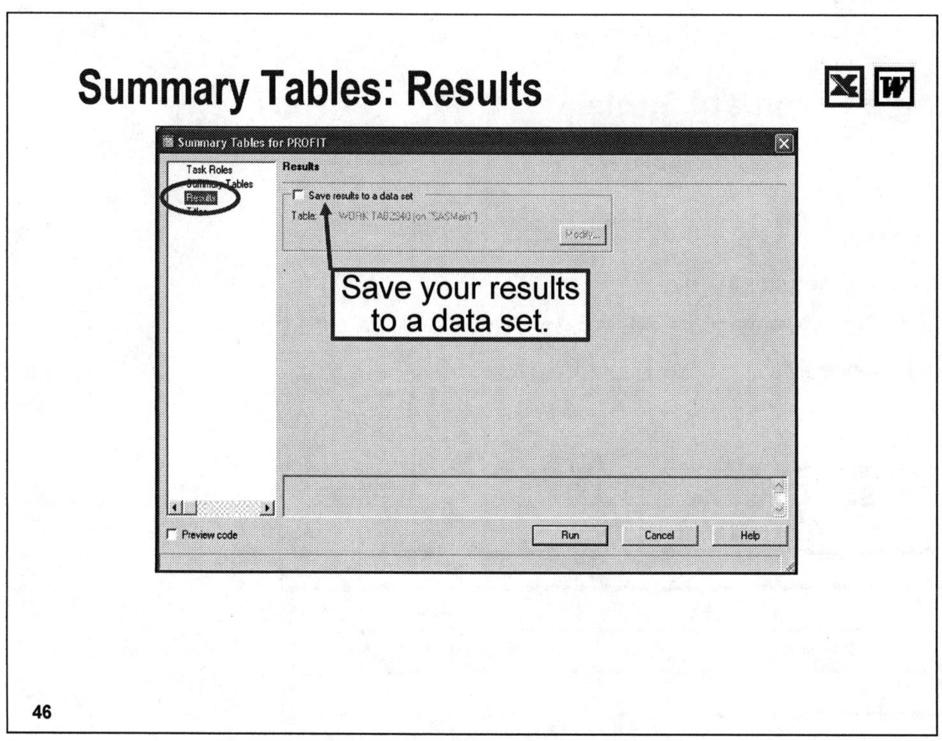

46

Creating a Summary Table

For this demonstration, you will

- filter data to subset only the Orion companies
- create a summary report of the average and total costs and sales
- add formats, labels, and change fonts.

Output:

	A	B	C	D	E
1	Summary Tables				
2					
3		Cost		Sales	
4		Average	Total	Average	Total
5	Company				
6	Orion Australia	$47,806	$2,868,340	$101,740	$6,104,407
7	Orion Belgium	$26,174	$1,256,368	$55,691	$2,673,164
8	Orion Denmark	$16,016	$960,964	$34,820	$2,089,222
9	Orion France	$90,590	$5,435,393	$193,617	$11,617,011
10	Orion Germany	$109,770	$6,586,173	$236,403	$14,184,178
11	Orion Holland	$51,872	$3,112,292	$109,420	$6,565,209
12	Orion Italy	$85,212	$5,112,743	$182,985	$10,979,076
13	Orion Spain	$70,236	$4,214,150	$148,814	$8,928,848
14	Orion UK	$88,772	$5,326,325	$190,037	$11,402,196
15	Orion USA	$167,737	$10,064,216	$356,581	$21,394,856

Accessing SAS Data in Excel

1. Return to Microsoft Excel. (If it is closed, invoke the Excel program by selecting **Start** ⇨ **Programs** ⇨ **Microsoft Office** ⇨ **Microsoft Excel**.

2. Select **Active Data** ⇨ **Active Worksheet**.

   Active Data: Active Worksheet

3. Select **SAS** ⇨ **Open SAS Data Source** from the pull-down menus, or select on the SAS Data Analysis toolbar.

4. In the Open SAS Data Source window, select **Servers** ⇨ **SASMain** and select Open.

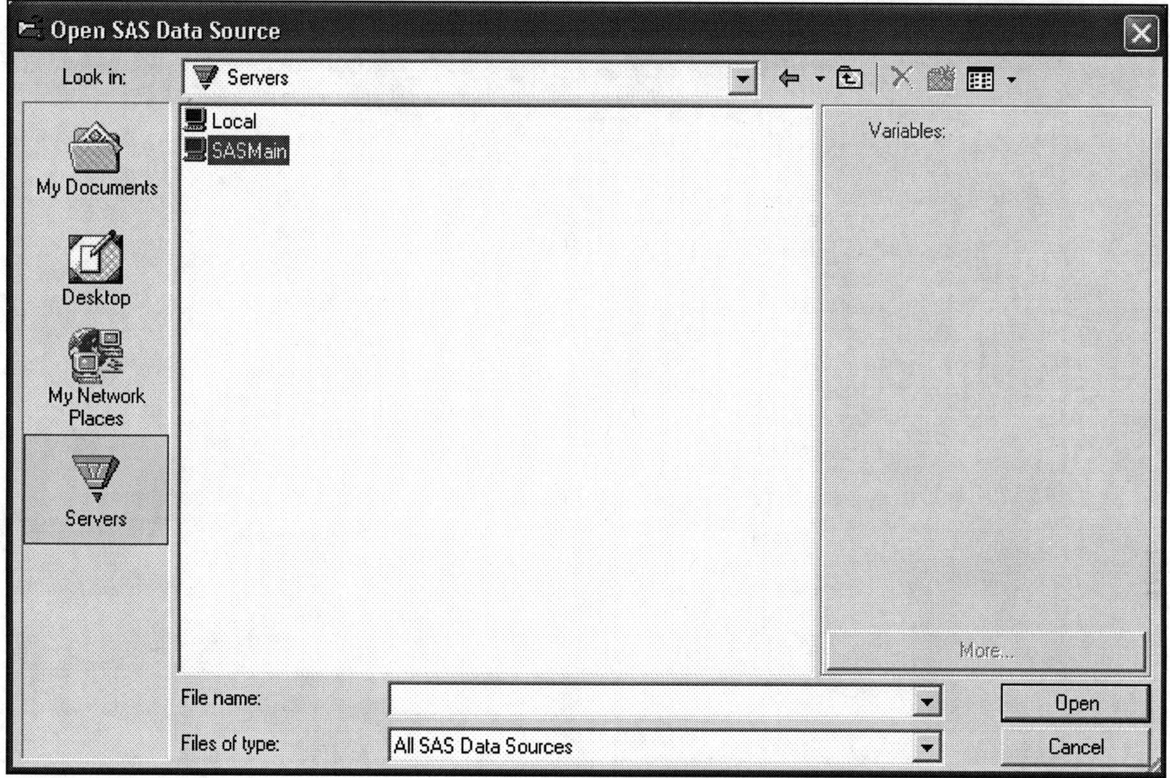

a. Choose **AMO Orsum Data** and select Open.

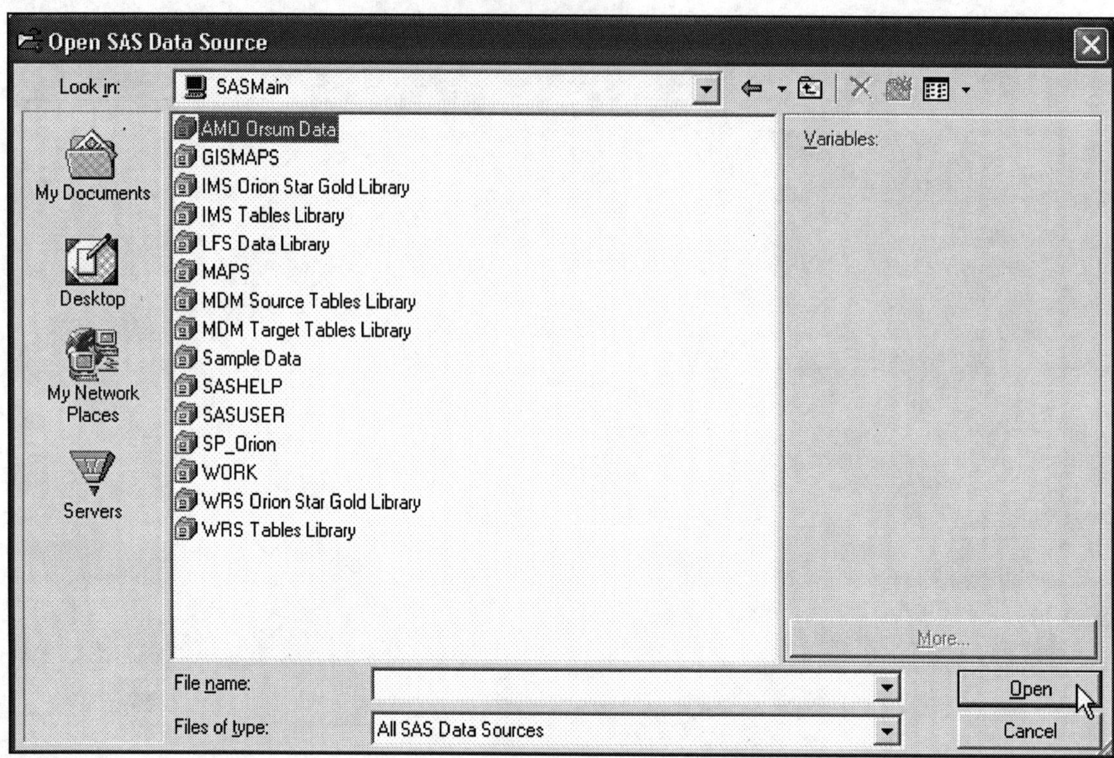

b. Select the PROFIT table and then select Open.

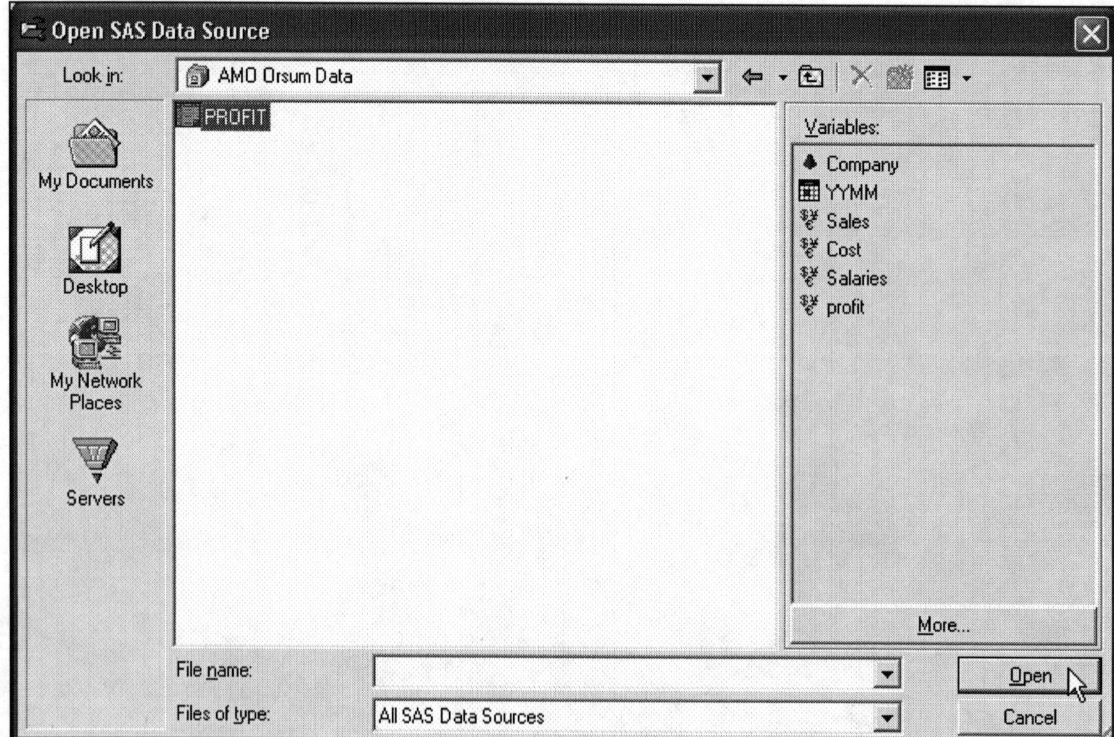

Filtering SAS Data in Excel

1. Filter the data to display only the Orion companies.

   a. Select [filter icon] on the SAS Data Analysis toolbar (or select **SAS** ⇨ **Filter SAS Data Source**).

   b. Build the filter to subset the Orion companies.

      1) Select [▼] in the first box and select **`Company`**.

      2) Select [▼] in the second box and scroll down to specify the filter criterion **Contains**.

      3) Type **`Orion`** in the third box and select [OK].

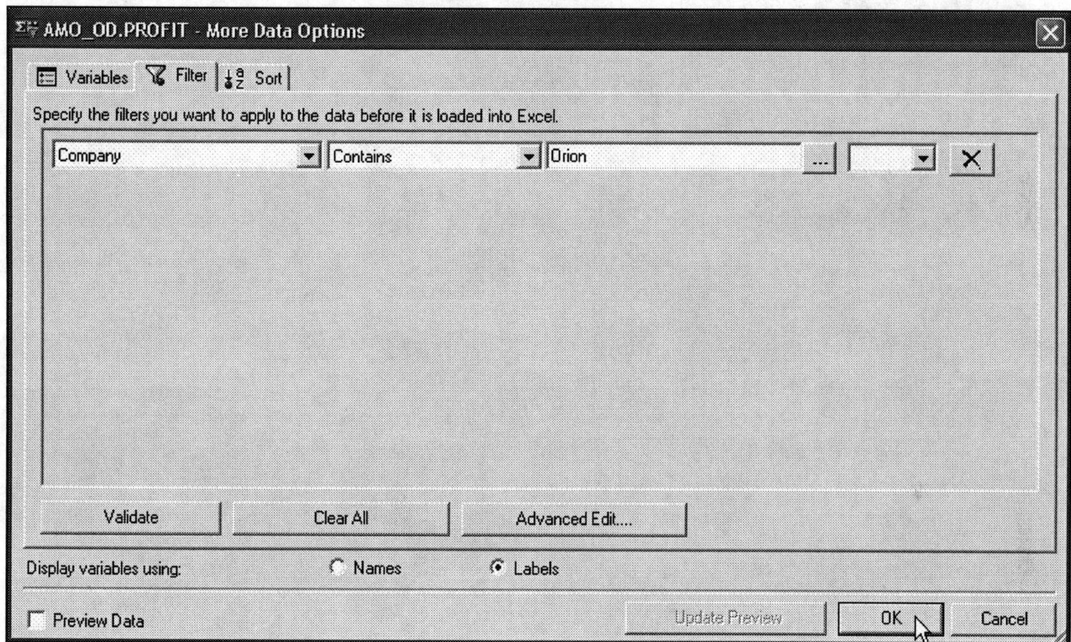

2. The data is filtered on the SAS Workspace Server and returned to Excel. The original data contained 960 rows. The worksheet now displays the 600 rows that match the filter criterion.

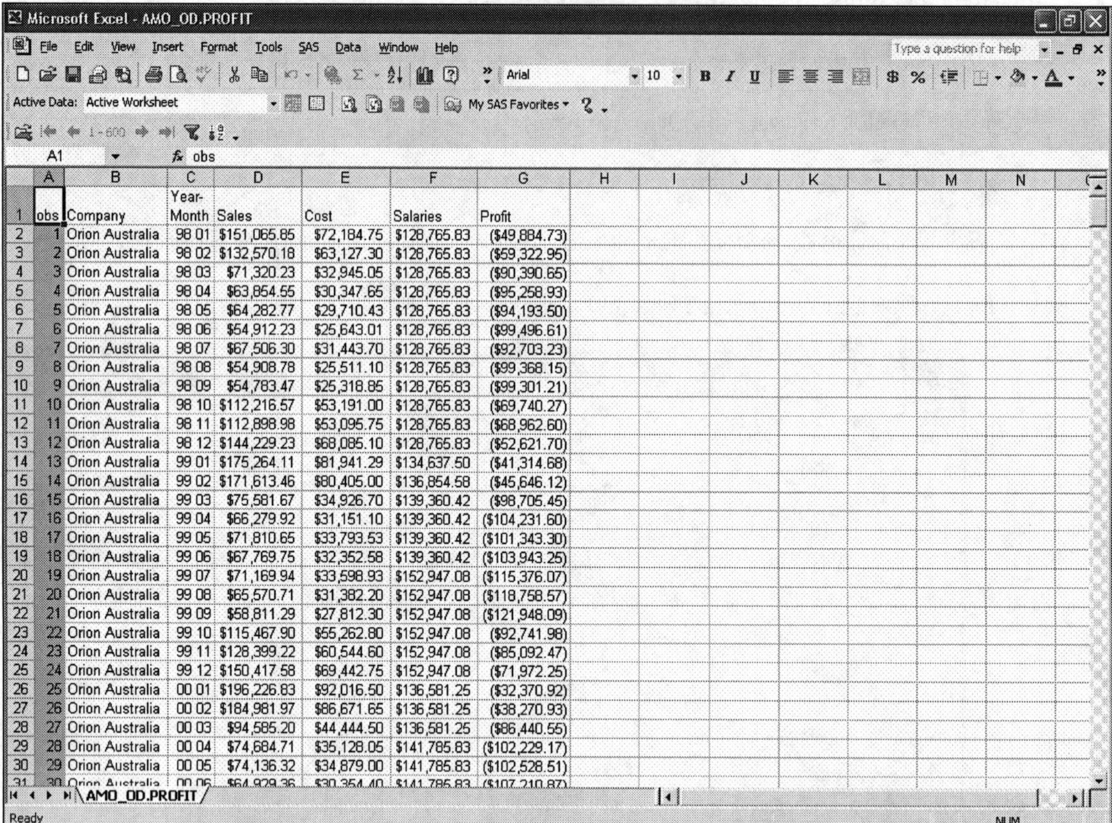

obs	Company	Year-Month	Sales	Cost	Salaries	Profit
1	Orion Australia	98 01	$151,065.85	$72,184.75	$128,765.83	($49,884.73)
2	Orion Australia	98 02	$132,570.18	$63,127.30	$128,765.83	($59,322.95)
3	Orion Australia	98 03	$71,320.23	$32,945.05	$128,765.83	($90,390.65)
4	Orion Australia	98 04	$63,854.55	$30,347.65	$128,765.83	($95,258.93)
5	Orion Australia	98 05	$64,282.77	$29,710.43	$128,765.83	($94,193.50)
6	Orion Australia	98 06	$54,912.23	$25,643.01	$128,765.83	($99,496.61)
7	Orion Australia	98 07	$67,506.30	$31,443.70	$128,765.83	($92,703.23)
8	Orion Australia	98 08	$54,908.78	$25,511.10	$128,765.83	($99,368.15)
9	Orion Australia	98 09	$54,783.47	$25,318.85	$128,765.83	($99,301.21)
10	Orion Australia	98 10	$112,216.57	$53,191.00	$128,765.83	($69,740.27)
11	Orion Australia	98 11	$112,898.98	$53,095.75	$128,765.83	($68,962.60)
12	Orion Australia	98 12	$144,229.23	$68,085.10	$128,765.83	($52,621.70)
13	Orion Australia	99 01	$175,264.11	$81,941.29	$134,637.50	($41,314.68)
14	Orion Australia	99 02	$171,613.46	$80,405.00	$136,854.58	($45,646.12)
15	Orion Australia	99 03	$75,581.67	$34,926.70	$139,360.42	($98,705.45)
16	Orion Australia	99 04	$66,279.92	$31,151.10	$139,360.42	($104,231.60)
17	Orion Australia	99 05	$71,810.65	$33,793.53	$139,360.42	($101,343.30)
18	Orion Australia	99 06	$67,769.75	$32,352.58	$139,360.42	($103,943.25)
19	Orion Australia	99 07	$71,169.94	$33,598.93	$152,947.08	($115,376.07)
20	Orion Australia	99 08	$65,570.71	$31,382.20	$152,947.08	($118,758.57)
21	Orion Australia	99 09	$58,811.29	$27,812.30	$152,947.08	($121,948.09)
22	Orion Australia	99 10	$115,467.90	$55,262.80	$152,947.08	($92,741.98)
23	Orion Australia	99 11	$128,399.22	$60,544.60	$152,947.08	($85,092.47)
24	Orion Australia	99 12	$150,417.58	$69,442.75	$152,947.08	($71,972.25)
25	Orion Australia	00 01	$196,226.83	$92,016.50	$136,581.25	($32,370.92)
26	Orion Australia	00 02	$184,981.97	$86,671.65	$136,581.25	($38,270.93)
27	Orion Australia	00 03	$94,585.20	$44,444.50	$136,581.25	($86,440.55)
28	Orion Australia	00 04	$74,684.71	$35,128.05	$141,785.83	($102,229.17)
29	Orion Australia	00 05	$74,136.32	$34,879.00	$141,785.83	($102,528.51)
30	Orion Australia	00 06	$64,929.36	$30,354.40	$141,785.83	($107,210.87)

Running a Summary Tables Task

1. Open the Summary Tables task to create a table of sales and costs.

   a. Select [icon] on the SAS Analysis Tools toolbar (or select **SAS** ⇨ **Browse SAS Programs**).

   b. Expand the group **SAS Tasks** and select the folder **Describe** ⇨ **Summary Tables**. Then select Run.

2. Drag the `Company` column from the Variables pan and drop it on the Classification variables role in the Role pane. Drag the `Sales` and `Cost` columns and drop them on the Analysis variables role.

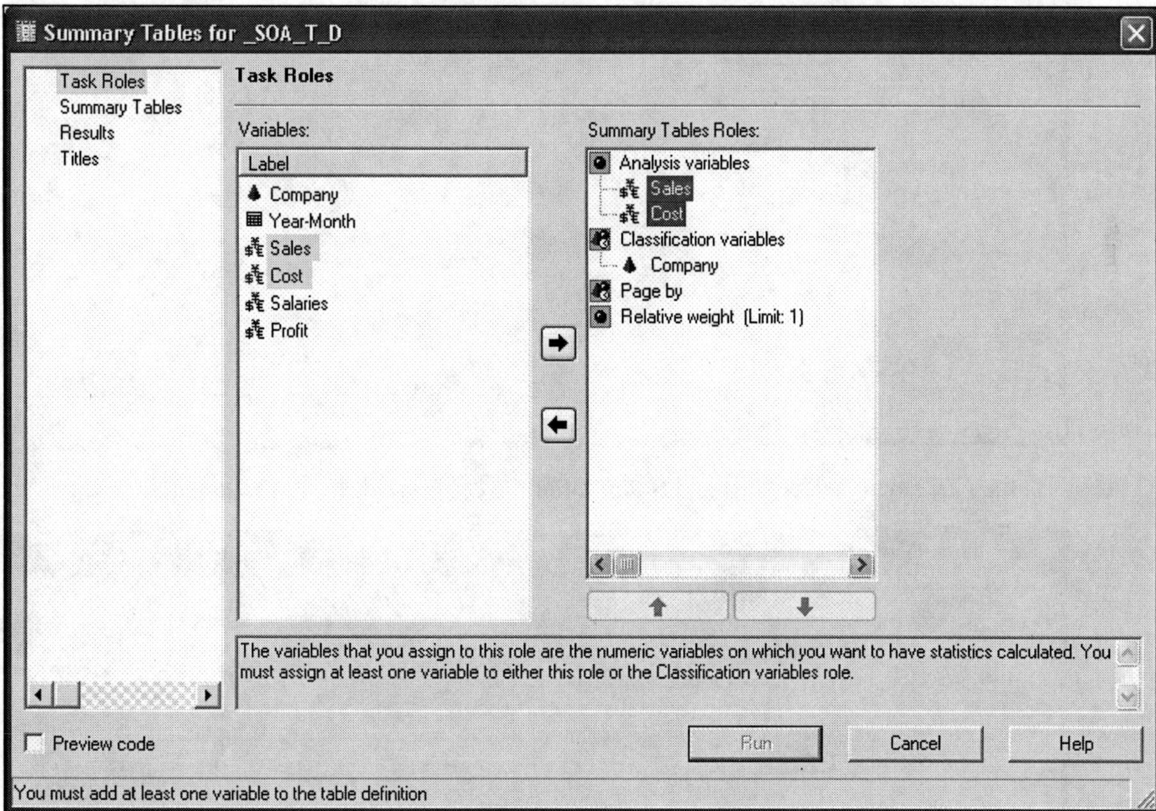

3. Select **Summary Tables** in the Selection pane.

a. Drag the **Company** column into the row under the Box Area.

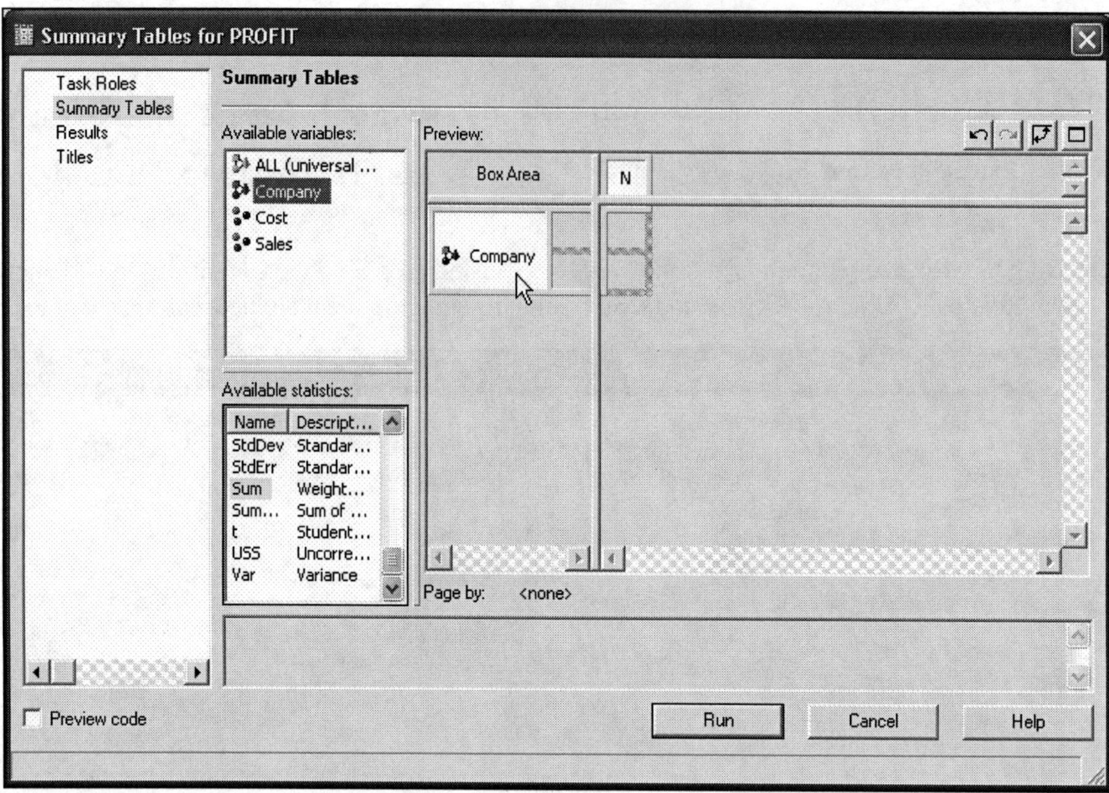

b. Use the Ctrl key to select **Cost** and **Sales**. Drag the columns above the N statistic.

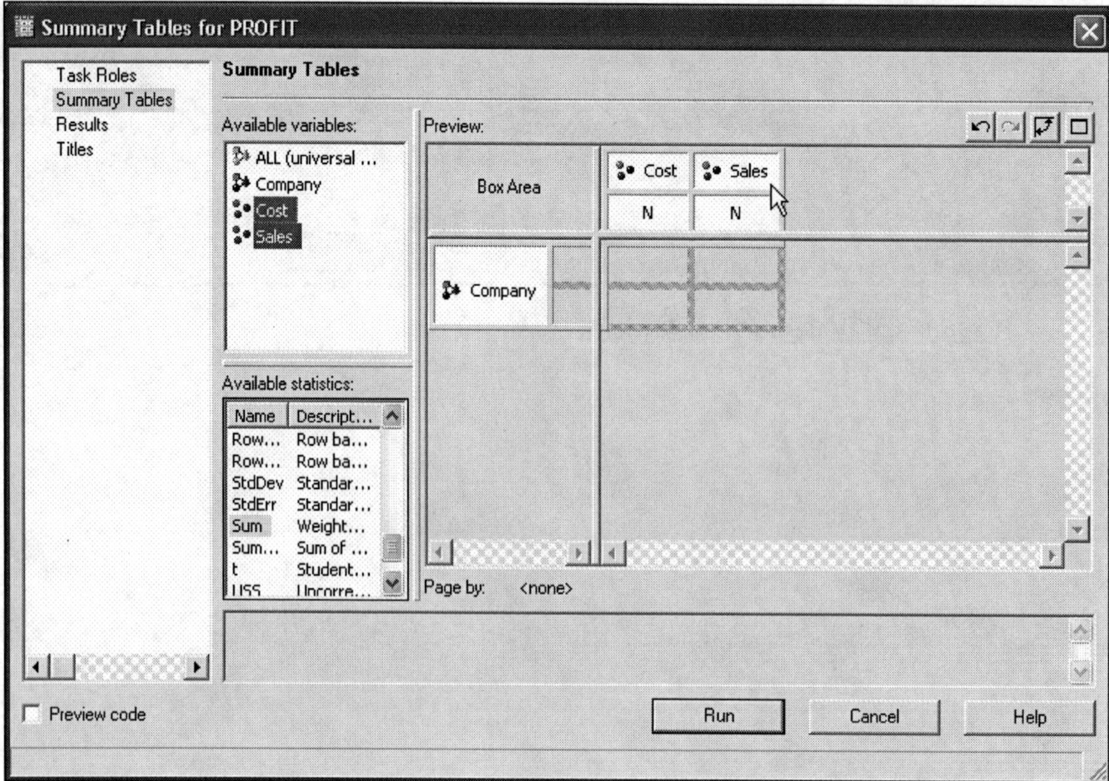

c. Use the Ctrl key to select **Mean** and **Sum** under the Available statistics pane and drag them directly on top of the N statistic to replace the N statistic under `Cost`. Repeat for `Sales`.

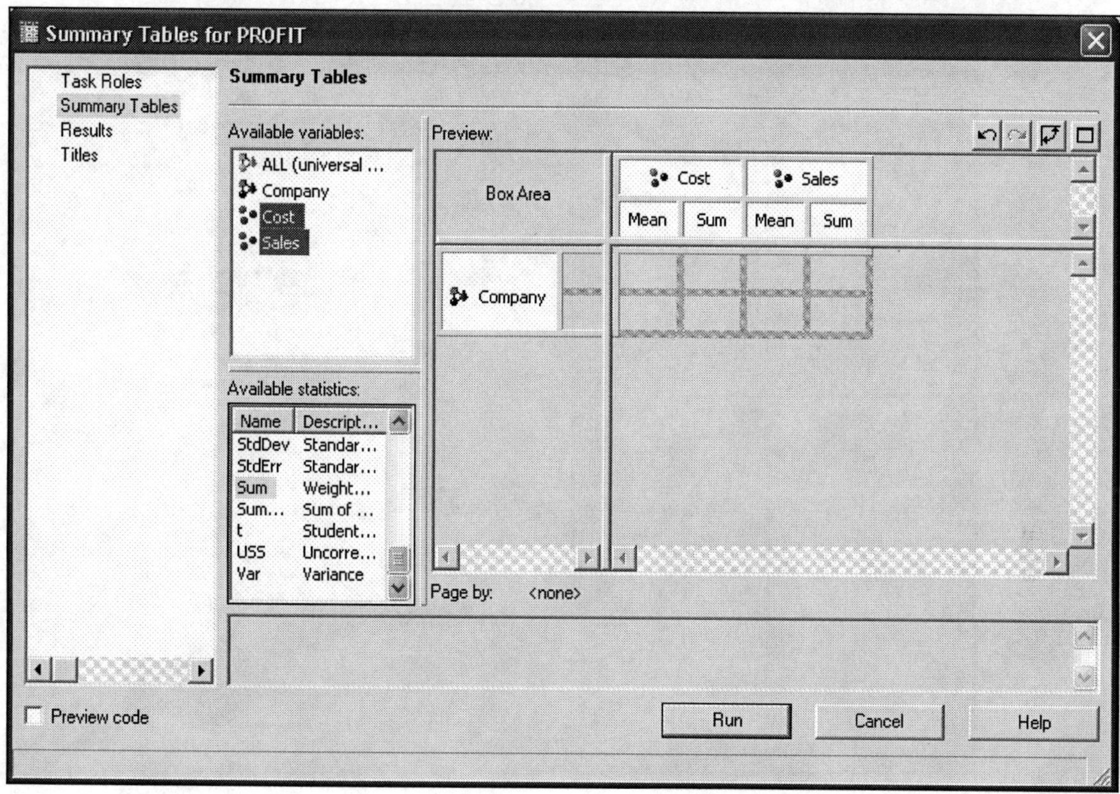

To remove an unwanted column, you can right-click the column name, then select **Remove Cells**.

d. Format the Sum and Mean statistics as currency.

1) Right-click the table and select **Table Properties…**.

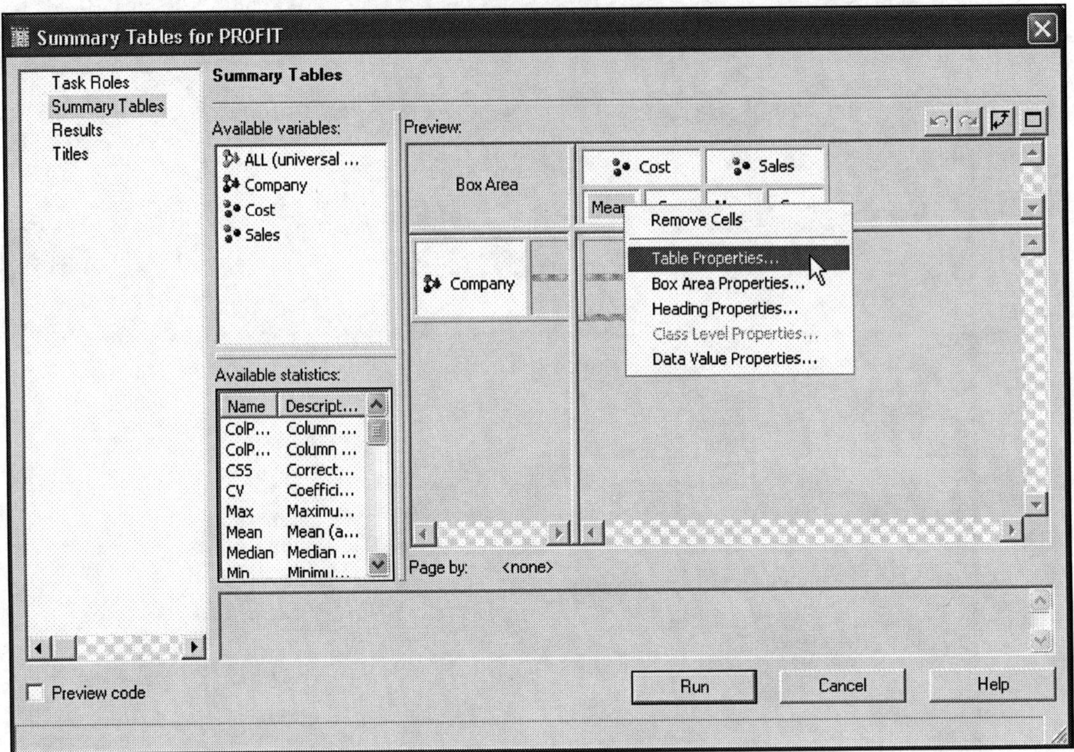

2) Select the **Format** tab and select **Currency** under the Categories menu.

3) Select **DOLLARw.d** under Formats and change the Overall width to 10.

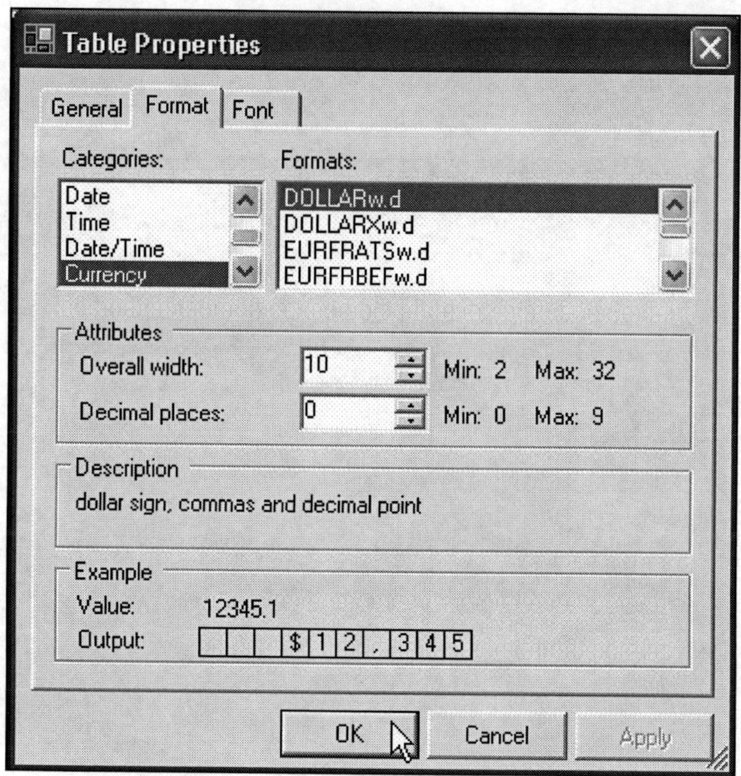

4) Select OK.

e. Right-click the **Sum** statistic under `Cost` and select **Heading Properties…**.

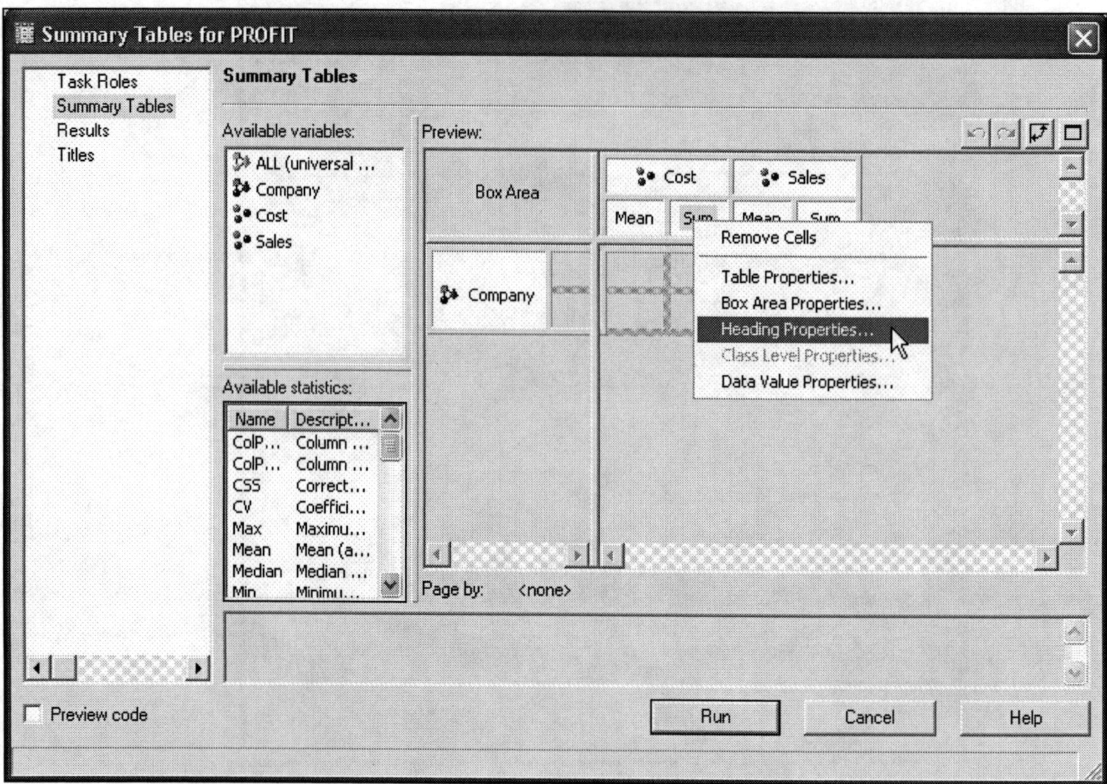

1) Type `Total` for the label.

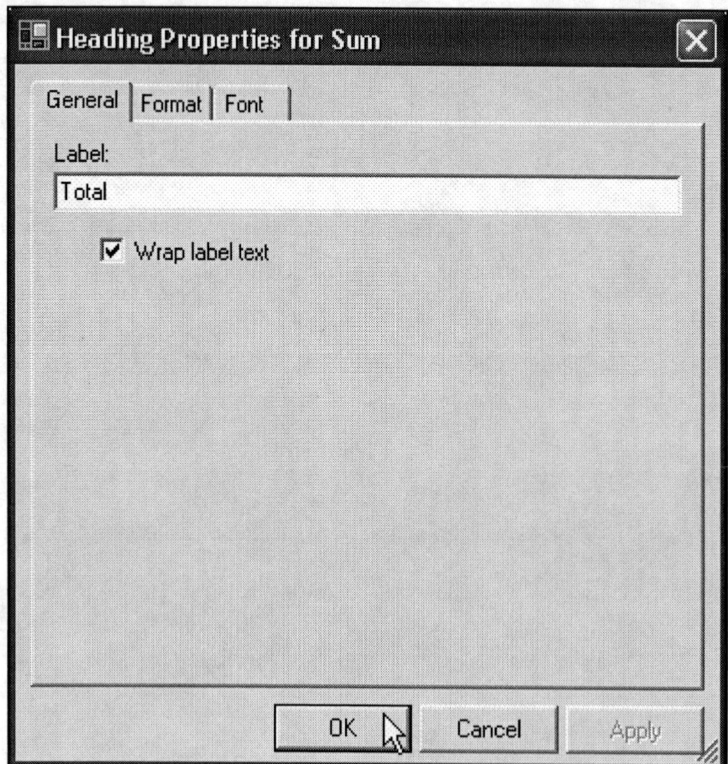

2) Select OK to exit the Heading Properties window.

f. Right-click the **Sum** statistic under `Sales` and select **Header Properties…**.

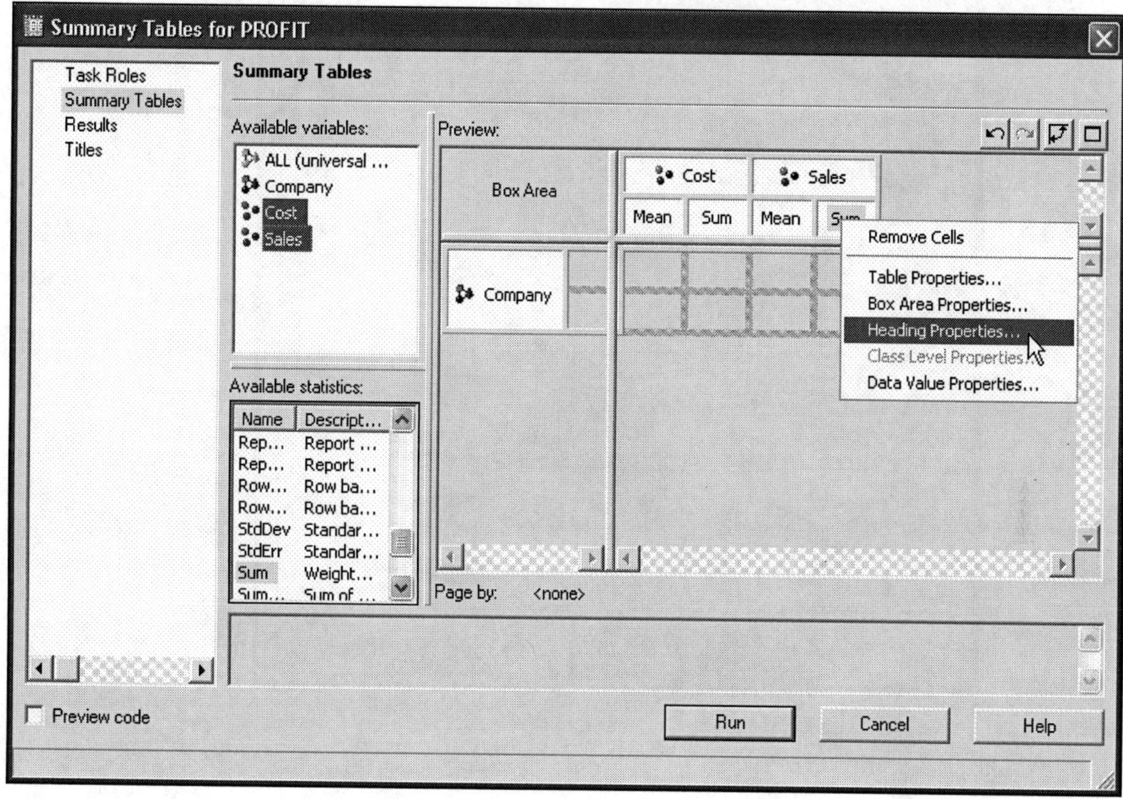

1) Type **Total** for the label.

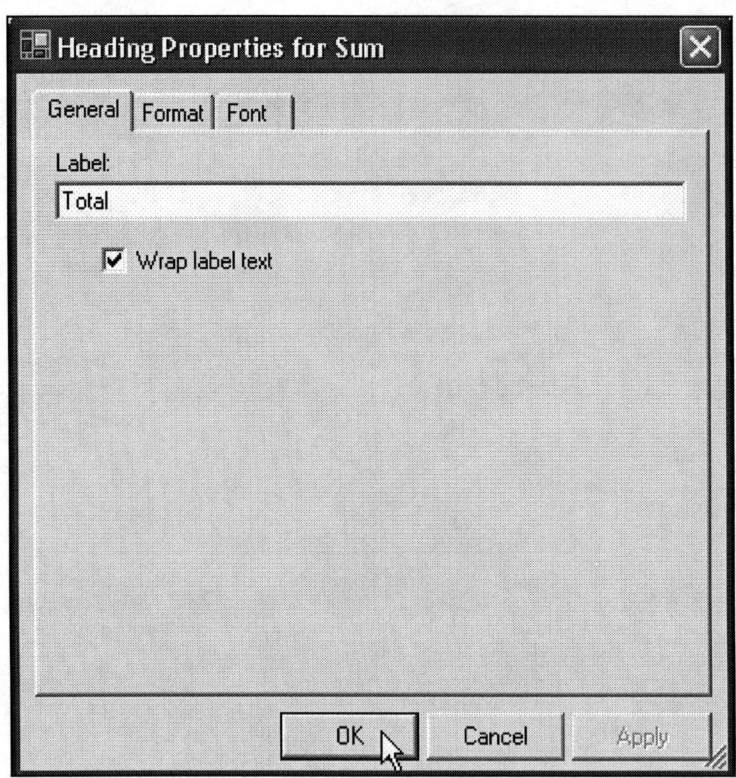

2) Select OK to exit the Heading Properties window.

g. Select Run to generate the table.

	A	B	C	D	E
1	**Summary Tables**				
2					
3		**Cost**		**Sales**	
4		**Mean**	**Total**	**Mean**	**Total**
5	**Company**				
6	**Orion Australia**	$47,806	$2,868,340	$101,740	$6,104,407
7	**Orion Belgium**	$26,174	$1,256,368	$55,691	$2,673,164
8	**Orion Denmark**	$16,016	$960,964	$34,820	$2,089,222
9	**Orion France**	$90,590	$5,435,393	$193,617	$11,617,011
10	**Orion Germany**	$109,770	$6,586,173	$236,403	$14,184,178
11	**Orion Holland**	$51,872	$3,112,292	$109,420	$6,565,209
12	**Orion Italy**	$85,212	$5,112,743	$182,985	$10,979,076
13	**Orion Spain**	$70,236	$4,214,150	$148,814	$8,928,848
14	**Orion UK**	$88,772	$5,326,325	$190,037	$11,402,196
15	**Orion USA**	$167,737	$10,064,216	$356,581	$21,394,856

h. Select **SAS** ⇨ **Refresh** (or select [icon] from the SAS Analysis Tools toolbar) to change Mean to Average.

1) Select Summary Table. Right-click the **Mean** statistic under `Cost` and select **Heading Properties…**.

2) Type **`Average`** for the label and select **OK**.

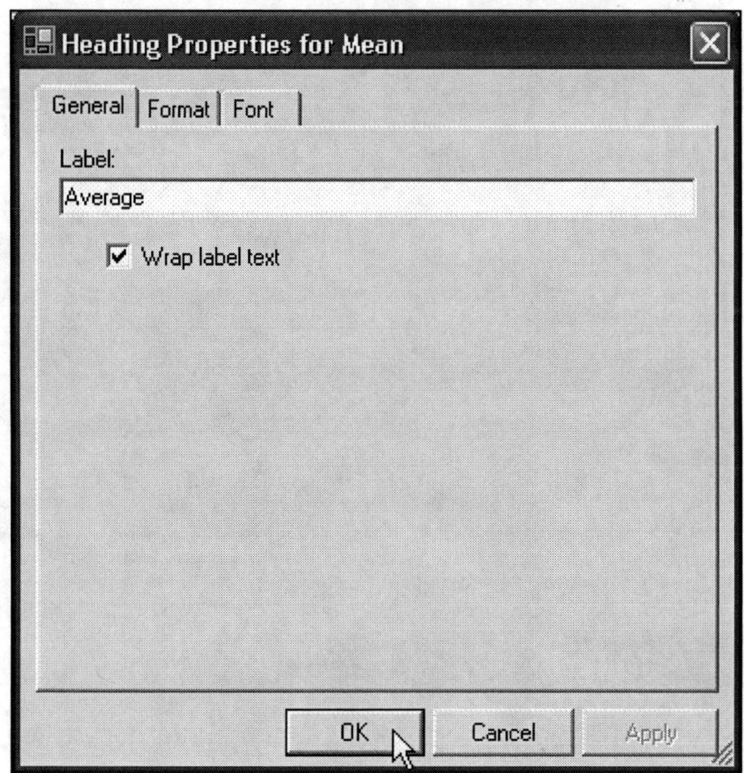

3) Right-click the **Mean** statistic under `Sales` and select **Heading Properties…**.

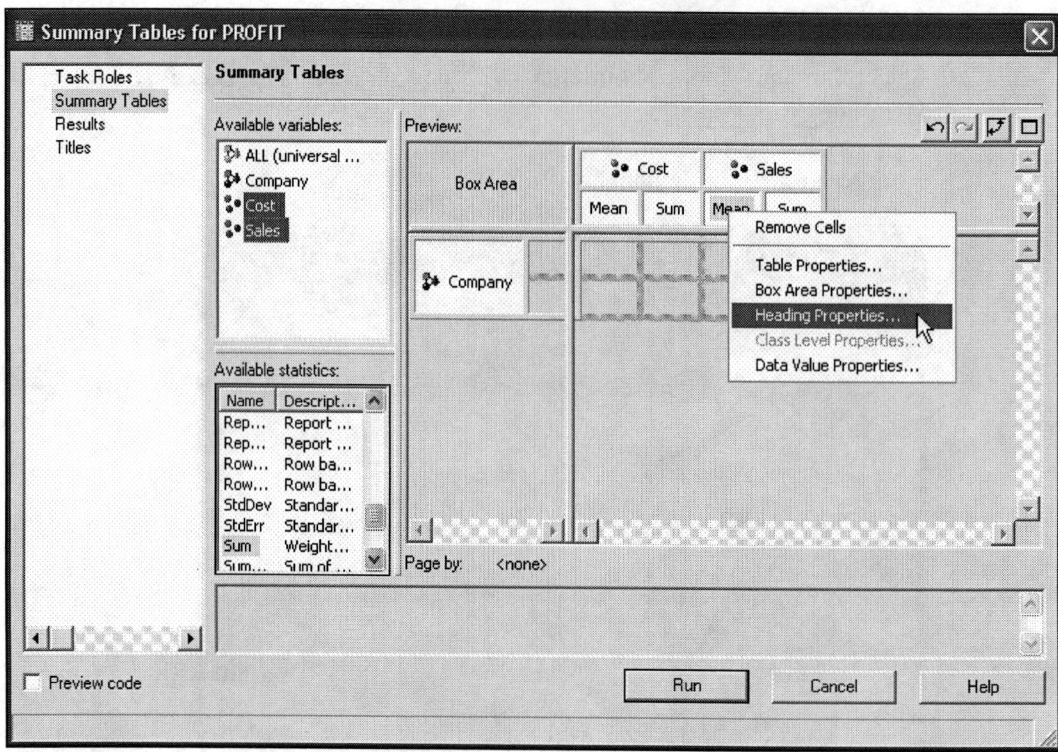

4) On the General tab, type `Average` for the label and select OK.

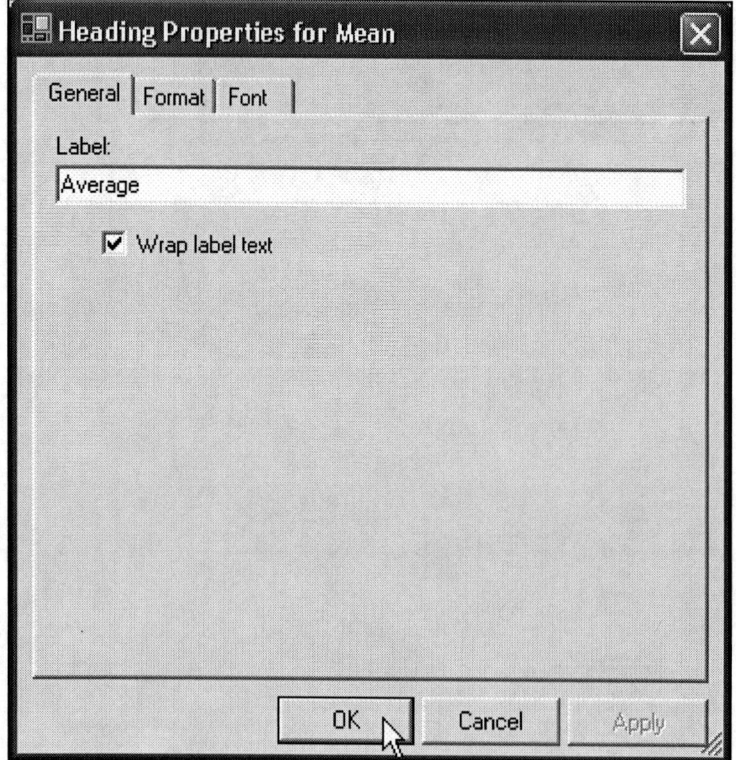

i. Right-click **Company** and select **Class Level Properties…**.

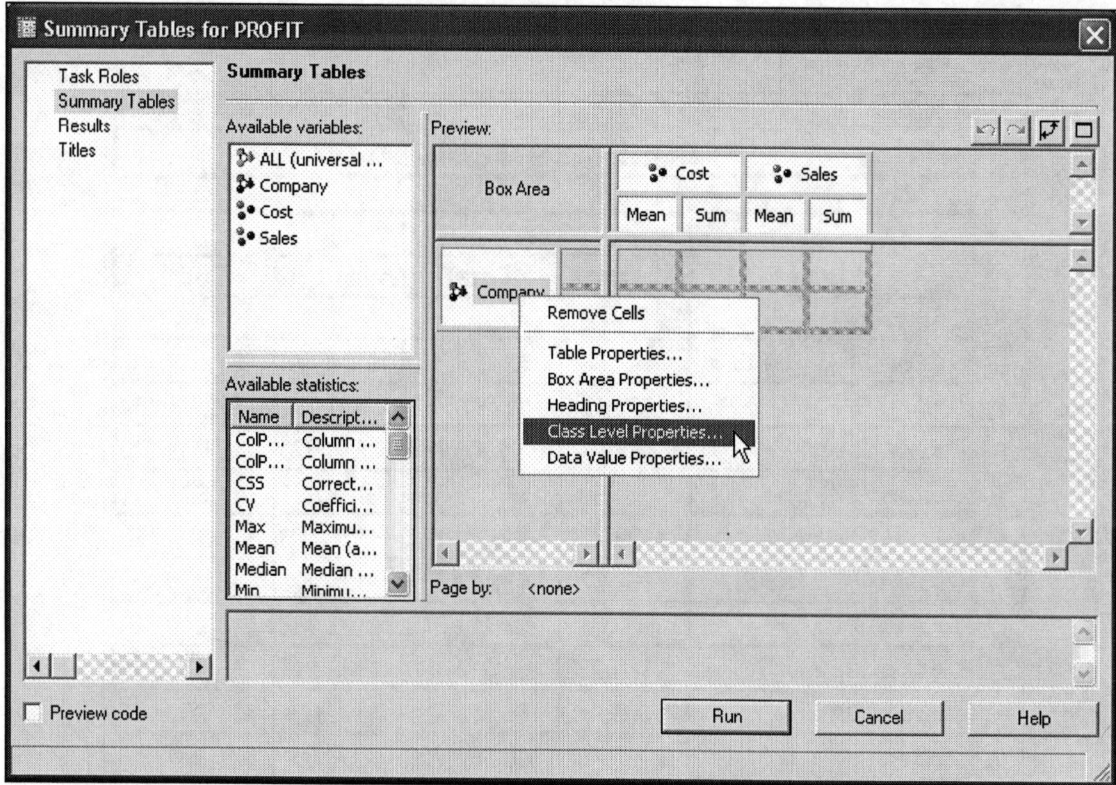

1) Select the **Font** tab ⇨ **Courier New** ⇨ **Italic**.

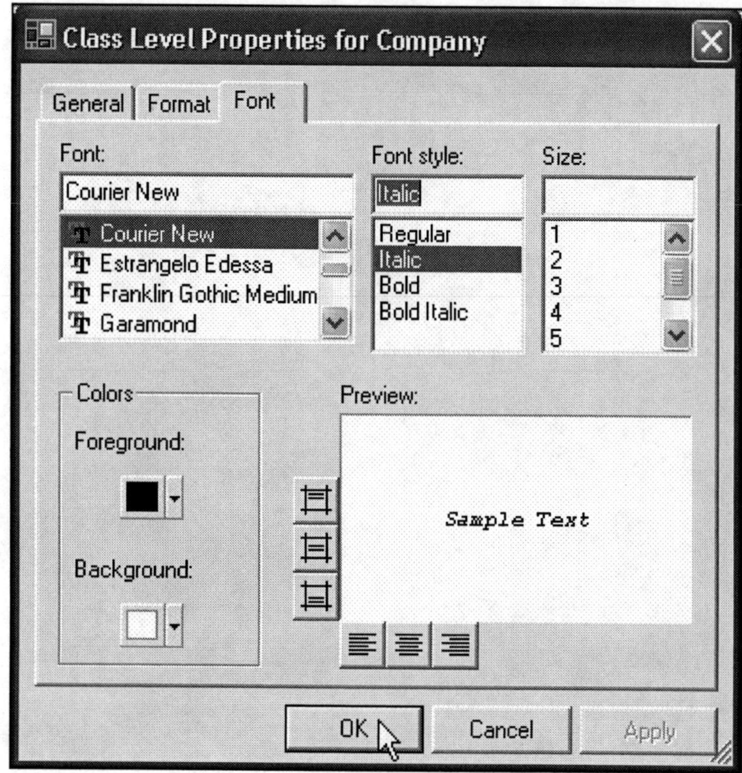

2) Select OK.

j. Select Run to generate the table.

	A	B	C	D	E
1	**Summary Tables**				
2					
3		**Cost**		**Sales**	
4		**Average**	**Total**	**Average**	**Total**
5	**Company**				
6	*Orion Australia*	$47,806	$2,868,340	$101,740	$6,104,407
7	*Orion Belgium*	$26,174	$1,256,368	$55,691	$2,673,164
8	*Orion Denmark*	$16,016	$960,964	$34,820	$2,089,222
9	*Orion France*	$90,590	$5,435,393	$193,617	$11,617,011
10	*Orion Germany*	$109,770	$6,586,173	$236,403	$14,184,178
11	*Orion Holland*	$51,872	$3,112,292	$109,420	$6,565,209
12	*Orion Italy*	$85,212	$5,112,743	$182,985	$10,979,076
13	*Orion Spain*	$70,236	$4,214,150	$148,814	$8,928,848
14	*Orion UK*	$88,772	$5,326,325	$190,037	$11,402,196
15	*Orion USA*	$167,737	$10,064,216	$356,581	$21,394,856

5.7 Bar Chart Task

Objectives

- Name the types of graphs supported with SAS tasks.
- State the differences between the output formats that are supported.
- Create a bar chart.

49

Graphs Using SAS Tasks

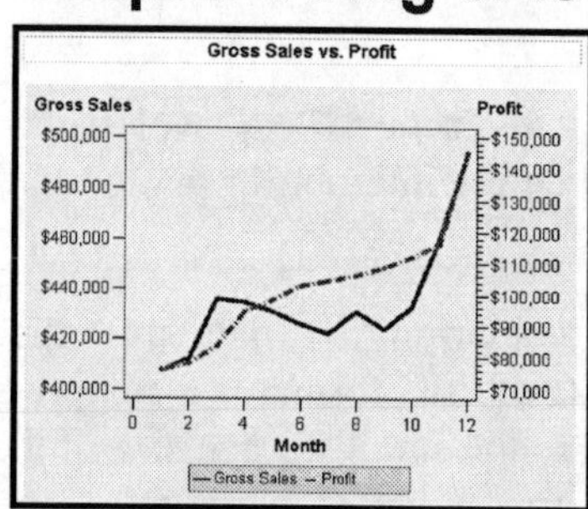

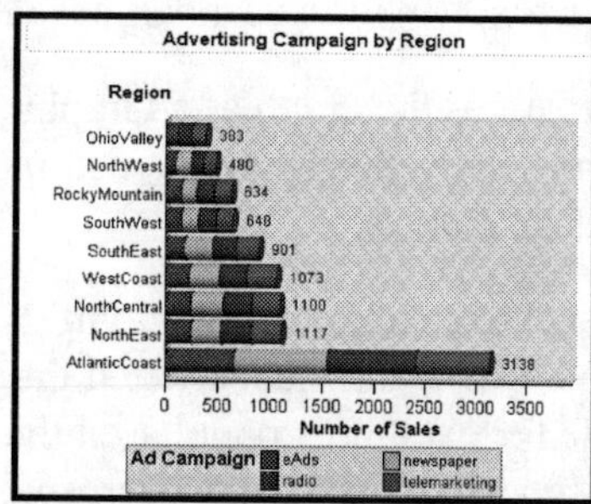

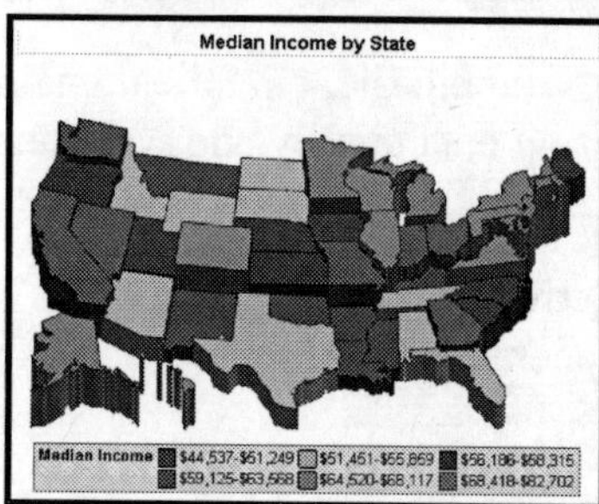

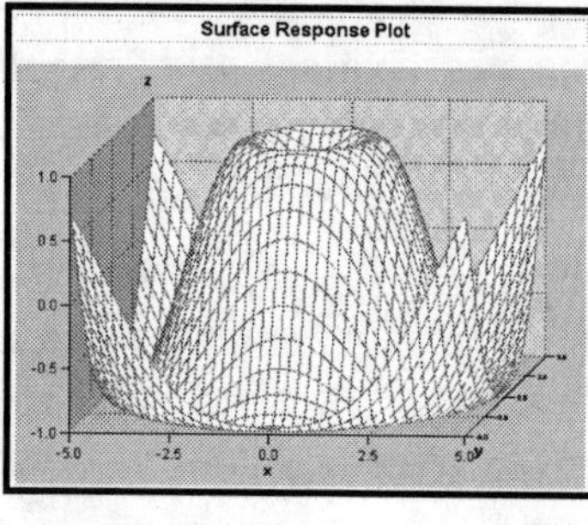

50

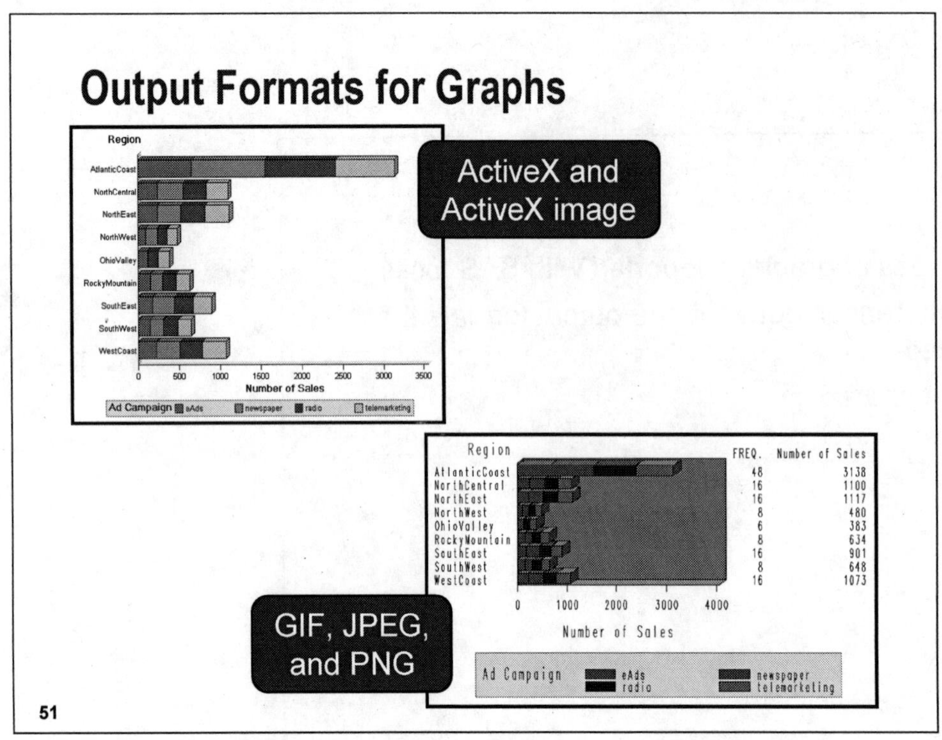

SAS Add-In for Microsoft Office has five different graphics output formats. You can select the graphics output format by going to **SAS** ⇨ **Options** ⇨ **Graph** from the menu bar.

ActiveX generates the graph as an ActiveX control, a set of technologies that allow software components to interact with one another. ActiveX is typically used on the Web to produce animation and other multimedia effects. This is the default output format, and you can view it in Microsoft Internet Explorer on Microsoft Windows machines only.

GIF generates the graph as a Graphics Interchange Format file. Developed in the mid-1980s, this format is commonly used on the Internet for photo-quality image display.

JPEG generates the graph as a Joint Pictures Expert Group file (named for the committee that standardized the format). The JPEG format is a compressed file format that is popular on the Web due to the small storage size of the displayed object. However, some picture quality is lost in compression.

PNG generates the graph as a Portable Network Graphic file, a public domain format that compresses images without losing data quality and was created to replace GIF imaging.

ActiveX image (SAS®9) generates the graph as a PNG file using ActiveX technology. Only the SAS®9 for Windows Server or later can generate this format.

The ActiveX output format is interactive. You can right-click on any graphic output generated in this format and change the chart type and many other options. Any options that you change are reflected in the output only and not in the task dialog selections you made to set up the chart.

While the ActiveX image output has a small degree of interactivity, the GIF, JPEG, and PNG output formats are non-interactive; you cannot change the appearance of a chart after you generate it.

In Microsoft Word with RTF results format, the ActiveX output format for graphs is not supported.

If your stored process returns streaming output and you specify a graphics output format other than ActiveX, the results may not display correctly.

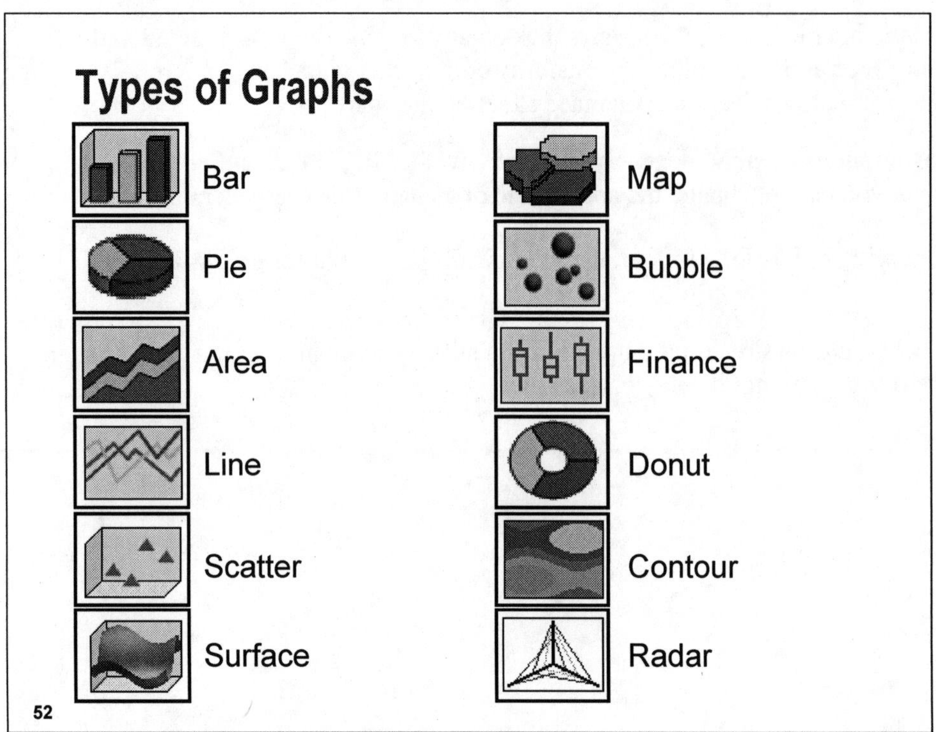

Description of the most common charts:

Bar charts

vertical, horizontal, or 3D block charts that compare numeric values or statistics between different values of a chart variable

Pie charts

simple, group, or stacked charts that represent the relative contribution of the parts to the whole by displaying data as wedge-shaped slices of a circle

Line charts

line, spline, needle, step, regression, smooth, STD, Lagrange interpolation, or overlay charts that show the mathematical relationships between numeric variables by revealing trends or patterns of data points

Scatter charts

2D scatter charts, 3D scatter charts, or 3D needle charts that show the relationships between two or three variables by revealing patterns or a concentration of data points

Finance charts

box plots, hi-lo charts, or hi-lo-close charts that display multiple summary statistics for some numeric variable across different values of a chart variable.

For a description of charts not listed here, select **Help** in any graph task dialog box.

Bar Chart

The Bar Chart task creates vertical, horizontal, or 3D block charts that compare numeric values or statistics between different values of a chart variable.

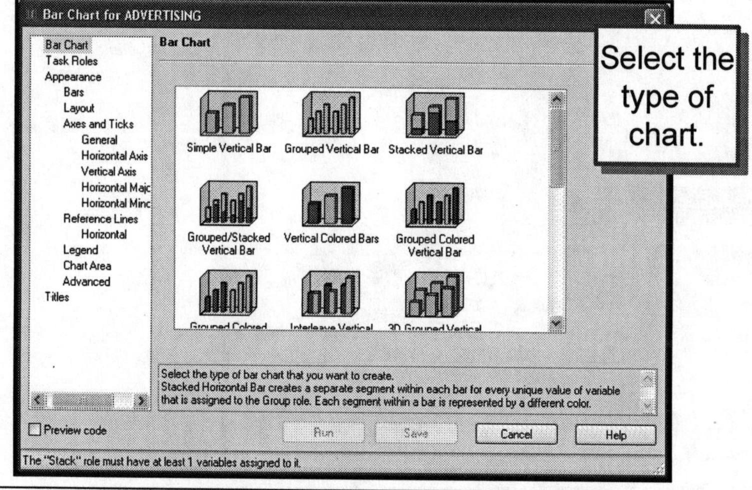

53

To access the Bar Chart task, select **SAS** ⇨ **Browse SAS Programs…** from the menu bar. Then select **SAS Tasks** ⇨ **Graph** ⇨ **Bar Chart**.

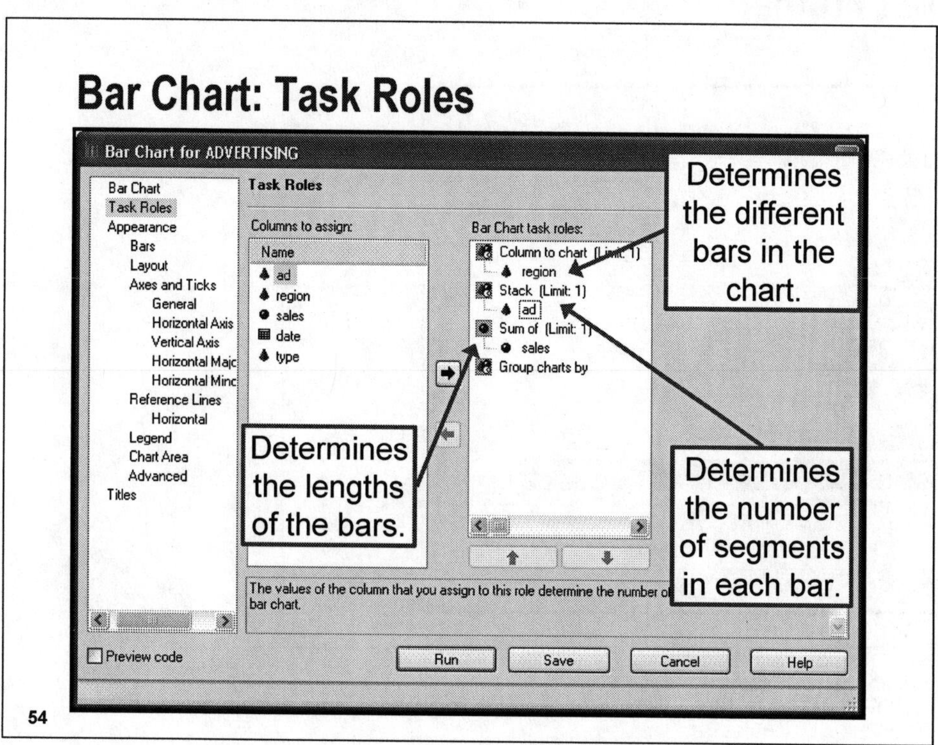

The task roles change depending on the type of chart selected.

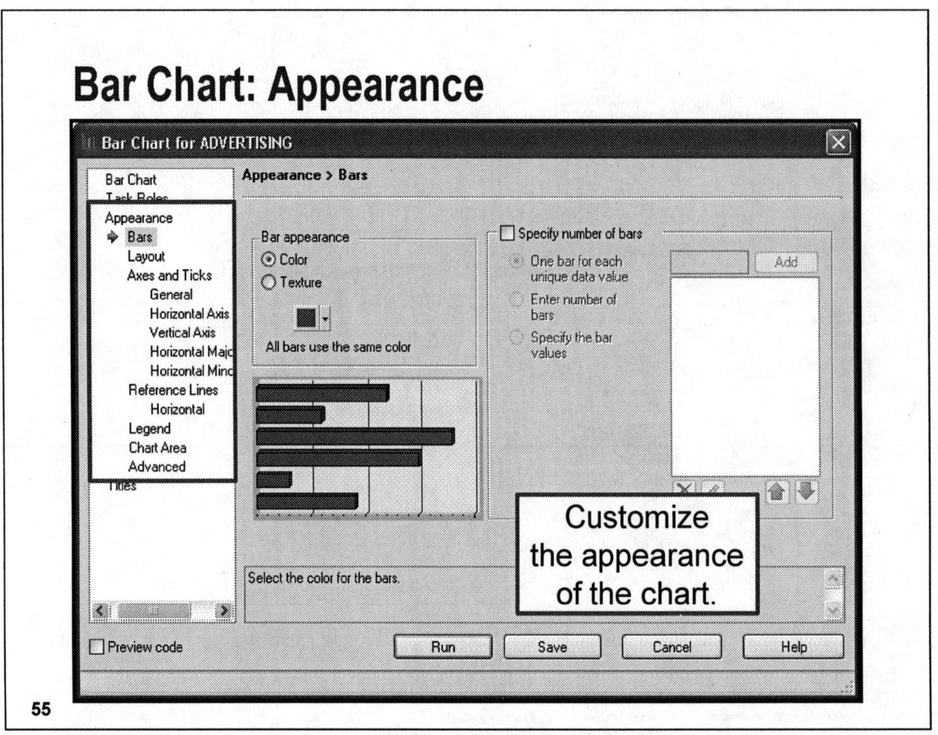

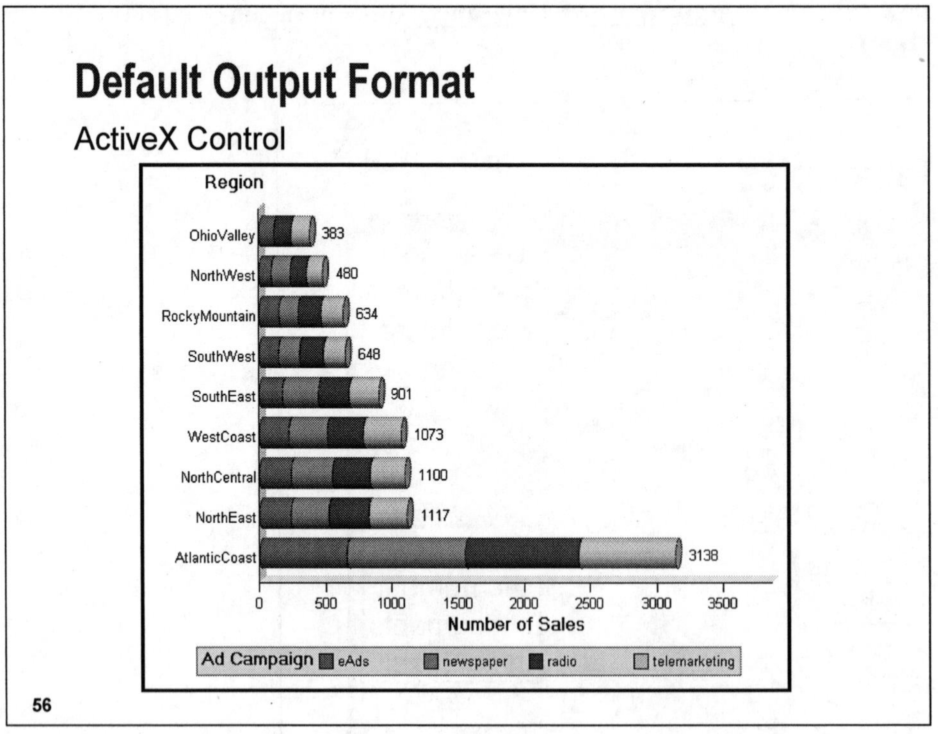

Complex graphs created in the ActiveX format may take additional time to render.

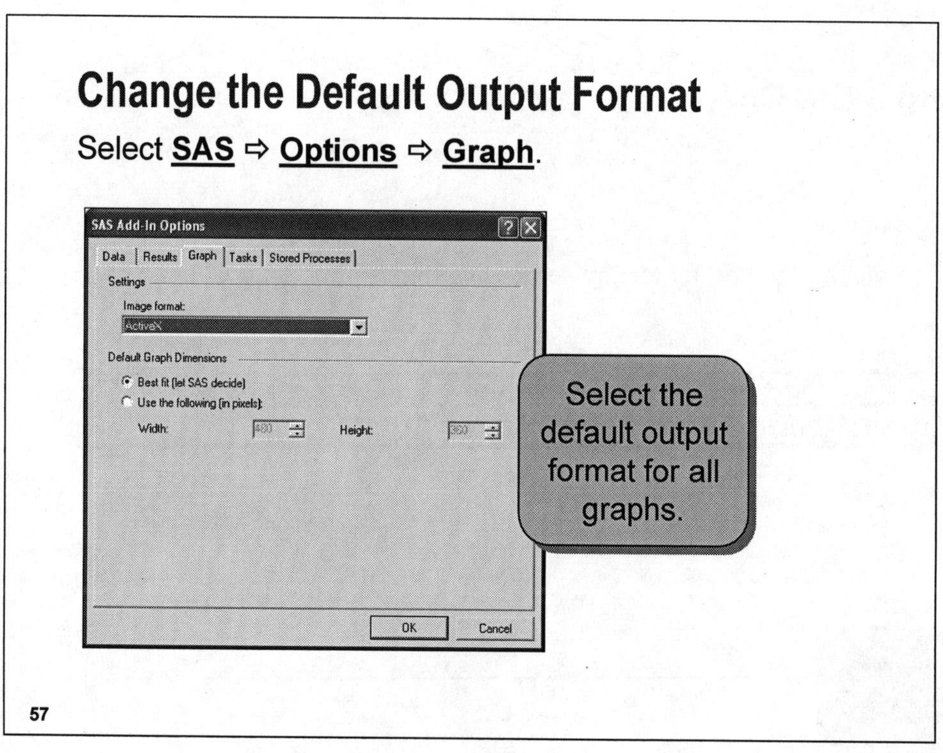

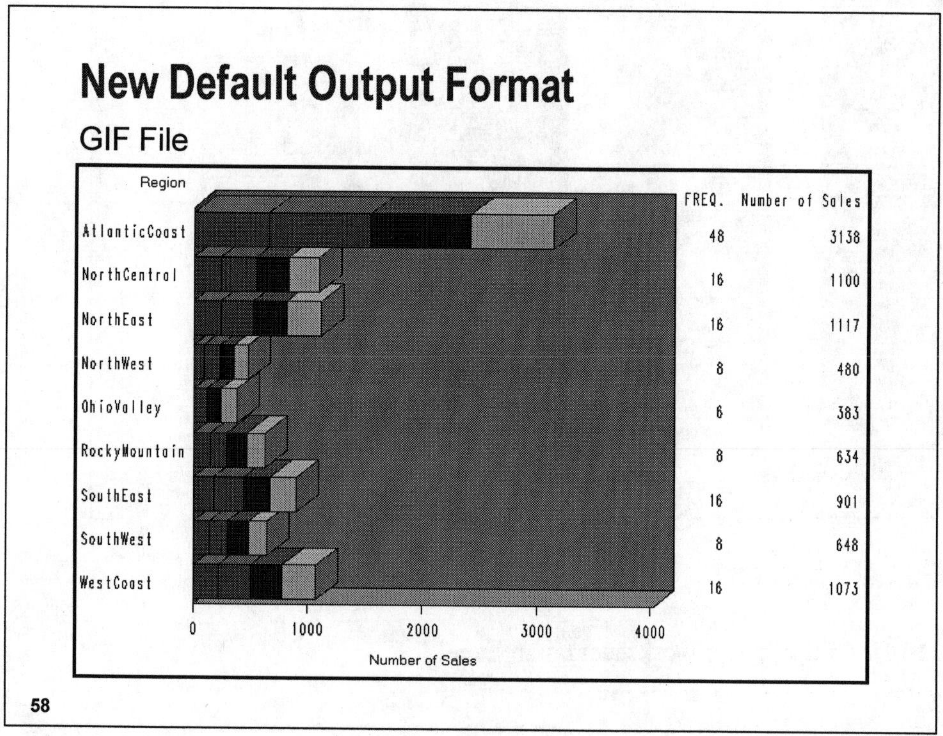

You must rerun the task so that the graph can be generated in the new output format. To do this, select **SAS** ⇨ **Refresh** after the new format has been specified.

Creating a Bar Chart

For this demonstration, you will

- create a bar chart of customer age groups in order by descending frequency.

Output:

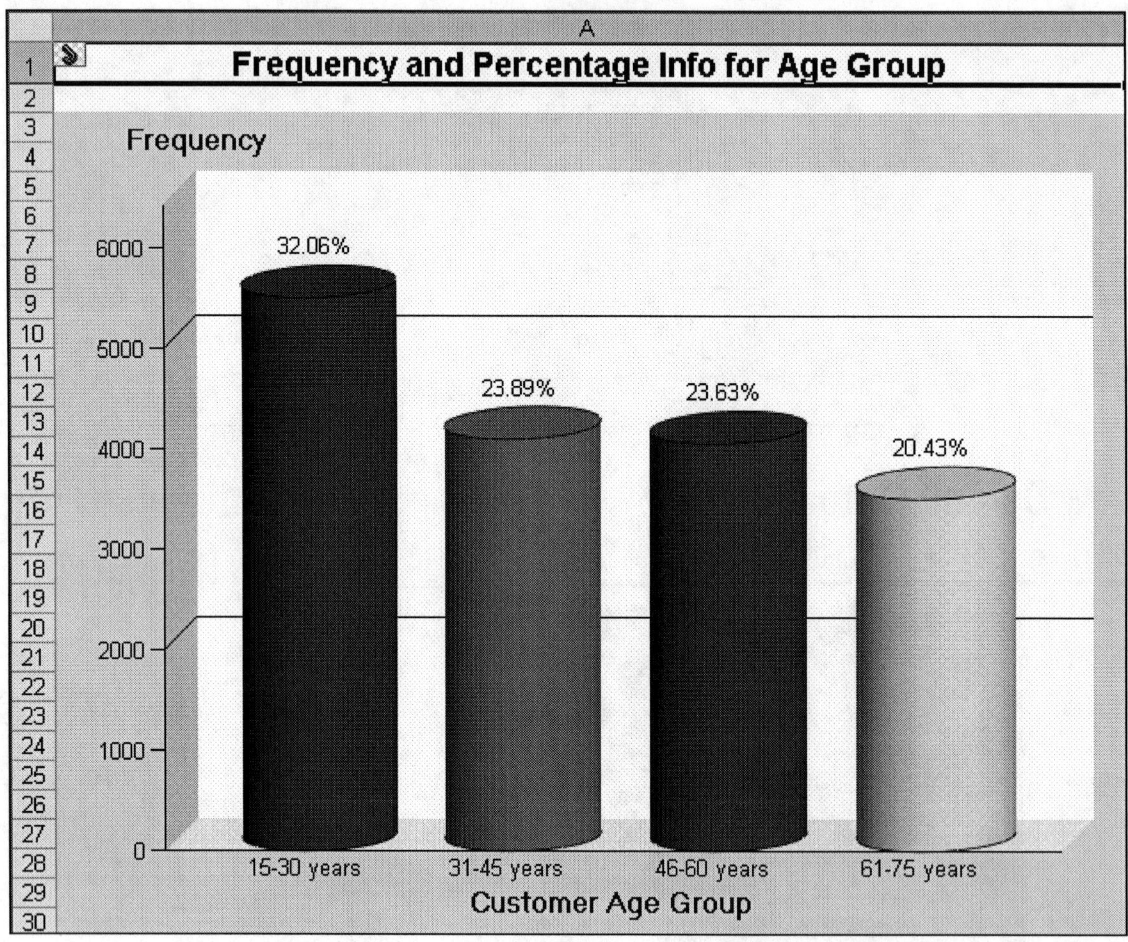

Running a Bar Chart Task

1. Return to the **`MDMT.MDM_OrderFact`** worksheet tab in Excel.

2. Verify that the **MDM_CUSTOMER_DIM** table is still the active data source.

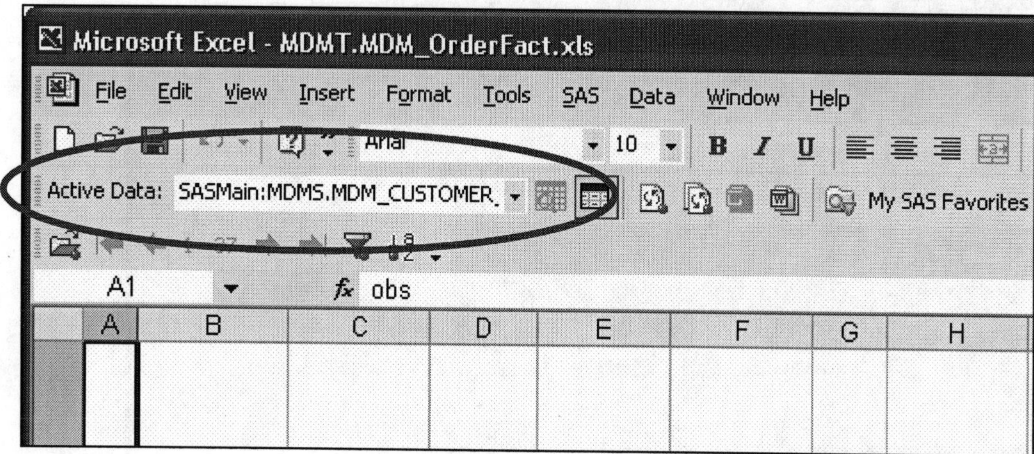

If the Active Data is set to Active Worksheet, you will get unexpected column names when you attempt to assign Task Roles in a task.

3. Open the Bar Chart task.

   a. Select [icon] on the SAS Analysis Tools toolbar (or select **SAS ⇨ Browse SAS Programs**).

   b. Expand the group **SAS Tasks** and select **Graph ⇨ Bar Chart**. Then select [Run].

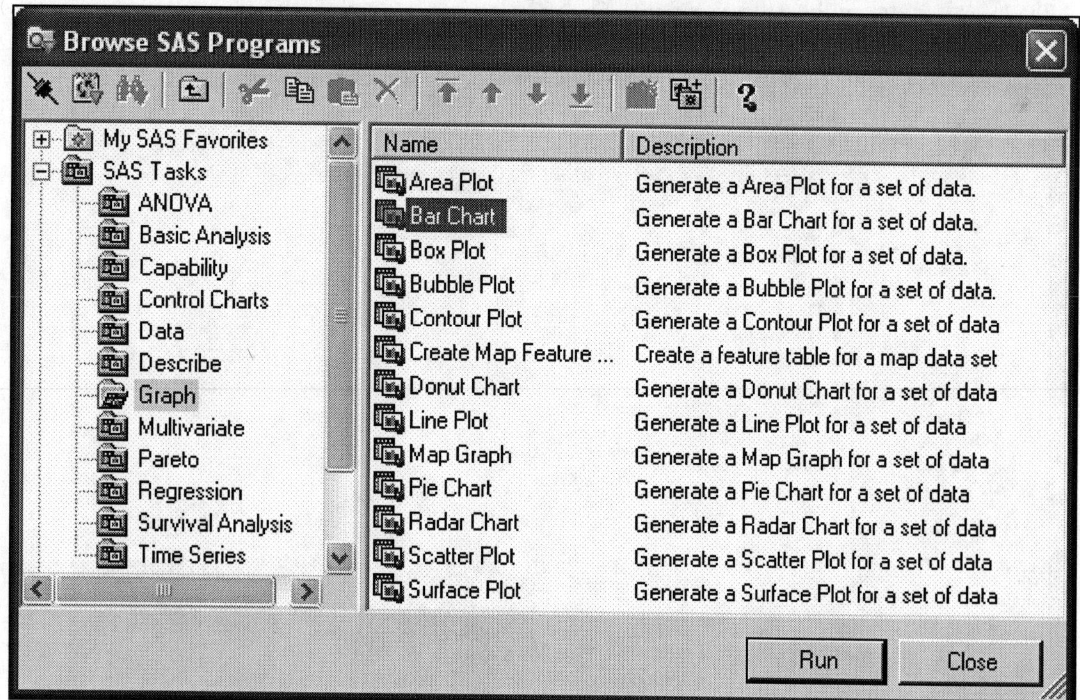

A Bar Chart dialog box opens where you select the type of chart to create, select the columns to include in the report, and specify how the columns will be used. In this dialog box, you can also change output formatting options.

4. In the Bar Chart pane, select **Vertical Colored Bars**.

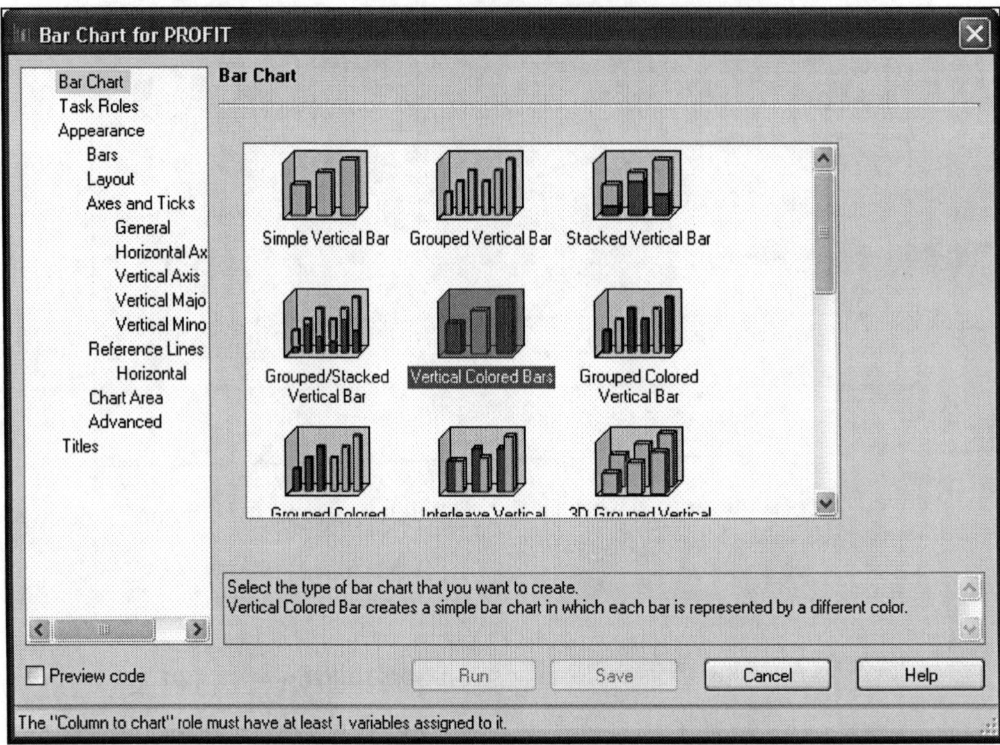

5. Select **Task Roles** in the Selection pane. Drag **Customer Age Group** to the Column to chart role.

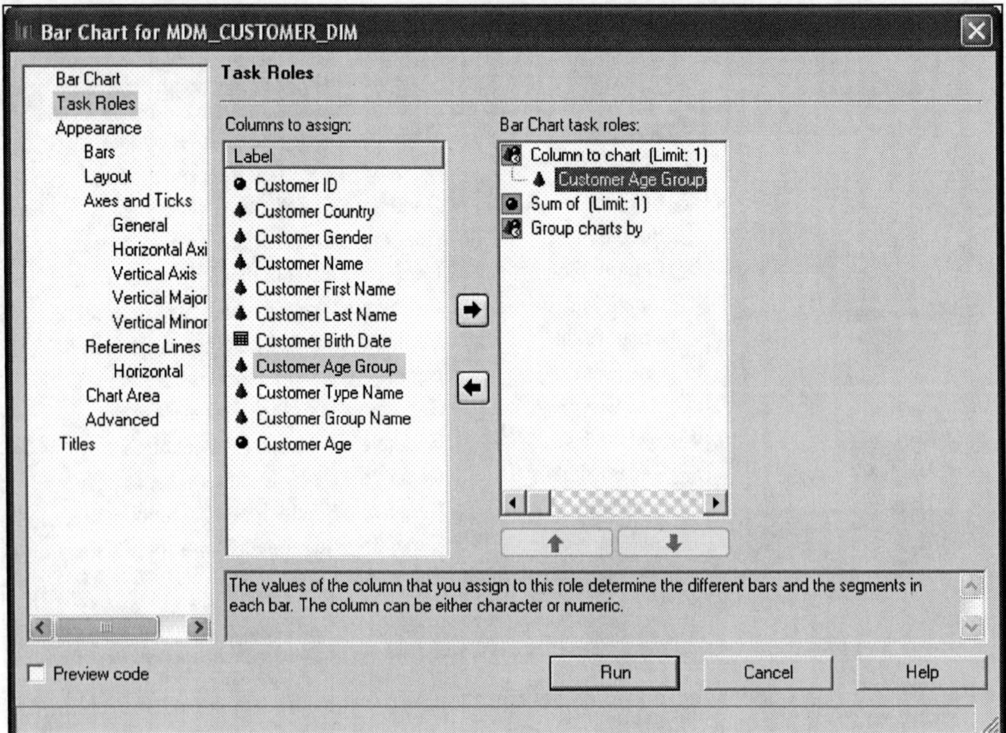

6. Select **Bars** under the Appearance category in the Selection pane.

7. Select **Finance** as the color scheme for the bar colors.

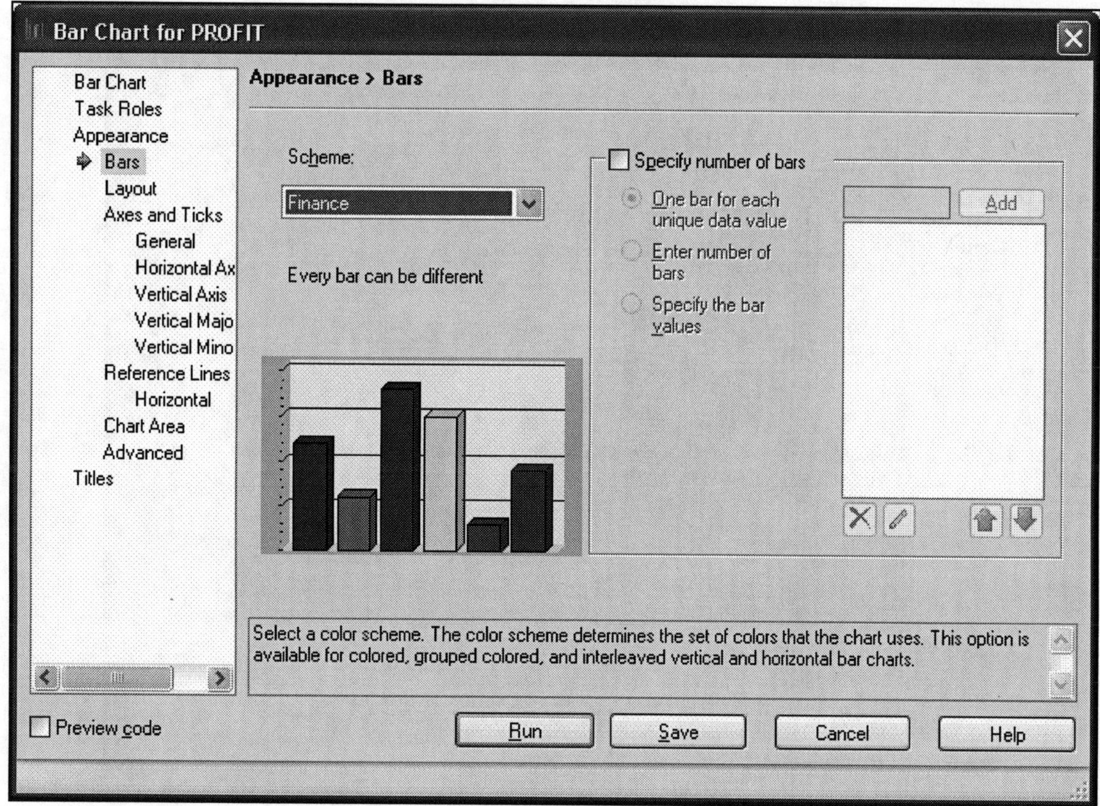

8. Select **Layout** in the Selection pane. In the `Shape` field, use the drop-down list to select **Cylinder** as the shape for the bars. In the `Order` field, select **Descending** to arrange the bars in descending order of height.

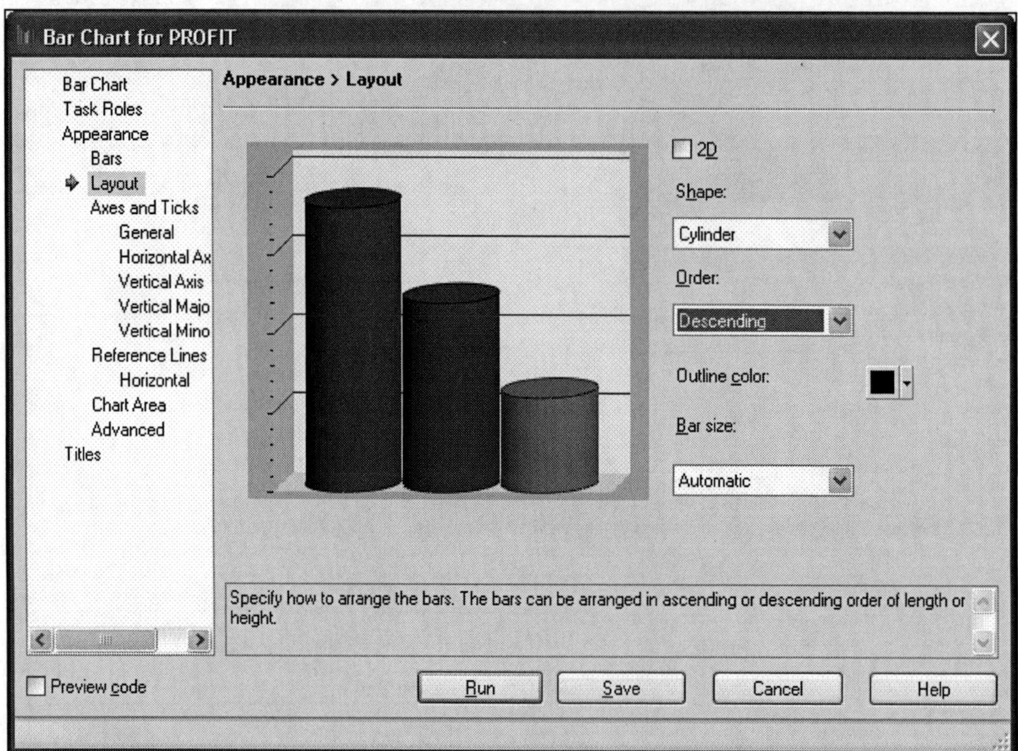

9. Select **Horizontal Axis** in the Selection pane. Type **`Age Group`** in the Label box.

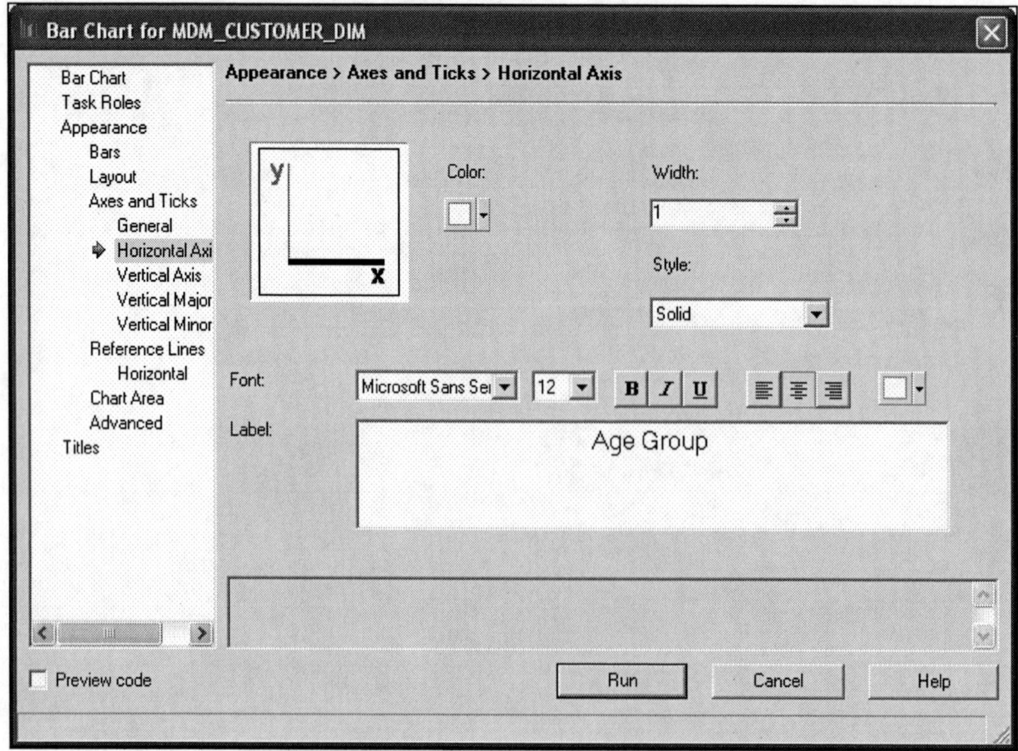

10. Select **Advanced** from the Selection pane. Verify that Frequency is the statistic used to calculate the bars. To display the percentages in the chart area, select the Additional statistical value to show next to bar check box and select **Percentage** from the drop-down list.

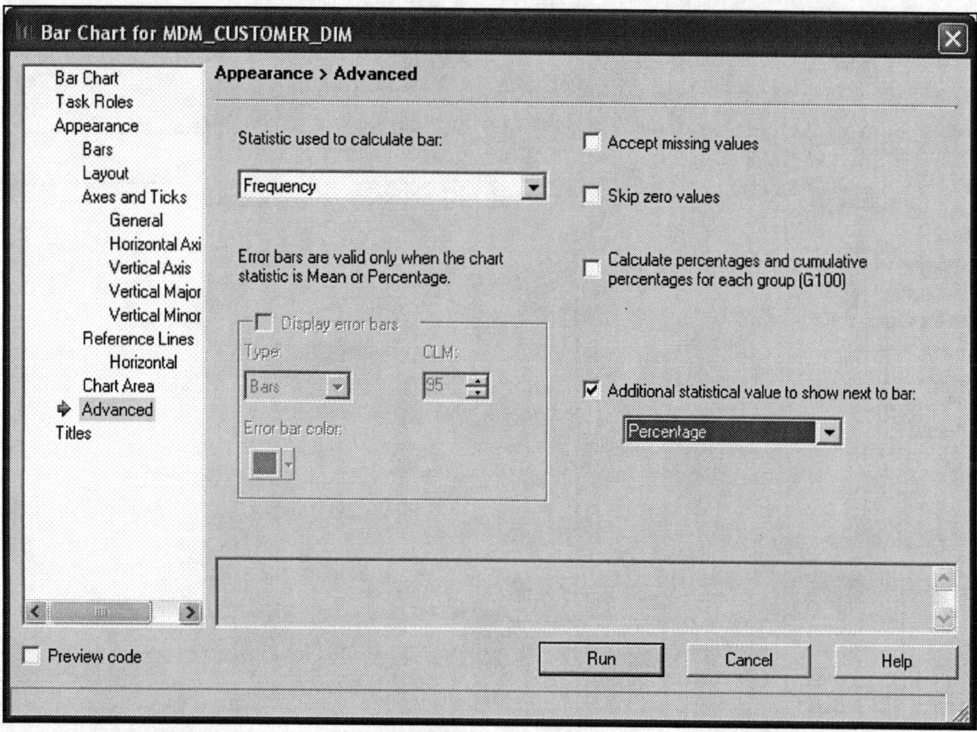

11. Select **Reference Lines** in the Selection pane. To provide your own reference lines at 2,000 and 5,000, select **Specify values for lines**. Type **2000** and select **Add**. Repeat the process to add a line for **5000**.

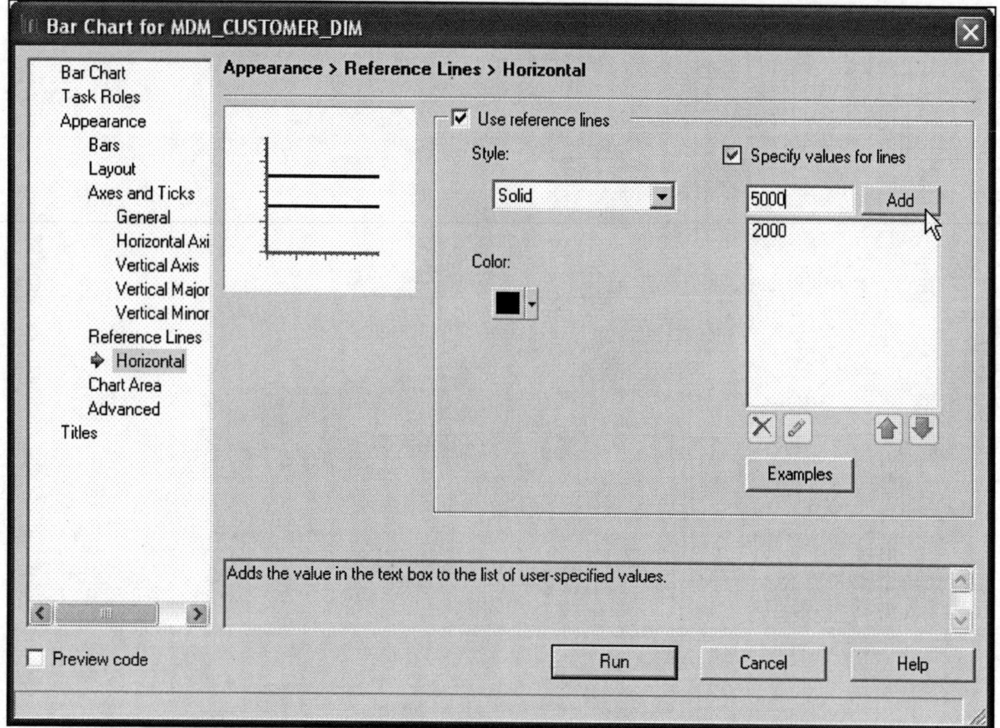

12. Select **Titles** in the Selection pane. Deselect the Use default text check box and type **`Frequency and Percentage Info for Age Group`**.

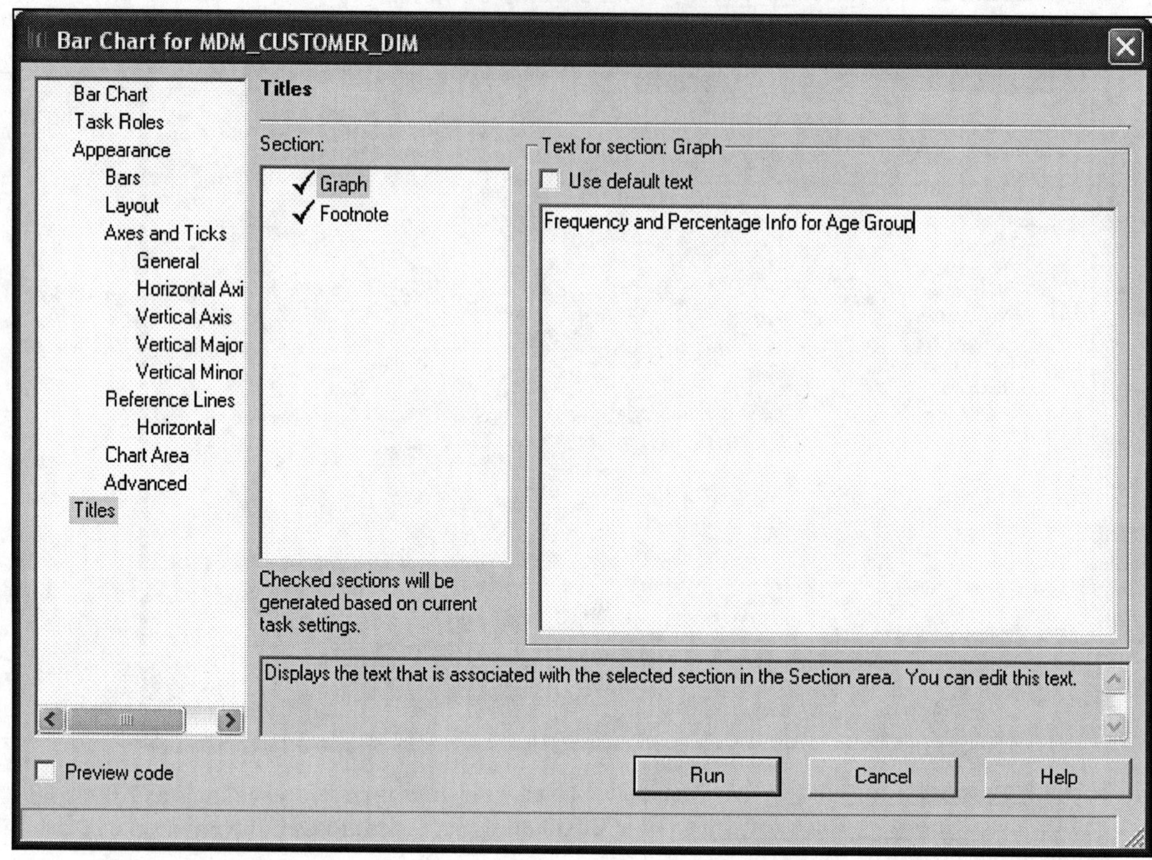

13. Select Run and examine the results.

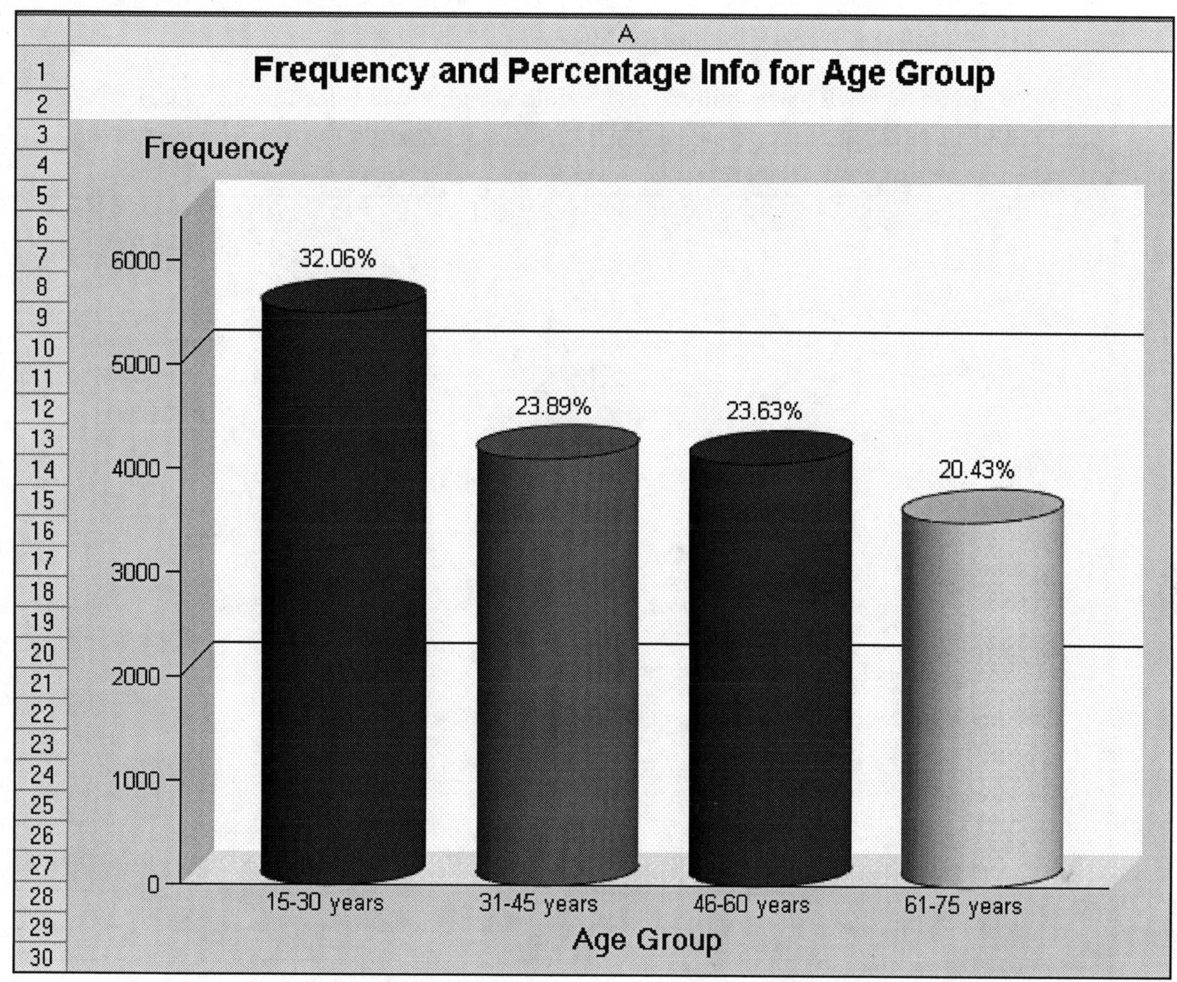

Once created, a chart can be modified by selecting **Refresh** or by selecting [icon] from the SAS Analysis Tools toolbar. This reopens the task dialog box where variable roles and attributes, as well as graphics options, are modifiable.

Sending Multiple Results to Microsoft Word

1. Select **SAS** ⇨ **Options**. Then select the **Results** tab.
2. Enable the option that will place multiple results into separate Word documents. Select **When sending multiple results to Word, place each result in a separate document.** under Settings.

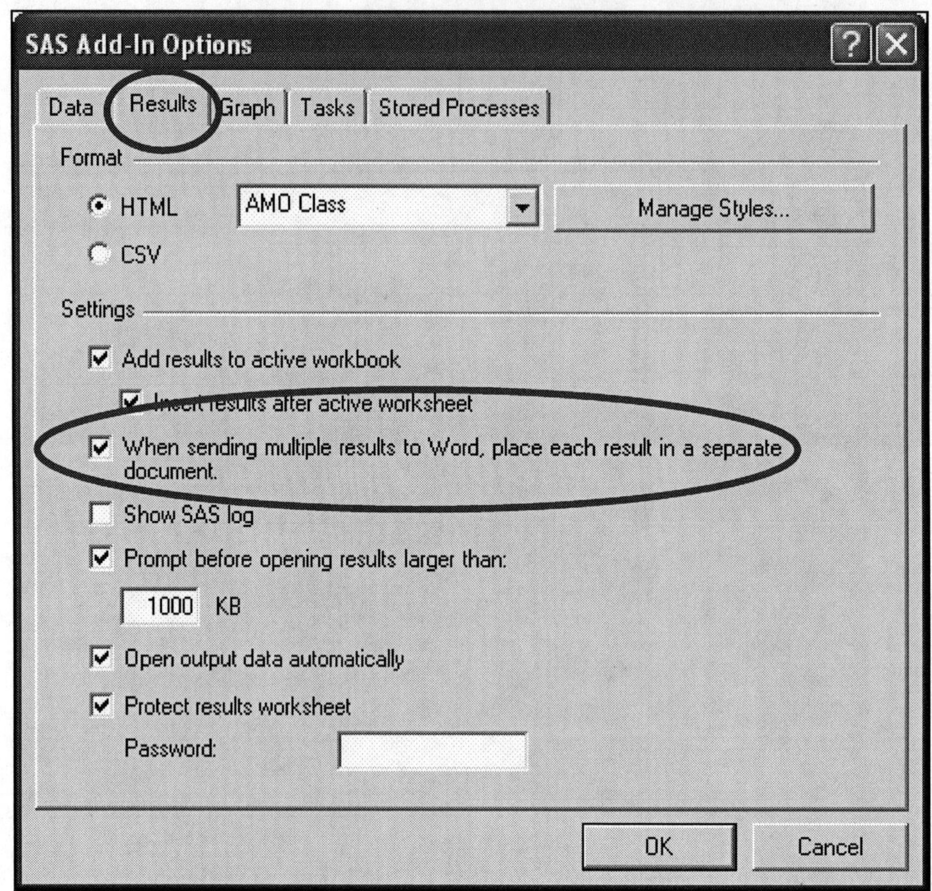

3. Select [OK] to close the SAS Add-In Options window.
4. Select [icon] on the SAS Analysis Tools toolbar (or select **SAS** ⇨ **Send Multiple Results to Microsoft Word**).

5. Of the four possible results to send to Word, select only the following three: **Table Analysis**, **Bar Chart**, and **List Data**.

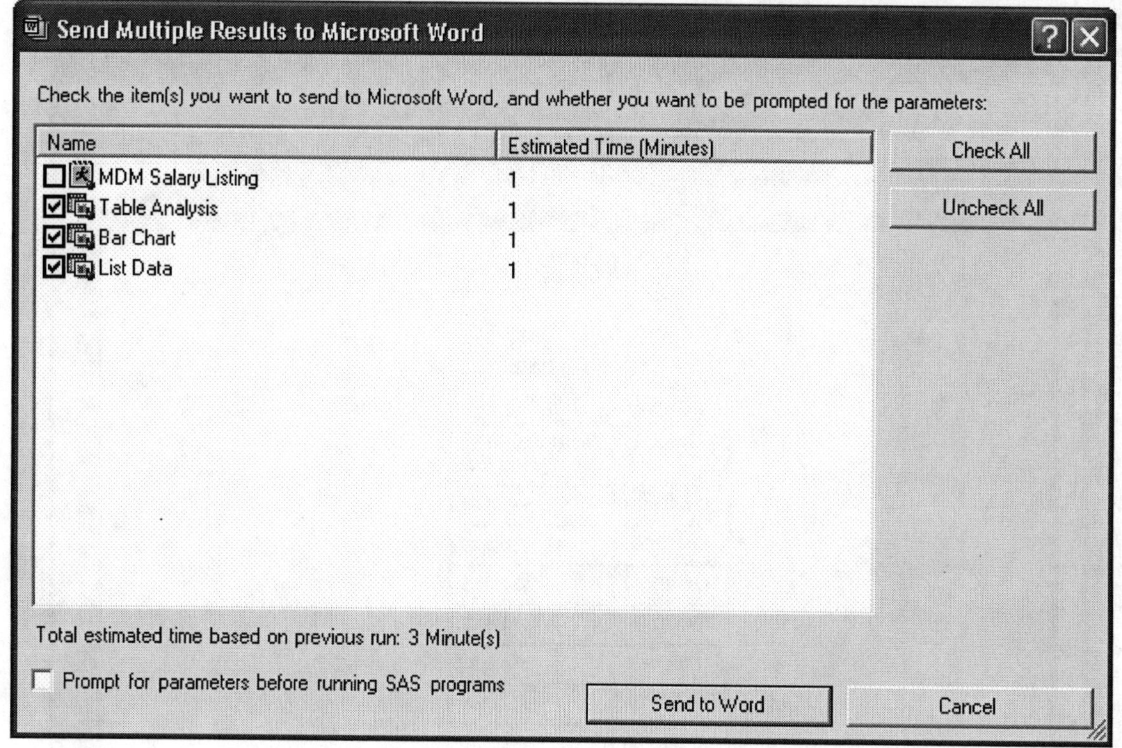

6. Select Send to Word and examine the results.

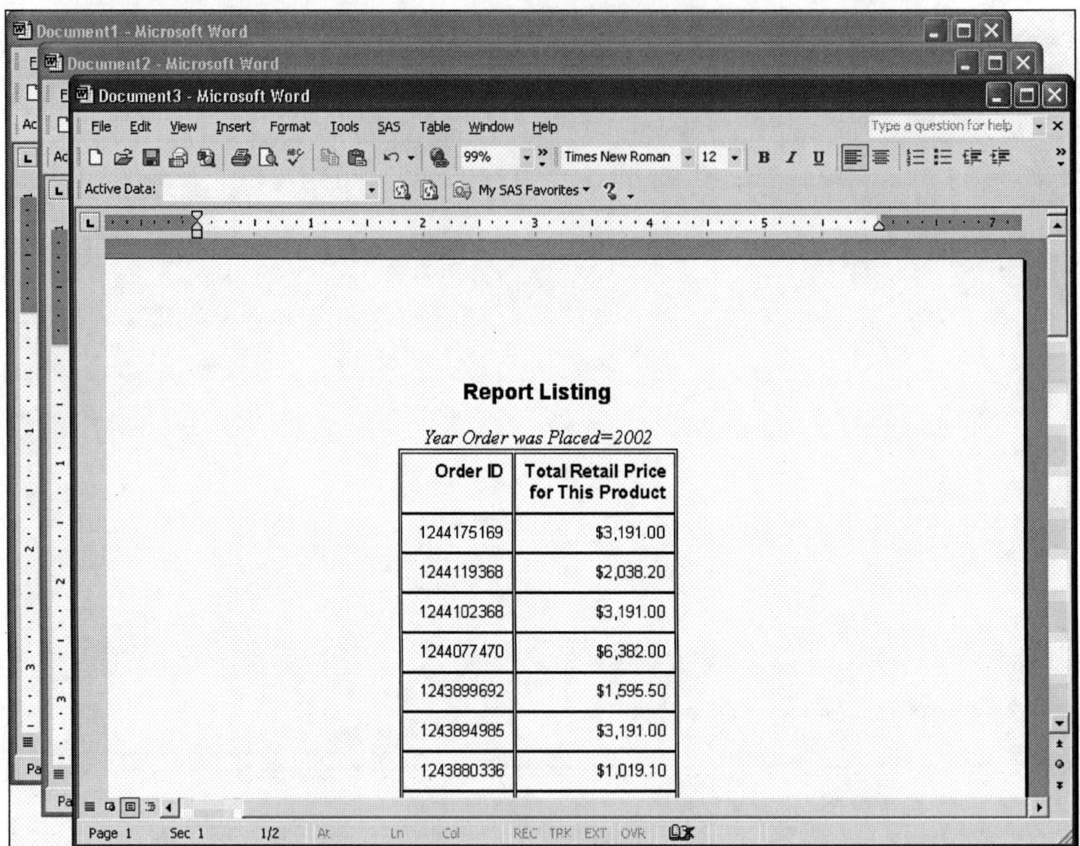

5.8 Interacting with an ActiveX Graph (Self-Study)

Objectives

- Subset the graph data.
- Change the chart type to a pie chart.
- Modify the labels of the pie slices.
- Change the graphics output format.

61

Modifying a Bar Chart

Modify the vertical bar chart to display the frequency count for each age group as a slice in a pie chart, and change the labels of the slices.

1. Find the Microsoft Word document that contains the bar chart.

2. To make modifications to the graph, right-click on the graph.

3. From the pop-up menu, select **Graph Toolbar** and select the **Subset** button.

If Graph Toolbar is not an option, SAS might be using an alternative version of Graph Control. Instead, select **Mouse Control** from the pop-up menu.

4. Position the cursor to the left of the tallest cylinder. While pressing the left mouse button, drag the cursor to the right so that it crosses over the three highest age group category cylinders. Release the mouse button.

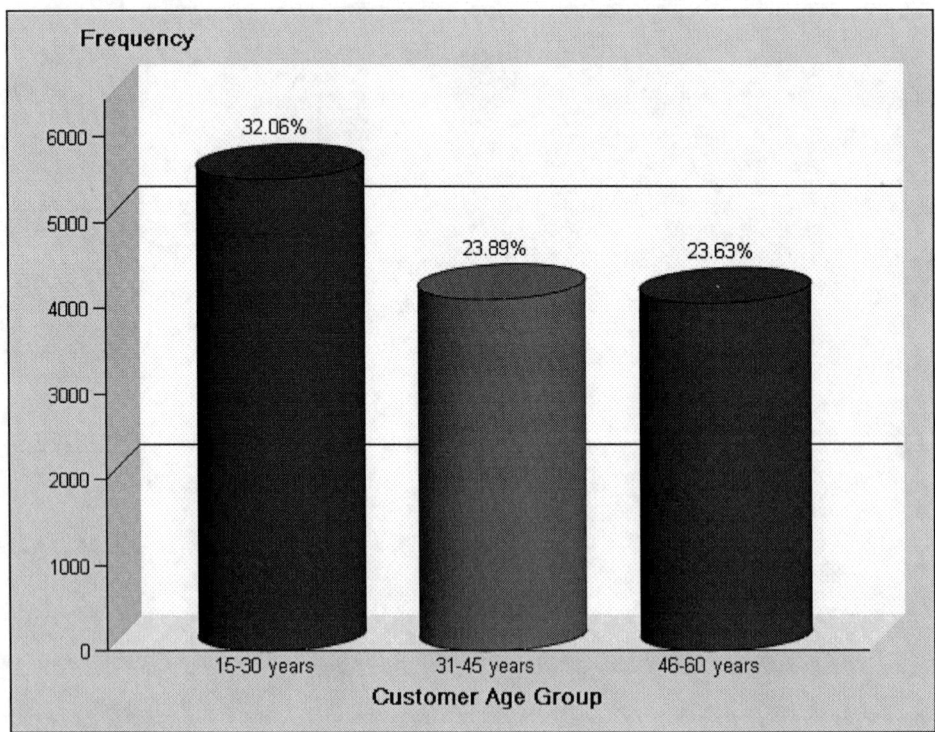

5. Close the Graph Toolbar menu bar.

6. Right-click on the bar chart and select **Chart Type** ⇨ **Pie**.

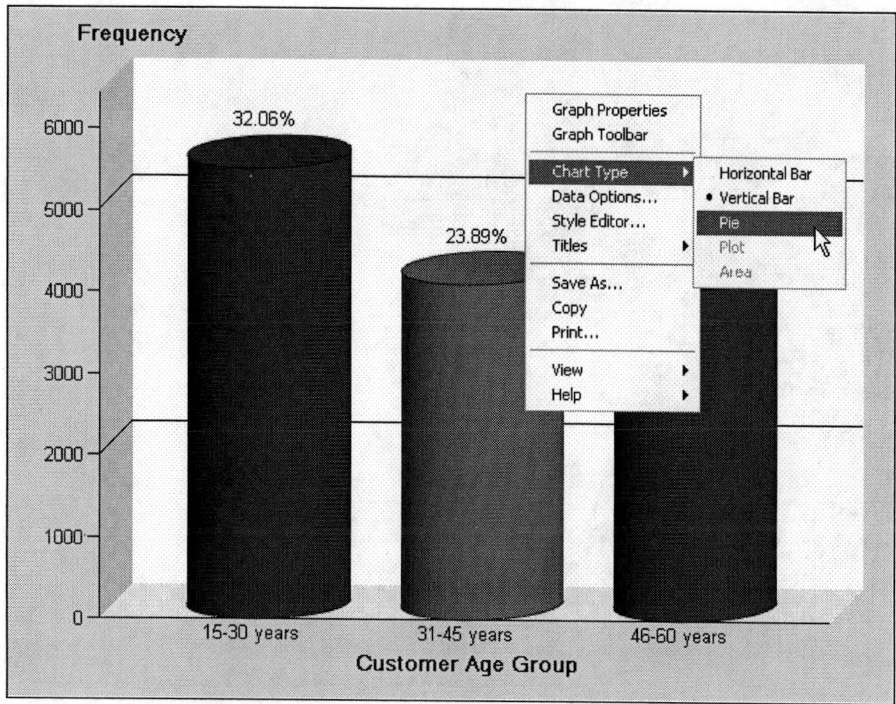

7. The frequency count of age group now appears as a pie chart.

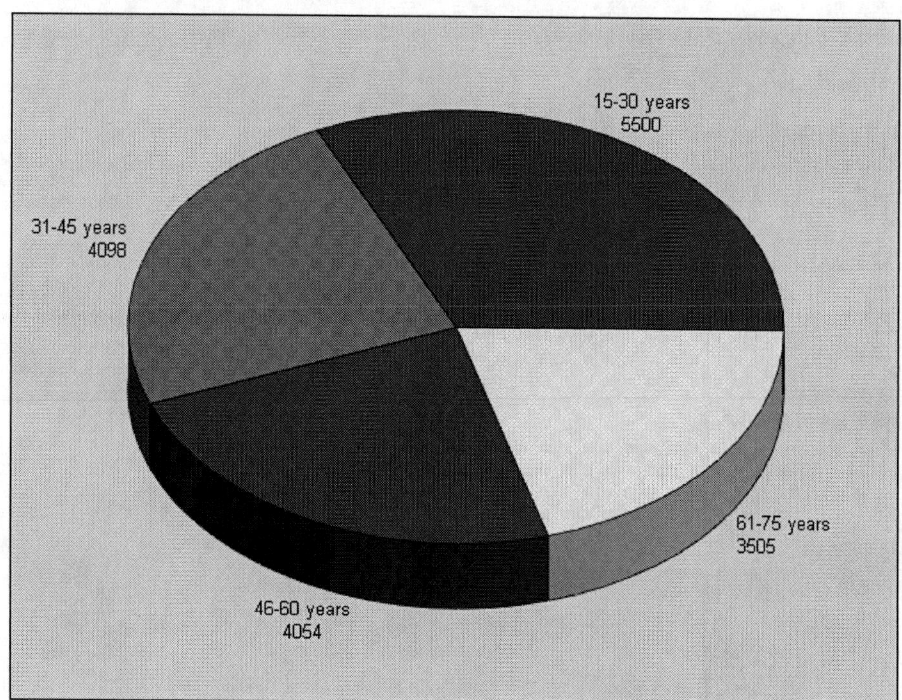

The subsetting criterion is lost when moving between chart types.

8. Right-click on the pie chart and select **Pie Properties**.

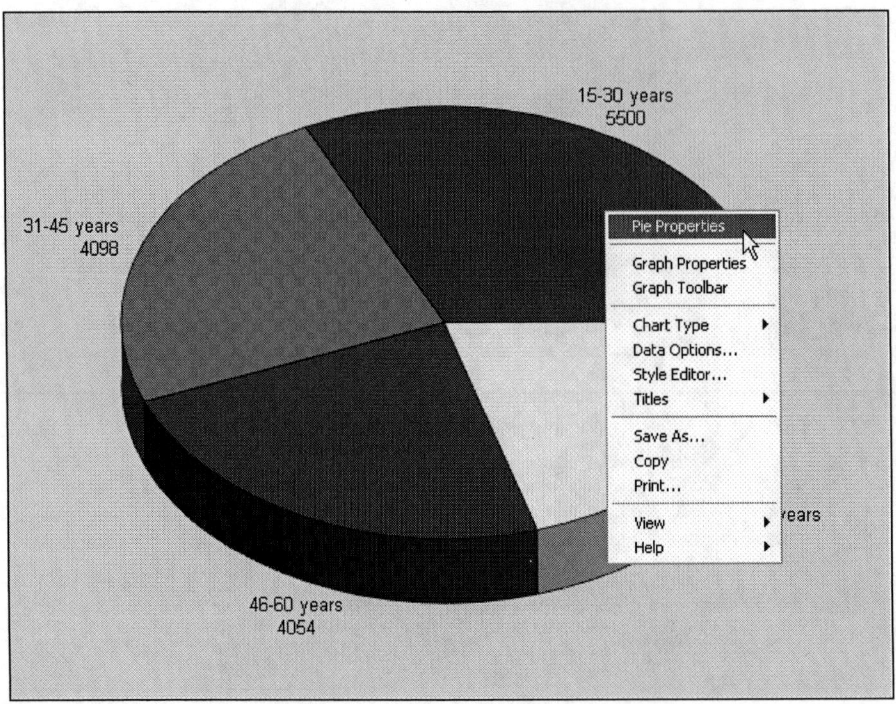

If Pie Properties is not an option, select **Options** ⇨ **Pie…**.

9. Change the value in the `Percent` field from `None` to `Inside` to display the percent of profit that corresponds to each slice. Select OK.

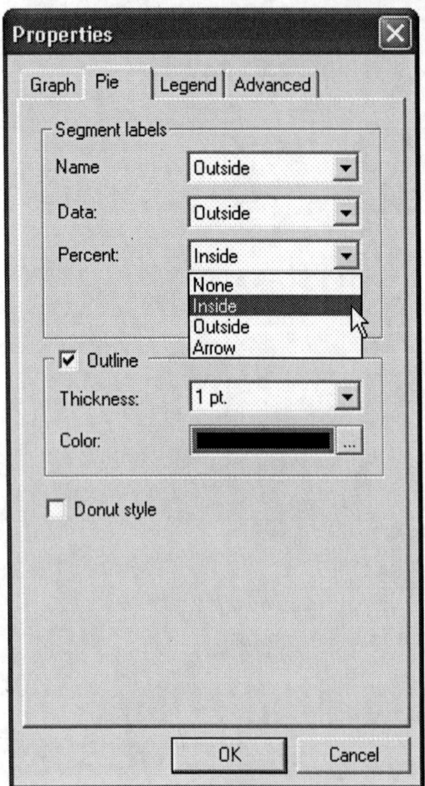

The percentages appear within the pie chart.

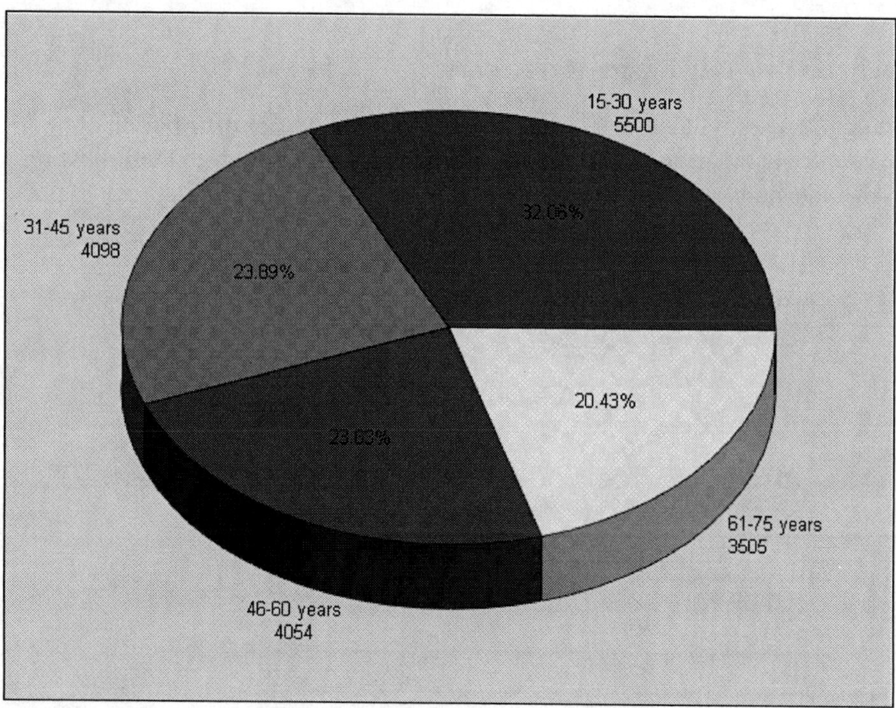

10. Save the pie chart as a .JPG file. Right-click on the graph and select **Save as…**. In the Save As… dialog box, navigate to S:\workshop\winsas\sbiamo and name the file **`MyPieChart.jpg`**. Select **Save**.

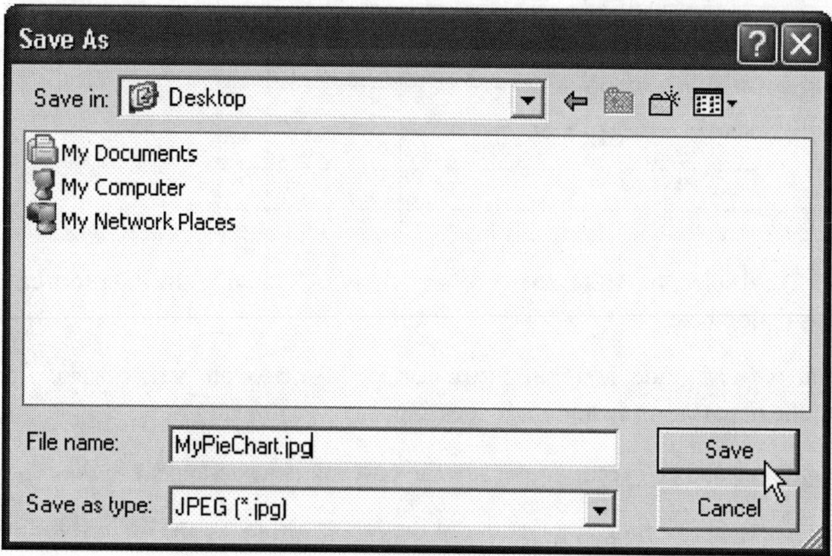

5.9 Exercises

7. Creating a Table Analysis (Two-Way Frequency) Report

a. For future marketing purposes, you are interested in analyzing the gender distribution of your customers by the country of residence. Use the Table Analysis task to produce the following report using the AMODefault output style.

Partial Output

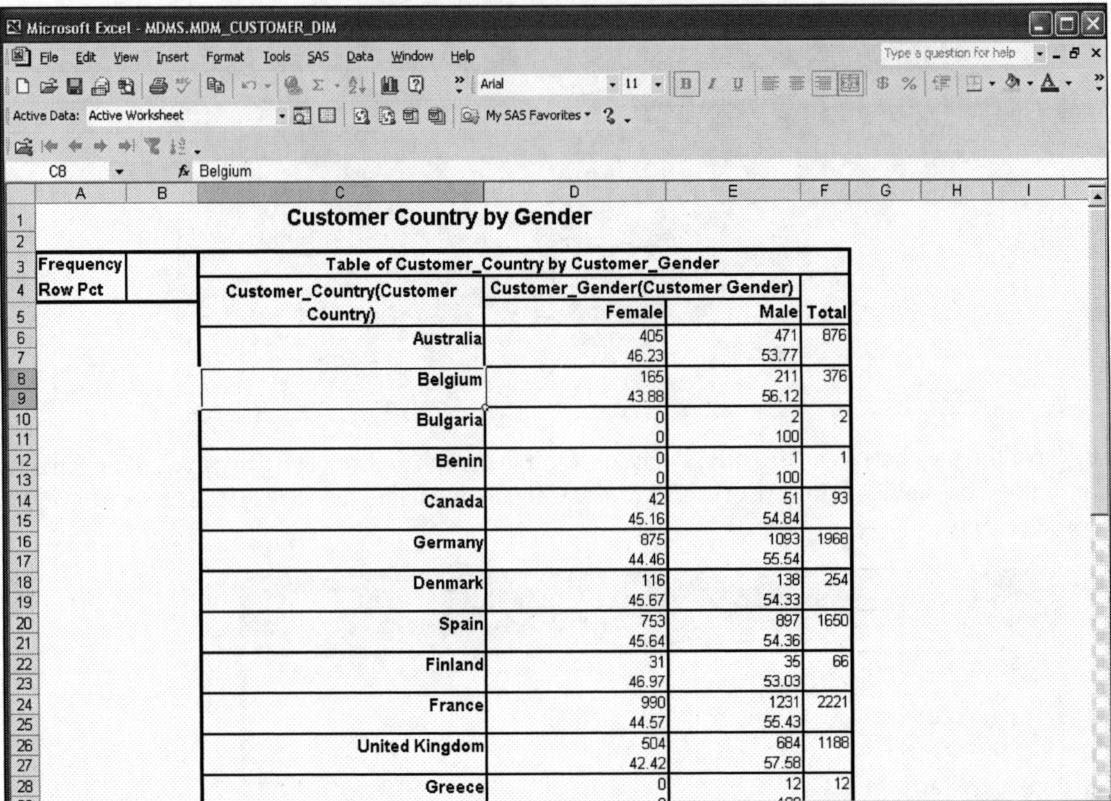

Customer Country by Gender

Frequency Row Pct	Table of Customer_Country by Customer_Gender			
	Customer_Country(Customer Country)	Customer_Gender(Customer Gender)		
		Female	Male	Total
	Australia	405 46.23	471 53.77	876
	Belgium	165 43.88	211 56.12	376
	Bulgaria	0 0	2 100	2
	Benin	0 0	1 100	1
	Canada	42 45.16	51 54.84	93
	Germany	875 44.46	1093 55.54	1968
	Denmark	116 45.67	138 54.33	254
	Spain	753 45.64	897 54.36	1650
	Finland	31 46.97	35 53.03	66
	France	990 44.57	1231 55.43	2221
	United Kingdom	504 42.42	684 57.58	1188
	Greece	0	12	12

b. From within Microsoft Excel select the **`MDM_Customer_Dim`** SAS table as the data source and open the Table Analysis dialog box.

c. Using the output from above as a guide, assign the **`Customer Gender`** and **`Customer Country`** variables to the necessary role and table location.

d. Specify that **row percentages** and **cell frequencies** are the only statistics to appear in the report.

e. Add a title with the text Customer Country by Gender to the report. Remove the default footnote.

f. Generate the report and answer the following question:

1) Which countries have a higher percentage of female customers than male customers?

8. Producing a Summary Table from the `MDM_Customer_Dim` Table

a. Use the **`MDM_Customer_Dim`** table in the MDM Source Tables Library to create a summary table that shows the number of customers and average age for each gender in each country.

b. Use the COMMAw.d format with a total width of 8 for the N statistic and the w.d with a total width of 6 for the MEAN statistic.

c. Refresh the table to add the title **`Average Customer Age by Gender and Country`**. Label the N statistic as **`Total`**.

Partial output

	A	B	C	D	E
1	**Average Customer Age by Gender and Country**				
2					
3		Total	Customer Gender		
4			Female	Male	
5			Customer Age	Customer Age	
6			Mean	Mean	
7	Customer Country				
8	Australia	876	43	44	
9	Belgium	376	46	45	
10	Bulgaria	2	.	31	
11	Benin	1	.	28	
12	Canada	93	40	43	
13	Germany	1,968	44	45	
14	Denmark	254	43	42	
15	Spain	1,650	44	42	
16	Finland	66	44	43	
17	France	2,221	42	44	
18	United Kingdom	1,188	44	44	

9. Producing a Bar Chart from the `MDM_OrderFact` Table

a. Use the **`MDM_OrderFact`** table to produce a bar chart that compares the average and overall total retail price for products provided through each of your sales channels.

Use the Bar Chart task to produce the following report that shows the average and overall total retail price (**`Total Retail Price for This Product`**) by **`Order Type`**.

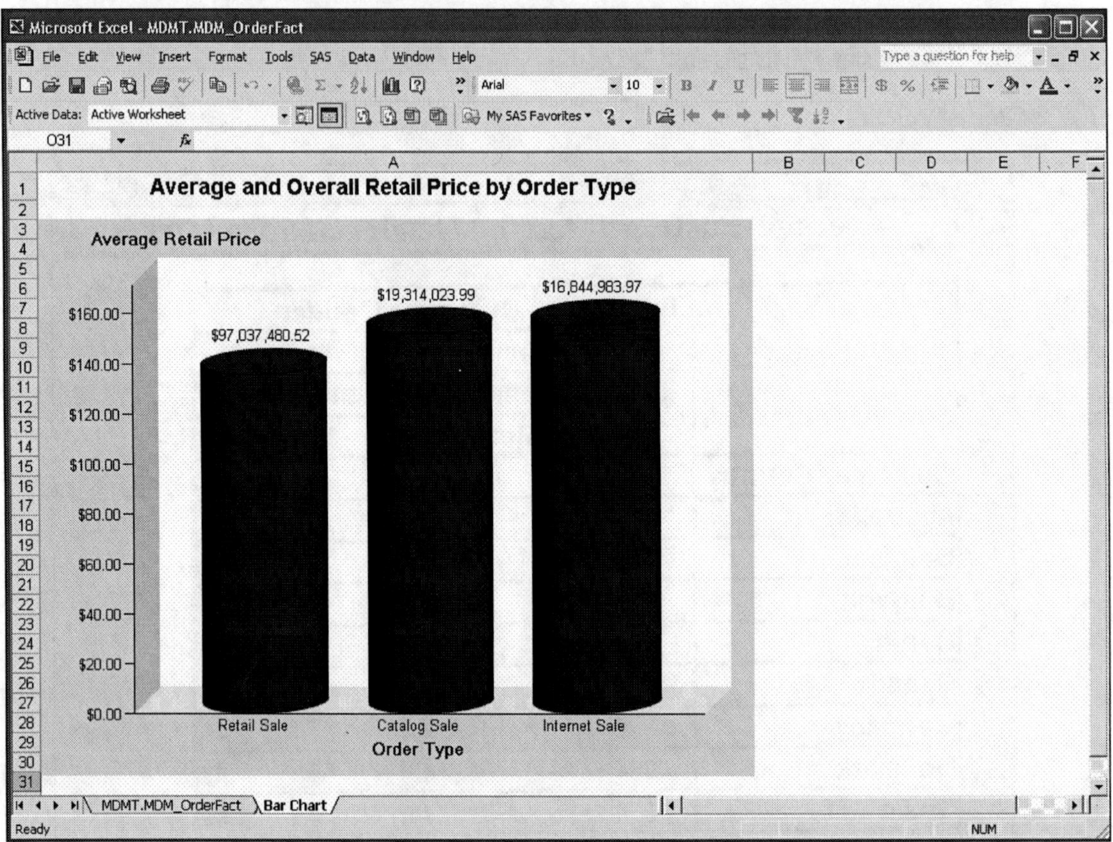

1) Select the **MDM_OrderFact** table as the data source and open the Bar Chart task. Select the simple vertical bar chart as the type of graph.

b. Assign the Chart variables and produce the graph.

1) Assign **`Order Type`** as the Column to chart and **`Total Retail Price for This Product`** as the column that determines the length of the bars.

2) Specify that the report contains one blue cylindrical bar for each unique value of **`Order Type`** with no reference lines.

3) Specify **`Average Retail Price`** as the Vertical Axis Label.

4) Specify that the height of each bar be determined by the average (**mean**) overall **`Total Retail Price for This Product`** and that the sum values of this column be included in the report next to each bar.

   a) Specify the format DOLLAR15.2 for the **`Total Retail Price for This Product`**.

5) Add a title with the text **`Average and Overall Retail Price by Order Type`** and delete the default footnote.

c. Generate the report and answer the following questions:

1) Products sold through which sales channel have the lowest average total retail price?

2) Products sold through which sales channel generate the greatest overall retail price?

10. Displaying a Pie Chart (Optional)

a. Use the Products.xls spreadsheet to produce the following pie chart that displays the proportional breakdown of men's shoe products by group.

Output

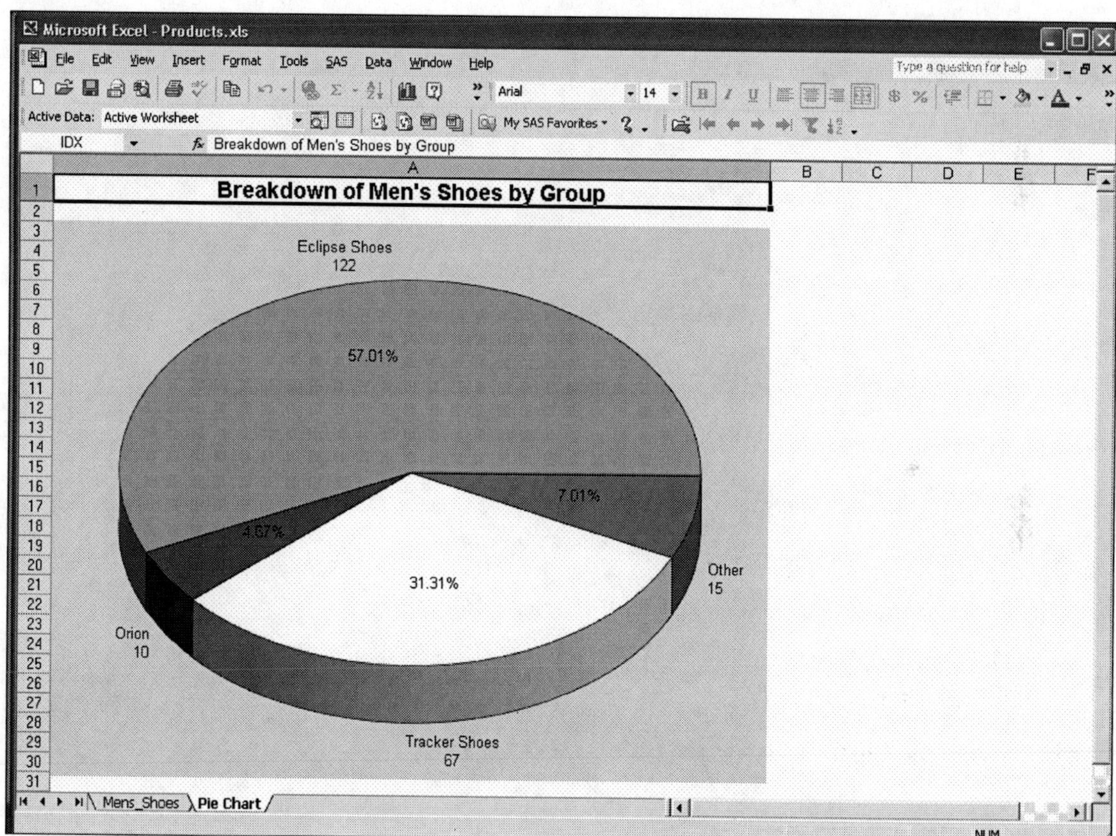

The Products.xls Excel spreadsheet is stored in S:\workshop\winsas\sbiamo.

b. Open the Products.xls Excel spreadsheet and create a simple pie chart.

1) Verify that the SAS option **Labels in First Row** is selected.

c. Create the pie chart.

1) Assign `Product Group` as the Column to chart.

2) Select the **Beach** color scheme.

3) Specify that the Frequency is used to calculate the size of each slice and that the frequency value is displayed outside of the slice.

4) Specify that Percentages be displayed within each pie slice.

5) Specify the title Breakdown of Men's Shoes by Group and no footnote.

5.10 Solutions to Exercises

1. **Preparing a Data Source for SAS Tasks**

   a. In Excel, open and filter the `MDM_Order_fact` table.

      1) Select **SAS** ⇨ **Options**.

      2) On the Tasks tab, deselect the option **Include SAS procedure titles in results**.

      3) Select **SAS** ⇨ **Open SAS Data Source** from the pull-down menus, or select [icon] on the SAS Data Analysis toolbar.

      4) In the Open SAS Data Source window, select **Servers** from the shortcut bar.

      5) If prompted, enter the user name and password provided by the instructor.

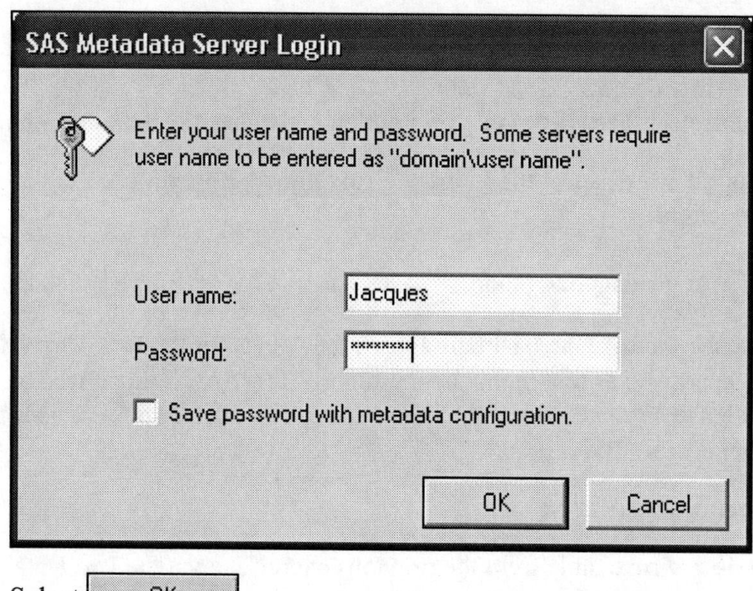

      Select [OK].

      6) Choose **SASMain** and select [Open] (or double-click **SASMain**).

      7) Select **MDM Target Tables Library**, then select [Open] (or double-click **Source Tables Library**).

      8) Select **MDM_OrderFact**, then choose [Open] (or double-click **Customer_Dim**). The data from the server is retrieved into the worksheet.

      9) Select the filter icon [icon] on the SAS Data Analysis toolbar (or select **SAS** ⇨ **Filter SAS Data Source**).

      10) Using the drop-down menus, specify an expression of `Delivery_Time Is greater than 21`.

      11) Select [OK] to apply the filter.

How many orders took over 21 days to deliver? **142**

2. **Creating a Listing Report**

   a. Using the filtered `Order_fact` table from the previous exercise, open the List Data task, and assign List variables and a Group analysis by variable.

      1) Navigate to the filtered `Order_fact` table by selecting the appropriate sheet in Excel.

      2) Select **SAS** ⇨ **Browse SAS Programs**.

      3) Expand the SAS Tasks menu and select **Describe** ⇨ **List Data** to open the List Data task dialog box. Select Run.

      4) Drag **Order_ID**, **Quantity**, **Order_Type**, and **Delivery_Time** to the List variables role.

      5) Drag **Order_Qtr** to the Group analysis by role.

      6) Select the **Titles** tab and select **Report Titles**. Deselect the **Use default text** option and specify the title text `Delayed Deliveries by Quarter`.

      7) Select **Footnote**. Deselect the **Use default text** option and delete the default footnote text.

      8) Select the **Options** tab and deselect the **Print the row number** option. Select the **Print number of rows** option.

      9) Select Run to generate the report.

   When you opened the `MDM_OrderFact` table in Excel, the values for `Order Type` were numeric. Why are they appearing as text in this listing report? **The SAS data source has a permanent format assigned to the `Order_Type` variable. The List Data task uses that format automatically when generating the report.**

3. **Creating a Listing Report**

   a. Using the filtered `Order_fact` table from the previous exercise, open the List Data task and assign List variables and a Group analysis by variable.

      1) Navigate to the filtered `Order_fact` table by selecting the appropriate sheet in Excel.

      2) Select **SAS** ⇨ **Browse SAS Programs**.

      3) Expand the SAS Tasks menu and select **Describe** ⇨ **List Data** to open the List Data task dialog box. Select Run.

      4) Drag **Order_ID**, **Quantity**, and **Delivery_Time** to the List variables role.

      5) Drag **Order_Type** to the Group analysis by role.

      6) Select the **Titles** tab and select **Report Titles**. Deselect the **Use default text** option and specify the title text `Delayed Deliveries by Order Type`.

      7) Select **Footnote**. Deselect the **Use default text** option and delete the default footnote text.

8) Select the **Options** tab and deselect the **Print the row number** option. Select the **Print number of rows** option.

9) Select Run to generate the report.

4. **Sending Multiple Results to Word**

a. Verify that the SAS option **When sending multiple results to Word, place each result in a separate document** is deselected.

1) Select **SAS** ⇨ **Options**.

2) On the Results tab, verify that the **When sending multiple results to Word, place each result in a separate document** is deselected.

b. Send both of these listing reports to a single Microsoft Word document.

1) Select **SAS** ⇨ **Send Multiple Results to Microsoft Word**.

2) Make sure both List Data output items are selected.

3) Select Send to Word.

5. **Creating a One-Way Frequency Report**

a. Using the filtered `MDM_OrderFact` table from the previous exercises, execute the One-Way Frequency task in Microsoft Excel to display the number of delayed deliveries by quarter. Open the One-Way Frequencies task dialog box and assign an analysis variable.

1) Make sure that **Active worksheet** is selected as the data source. Navigate to the filtered `Order_fact` table by selecting the appropriate sheet in Excel.

2) Select **SAS** ⇨ **Browse SAS Programs**.

3) Expand the SAS Tasks menu and select **Describe** ⇨ **One-Way Frequencies** to open the One-Way Frequencies for order_fact task dialog box.

4) Drag **ORDER_QTR** to the Analysis variables role.

5) Select the **Statistics** tab and select **Frequencies and percentages** under the Frequency table options.

6) To specify a vertical bar chart, select the **Plots** tab and select **Vertical**.

7) Select the **Titles** tab and select **Anaylsis**. Deselect the **Use default text** option and specify the title text `Frequency of Delayed Orders by Quarter`.

8) Select the **Titles** tab and select **Plots**. Deselect the **Use default text** option and specify the title text `Plot of Delayed Orders by Quarter`.

9) Select **Footnote**. Deselect the **Use default text** option and delete the default footnote text.

10) Select Run.

Which Quarter experienced the most delayed deliveries? **Quarter3**

6. Running Tasks from Microsoft Word

a. You are interested in identifying your most important suppliers. Use the One-Way Frequency task to identify the number of products obtained from each supplier.

1) Make sure the SASAddin style is active.

a) Select **SAS** ⇨ **Style Manager**.

b) Highlight the SASAddin style and select Set as Default.

2) Make sure the option **Include SAS procedure titles in results** is deselected.

a) Select **SAS** ⇨ **Options.**

b) On the Tasks tab, deselect the option to **Include SAS procedure titles in results**.

c) Select OK to close the Style Manager window.

3) Use `MDM_Product_List` to create a one-way frequency table of `Supplier_ID`.

a) From within Word, select **MDM_Product_List** as the active data source.

(1) Select **SAS** ⇨ **Active Data** ⇨ **Select SAS Data Source**

(2) Select **Servers** from the shortcut bar.

(3) If prompted, enter the user name and password provided by the instructor.

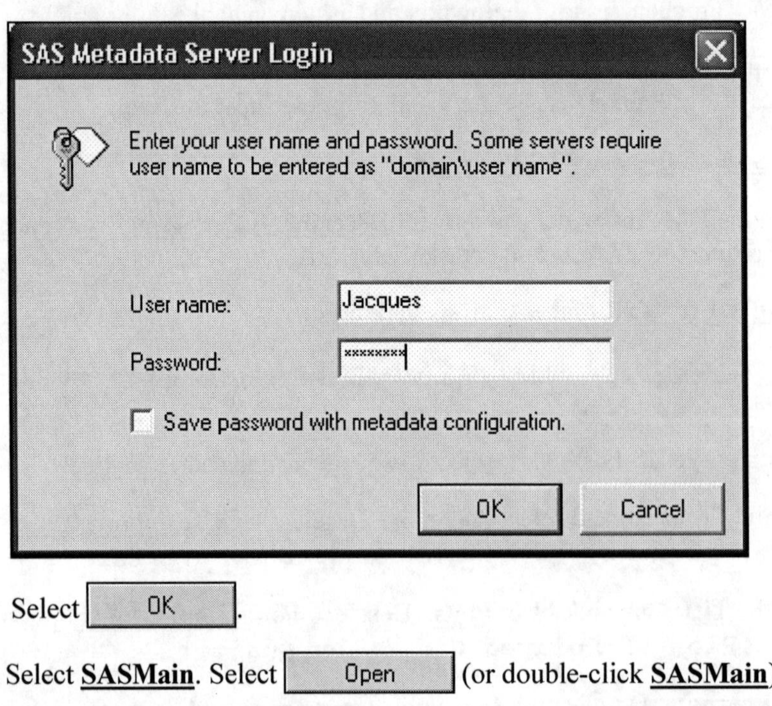

Select OK.

(4) Select **SASMain**. Select Open (or double-click **SASMain**).

(5) Select **MDM Source Tables Library**, then select Open (or double-click **MDM Source Tables Library**).

(6) Select the **MDM_Product_List** table and select Open.

b. Create a one-way frequency table of `Supplier_ID`.

1) Select **SAS** ⇨ **Browse SAS Programs**.

2) Expand the SAS Tasks menu and select **Describe** ⇨ **One-Way Frequencies** to open the One-Way Frequencies task dialog box. Select [Run].

3) Drag **Supplier_ID** to the Analysis variables role.

4) On the Statistics tab, select **Frequencies and percentages** under the Frequency table options.

5) On the Results tab, use the Order output data by drop-down menu to select **Descending frequencies** and select [Run].

Which Supplier ID references the supplier that provides us with 30 different products? **13199**

c. Enhance the report by refreshing the output.

1) Specify that the sasweb output style is used.

a) Select **SAS** ⇨ **Style Manager**.

b) Highlight the **sasweb** style and select [Set as Default].

c) Select [OK] to close the Style Manager window.

2) Make sure the cursor is positioned in the body of the report and then select **SAS** ⇨ **Refresh**.

3) Specify the title Number of Products from each Supplier with no footnote.

a) Select the **Titles** tab and select **Analysis**. Deselect the **Use default text** option and specify the title text `Number of Products from each Supplier`.

b) Select **Footnote**. Deselect the **Use default text** option and delete the default footnote text.

7. Creating a Table Analysis (Two-Way Frequency) Report for the `MDM_Customer_Dim` Table

a. From within Excel open the `MDM_Customer_Dim` data source.

1) Select **SAS** ⇨ **Open SAS Data Source** from the pull-down menus, or select [icon] on the SAS Data Analysis toolbar.

2) Select the **MDM Source Tables Library**.

3) Select the **MDM_Customer_Dim** table.

4) Open the Table Analysis dialog box by selecting **SAS** ⇨ **Browse SAS Programs**.

5) Expand the Describe category and select **Table Analysis**.

6) Select [Run] to generate the table.

b. Assign the table variables and generate the report.

1) Drag the **Customer_Gender** and **Customer_Country** variables to the Table variables role.

2) On the Tables tab, drag and drop **Customer_Gender** onto the table in the Preview pane.

3) Next, drag **Customer_Country** onto the table in the Preview pane.

Hint: The first variable dragged onto the table represents the column dimension and the second represents the row dimension.

c. On the Cell Statistics tab, deselect the option to display **Column percentages** and select the option to display **Row percentages**.

d. Add a title with the text Customer Country by Gender to the report. Remove the default footnote.

1) Select the **Titles** tab and select **Table Anaylsis**. Deselect the **Use default text** option and specify the title text `Customer Country by Gender`.

2) Select **Footnote**. Deselect **Use default text** and delete the default footnote text.

e. Select [Run] to generate the report.

Which countries have a higher percentage of female customers than male customers? **Croatia, Ireland, Lithuania, Luxembourg,** and **Macedonia.**

8. Producing a Summary Table from the `MDM_Customer_Dim` Table

a. Use the **`MDM_Customer_Dim`** table in the MDM Source Tables Library to create a summary table that shows the number of customers and average age for each gender in each country.

1) From Excel, select **SAS** ⇨ **Open SAS Data Source** from the pull-down menu, or select [icon] on the SAS Data Analysis toolbar.

2) Select the **MDM Source Tables Library** and select the **MDM_Customer_Dim** table.

3) Open the Summary Tables task by selecting **SAS** ⇨ **Browse SAS Programs** ⇨ **SAS Tasks**.

4) Expand the Describe category, select **Summary Tables**, and select [Run].

5) On the Task Roles pane, drag **Customer Age** to the Analysis variables role and **Customer Country** and **Customer Gender** to the Classification variables role.

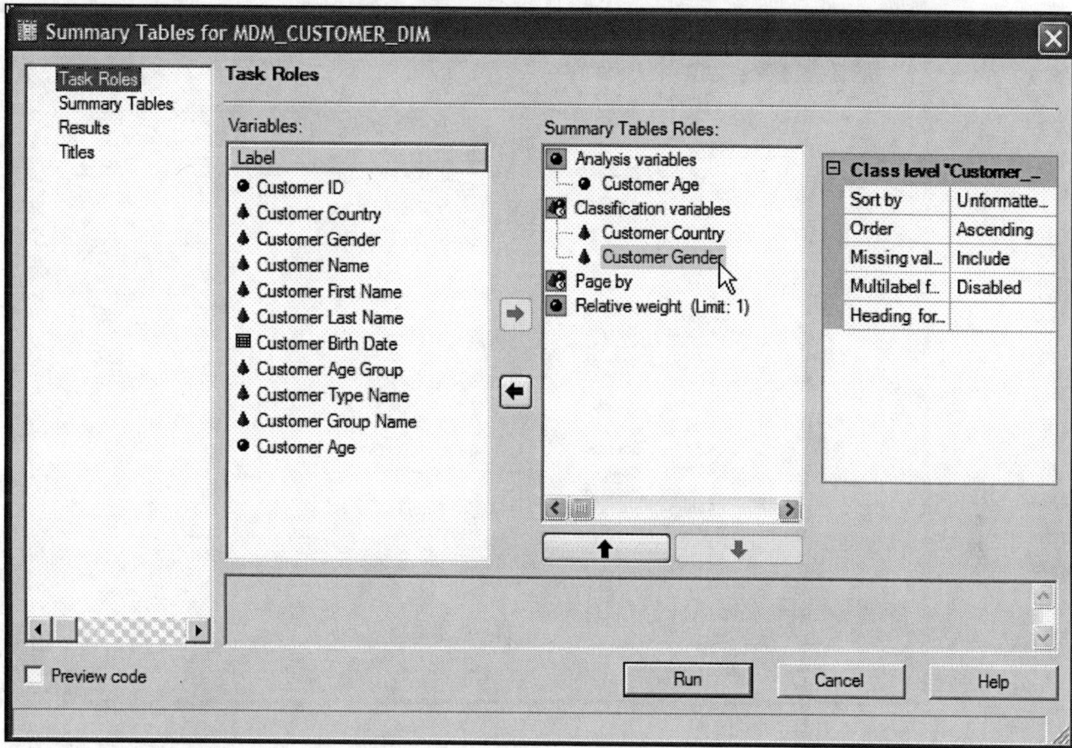

6) Select **Summary Tables** and drag **Customer Country** to the row box under Box Area. The N statistic is placed in the column area by default.

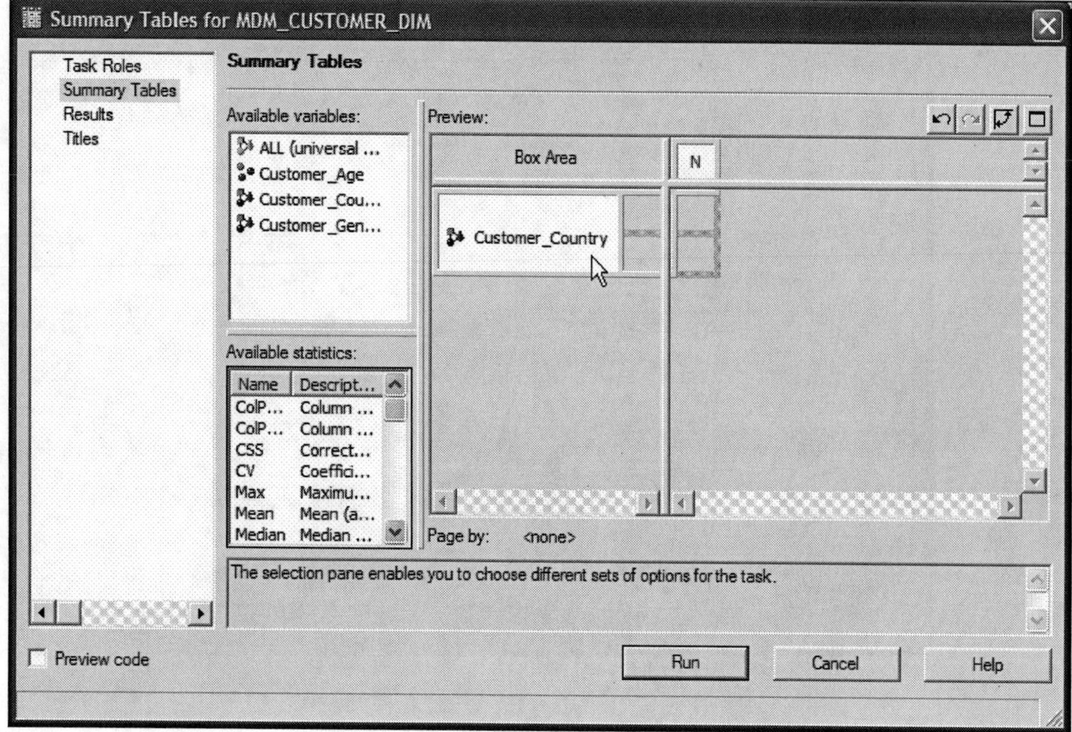

7) Drag **Customer Gender** to the column area to the right of the N statistic.

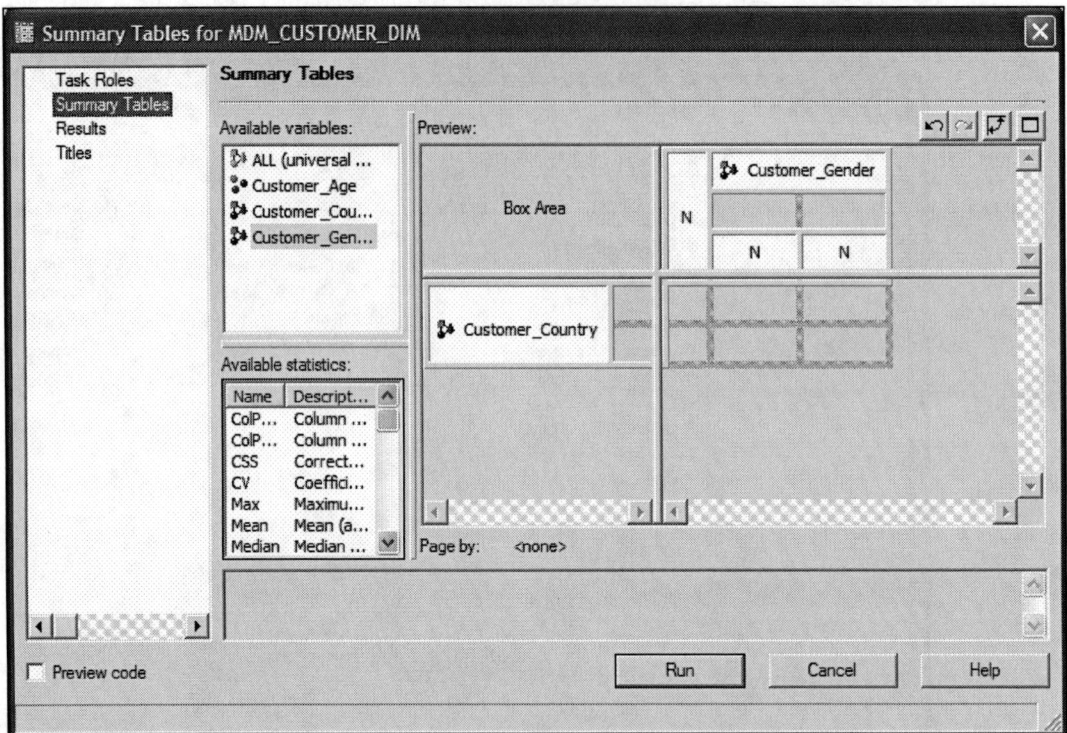

8) Drag **Customer Age** directly above the N statistic listed under **Customer Gender**.

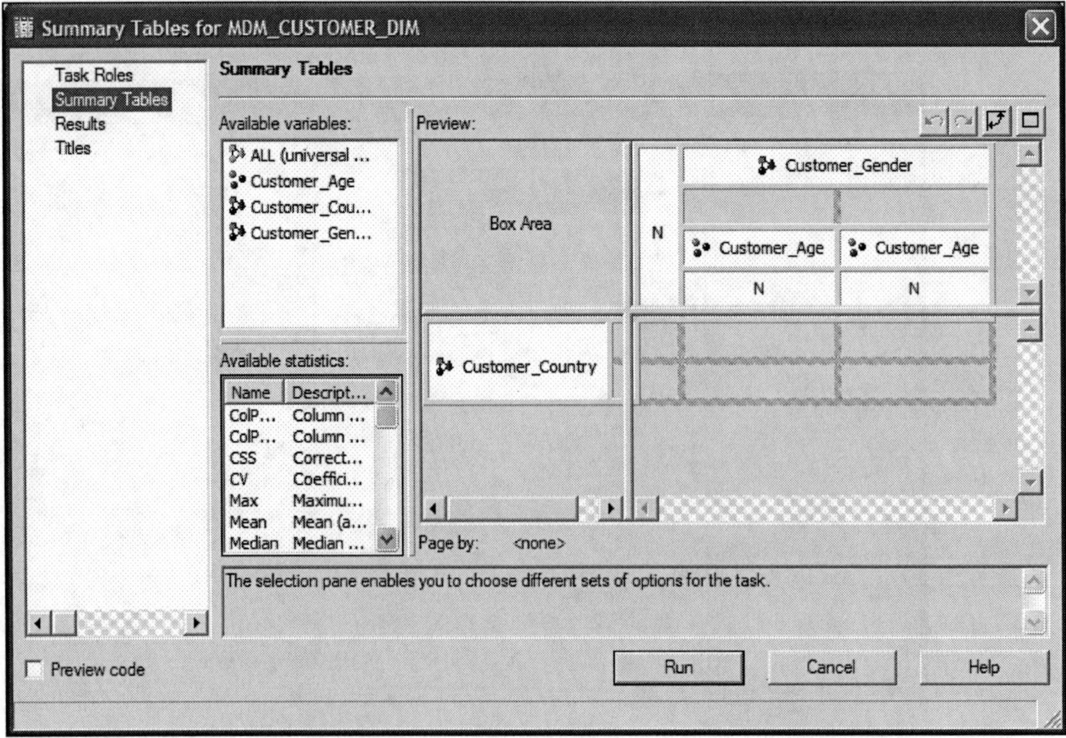

9) Select **Mean** under the Available statistics pane and drop it on top of the N statistic under the `Customer Age` column.

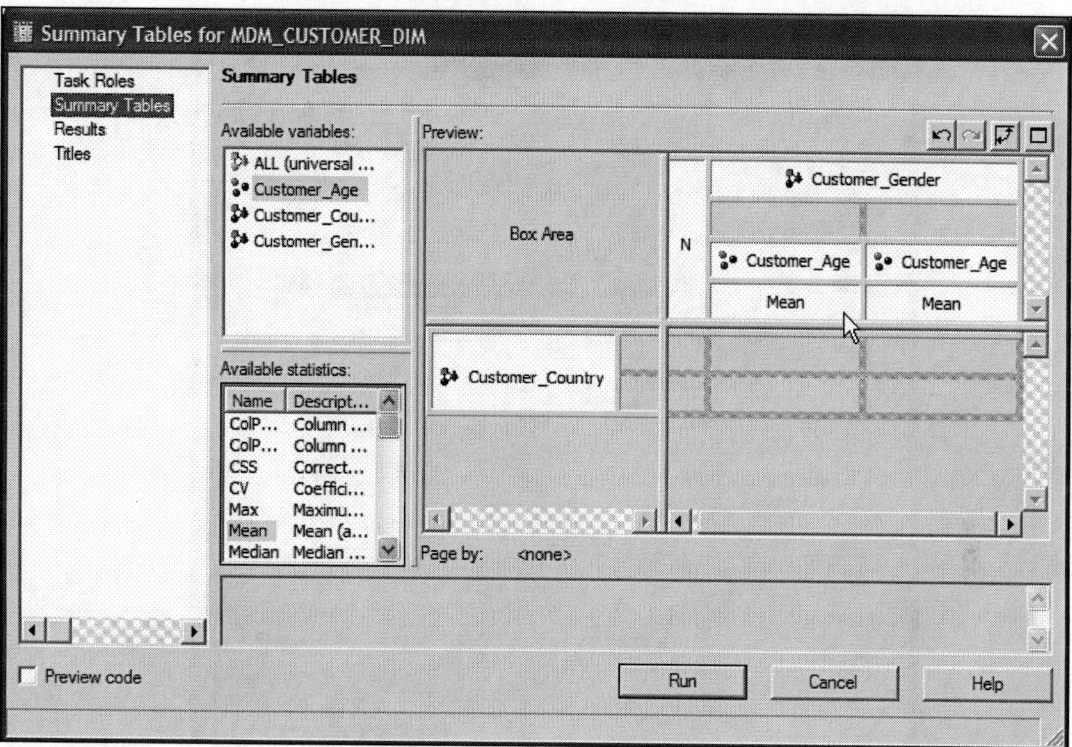

b. Use the COMMA*w.d* format with a total width of 8 for the N statistic and the BEST*w.d* format with a total width of 6 for the MEAN statistic.

1) Right-click the **N** statistic and select **Data Value Properties…**.

2) Select **Format** ⇨ **Numeric** ⇨ **COMMAw.d**. Make the Overall width 8 and select OK.

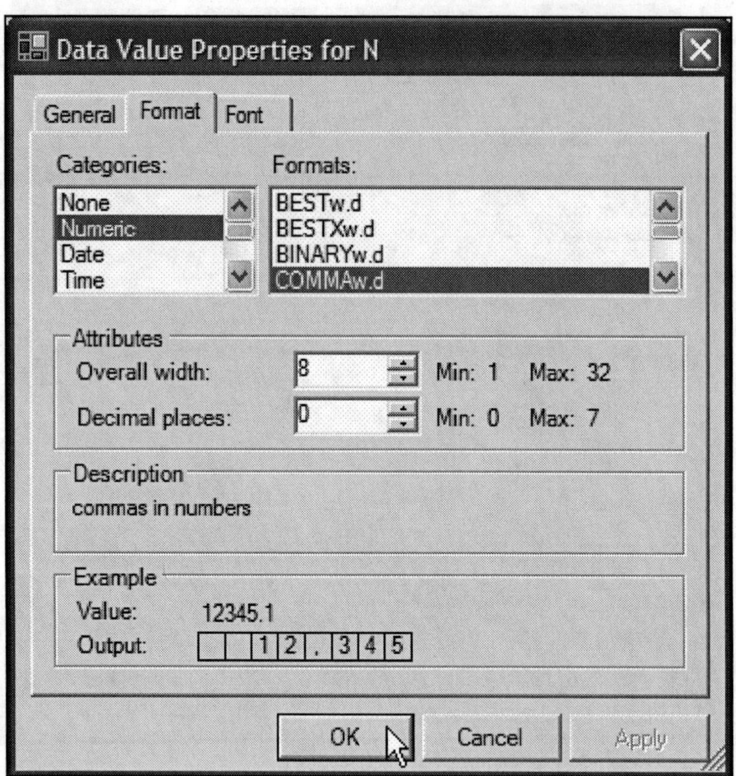

3) Right-click the Mean statistic and select **Data Value Properties…**.

4) Select **Format** ⇨ **Numeric** ⇨ **w.d**. Type in **6** for the overall width, or use the down arrow to navigate to 6. Then select OK.

5) Select **Run** to create the table.

Partial output

	A	B	C	D
1	Summary Tables			
2				
3		N	Customer Gender	
4			Female	Male
5			Customer Age	Customer Age
6			Mean	Mean
7	Customer Country			
8	Australia	876	43	44
9	Belgium	376	46	45
10	Bulgaria	2	.	31
11	Benin	1	.	28
12	Canada	93	40	43
13	Germany	1,968	44	45
14	Denmark	254	43	42
15	Spain	1,650	44	42
16	Finland	66	44	43
17	France	2,221	42	44
18	United Kingdom	1,188	44	44

c. Refresh the table to add the title Average Customer Age by Gender and Country. Label the N statistic as `Total`.

1) Select **SAS** ⇨ **Refresh**, or select the Refresh icon from the SAS Analysis Tools toolbar.

2) Select **Titles** ⇨ **Table Titles** and deselect **Use default text**.

3) Type `Average Customer Age by Gender and Country` for the title text.

4) Select **Summary Tables**, right-click the **N** statistic, and select **Heading Properties…**.

5) Select the **General** tab and type **`Total`** for the label. Select OK.

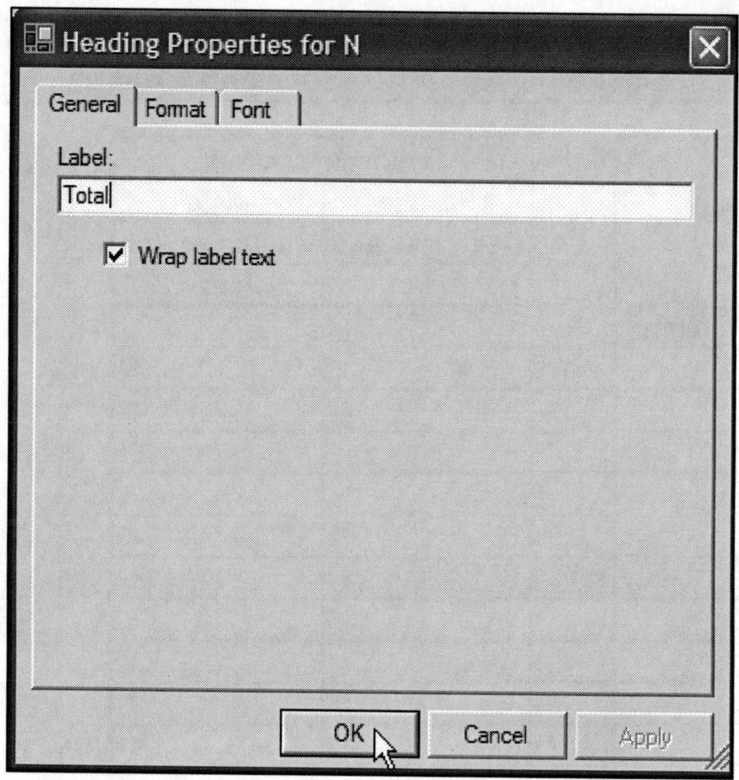

6) Select Run to create the table.

	A	B	C	D	E
1	**Average Customer Age by Gender and Country**				
2					
3		**Total**	**Customer Gender**		
4			**Female**	**Male**	
5			**Customer Age**	**Customer Age**	
6			**Mean**	**Mean**	
7	**Customer Country**				
8	**Australia**	876	43	44	
9	**Belgium**	376	46	45	
10	**Bulgaria**	2	.	31	
11	**Benin**	1	.	28	
12	**Canada**	93	40	43	
13	**Germany**	1,968	44	45	
14	**Denmark**	254	43	42	
15	**Spain**	1,650	44	42	
16	**Finland**	66	44	43	
17	**France**	2,221	42	44	
18	**United Kingdom**	1,188	44	44	

To remove any column headings, right-click the column and select **Heading Properties…** and delete the text in the label.

9. Producing a Bar Chart from the `MDM_OrderFact` Table

a. From within Excel, open the **`MDM_OrderFact`** data source.

1) Select **SAS** ⇨ **Open SAS Data Source** from the pull-down menus, or select the icon on the SAS Data Analysis toolbar.

2) Select the **MDM Target Tables** library.

3) Select the **MDM_OrderFact** table.

4) Open the Bar Chart task dialog box by selecting **SAS** ⇨ **Browse SAS Programs** ⇨ **SAS Tasks**.

5) Expand the Graph category, select **Bar Chart**, and select Run.

6) On the Bar Chart tab, select **Simple Vertical Bar** as the type of graph to produce.

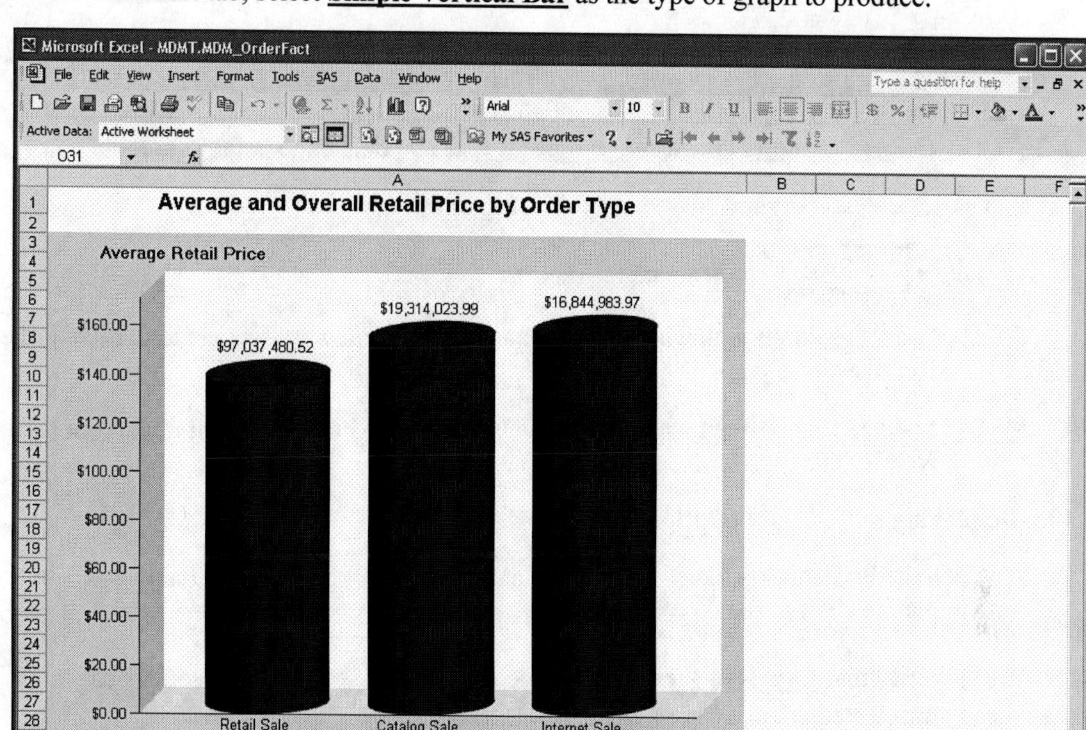

b. Assign the chart variables and produce the graph.

1) On the Task Roles tab, drag **Order_Type** to the Column to chart role and **Total_Retail_Price** to the Sum of role.

2) Right-click on `Total_Retail_Price`, select **Properties**, and select [Change...] to change the format to DOLLAR15.2.

3) Select [OK] to close the Formats Window. Select [OK] to close the Properties window.

4) In the **Appearance** ⇨ **Bars** dialog box, with the **Color** radio button selected in the Bar appearance pane, use the drop-down menu to select one of the blue color options.

5) Select the option **Specify number of bars** and select **One bar for each unique data value**.

6) On the Layout tab, select **Cylinder** from the Shape drop-down menu.

7) On the Reference Lines tab, deselect the option **Use reference lines**.

8) On the Vertical Axis tab, enter the text `Average Retail Price` in the Label area.

9) On the Advanced tab, select **Mean** as the Statistic used to calculate bar.

10) Then, select **Sum** as the Additional statistical value to show next to bar.

11) Select **Titles** ⇨ **Graph**. Deselect **Use default text** and specify the title text `Average and Overall Retail Price by Order Type`.

12) Select **Footnote**. Deselect **Use default text** and delete the default footnote text.

c. Generate the report and answer the following questions:

Select **Run** to generate the report.

1) Products sold through which sales channel have the lowest average total retail price?
Retail Sale

2) Products sold through which sales channel have the highest overall total retail price?
Retail Sale

10. Displaying a Pie Chart (Optional)

a. Open the Products.xls Excel spreadsheet and open the Pie Chart task dialog box. Select the Simple pie chart as the type of pie chart.

1) Verify that **Labels in First Row** is selected. (When selected, the icon appears as ; unselected, it appears as .)

a) Select **SAS** ⇨ **Labels in First Row**.

b) The icon should appear indicating that labels are in the first row.

b. Create the Pie Chart.

Select **SAS** ⇨ **Browse SAS Programs**. Expand the Graph category and select **Pie Chart**. On the Pie Chart tab, select **Simple Pie**.

1) On the Task roles tab, drag **Product_Group** to the Column to chart role.

2) On the Appearance tab, select the **Beach** color scheme.

3) On the Advanced tab, specify that **Frequency** is used to calculate the size of each slice. On the Layout tab, specify that the Statistic value is displayed **Outside** of the slice.

4) On the Layout tab, specify that Percentages are displayed **Inside** the slice.

5) Select **Titles** ⇨ **Graph**. Deselect **Use default text** and specify the title text `Breakdown of Men's Shoes by Group`. Select **Footnote**. Deselect **Use default text** and delete the default footnote text.

6) Select **Run** to generate the report.

Appendix A SAS®9 Business Intelligence Training

SAS®9 Business Intelligence Training

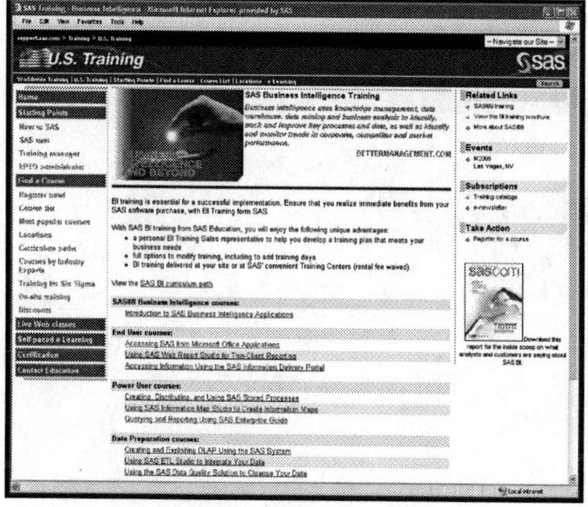

http://support.sas.com/training/bi/

2

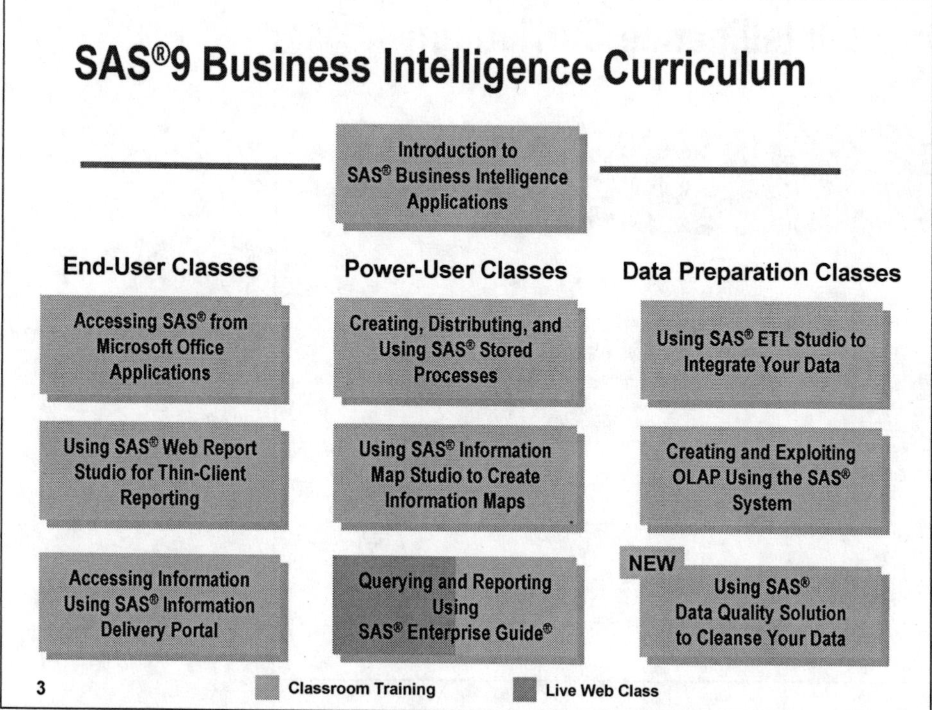

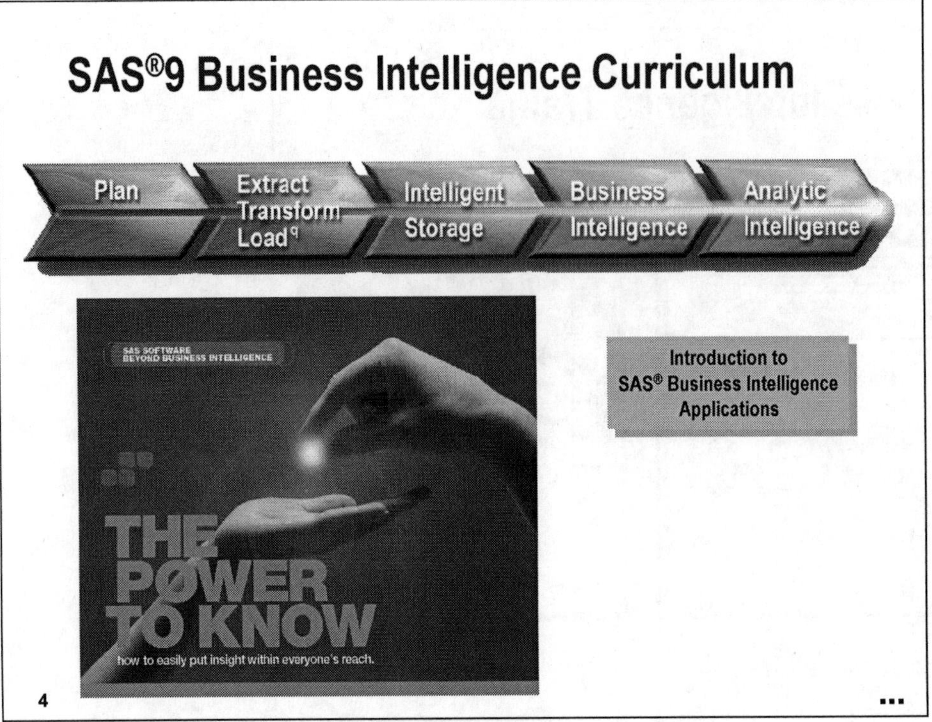
SAS®9 Business Intelligence Curriculum
Plan
Extract Transform Load
Intelligent Storage
Business Intelligence
Analytic Intelligence
SAS SOFTWARE BEYOND BUSINESS INTELLIGENCE
THE POWER TO KNOW
how to easily put insight within everyone's reach.
Introduction to SAS® Business Intelligence Applications
4

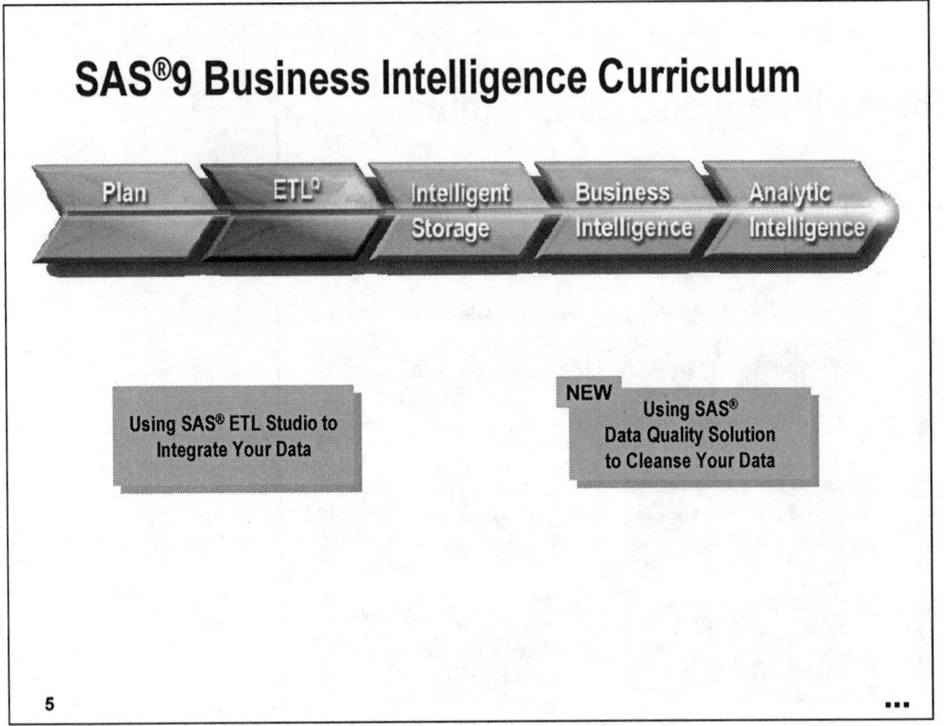
SAS®9 Business Intelligence Curriculum
Plan
ETL
Intelligent Storage
Business Intelligence
Analytic Intelligence
Using SAS® ETL Studio to Integrate Your Data
NEW
Using SAS® Data Quality Solution to Cleanse Your Data
5

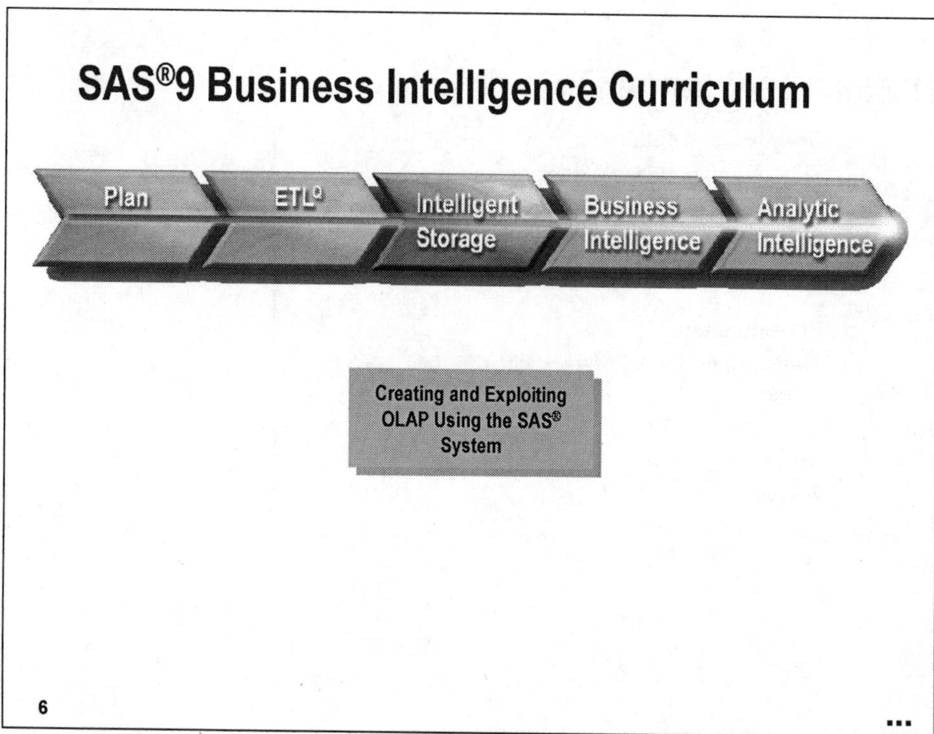
SAS®9 Business Intelligence Curriculum
Plan
ETLQ
Intelligent Storage
Business Intelligence
Analytic Intelligence
Creating and Exploiting OLAP Using the SAS® System
6
...

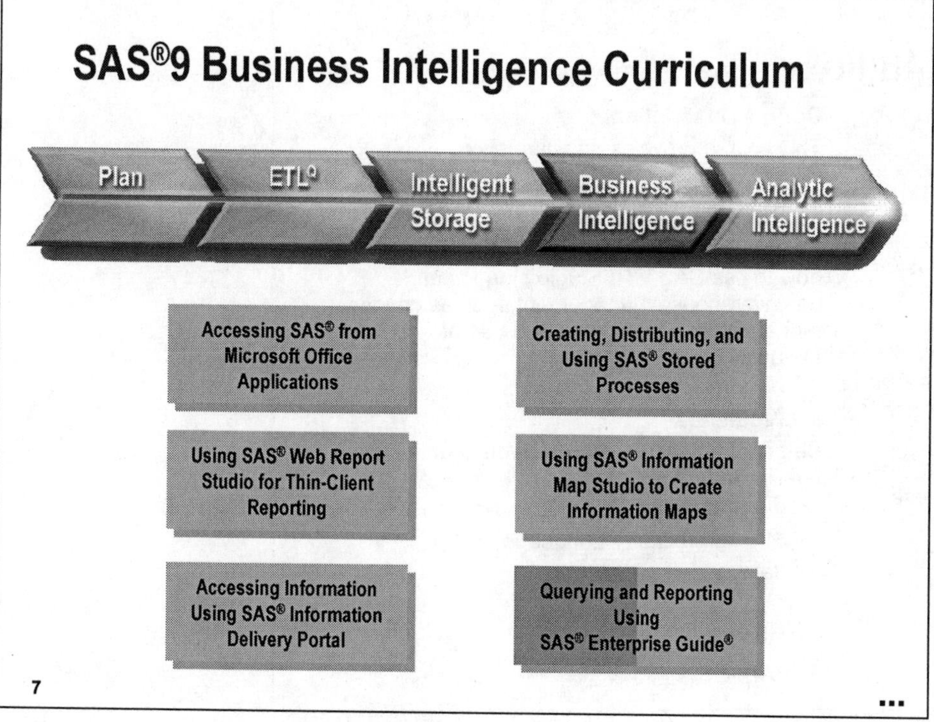
SAS®9 Business Intelligence Curriculum
Plan
ETLQ
Intelligent Storage
Business Intelligence
Analytic Intelligence
Accessing SAS® from Microsoft Office Applications
Creating, Distributing, and Using SAS® Stored Processes
Using SAS® Web Report Studio for Thin-Client Reporting
Using SAS® Information Map Studio to Create Information Maps
Accessing Information Using SAS® Information Delivery Portal
Querying and Reporting Using SAS® Enterprise Guide®
7
...

SAS®9 Business Intelligence Overview

Introduction to the SAS® Business Intelligence Applications

This Level I course is designed for anyone who wants a hands-on overview of the new SAS®9 Business Intelligence applications. This course requires the SAS®9 Intelligence Platform.

Course Description

This course provides participants with a hands-on overview of the features and functionality available in the applications of the SAS®9 Intelligence Platform.

Prerequisites

There are no formal prerequisites for this course.

Duration

2 days

8

SAS® ETL Studio

Using SAS® ETL Studio to Integrate Your Data

This Level III course is for data warehouse project leaders, ETL designers, systems experts, and/or data modelers who will be involved in the extraction, transformation, and loading of data into a warehouse. This course requires the SAS®9 Intelligence Platform.

Course Description

This course provides an overview of SAS ETL Studio. You learn how to navigate through the SAS ETL Studio interface and to extract, transform, and load data using SAS ETL Studio. Additional topics include how to use SAS ETL Studio plug-ins and data warehouse management such as change management, scheduling, and use of metadata.

Prerequisites

Before attending this course, you should be familiar with

- the SAS programming language
- Structured Query Language (SQL)
- data modeling concepts.

Duration

3 days

9

SAS®9 Data Quality Solution

NEW

Using SAS® Data Quality Solution to Cleanse Your Data

This Level III course is designed for data quality analysts, warehouse consultants, and ETL specialists who want to learn the tools and techniques of using SAS Data Quality Solution to cleanse data. This course requires the SAS®9 Intelligence Platform.

Course Description

This course introduces you to the issues relating to data quality and provides hands-on experience using SAS Data Quality Solution and SAS ETL Studio. You gain an understanding of the essentials of data quality and gain specific knowledge of data profiling and analysis, standardization and scheme building, duplicate elimination and match code generation, and data augmentation and enhancement.

Prerequisites

Knowledge of data cleansing issues, SAS programming, and SAS ETL Studio is helpful, but not required.

Duration

2 days

10

SAS® OLAP Cube Studio

Creating and Exploiting OLAP Using the SAS® System

This Level II course is designed for data modelers and system experts who want to understand, create, and exploit Online Analytical Processing (OLAP) using the SAS System. This course requires the SAS®9 Intelligence Platform.

Course Description

This course defines SAS OLAP cubes and explores their characteristics. This course also demonstrates how to create and exploit SAS OLAP cubes using a variety of SAS products, including SAS OLAP Cube Studio, SAS Enterprise Guide, SAS Information Delivery Portal, and Microsoft Excel with the SAS OLAP Data Provider.

Prerequisites

Familiarity with SAS programming and table structures is helpful but not required.

Duration

2 days

11

SAS® Add-In for Microsoft Office

Accessing SAS® from Microsoft Office Applications

This Level I course is intended for users with little or no programming experience who want to access the power of SAS directly from Microsoft Excel and Microsoft Word. This course requires the SAS®9 Intelligence Platform.

Course Description

This course provides an overview of SAS Add-In for Microsoft Office and shows how it can be used to directly access SAS information from Microsoft Office applications. You learn how to run SAS Stored Processes and use SAS tasks for processing data directly from inside a Microsoft Excel or Microsoft Word document. In addition, you learn how to access and work with existing SAS data from Microsoft Excel.

Prerequisites

There are no formal prerequisites for this course.

Duration

1 day

12

SAS® Web Report Studio

Using SAS® Web Report Studio for Thin-Client Reporting

This Level I course is intended for users with little or no experience in other reporting tools or database technology. This course requires the SAS®9 Intelligence Platform.

Course Description

This course provides an overview of SAS Web Report Studio. SAS Web Report Studio enables non-technical business users to find, interact with, create, and share reports based on corporate data. You learn how to navigate the SAS Web Report Studio interface and how to build simple and complex reports that surface information from tables and OLAP cubes.

Prerequisites

There are no formal prerequisites for this course.

Duration

1 day

13

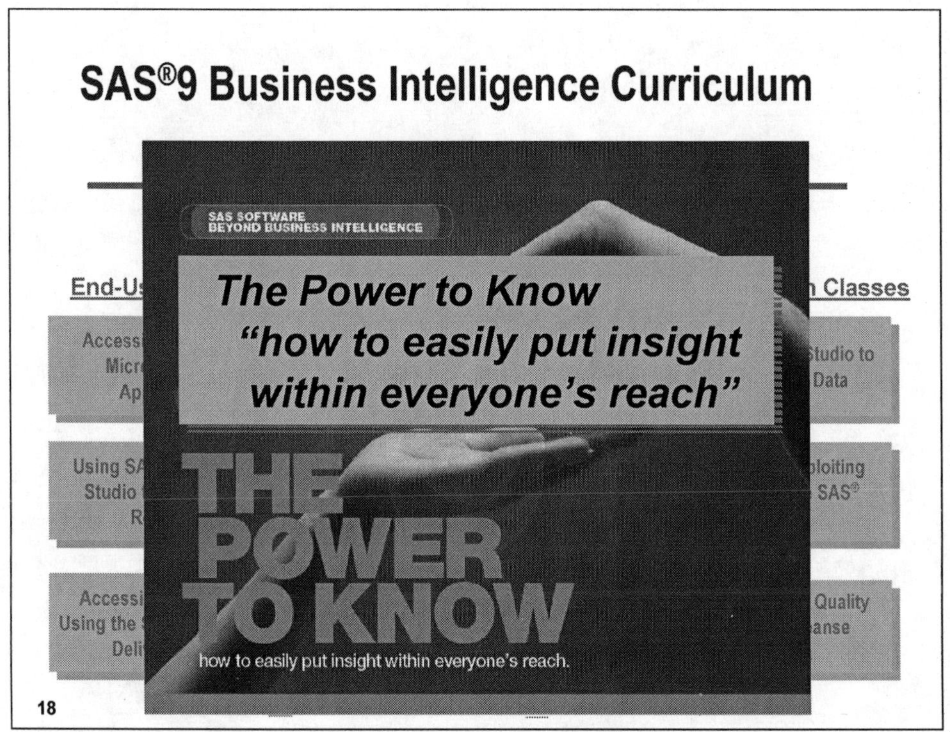
SAS®9 Business Intelligence Curriculum
SAS SOFTWARE
BEYOND BUSINESS INTELLIGENCE
The Power to Know
"how to easily put insight within everyone's reach"
THE POWER TO KNOW
how to easily put insight within everyone's reach.
18

SAS® Information Delivery Portal

Accessing Information Using SAS® Information Delivery Portal

This Level I course is for end users of the SAS Information Delivery Portal who want to customize their view of their organization's existing SAS Information Delivery Portal. This course requires the SAS®9 Intelligence Platform.

Course Description

This course focuses on using SAS Information Delivery Portal to view content developed in the SAS Business Intelligence environment. You learn how to navigate through the pages and portlets of the portal, how to add new pages and portlets to your view of the portal, as well as how to add SAS Information Maps, SAS Web Report Studio reports, and SAS Stored Processes to your portal pages.

Prerequisites

There are no formal prerequisites for this course.

Duration

1 day

14

SAS® Stored Processes

Creating, Distributing, and Using SAS® Stored Processes

This Level III course is designed for programmers and analysts who want to understand, create, and exploit SAS Stored Processes. This course requires the SAS®9 Intelligence Platform.

Course Description

This course defines SAS Stored Processes and demonstrates how to create and use them. SAS products such as SAS Enterprise Guide and SAS ETL Studio, as well as the SAS windowing environment, can be used to create Stored Processes. The course also illustrates how SAS Stored Processes can be used from SAS Add-In to Microsoft Office and SAS Information Delivery Portal.

Prerequisites

Familiarity with SAS programming is required.

Duration

2 days

15

SAS® Information Map Studio

Using SAS® Information Map Studio to Create Information Maps

This Level II course is for data modelers and data architects who have experience in data modeling, know the physical data, and have a strong understanding of the business domain. This course requires the SAS®9 Intelligence Platform.

Course Description

This course provides an overview of SAS Information Map Studio. You learn how to navigate the SAS Information Map Studio interface, how to create information maps from simple to complex on single or multiple data sources, and how to create information maps on OLAP cubes. Additional topics include exporting and importing information maps as XML, using SAS Stored Processes with an information map, and using information maps in SAS Web Report Studio and SAS Information Delivery Portal.

Prerequisites

A general understanding of Structured Query Language (SQL) and Multidimensional eXpressions (MDX) is helpful but not required.

Duration

2 days

16

SAS® Enterprise Guide®

Querying and Reporting Using SAS® Enterprise Guide®

This Level I course is designed for end users who are not programmers but who need to retrieve information from different sources, summarize it, and present it in tables and graphs.

This course is available in the classroom (2 days) or as a Live Web course (a series of 5 sessions, each approximately 3.5 hours long).

Course Description

This course focuses on how to access, manage, summarize, and present data using SAS Enterprise Guide. The course teaches students how to navigate the menu-driven interface of SAS Enterprise Guide to accomplish tasks such as accessing local SAS and Microsoft Excel tables and remote relational databases; creating user-defined formats; managing, manipulating, and joining data using the SQL query builder; generating descriptive statistics, tabular summary reports, and ActiveX graphs; and automating and scheduling tasks. This course does not cover statistical analysis tasks.

Prerequisites

This course is designed for end users with no programming experience or SAS knowledge.

17